Behaviour Modification
with the Severely Retarded

The Institute for Research into Mental and Multiple Handicap, 16 Fitzroy Square, London W1P 5HQ, England is a charitable foundation devoted to stimulating and coordinating research into the prevention and treatment of handicapping disorders and into the improved provision of services for the handicapped.

Titles of previously published Study Groups are:

1. *Infantile Autism: Concepts, Characteristics and Treatment*
2. *Cellular Organelles and Membranes in Mental Retardation*
3. *The Brain in Unclassified Mental Retardation*
4. *Mental Retardation and Behavioural Research*
5. *Assessment for Learning in the Mentally Handicapped*
6. *Experiments in the Rehabilitation of the Mentally Handicapped*
7. *Language, Cognitive Deficits, and Retardation*

Study Groups 1–5 were published by Churchill Livingstone, London; 6 and 7 by Butterworths, London

Associated Scientific Publishers, P.O. Box 211, Amsterdam

Behaviour Modification
with the Severely Retarded

Study Group 8 of the
Institute for Research into Mental and Multiple Handicap

Edited by

C.C. KIERNAN

Assistant Director, Thomas Coram Research Unit, Institute of Education,
University of London

and

F. PETER WOODFORD

Executive Director, Institute for Research into Mental and Multiple Handicap,
London

1975

Elsevier · Excerpta Medica · North-Holland
Associated Scientific Publishers · Amsterdam · Oxford · New York

ISBN Excerpta Medica 90 219 5000 6
ISBN American Elsevier 0-444-15191-5

Published in November 1975 by Associated Scientific Publishers, P.O. Box 211, Amsterdam, and American Elsevier, 52 Vanderbilt Avenue, New York, N.Y. 10017

Suggested publisher's entry for library catalogues: Associated Scientific Publishers

Printed in The Netherlands by Mouton & Co, The Hague

Contents

Part I: Fundamental research

Part II: Applications

Part III: The context of programmes

Contributors and Participants

The Study Group on *Behaviour Modification with the Severely Retarded* was held at Cumberland Lodge, Windsor Great Park on 2–4 December 1974

ELIZABETH SPINDLER BARTON   Department of Psychology, Meanwood Park Hospital, Tongue Lane, Leeds LS6 4QB

MICHAEL BERGER   Department of Psychology and Child Development, Institute of Education (London University), 55 Gordon Square, London WC1

MARIA CALLIAS   Hilda Lewis House, Bethlem Royal Hospital, 579 Wickham Road, Shirley, Croydon, Surrey CRO 8DR

JANET CARR   Hilda Lewis House, Bethlem Royal Hospital, 579 Wickham Road, Shirley, Croydon, Surrey CRO 8DR

KEVIN CONNOLLY   Department of Psychology, Sheffield University, Sheffield S10 2TN

JOHN CORBETT   Hilda Lewis House, Bethlem Royal Hospital, 579 Wickham Road, Shirley, Croydon CRO 8DR

CLIFF CUNNINGHAM   Hester Adrian Research Centre, Manchester University, Manchester M13 9PL

NICK GEORGIADES   Department of Occupational Psychology, Birkbeck College, London University*

PETER HARZEM   Department of Psychology, University College of North Wales, Bangor

JAMES HOGG   Hester Adrian Research Centre, Manchester University, Manchester M13 9PL

MIKE JACKSON   Institute of Mental Subnormality, Wolverhampton Road, Kidderminster, Worcs. D410 3PP

MALCOLM JONES   Meldreth Manor School, nr. Royston, Herts. SG8 6LG

RITA JORDAN   Hornsey Centre for Handicapped Children, 26A Duke's Avenue, Muswell Hill, London N10

CHRIS KIERNAN   Thomas Coram Research Unit, Institute of Education (London University), 41 Brunswick Square, London WC1N 1AZ

ALBERT KUSHLICK   Health Care Evaluation Research Team, Highcroft, Romsey Road, Winchester SO22 5DH

* Present address: Work Research Unit, Department of Employment, Steel House, 11 Tothill Street, London SW1H 9LN.

PETER MITTLER   Hester Adrian Research Centre, Manchester University, Manchester M13 9PL

CHRIS SAUNDERS   Hornsey Centre for Handicapped Children, 26A Duke's Avenue, Muswell Hill, London N10

GEOFF THORPE   The Manor Hospital, Epsom, Surrey

JACK TIZARD   Thomas Coram Research Unit, Institute of Education (London University), 41 Brunswick Square, London WC1N 1AZ

STEVE WALKER   Department of Psychology, Birkbeck College (London University), Malet Street, London WC1E 7HX

CHRIS WILLIAMS   Institute of Mental Subnormality, Wolverhampton Road, Kidderminster, Worcs. D410 3PP

PAUL WILLIAMS   Castle Priory College, Wallingford, Berks. OX10 0HE

WILLIAM YULE   Department of Psychology, Institute of Psychiatry (University of London), De Crespigny Park, Denmark Hill, London SE5 8AF

Acknowledgements

We would like to thank the Board of Governors and staff of the Institute for Research into Mental and Multiple Handicap for initiating the Study Group which has led to this book. We are also most grateful to the anonymous Trust which donated funds to allow the Study Group to take place, as well as the Programme Coordinator (Miss Ruth Norton) and staff of the King George VI and Queen Elizabeth Foundation of St Catharine's, Cumberland Lodge, Great Park, Windsor, for the organization and hospitality which allowed the conference to achieve its aim of bringing people together in a comfortable and stimulating environment. Finally we thank the contributors whose hard work has allowed the rapid production of the book, and the staff in the Institute for Research into Mental and Multiple Handicap and in the Institute of Education for much patient typing and bibliographical work.

C. C. KIERNAN
F. PETER WOODFORD

Introduction

C.C. KIERNAN

This volume contains the proceedings of Study Group 8 of the Institute for Research into Mental and Multiple Handicap, held in December 1974. Each of the papers presented was followed by a formal commentary by an appointed discussant and then by a general discussion. Most of the commentaries and discussions have been edited and are included in this volume. Occasionally, the quality of recording of discussions rendered them incomprehensible. This accounts for regrettable omissions of discussion which may otherwise have been of value to the reader.

The last paper in the volume, by Nicholas Georgiades, was presented at an Action Workshop, also organized by the Institute for Research into Mental and Multiple Handicap, in October 1974. The workshop was concerned with the implementation of behaviour modification programmes. It has been added because we believe it makes a valuable contribution to our subject.

The aim of the conference was to discuss issues arising from the application of behaviour modification techniques to the severely mentally handicapped. There is no doubt at all that we now know enough about mental handicap and about methods of changing behaviour to substantially change the status of the mentally handicapped. To an extent all that is needed is hard work in applying, in existing services, what is already known. However, as soon as we begin to teach or advise, several levels of problem emerge. What needs to be taught, what sequence is optimal for teaching, what are the best service settings for implementation? Given that service contexts are not optimal, how do we go about changing them? How do we evaluate complex programmes? At each level we can, and do, use rule-of-thumb or provisional solutions to the problems. This book examines the problems in relation to relevant research and conceptualizations, with the object of suggesting guidelines for the development both of applications and of thinking.

In the course of the meeting differences of opinion on the value of relating research to its application emerged. Some participants felt that much of the research discussed was of questionable practical value. "Will it change what I do next week?" Academics are notorious for complicating things unnecessarily, for being overly concerned with factors which may only contribute 2% to the variance of everyday behaviour. The conference participants were nearly all practitioners of one sort or another. Their concern for relevance differed only in time scale. Some were more concerned with longer-term relevance and with the risky operation of researching the possible value of innovations guided by conceptual frameworks which had evolved outside direct applied research. All practitioners shared the concern for changing the behaviour of the mentally handicapped within realistic service contexts. And all shared the assumption that application represents both a critical source of hypotheses for controlled research and a touchstone for the value of pure research.

A second divergence of thinking appeared during the meeting. Participants tended to define behaviour modification in different ways. At one extreme, behaviour modification was seen as a relatively restricted set of techniques interpreted within reinforcement theory. Techniques like prompt and fade, shaping, the use of reward and Time Out were seen as prime. At the other extreme the conceptual framework of behavioural analysis was offered as the defining characteristic. From this viewpoint, analysis in behavioural terms could be applied to *any* setting or *any* technique. Thus, dynamic psychotherapy might be interpreted within a behavioural framework without 'claiming dynamic psychotherapy' as within the scope of behaviour modification. This approach is not unusual; other 'schools' of psychology have followed the same strategy.

The current volume follows the suggestion that it is potentially valuable to analyse behaviour within the conceptual framework offered by a behavioural approach. By this we mean an approach which analyses behaviour in terms of antecedents, setting and discriminative stimuli, behaviour and consequences (cf. Kiernan 1973). Thus, the behaviour of a teacher in the classroom or an administrator in the committee room may be analysed within the same model despite the fact that neither sees himself as operating within a behavioural model (Krasner and Ullman 1966).

The value of a theory lies in its ability to generate new hypotheses and ideas, its deductive heuristic functions, and the degree to which people find they can use it—a primarily sociological function. The reader will be able to judge for himself the value of the behavioural approach in this book. Only the long-term evaluation of the theory in practice will answer the questions completely.

This book is, therefore, a discussion of issues arising from the application of behaviour modification to the education of the severely retarded. It is not an introductory text on behaviour modification or a general review of literature on it. There are now several such reviews (Bandura 1969, Gardner 1971, Kiernan 1974). The book is directed at clinical and educational psychologists, senior nurses, psychiatrists, social workers, administrators and teachers who are already familiar with the basic principles of behaviour modification. In particular, it is directed at those responsible for innovating and planning programmes. The book does not pretend to be a text for parents or practising nurses and teachers, although many people in these groups would probably gain not a little from reading it.

REFERENCES

BANDURA, A. (1969) *Principles of Behaviour Modification.* Holt, Rinehart and Winston, New York

GARDNER, W.I. (1971) *Behaviour Modification in Mental Retardation.* Aldine Atherton, Chicago

KIERNAN, C.C. (1973) Functional analysis. In *Assessment for Learning in the Mentally Handicapped* (Mittler, P., ed.). Churchill Livingstone, London

KIERNAN, C.C. (1974) Behaviour modification. In *Mental Deficiencies: The Changing Outlook* (Clarke, A.M. and Clarke, A.D.B., 3rd ed.). Methuen, London

KRASNER, L. and ULLMAN, L.P. (1966) *Research in Behaviour Modification.* Holt, Rinehart and Winston, New York

I Fundamental Research

Part I consists of two groups of papers. The first five papers may be roughly grouped together; the last two deal with animal research and form a group on their own.

Behaviour modification represents a range of techniques and a way of conceptualizing behaviour. The approach does not of itself dictate the content of teaching or therapy or the sequence of steps in teaching. The papers in the first group consider important issues arising out of this situation. Hogg, Connolly, Yule and Berger and Jordan and Saunders deal with the method of deriving content for behaviour modification programmes from our knowledge of normal development and from pure and applied research. Kiernan addresses some problems in the evaluation of behaviour modification programmes.

Normative Development and Educational Programme Planning for Severely Educationally Subnormal Children

JAMES HOGG

Hester Adrian Research Centre, The University, Manchester M13 9PL

Developmental psychology sets out to establish the characteristics of behavioural change and the processes affecting such change from infancy to adolescence. It is an area of psychology that is diverse in its subject matter. At one extreme it is concerned with the development of visually controlled reaching in the young infant and at the other in the evolution of complex symbolic skills and social behaviour. The nature of the processes affecting development may alter with increasing chronological age. It is possible that certain behaviours are inherent in the neonate (e.g. some degree of auditory–manual coordination, see Bower 1974, p.170). Others may reflect neurological maturation (e.g. breadth of attention, see Bower 1974, pp. 130–134). Both innate and maturational influences will interact with environmental events in the elaboration of complex skills. In addition, the balance between such contributory influences will shift with age. Much of the scientific work that has been carried out in this area is concerned with establishing typical patterns of developmental change and is therefore concerned with normative aspects of behavioural developments. The term 'normative' should not be taken here to imply that all workers are concerned with establishing statistical norms in the conventional sense. Much of the work is implicitly normative in the statement of its findings on development.

At one level, therefore, it is impossible to specify in general terms what the relevance of normative development for education planning is. Any comment on such a relation must be made about specific areas of development for which a clear statement on the connection between normative development and a programme objective can be made. Such a proposed connection, however, will depend in turn on a broader view of the relation of information on normative development and educational objectives. In the case of severely educationally subnormal children two views may be distinguished. The first suggests that information on normative development can provide educational objectives in a direct fashion. The second suggests that an adequate educational theory must establish content prior to implementing developmental information in educational procedures. The former view looks to developmental information for content. The latter suggests that such information may, under carefully stated conditions, influence technique.

7

This article presents the background to the former position and argues that it is got tenable, i.e. information on normative development cannot provide programme content. It then goes on to examine a selected area of behaviour that develops in the first year of life in a normal child, namely visually controlled reaching. Questions are raised about the way in which this behaviour and its evolution might be used in a programme of intervention with profoundly retarded nonambulant individuals. In doing this I hope to demonstrate by a concrete example ways in which developmental information can be embedded in a behaviour modification programme and to support the more abstract points made earlier in the article.

THE DEVELOPMENTAL PROCESS: ATTITUDES AND IMPLICATIONS

The contribution of a child's interaction with his or her environment to a variety of developmentally significant behaviours is acknowledged by proponents of a number of theoretical viewpoints regarding development. Such positions are generally contrasted with those involving what Hunt (1966) has referred to as 'the belief in predetermined development', and Gesell (1928), with his view of development as 'intrinsic growth', is often cited as a representative of this view. In contrast, those adopting an interactionist position argue for the modifiability of developmentally significant behaviours, i.e. behaviours that have been regarded as of theoretical interest by developmental psychologists, and/or of adaptive importance to the child. At one extreme, Bijou and Baer (1966) have proposed a speculative account of behavioural development employing the concepts of operant and respondent conditioning. Bijou (1966) has extended this analysis to behaviour that is retarded developmentally, i.e. in which there is a socially unacceptable discrepancy between a child's chronological age (CA) and the behaviour that is explicitly or implicitly considered to be normative at that CA.

Not all learning-based theories of development have been evolved strictly within an operant-respondent learning framework. Gagné (1968) has also analysed development in terms of learning, emphasizing the hierarchical nature of complex behaviours associated with development. Though Piaget is sometimes grouped with Gesell in the controversy noted above, Gagné acknowledges that Piaget does give the child's interaction with his or her environment a specific place in his theory, though only assigning a contributory place to learning. Pascual-Leone and Smith (1969), however, have produced a more formal neo-Piagetian analysis of the development of schemes that deals explicitly with the contribution of learning to their evolution. Case (1972) compares Pascual-Leone's analysis directly with that of Gagné. He notes, however, that the latter does not have a specific growth factor, while the former proposes a 'mental space' which refers to the contribution of CA to the number of schemes which a child can coordinate.

It may be seen that there is a range of positions with differing constructs and emphases, all of which acknowledge the contribution of learning and experience to developmentally significant behaviours. The implication of this is that such behaviours may be modified, given that effective techniques are available. Bijou and Baer's position is inextricably bound up with the mainstream of behaviour modification. Here relevant procedures have been applied to behaviours that have been the traditional concern of developmental psychologists and psycholinguists and systematic changes have been reported, e.g. Bucher and Schneider (1973) on conservation, and Whitehurst (1972) on novel and grammatical utterances. Baer (1973) has emphasized the potential contribution of information gathered in behaviour modification studies to an understanding of the developmental process. He has also questioned whether there is such a field as developmental psychology (Baer and Wright 1974). He suggests that 'child psychology' may be an adequate description indicating that there are no qualitative differences in the factors leading to behavioural change in populations differing in CA. The general laws of learning apply throughout the population. Studies of change in developmentally significant behaviours have not been limited to operant studies: Pascual-Leone's analysis has also received a direct test involving controlled intervention by Case (1972).

Thus, both behaviour modification and general programme training have in common the attempt to produce specific measurable changes in developmentally significant behaviours. In the light of currently available evidence it is open to question whether a thoroughgoing learning analysis of development can be maintained, especially when one is considering early infancy. Equally, however, there is ample evidence on the effects of experience on development. White's (1971) observation may be used to summarize the position: "The modern view seems to be that man is an unfinished creature at birth, with many fragments of instinct-like behavior and basic drives which are biologically guaranteed but are subsequently molded and differentiated by experience" (p. 23).

DEVELOPMENTAL CHANGE AND THE EDUCATION OF SEVERELY EDUCATIONALLY SUBNORMAL CHILDREN

We have already noted that Bijou (1966) has applied a learning analysis to the discrepancy in a child's behaviour between his CA and his actual performance. This is of course lower than anticipated in the case of the Severely Educationally Subnormal (SESN). We have also noted that the modifiability of developmentally significant behaviours has been demonstrated in a number of studies. Taken together these facts have led to the position being established among some workers that behaviours that are normative developmentally can serve as objectives for SESN children. Thus Bricker (1970) adopted the term 'developmental retardation' and defends the proposition "... that the primary method for studying and understanding developmental retardation is to develop a process to teach such children or adults to behave 'normally'" (p. 16). In the case of Bricker and Bricker (1974), language development and its functionally related precursors have provided a major area to which such an effort is directed. Here information from psycholinguistic analyses of language development has

9

provided the starting point for evolving programmes of language facilitation in SESN children.

The internal logic of this view is clear and for many workers compelling. Indeed, at face value it would seem sheer casuistry to question the value of training an 'important' set of behaviours such as language. However, the equation 'normative developmental information + behaviour modification = an educational theory for the retarded' is open to several criticisms, some of which relate to educational theory, and others to the stability of the norms of development.

NORMATIVE DEVELOPMENT AS AN EDUCATIONAL AIM

First, let us consider educational theory and the setting of developmentally significant behaviours as educational objectives. Spodek (1972), in a discussion of the education of normal pre-school children and normative development, and Cunningham (1974), in a consideration of educational objectives for SESN children, have both emphasized that educational objectives are not determined by what is, but by what ought to be. Such decisions clearly involve value judgements. McMaster (1973) has provided a clear account of what is involved in formulating an educational theory for the mentally handicapped or a sub-group within that population. The construction of such a theory is based upon a variety of essential components that inform the theory which McMaster considers a 'practical theory' (p. 20). Experience, history, psychology, philosophy, sociology, medicine and psychiatry, as well as political, economic and social studies, all contribute. The information derived from these conceptual components is integrated and informs operational aspects of the theory which in turn involve establishing aims and then objectives, followed by an evaluation of methods, implementation skills, assessment and evaluation. The formulation of such a theory is discussed further below.

Clearly, the outcome of evolving a practical educational theory may be that objectives are set that will entail closing the CA (observed)–CA (expected) discrepancy. If this is formulated in terms of teaching developmentally significant behaviours, two further points must have been made in the formulation of the theory and should be explicit. On the one hand what is normative in the developing behaviour of children in the majority (normal) culture must be considered not only acceptable but actually desirable. Given this, the desirable norm must also be deemed desirable for the minority group, that is for SESN individuals. In this case not only what is should be, but by extension to others will be made more so.

Objections may be made to these judgements. While in infancy and early childhood developmentally significant behaviours seem so basic to the child's interaction with the environment that they may serve as educational objectives, with increasing CA the face validity of this will decline. It is unlikely that proponents of a developmental curriculum would maintain that all behaviours exhibiting development in childhood are of equal significance or desirability. While the importance of language may seem paramount to many (but not all—as

10

Furth, 1974, has indicated), are we to invest certain aspects of social development within our culture that are probably of equal significance as conceptual developments with a similar educational status? For example, the development of sexual identity in our own culture is a legitimate area of developmental research (Kagin 1964). Are we then to teach sexual identity in the case of those who on some appropriate criterion fail to attain a normative and suitable identity? Clearly the implications of such a view would be profound, and in the last analysis, as with all educational decisions, political (Millett 1971). Lest this example seem fanciful, work is already beginning to appear in this area with children whose behaviours seem inappropriate to their gender (e.g. Rekers and Lovaas 1974). Similarly, we might ask whether it is a desirable objective to maintain the normative level of aggressive behaviour in our culture. Even in the event of adopting a conservative view of the acceptability of the status quo, the desirability of applying it to a minority group is open to further questions. Training sexual identity or aggressive behaviour in normal children might be justified by some on the grounds that it will lead to adaptive behaviour in the culture in which the child grows up and with which he or she interacts. While in one sense the SESN child may be growing up in the same culture, his interaction with that culture is clearly different in terms of provision, social attitudes and expectations. There is no guarantee that in the light of this differing interaction a behaviour that is adaptive for a normal child will be similarly adaptive for an SESN person. Ultimately the choice of what is to be taught must be considered in relation to the development of actual provisions for those taught at later stages in their development, not the majority cultural norm.

The second, factual, problem in adapting normative developmental information for educational objectives relates to the stability of such development. "For the so-called normal individual, the succession of effective environmental events in development are more or less typical for his culture. The opportunities for him to interact with social and physical events have been within normal limits; his biological structure and physiological functioning are adequate and are maturing at the usual rates" writes Bijou (1966) (p. 2). However, the whole interactionist position is that different 'effective environmental events' will alter the nature of the child's interaction with his culture. The extent and limits of such change are as yet by no means defined, though they undoubtedly reach back into the first year of life, and a specific example is given later. Whether such change is altered systematically through educational procedures, or reflects the influence of general cultural change, we find ourselves confronting normative developmental information that, probably within limits, will vary depending on circumstances. Thus, in terms of educational aims, normative development may present us with an unstable norm, the trends in which are both unpredictable and difficult to monitor. Again, the only decision is to abandon behaviours of developmental significance as educational objectives because they happen to be significant to students of development, and establish our curriculum in line with the type of decision making described by Spodek, Cunningham and McMaster.

NORMAL DEVELOPMENT AND EDUCATIONAL AIMS

The conclusion to be drawn from the arguments presented is not necessarily that a knowledge of normal development is irrelevant to developing educational programmes. Certainly many teachers of both normal and handicapped children would look askance at such a suggestion. Those with clear educational objectives have long sought to utilize what information developmental psychologists could supply. They have, however, drawn upon the information to inform procedures that aim at realizing curriculum objectives. Thus, Mitchell (1973, pp. 122–139) discusses how basic developments in a child's behaviour contribute, or fail to contribute, to a variety of familiar objectives set for children in primary schools such as model making, painting, drawing, writing, and so forth. The task for the behaviour modifier is to state how developmental information is implemented in the educational theory that informs his activities. As we indicated earlier, there is probably no general answer to the questions raised in making such an attempt. Here I shall try, very tentatively, to indicate what might be involved. Specifically, I will consider how we might devise meaningful objectives for profoundly multiply handicapped children, focusing eventually on the development of visually controlled reaching.

As we have seen, McMaster (1973) suggests a number of conceptual areas which will contribute to an educational theory. They include: (1) Experience (of the target population and their situation); (2) History (of the treatment of the target population); (3) Psychology (i.e. available information derived from assessment of all relevant functions and potential intervention procedures); (4) Philosophy (essentially involving the value judgements that inform our attitude to the target population); (5) Medicine. Any one of these factors (selected, it will be noted, from a longer list) would merit a chapter in its own right in relation to the profoundly multiply handicapped, and the relation among them requires still further treatment. Briefly, the following observations may be made:

(1) Experience: Here we may consider the experience of those who are involved in planning programmes for children in the ward and school, and the verbal or written reports that they may derive from other professionals. This information relates not only to individual children, but to the general environment the children confront. Information of the following sort may be gathered: (a) the children do (in general) develop both in motor behaviour and socially. Such development, however, may be seen over years rather than weeks or months; (b) Active intervention with children by teachers, nurses or parents may occur for only a short part of the day; discontinuities in approach to the children may emerge; (c) The physical environment of the child may limit the possibility of each child experiencing differential stimulation.

(2) History: in the past the multiply handicapped, profoundly retarded child has in many instances been considered ineducable. Such a view has not been restricted to educational provision in the conventional sense but on occasions to basic medical provision such as physiotherapy. Legislative change necessitating educational provision for such children was clearly an important historical

development in both stimulating provision and affecting our basic approach.

(3) Psychology will enter educational theory in at least two ways. First, there is the contribution of assessment procedures to the evaluation of a child. Here developmental testing provides an organized observational framework in which to consider the range and pattern of a child's behaviours (Foxen and Hogg 1972). Such testing is not necessarily aimed at placing the child within a normative framework. In addition, specialized techniques employing operant or respondent functions may be used to test sensory functions (Remington 1974). Second, psychological information will also inform intervention procedures. In reality, such procedures are already in use and suggest themselves in a fairly obvious way—behaviour modification, with which we are concerned here, being an important technique.

(4) Philosophy: according to McMaster, a discussion of the philosophy of education involves a detailed and rigorous 'derivation' of the value judgements that will inform practice. At one extreme the outcome of such a consideration might lead to advocacy of euthanasia for some children showing a high degree of impairment (a view not unvoiced among some dedicated teachers who see the eventual lack of provision in adult life as negating anything they may achieve in childhood). At the other extreme the children may not even be differentiated from normal children in terms of the provision to which they are entitled. Here we shall not attempt a rigorous derivation of our position and we shall content ourselves with some general judgements that might inform practice. First, it is of value to initiate systematic and reliable changes in the behaviour of such children, however limited and however slow progress is. Second, such behaviour must be adaptive and progressive even if the environment to which the child adapts and in which he progresses is artificially established and maintained.

(5) Medicine: Medical assessment is clearly complementary to psychological assessment. Many children are severely spastic and are also maintained on anticonvulsant drugs. Sensory impairment is both marked and multiple in many. Clearly, all such information is potentially relevant to establishing educational aims for the children and it will also affect the form any programme takes.

If we integrate the information that has just been provided the following picture emerges: we are concerned with a population whose interaction with the environment is inherently different from that of an ambulant child, normal or retarded, who lacks multiple handicaps. The particular pattern of interaction varies from child to child depending upon the components of the handicap, degree of deprivation, and the extent to which interactions within the environment have been stereotyped or inconsistent. Behavioural development, however, is discernible, and progress attributable to teaching is frequently reported. In addition, such children should be considered within an educational context which implies that specific objectives must be set which must be implemented through appropriate procedures and adequately evaluated.

Taken together, these points suggest that an essential starting point for the education of the non-ambulant profoundly retarded child must be to establish a structured and reliable interaction between the child and his or her environment. Such an interaction may then serve for developing more complex behaviours which will not be discussed here. In addition, whatever can be achieved educationally will be enhanced by improvement in motor performance and development. The slow development of behaviour and the difficulty of eliciting it reliably suggest two determinants of technique. First, development must be adequately monitored, and second, some form of reliable control must be established prior to implementing the main programmes. The need for motor development suggests that we apply whatever relevant procedures for encouraging improvement in this area are available in medical practice. The need to monitor and control behaviour would suggest the use of behaviour modification techniques. The encouragement of motor development may be achieved through physiotherapy. These two areas should be regarded as complementary, interacting but distinguishable.

Our aim is then to develop a structured and adaptive interaction between child and environment employing two available procedures. McMaster (p. 117) suggests that we should have developed our objectives before discussing techniques. However, the object of this excursion into educational theory has been to lead us in a rational fashion to a consideration of the significance of a behaviour of importance in normal development for educational programming. In order to establish a structured interaction between child and environment we must, then, define a response that will serve as a starting point. For children whose assessment indicates that they have the motor and sensory ability, visually controlled reaching might provide such a point. For other children with a different pattern of handicap, alternative responses and sensory modalities may serve the same general aim. For purposes of discussion, however, we will limit ourselves to a behaviour that has received much attention in the developmental literature. Thus, we have a child who can move his arms, who is sighted, but who does not reach out for objects in his field of vision. We therefore set the objective, or group of objectives, which will lead to visually controlled reaching. Two questions may now be raised: First, what is known about the development of visually controlled reaching in normal infants? Second, what are the implications of this information for the detailed development of our programme which has drawn in this behaviour not because it has been studied by developmental psychologists, but because it is a justified educational objective?

We are fortunate in having available a recent analysis of visually controlled reaching which, though not couched in terms of a functional analysis, must be considered as going some way towards such an analysis. Bower (1974) reviews recent work in this area and considers two allegedly distinct accounts of the development of the behaviour. The first is the influential work of White (1971) and his associates. White's account is of the development of visually controlled reaching in normal infants in an institution. It begins with the assumption that at the outset the infant has reflexive grasps in response to touch (White 1971, p. 63) and some innate visual attentional behaviour (p. 63), the two being initially independent. Attentional behaviour improves through the first $3\frac{1}{2}$ months, partly as a result of improved visual accommodation (pp. 56–59).

Reaching develops through the child regarding his own hands, thus generating eye–hand coordination. At this stage rapid swiping at objects occurs though the hand is closed prior to contact (pp. 58, 62, 64). Next, the child catches sight of its own hand and begins to look from it to the object, developing an integration of eye–hand and eye–object behaviour (pp. 60, 63, 64). Mutual hand grasping then 'spontaneously' occurs and the child discovers that the seen hand is the grasping hand. Further coordination between eye–hand, eye–object, and tactual–motor behaviours lead to visually controlled reaching (p. 64). This involves the hand opening prior to grasping, and the behaviour starting from outside the visual field.

Bower suggests that this theory of the development of visually directed reaching implies certain necessary prerequisites. If hand regard is essential to its development, anything that facilitates hand regard will facilitate the development of the behaviour. Similarly, the facilitation of swiping will develop grasping and facilitate mature reaching. White's study involved a direct intervention which provides information relevant to these suggestions (White 1971, pp. 89–106). He massively enriched the environment of some infants, providing an object that could be looked at and swiped at. In contrast to a control group hand regard was delayed until after the development of swiping. This finding is clearly inconsistent with the view that hand regard is a necessary precursor of swiping. In addition, top-level reaching was accelerated, and occurred before tactually elicited grasping. This is also incompatible with the sequence of events described since reaching is supposed to develop from tactually elicited grasping.

Bower interprets these inconsistencies as a refutation of White's 'theory'. For someone looking at this field with a view to programme development, however, a somewhat different slant may be put upon the so-called inconsistencies. First, White has conclusively shown that however narrow the gate, the ways are many by which a terminal behaviour may be reached. Second, Bower's criticism seems to be directed to a *theory* that was never actually proposed by White, who does not suggest a rigid or invariant developmental sequence. Indeed, he acknowledges that his study demonstrates "the plasticity of several visual–motor developments" (p. 97) and explicitly rejects "elaborate theorizing" (p. 89).

It is unlikely, therefore, that White would necessarily take exception to Bower's account of the development of visually controlled reaching under other environmental conditions. First, Bower notes that White's infants were 4 weeks old at the start of his study though the components of reaching and grasping may be elicited 14–16 weeks after conception. Further, visually initiated reaching may be observed under certain conditions in newborns. From 4 to 20 weeks this behaviour does not occur, however, though after 20 weeks it is again observed and is more accurate than in the newborn and occurs in a wider range of postures; the time taken for the hand to close on the object is longer in the older infant. At 26 weeks the child can reach and *not* grasp, i.e. reaching and grasping have become differentiated. In addition, infants over 20 weeks can correct the course of the hand during reaching, thus displaying true visually directed reaching as against visually initiated reaching. Bower suggests that in

15

part the developments reflect learning. First, visually initiated reaching, it is assumed, is reinforced by contact with the object. Second, visually initiated grasping will not always be reinforced, as in some cases an object that is not fixed will move when touched, thus preventing grasping. Third, tactually initiated grasping will always be reinforced, e.g. grasping clothes and so forth. It may be suggested that while visually initiated reaching and tactually initiated grasping will be reinforced, visually initiated grasping will be extinguished. The change from visually initiated reaching to visually controlled reaching will involve simultaneous attention to both hand and object, and with the differentiation of functions as a result of learning as noted, visually controlled reaching will become possible. It is suggested (Bower 1974, pp. 130–143) that the simultaneous attention is dependent upon neurological maturation of the brain, though the possibility of experience contributing to this is not ruled out.

From these relatively complex accounts of the development of visually controlled reaching let us turn to some simple questions that will help us to decide on the relevance of such developmental information to our educational objective. First, is there anything inherent in the differing accounts that would indicate that if one were 'correct' and the other 'incorrect', this would have any definite implication for evolving our programme? Clearly both lay great emphasis on learning and experience. Indeed, Bower specifically implicates positive reinforcement and extinction, though here a functional demonstration of this is called for. (Why should grasping that is not always reinforced be considered as extinguishing rather than being maintained by intermittent reinforcement?) In this, then, both are compatible with a behaviour modification approach, i.e. they do not suggest that the process is endogenously generated. Indeed both White and Bower demonstrate that environmental intervention does produce specific and predictable changes in the course of behavioural development. Second, both involve behaviours that appear to be inherent rather than learnt. This raises the question of whether with retarded subjects we must wait for those given behaviours to manifest themselves before influencing development through learning. I am not aware that anyone has as yet shown that an intervention programme has failed because it was initiated in the absence of behaviours inherent in normal infants. However, this is a possibility that, as we become more sophisticated in behavioural intervention, might have to be evaluated in cases where a programme consistently breaks down. In the meantime the behaviour modification approach would lead us to attempt to develop such behaviours if they were absent and we would be unlikely to refrain from intervening because of this. Third, if maturational processes are involved, the same comments apply. Our starting point would be to train increasing attention span, for example, rather than account for its limitation by recourse to a maturational explanation. Again, increasing sophistication in assessment and programme evaluation may change our view on this point. In summary, then, there is nothing in either account that would deter us from attempting to train visually controlled reaching and much that would positively encourage such an approach. Where inherent or maturational processes are implicated, we would do well to bear these in mind as our techniques evolve—though with the profoundly retarded it is doubtful that normative information on central nervous system factors can be easily interpreted given the extensive CNS damage.

What has been said so far may seem like damning with faint praise. Can we be more positive and ask the question whether the account of the structure of the development of visually directed reaching constrains or guides our formulation of a programme? Having spent some time considering White's account in relation to possible programme development one might be led to the conclusion that if hand regard is crucial to the development of visually controlled reaching, we should perhaps train it as a component of the programme. It would therefore be disconcerting to confront Bower's suggestion that it is possibly "an epiphenomenon—an accidental consequence of other processes—rather than a direct precursor of later behaviour" (p. 169). However, to over-emphasize the fact that developmental psychology is itself developing and that alternative accounts may be given of the same phenomenon is to beg the issue, which is whether knowledge of a developmental sequence occurring in a given environment can inform our programme. There are two aspects to our answer in the present case. First, the knowledge provided by a White or a Bower may draw our attention to the essential components in the skill. For example, Bower's implication of attention span in visually directed reaching could usefully inform a programme. Second, there appears to be nothing in the information provided in the two accounts that suggests that the knowledge of the sequence and integration of the behaviours itself must of necessity determine the course of the programme—other than insofar as there is an inherent logical structure to the behaviour. For example, visual fixation of the object would seem to be a logical prerequisite for the skill. The logical structure of a programme, however, may be developed independently of the structure of the observed 'natural' development. Indeed, if we are to optimize the learning situation by employing the techniques available within behaviour modification this would seem desirable. A backward chaining procedure might be employed in which the starting point for the reach was determined by the teacher holding the child's hand in positions progressively farther from the object. The delay between termination of the reach and grasping might be established using a DRL contingency and so forth. Neither of these occurrences is necessarily observed in the development of the behaviour in the natural environment.

The position arrived at in the example that we have given might, after suitable analysis, apply to other behaviours. Bricker and Bricker (1974) argue that even if psycholinguists are correct in suggesting that imitation by children is not involved in normal language acquisition, this does not preclude its use as a tool in language training programmes. In addition, we must bear in mind that physical and sensory handicaps will probably produce non-normative acquisition of a behaviour though often eventuating in an appropriate terminal behaviour. For children with certain handicaps the logical structure of the programme will inevitably differ from that for non-handicapped children.

CONCLUSIONS

This article has in its early sections suggested that developmental information as content cannot be simply introduced into a curriculum for the mentally handicapped. It has gone on to show, however, that developmental information can be implemented in a total educational theory; indeed should be implemented in a curriculum by developing such a theory. One example, visually controlled reaching, was then considered against the background of a simplistic attempt to consider some facets of a theory of the education of profoundly retarded multiply handicapped people. The conclusion derived from a brief report on the present state of knowledge concerning the development of this behaviour was that such information could prime us to consider the component behaviours that might be relevant to developing a programme. It seemed unnecessary, however, to take into account what actually occurs by way of sequence and learning experience in the natural environment (or unnatural environment, as White's infants were actually in an institution). However, it was suggested that at some future date, information on the inherent components of behaviour and maturation might be relevant to evaluating programme failure. The way in which such information, and other findings relating to constraints on learning, can be implicated in behaviour modification at present is difficult to determine, but clearly merits serious consideration.

REFERENCES

BAER, D.M. (1973) The control of development process: why wait? In *Life Span Developmental Psychology: Methodological Issues* (Nesselroade, J.R. and Reese, H.W., eds.). Academic Press, New York

BAER, D.M. and WRIGHT, J.C. (1974) Developmental psychology. In *Annual Review of Psychology*, 25, pp. 1–82. Annual Reviews Inc., Palo Alto, Calif.

BIJOU, S.W. (1966) A functional analysis of retarded development. In *International Review of Research in Mental Retardation*, Vol.1 (N.R. Ellis, ed.), pp.1–19. Academic Press, New York

BIJOU, S.W. and BAER, D.M. (1966) Operant procedures and child behavior and development. In *Operant Behavior: Areas of Research and Application* (Honig, W.K., ed.), pp. 718–799. Appleton-Century-Crofts, New York

BOWER, T.G.R. (1974) *Development in Infancy*. Freeman, Reading, Berks

BRICKER, W.A. (1970) Identifying and modifying behavioral deficits. *Am. J. Ment. Defic.* 75, 16–21

BRICKER, W.A. and BRICKER, D.D. (1974) An early language training strategy. In *Language Perspectives – Acquisition, Retardation, and Intervention* (Schiefelbusch, R.L. and Lloyd, L.L., eds.), Macmillan, London/University Park Press, Baltimore

BUCHER, B. and SCHNEIDER, R.E. (1973) Acquisition and generalization of conservation by pre-schoolers using operant training. *J. Exp. Child Psychol.* 16, 187–204

CASE, R. (1972) Learning and development: a neo-Piagetian interpretation. *Hum. Devel.* 15, 339–358

CUNNINGHAM, C.C. (1974) The relevance of 'normal' educational theory and practice for the mentally retarded. In *Mental Retardation: Concepts of Education and Research* (Tizard, J., ed.), pp. 47–56. Butterworths, London

FOXEN, T. and HOGG, J. (1972) Behavioural variability and the problems of baseline assessment with subjects exhibiting minimal behavioural repertoires. Paper presented to the 2nd European Conference on Behaviour Modification

FURTH, H.G. (1974) On the role of language and speech in the development of the deaf child. Paper presented to Symposium: Aids to the Handicapped – Speech and Deafness. British Association for the Advancement of Science Annual Meeting, Stirling, 2–7 September 1974

GAGNÉ, R.M. (1968) Contributions of learning to human development. *Psychol. Rev. 75*, 177–191

GESELL, A. (1928) *Infancy and Human Growth.* Macmillan, New York

HUNT, J.McV. (1966) The psychological basis for using preschool enrichment as an antidote for cultural deprivation. In *Experience, Structure and Adaptability* (Harvey, O.J., ed.), Springer, New York

KAGIN, J. (1964) The acquisition and significance of sex-typing. In *Review of Child Development Research* (Hoffmann, M. and Hoffman, L.W., eds.). Russell Sage Found., New York

MCMASTER, J.McG. (1973) *Toward an Educational Theory for the Mentally Handicapped.* Edward Arnold, London

MILLETT, K. (1971) *Sexual Politics.* Hart Davis, London

MITCHELL, C. (1973) *Time for School: A Practical Guide for Parents of Young Children.* Penguin Books, Harmondsworth, Middx.

PASCUAL-LEONE, J. and SMITH, J. (1969) The encoding and decoding of symbols by children: new experimental paradigm and a neo-Piagetian model. *J. Exp. Child Psychol. 8*, 832–355

REKERS, G.A. and LOVAAS, O.I. (1974) Behavioral treatment of deviant sex-role behaviors in a male child. *J. Appl. Behav. Anal. 7*, 173–190

REMINGTON, R.E. (1974) Classical eyeblink conditioning in profoundly retarded non-ambulant children. *Bull. Br. Psychol. Soc. 27*, 177–178

SPODEK, B. (1973) What are the sources of early childhood curriculums? In *Early Childhood Education* (Spodek, B., ed.). Prentice-Hall, Englewood Cliffs, NJ

WHITE, B.L. (1971) *Human Infants: Experience and Psychological Development.* Prentice-Hall, Englewood Cliffs, NJ

WHITEHURST, G.J. (1972) Production of novel and grammatical utterances by young children. *J. Exp. Child Psychol. 13*, 502–515

Commentary

JANET CARR

I would like to focus on three points in Dr Hogg's paper.

1. What are the developmental stages and sequences to be derived from the study of development in normal children?

2. Which of these stages and sequences are essential prerequisites for the development of more advanced skills in normal children, and which are little more than developmental coincidences?

3. Which are essential in the development of skills in handicapped children?

Before attending this Study Group I had thought that the answers to the first question were reasonably well established through a wealth of research, both observational and experimental. Since hearing Professor Connolly's views (see p. 25) I realize that much research remains to be done.

Going on to the second question, it seems to me important to get over to a wider audience that this is a question that deserves consideration. Certain workers with handicapped children, especially those who have studied child development, tend to work rather rigidly through a developmental programme, insisting that each stage or sequence must be acquired in the order in which they appear in normal children. They may not allow for the possibility that some stages can be skipped or that in some cases the order of the sequence may be varied if this will make for more appropriate learning in the handicapped child.

After one has said that not all the stages and sequences must invariably be gone through, one must ask which of them *are* essential for the development of further skills? For instance, most children will first crawl and then stand before walking; probably all children need to go through the stage of standing but they certainly do not need to crawl. Reading offers another example: most children will learn letters before they learn to read words, but this is not always necessary. For any skill that we wish to teach a child it would be immensely helpful if we knew which 'pre-skills' we must first teach. We might in this way save the child and ourselves some time spent on teaching things which are not essential.

Conversely, Dr Hogg has drawn attention to the fact that we may have to teach handicapped children skills that are not important to the normal child in the achievement of a particular goal. Imitation may not be involved in normal language acquisition, but it certainly appears essential in teaching handicapped children the elements of speech (though it seems less useful in promoting the spontaneous use of speech, and we have used other methods, such as stimulating the expression of needs and wants which are then gratified).

In relation to the third question Dr Hogg points out the value judgement involved in determining that what is normative in the normal child population is ipso facto desirable, and I would like to make three points about this. First, we might notice that so far as the normal child is concerned it is the minimum attainment of the norms that is aimed for, that children should reach a stage not much later than does the normal child; few people are concerned if a child reaches a stage remarkably earlier than do his peers, nor do they try to restrain him from doing so in order that he may conform to the norm.

Secondly, it is quite possible to find areas (especially perhaps in social behaviour) in which the norm is not one that we should wish to encourage even in normal children. Swearing for instance is normal in some cultures, and may serve some quite useful function such as facilitating a child's acceptance by his fellows, and yet it is highly unlikely that we should ever deliberately try to train up a child's vocabulary of swear words. So even among normal children we may be selective about which norms of child behaviour we seek to encourage.

When we come to handicapped children the limitations on our acceptance of the principle 'norm is necessary' are more considerable. I should like to illustrate this with reference to Dr Hogg's example of aggression. If a child is going to live in a certain society he will need to be equipped to function in that society. If a certain range or minimum of aggressive behaviour is normal in a society it may be important for a particular child to have it developed. Parents on the whole want their children to be sufficiently aggressive to hold their own when they go to school. If, however, the child is not going to live in that society, but in one where the requirements for the variable under consideration —e.g. aggression—are different, he does not need to acquire normal levels of aggression. Indeed he may need to be *less* aggressive if he is likely to live in situations where control is maintained from above, such as an ESNS school, and in relation to this it may be noted that fewer mothers of 4-year-old Down's syndrome children than of normal children would encourage their children to be aggressive in any way (Carr 1975). It is possible, however, to imagine a situation where an aggressive level higher than normal would be appropriate. As Dr Hogg has emphasized, what the child needs to learn, and what it is appropriate to teach him, depends at least in part on the environment in which he will live. Developmental norms can offer guidelines, not rules.

REFERENCE

CARR, J. (1975) *Young Children with Down's Syndrome*. Butterworths, London

Discussion

Thorpe: The main question to my mind is not so much whether one should use aversion techniques but how one is to select target behaviours. Krasner (1969) has drawn attention to the tremendous responsibilities involved in behaviour modification. It seems to me that most of us are pretty inadequately qualified to carry this burden of responsibility in selecting appropriate target behaviours. Janet Carr has just said that in doing this you should look at society or the sub-society of which each individual is a member. But to take just one small problem, what about the child's parents? Maybe they don't want that child to be aggressive, whether or not aggressiveness is the norm for society or for the sub-society. To what extent are we able to deal with this?

Hogg: I personally feel very ill-equipped to deal with it. I would welcome guidelines reached by consensus. At present different groups working in isolation are setting objectives which may be unimpeachable at this stage of the development of behaviour modification, but will have to be thought about more as the techniques become more widely applied. This worry about what are the ultimate objectives of education is of course no greater a problem for behaviour modifiers than for other educationists, but it is not less of a problem, either.

Thorpe: It seems to me that the problem remained hidden while treatment of the severely retarded was regarded as a medical matter, and has only come to light with the transformation into an educational one.

Harzem: The ethical responsibilities in behaviour modification seem to me no more tremendous than those faced by, say, a neurosurgeon, but they seem awesome to us because they are of a different kind. They raise questions about the future of mankind which behaviour modifiers are no more adequate to deal with than the next man—but no *less* adequate, either. The best we can do, surely, is to take neither of the two extreme attitudes, i.e. make all the decisions ourselves *or* refer every decision to others, but try to strike a happy mean between the two. I don't believe that an outside body will necessarily produce wiser guidelines than we ourselves can.

Yule: As a group, behaviour modifiers have probably spent more time discussing the ethics of intervention than any other group at a similar stage in their development, probably because at the moment the techniques look extremely powerful. Now the ethics are exactly the same as in any other form of intervention. One's got to decide who gives you the right to do what to and with another person. And because we are working with the profoundly retarded who are unable to give informed consent themselves, we've got to think of all the safeguards that are necessary before embarking on any intervention, whatever the theoretical basis. Now, James Hogg is asking for someone to take this over and give him guidelines. The DHSS has a working party

21

right now which is aiming to do just that, and I hope that everyone has submitted their evidence to it, because otherwise the guidelines may well come out in a form no-one will like.

Hogg: You've overstated my position slightly: I would like to be involved in decision making, but I wouldn't want to make it in isolation.

P. Williams: Why are we talking about responsibility as though it were the responsibility of one person to determine what the goals in any service should be? Surely this is the main objection to the medical model: that too much responsibility is vested in one person. Nowadays we ought to agree that decisions should be taken by a team, to include the parents, and if possible the handicapped persons themselves.

Connolly: May I shift the discussion to Janet Carr's first point, and disagree with her? I don't think we need any more information about developmental norms, but we do need to know an awful lot more about developmental processes.

Berger: And about how these processes emerge sequentially! This is where a lot of work is needed. Which is not to say, of course, that in any behaviour modification approach one has to use the same sequences as in normal development. Chris Kiernan has a nice concept in his paper (p. 83), namely over-riding, and it may be possible through using devious routes or over-riding procedures to shortcut some of the processes which occur naturally.

Kiernan: One helpful strategy may be to treat societal norms as sources of hypotheses about processes. But norms give precious little help in devising developmental programmes for individual children.

Tizard: If I brought you a 10-month-old baby and said "I think he needs therapy because he can't sit up without support", what would you say? Isn't there *some* significance in developmental norms?

Connolly: More significant, to my mind, is what triggers off the transition from one developmental stage to another.

Harzem: Isn't there another hazard in talking about developmental stages? There may be stages, but not developmental. If you want to produce a certain behaviour pattern in an adult you may be obliged to go through certain sequences in every case. They are *not* necessarily sequences traversed during normal development in childhood.

Hogg: Right, and on that score I would like to challenge Kevin Connolly, who seems to be saying that the processes which would be observed in a normally functioning organism or a normal child are actually relevant to the logical analysis of behaviour and how to teach it. Although this might well be true, it seems to me very much an abstract statement because nobody has yet demonstrated that programmes break down through ignorance of processes. Do you, in the light of your research, envisage a time when programmes will be so refined that when they break down we will have to have recourse to process information to cope with the breakdown?

Connolly: I'm not sure how to answer that question. What strikes me about development is that there are seemingly almost endless numbers of routes to a given endpoint, and I just think it would be valuable to know something about the mechanisms involved in arriving at that endpoint.

Hogg: Bricker has baldly stated his assumption that for language acquisition, at any rate, the way this happens in normal development is irrelevant to the programming itself. Whether imitation is involved in normal development or not, for example, is irrelevant as it may still legitimately be used in training.

Walker: This current behaviour modifier's view expressed by Hogg and Kiernan can be taken as a belief in the existence of standard sets of prerequisites for a behaviour which are, or can be, independent of and different from normal developmental processes. I think the idea of a standard set of prerequisites may prove to be unfounded. Individuals vary so much that it is highly unlikely that one can designate a set of prerequisites valid even for a whole class of individuals, let alone for everyone. So perhaps the traditional behaviour modifiers weren't too far wrong when they taught somebody typing just by leaving them in a room with a typewriter and giving rewards for progress. That might still be easier than asking detailed theoretical questions and making hypotheses about how we should go about it—should we teach him to place his fingers on the keys first, should we teach him the stimulus pattern first, etc. It may in practice be much better to allow for individual variations in what preliminary skills are necessary for some final accomplishment.

Mittler: Statements about prerequisites are in fact statements about *probability*, aren't they? We know that the probability that a child who is totally deaf will acquire language without very special help is rather low. On the other hand some have done so. The probability that a child with Down's syndrome will write a book is relatively low, but a few have done so, and I guess more will do so in the future. One of the things that worries me about the developmental approach is that it assumes that a child who has developed to point X in relation to one skill ought to be at a comparable point in relation so some other skill. Take, for example, a child brought for assessment by his parents who are worried that he's not talking. The answer is likely to be "Well, we've assessed him very carefully, and we find his level of mental development is such that he's unlikely ever to be able to talk." It's that sort of application of our developmental knowledge that worries me, and it happens in normal schools in relation to reading. "This child isn't reading. What do you expect, if his mental age is only $4\frac{1}{2}$? Children of $4\frac{1}{2}$ don't learn to read." We really don't have the knowledge to make statements like that.

Carr: We have experienced exactly the same thing: a child with a mental age of 18 months was having temper tantrums, and because normal infants of 18 months have such tantrums no effort was made to train the child out of them, even though the methods to do so were available and it could have been done.

Kiernan: However, it must be acknowledged that we really don't know what function temper tantrums have in the development of the child, and until we do we really can't make that kind of statement with any security, even though I am personally very much in sympathy with it. In the present state of our knowledge, your attitude is just as open to criticism as the other person's: they are saying "This behaviour is normal, and therefore must be right"; you're saying "It's not logical, so let's get rid of it"—thereby implying that it has no function, which may be incorrect.

Carr: Of course you're right, although I think it unlikely that temper tantrums have a developmental function.

Cunningham: We've all been attacking developmental scales, but let's face it, when we actually sit down and plan programmes in a particular situation, it's extremely useful to have something in your hands—and developmental scales do provide it.

Connolly: It's not my intention to attack developmental tests, only the view that they are the end of the road.

Jones: Let's cast our minds back to what we normally do when we discuss a programme for a child. Surely, we usually consider the child's most disturbing problem, and only rarely consider the developmental background. Most behaviour modification programmes in fact attack things like temper tantrums, throwing behaviours, soiling behaviours, and so on and it is most unusual to consider these in terms of developmental patterns. Isn't this issue something of a red herring?

Hogg: Although much behaviour modification work has been done on problem behaviours, my own impression is that the trend is now towards much more far-reaching educational use. If that is true, what we've been discussing is the central crucial issue.

Jones: What I would like to see trained are things like attention set or the ability to recognize novelty in a situation. Now it may be that there are developmental points at which such behaviour occurs, but I think it would be more practical to go directly for attention training, recognition of novelty value, than to trace the normal developmental sequencing of such things.

Hogg: I disagree. I have been involved in a programme which simply trained attention, and have strong doubts about the worthwhileness of that as an object in itself. One has to go beyond that, and to do so effectively one needs a framework and a structure.

Harzem: The question is, how relevant is the knowledge of developmental processes? I don't think Kevin Connolly is saying that you'll *never* train a child without a knowledge of developmental processes. What he's saying is that if you have such knowledge your programme may be more finely tuned and you may be more successful. Further, I am prepared to guess, without any clinical evidence, that on occasion it may actually be harmful to be entirely ignorant of these processes. Now this is not to say that we must all stop what we're doing until knowledge of developmental processes is complete, or at least a lot more advanced. You obviously have to work with what you have. But it is surely not very helpful to argue, like Bricker, that we don't need any more knowledge, we can just go ahead with what we are doing.

Hogg: I don't think that's quite what he said. He builds on information he regards as important (not 'relevant', the word you used). He does not build programmes on another kind of information: knowledge of process mechanisms. He's taking part of the information available but not the whole.

Kiernan: One of the difficulties in considering relevance is relevance to whom. It struck me very strongly when we worked in a hospital. If you had left the curriculum planning to some of the nurses, the curriculum would have consisted in training the inmates to sit and self-stimulate in a non-injurious way for most of the day, to respond to their names if called, and to come and stand in line for food and pills. The whole curriculum would have been determined by the pattern of the institution. This is why we have got to address ourselves most seriously to the fundamental problem of curriculum content, because if we leave it to those who have to look after the children, the content they will advocate will reflect in part the tremendous force of the environmental setting in which they are required to operate.

P. Williams: I want to put the opposite view. Part of the function of education for a handicapped person should be to equip him for life—whatever that life is going to be. Life in the short term at any rate is going to be life with his parents or with a nurse. These people should have some say in what is happening to their child at school. We can't leave it all to psychologists!

Thorpe: This is the point I was trying to make at the beginning of this discussion: parents should at the least have some say in what their child is being trained to do.

Behaviour Modification and Motor Control

KEVIN CONNOLLY

Department of Psychology, University of Sheffield

Behaviour modification is fundamentally a technology concerned with the production, shaping, control and suppression of behaviour. Inasmuch as behaviour of one kind or another is the prime focus, behaviour modification is at least indirectly concerned with movement. However, little attention has been devoted to the development of skill and the control of movement *per se*. So far the primary concern has been with the control of specific behaviours in relation to contextual cues. For example, the work of Johnston, Kelley, Harris and Wolf (1966), although directed specifically at what the authors called motor skills, was essentially concerned with motivation. They applied reinforcement techniques to developing climbing and play on a climbing frame in a 3-year-old child. The child whom they studied engaged in little physical activity and particularly avoided climbing equipment. The method used by Johnston and her colleagues was that of giving or withholding social reinforcement contingent upon certain responses. Initially, reinforcement was given whenever the child approached the climbing frame and gradually this was restricted to actual climbing behaviour. The operant level was extremely low, less than 1% of the child's outdoor activity being spent on the climbing frame, but 9 days after the reinforcement programme was instituted 67.4% of his outdoor activity was spent on the climbing frame. Behaviour changes consequent upon the reversal of reinforcement coupled with the generalization of motor responses provided adequate support for the contention that this behaviour was under stimulus control. This investigation, however, was not at all concerned with the fine structure or quality of the motor behaviour but simply with increasing the rate.

Meyerson, Kerr and Michael (1967), in an article on behaviour modification in rehabilitation, report three cases each concerned with motor behaviour specifically. In my view these cases are primarily reports of work concerning motivation and acquisition in a very broad sense. Again, attention is not directed to the structure of the skill, and the implication is that all the necessary components are present.

One of their patients, a mentally handicapped 9-year-old girl, was taught to walk with the use of food as a reinforcer. Although this child had no physical handicaps she did not walk and it was assumed that impoverished environmental

25

contingencies were responsible. Behaviour was shaped first by having the child stand with assistance and then gradually progressing to independent walking by successive approximations to the desired behaviour. After fifteen 45-minute training sessions the child was able to walk by herself. Six months later the walking still persisted. The same report describes how typing skill was improved in an 18-year-old youth suffering a traumatic quadriplegia. Prior to the behaviour modification programme the patient did not persist in typing, he frequently sought the therapist's attention, gained it and was thus reinforced. The behaviour modification programme consisted of placing him in a quiet room for typing, ignoring his demands for attention and reinforcing him for 30 minutes of typing. In this case the reinforcement was 5 minutes' conversation on a topic which interested him. As the programme progressed he was required to type a given number of lines before receiving any reinforcement. After 12 sessions of training his rate increased from 5 to 12 lines in 30 minutes, and errors decreased from an average of 3 per line to one every other line. The same authors report success in teaching a cerebral palsied boy to walk using a straightforward shaping procedure; in this case, tokens were used as reinforcers.

I have discussed elsewhere the application of operant conditioning principles to the measurement and development of motor skill in children (Connolly 1968). Here the concern was more with the use of these methods in shaping certain components of skilled motor behaviour. An apparatus and procedure designed to shape the accuracy and speed of a target response by cerebral palsied children was described. The task in question was relatively simple, and required a child to move his hand in response to a signal, from a start button to a target in a fixed position. From the child's viewpoint the apparatus is a clown's face with a large bright red button fixed to the base some 22 cm in front of it. The clown's nose, which is relatively very large, is the target area and can be divided into correct and incorrect zones. Initially the incorrect area is a thin annulus or ring around the large central, correct area. The relative size of the correct and incorrect zones can be changed by fitting a larger annulus, thus making the target smaller and more difficult to hit.

In order to shape a response some approximation to it must exist in the child's behavioural repertoire; hence the importance of providing a large target in the early stages. Similarly in the early stages of training unlimited time was allowed in which to make the response. The start signal was the clown's nose lighting up, in response to which the child had to strike the nose as quickly as he could. A correct response resulted in the nose light going off and a range of reinforcers followed; the clown's eyes flashed, it sang snatches of song and delivered sweets. All of these reinforcers could be delivered on various schedules. In addition to the frequency of hits and misses, measurements were made of reaction time and the flight time of the movement. Accuracy demands were systematically varied by changing the target size, and the speed of the movement was shaped by allowing only a specified time in which to make the response if reinforcement was to follow. This procedure was developed to train, in handicapped children, two important features of a motor skill: the accuracy and the speed of performance. The focus of the task is clearly on components of motor performance.

26

The results obtained by this training method with a number of spastic hemiplegic children revealed that the speed of a movement by an impaired limb could be greatly and reliably increased under conditions where accuracy is held constant.

Speed and accuracy are attributes of performance, and in many skills they are of great importance. However, if behaviour modification techniques are to be used in developing motor control and motor skill it is necessary to have a theory of skill development which can serve to direct the technology of behaviour modification. What shaping procedures to apply, to what components of skill, and when, is not self-evident and some framework within which to consider these questions is of great importance.

MOVEMENT AND SKILL

The literature on the growth of skill in infancy and childhood is sparse enough, but the position in respect of theory is worse. For the most part the literature on motor development is concerned with establishing norms specifying the age at which children are likely to acquire such behaviours as crawling, walking, etc. With few exceptions the concern has not been with the careful and detailed description of behaviour change.

Movements may be seen as making up acts which the individual uses to solve motor problems and as such they are of fundamental significance to any organism. The distinction between actions and movements is an important one which is often not fully appreciated. In speaking of skills such as walking, crawling or grasping we refer to the organization of movements into a purposeful plan. A key attribute of skill concerns its goal-orientated nature; skilled activity is *purposeful*. In a whole range of skills, for example swimming in a choppy sea or walking through snow, the individual is engaged in overcoming independent forces. Overcoming these external forces is a prerequisite for the solution of motor problems, and since they are not foreseeable they cannot be mastered in any stereotyped way. By its very nature, therefore, skilled behaviour is flexible.

To examine the relationship between movement, action and skill let me take an example. With the fingers of my right hand I can describe the letter C in the air; I can do it with my left hand and with a pencil held between my teeth. The result in each case is much the same, I write the letter C, but the movements involved are quite different and different sets of muscles are employed. The point is that there exists no necessary identity between movements and skill. Movement is rather an accompaniment of skill, not a defining characteristic of it; I can arrive at the same goal by quite different routes. If we consider a child learning to write we can see that this involves not only learning a sequence of appropriate postures and movements but also some higher-level description in which the child must learn about writing in terms of a temporal and spatial series of strokes. Presumably the brain accumulates some higher-level routines in terms of variously directed motions on the basis of relative position, without any specific reference to absolute position. Some form of higher-level programme is necessary to execute a series of acts which make up a skill such as picking up an object and positioning it somewhere else.

The ultimate smooth performance eventually shown by a normal healthy child on a task such as using a spoon depends upon his mastery of various sub-units or sub-routines which are combined in particular ways to perform a specific action. In achieving a specified goal or solving a motor problem the necessary sub-routines must be orchestrated into a general plan. Once the general plan emerges and the task is attempted, no matter how crudely, performance can be shaped and refined by practice. At this point the powerful technology of behaviour modification can be brought in. A given set of muscle contractions does not define a skill, because a skill is more than the sum of its constituent parts. The coordination of movements into purposeful goal-orientated programmes of action involves the intention to achieve a goal and the presence of a control system which can refine both the behaviour and the driving programme. I have explored these ideas in greater detail elsewhere (Connolly 1975). In connection with practice Bernstein (1967) makes an interesting and important point which I believe may have significant implications for behaviour modification, as applied to skills at least. He argues that practice does not consist of repeating the *means of solution* of a motor problem but repeating the *process of solving* by techniques which are changed and perfected from repetition to repetition. Thus "... practice is a particular type of repetition without repetition and motor training, if this position is ignored, is merely mechanical repetition by rote ... ." The process of practice then can be seen as the search for optimal motor solutions to appropriate problems. The central programme itself thus changes, not merely the means of its execution.

A crucially important consequence of practice is that the sub-routines themselves become increasingly reliable and predictable. As they are freed from a dependence upon a particular context they assume a modular quality, and become relatively constant in form, latency and the time required to execute them. They can confidently be employed in different action programmes and require much less of the child's processing capacity. This automatization of the components has the important consequence of freeing some of the child's processing capacity for further task analysis and the orchestrating of the sub-routines into increasingly complex programmes which form the basis of developed skills. An important feature of skilled behaviour to which Bartlett (1958) drew attention is timing. This is not so much the speed with which an action can be carried out as "... regulation of the flow from component to component in such a way that nowhere in the whole series is there any appearance of hurry and nowhere unnecessarily prolonged delay." The synchrony which is necessary for the efficient sequencing of modularized components is dependent upon coordination being established between internal feedback, feedback from peripheral sense organs, and knowledge of results.

To summarize this view of skill development: first, there is no necessary identity between movement and skill; controlled movements are themselves necessary in that they are accompaniments of action. Programmes of action are what we usually describe as skills such as walking, playing a piano and writing. These programmes are made up of components, sub-routines, which must be correctly deployed according to a plan. To achieve the flexibility which is a hallmark of skill the sub-routines must attain an integrity of their own and the driving programme of an action has itself to be evaluated and updated in response to the nature of the specific motor problem (Connolly 1973, 1975; Elliott and Connolly 1974). The process of task analysis is of crucial importance, especially during training and acquisition. A child must master and store an extensive repertoire of fairly precise movements and in performing any new task he must recognize the set which is relevant to the new task.

IMPLICATIONS FOR TRAINING THE HANDICAPPED

The performance of an action appropriate to the achievement of a specified goal involves the recognition and analysis of a problem, the choice of suitable response units and the execution of these. Each of these features may be accomplished with various degrees of success and efficiency. However, the evaluation of improvement in motor performance is often restricted to quite crude measurements of the speed and accuracy of the total process, as in the target task of the clown apparatus. In certain circumstances this may be adequate, but not so in designing training procedures for the handicapped. Such criteria fail to identify where difficulties lie and ignore the possibility that strategies which may in the long term be more effective can in the short term offer little or no benefit. Although speed and accuracy are important attributes of many motor skills they are by no means the only important ones. Several factors contribute to the time which a person takes to perform an action. For example, how certain he must be of a particular signal, how long it takes to select a given response, the precision of the motor programme and the synchrony which exists between different forms of feedback are all involved. The difficulties in respect of training are formidable. How do we know when to terminate training; when can we say an individual will not refine his performance further? From the standpoint of behaviour modification it is not even clear which strategies should be reinforced.

If an individual can isolate the cues relevant to the task in hand, he can perhaps be helped to ignore other changes. Long-term improvements in skilled behaviour may well come about if the individual can generalize from specific situations in such a manner as to improve his overall appreciation of motor control and motor programming. Any improved general understanding may well be the basis for a valuable reappraisal of old strategies and for alternative forms of approach to the solution of motor problems. As is evident from the model outlined above improvements in motor control may be a function of several factors, for example the individual's appreciation of environmental cues, the programming of an action or the utilization of feedback information.

The nature and extent of motor handicaps vary greatly. Even where one is dealing with a presumed single condition such as spastic cerebral palsy the aetiology and manifestation of the condition vary. The nature of the problem which the handicapped individual exhibits will determine the kind of remedial training which is appropriate. Procedures for training motor skills in a child handicapped as a result of an accident will differ from those appropriate to a child suffering from a wasting disease and may well differ quite fundamentally from the child with a congenital motor handicap.

Before deciding upon a form of training or rehabilitation it is necessary to know a good deal about the nature of the deficit which the handicap imposes. In the spastic the retention of 'primitive' reflexes and the presence of 'abnormal' reflex patterns are both difficulties which must be dealt with in some fashion before motor control and skill can be improved. Here hyperactivity of the motoneurons leads to a situation in which a muscle contraction can be triggered by sensory stimuli or by activity in related muscle groups. The spastic thus faces an enormously complex task in mapping the various pathways available in his neuromuscular system and in defining the interactions going on between the forces present. He has to plan movements not only to initiate specific action programmes but also to avoid concomitant unwanted activity which will hamper his achieving a particular goal.

An approach which offers promise in training individuals with spastic cerebral palsy concerns the provision of augmented feedback (Harrison and Connolly 1971). This involves augmenting the feedback normally available to a subject through an alternative input channel. Using surface electrodes to monitor the activity in the forearm flexor muscles Harrison (1973) showed that spastic subjects were unable to reliably repeat tension levels in a single muscle group and could not produce a set of significantly ranked tension levels. These findings point to a dual impairment in motor programming and in the evaluation of ongoing activity within the muscle. In a series of studies spastic subjects were given an index of muscular contraction on a voltmeter. This augmented feedback afforded an unambiguous measure of ongoing activity and provided a clear definition of error and improvement in performance. The results of a series of experiments indicate that through this training system spastic individuals can be enabled to execute with quite remarkable precision a range of responses of varying complexity (Connolly and Harrison 1975; Harrison 1975a and b).

I began this paper by suggesting that behaviour modification was in essence a technology. To take this point a stage further I shall suggest that it is a technology in search of theory. Here the theory that I refer to is not that of operant learning but rather theory related to whichever behavioural domain we are concerned with, and the purpose of such theory is to drive and direct the behaviour modification technology. To be sure, there is ample evidence to support the view that behaviour modification is efficacious in a number of ways but we might greatly increase this by sharpening the manner in which it is applied and the point at which it is used. In the case of motor skills, which are fundamental to developing an individual's competence and effectiveness in interacting with his environment, we need not only a theory of skill acquisition but also a theory of skill development. Much of the experimental psychology of skills is concerned with how we teach new, and often special, skills to persons who are already very skilled. Common everyday behaviours such as walking,

30

using simple tools and manipulating objects are dependent on the individual having at his command a range of finely tuned functions. Given these it is certainly possible to improve levels of performance and develop new skills. However, in the case of the handicapped it may be incorrect to assume that the building blocks are available and functioning. A knowledge of how simple, in the sense of common, skills are put together by a young child may go some way towards providing the necessary theory to guide the utilization of behaviour modification.

REFERENCES

BARTLETT, F.C. (1958) *Thinking: an Experimental and Social Study*. Allen and Unwin, London

BERNSTEIN, N. (1967) *The Co-ordination and Regulation of Movements*. Pergamon Press, Oxford

CONNOLLY, K. (1968) The applications of operant conditioning to the measurement and development of motor skill in children. *Develop. Med. Child Neurol. 10*, 697–705

CONNOLLY, K. (1973) Factors influencing the learning of manual skills by young children. In *Constraints on Learning* (Hinde, R.A. and Hinde, J.S., eds.). Academic Press, New York

CONNOLLY, K. (1975) Movement, action and skill. In *Movement and Child Development* (Holt, K.S., ed.). Spastics International Medical Publications/Heinemann, London

CONNOLLY, K. and HARRISON, A. (1975) The analysis of skill and its implications for training the handicapped. In *Mental Health in Children Vol. III* (Siva Sankar, D.V., ed.). PJD Publications, New York

ELLIOTT, J. and CONNOLLY, K. (1974) Hierarchical structure in skill development. In *The Growth of Competence* (Connolly, K. and Bruner, J. eds.), pp. 135–168. Academic Press, New York

HARRISON, A. and CONNOLLY, K. (1971) The conscious control of fine levels of neuromuscular firing in spastic and normal subjects. *Develop. Med. Child Neurol. 13*, 762–771

HARRISON, A. (1973) Studies of neuromuscular control in spastic persons. Unpublished PhD thesis, University of Sheffield

HARRISON, A. (1975a) Studies of neuromuscular control in normal and spastic individuals In *Movement and Child Development* (Holt, K.S., ed.). Spastics International Medical Publications/Heinemann, London

HARRISON, A. (1975b) Training spastic individuals to achieve better neuromuscular control using electromyographic feedback. In *Movement and Child Development* (Holt, K.S., ed.). Spastics International Medical Publications/Heinemann, London

JOHNSTON, M.K., KELLEY, C.S., HARRIS, F.R. and WOLF, M.M. (1966) An application of reinforcement principles to development of motor skills of a young child. *Child Devel. 37*, 379–387

MEYERSON, L., KERR, N. and MICHAEL, J.L. (1967) Behaviour modification in rehabilitation. In *Child Development: Readings in Experimental Analysis* (Bijou, S.W. and Boer, D.M., eds.). Appleton-Century-Crofts, New York

Commentary

J.A. CORBETT

We tend to pay lip service to the concept that a knowledge of child development is an essential prerequisite to the construction of any programme for the development of skills in the retarded child, by the use of behaviour modification techniques.

It is generally accepted that in any such programme the skill to be trained must be broken down into its components, and each step reinforced successively either by a process of forward or backward chaining accompanied by appropriate prompting, the prompts being faded precisely and each step being appropriately reinforced. We also know that normal children acquire skills by a fairly predictable developmental sequence characterized by an order in succession of stages, and that generally speaking one stage has to be successfully completed before the next occurs.

An appreciation of these two concepts is essential to the success of any training programme, and many have foundered because of failure to accurately identify the stage of development which the individual has reached and to devise a programme only to cover the next appropriate developmental sequence. Thus, unrealistic expectations of behaviour modification techniques have led to setbacks, particularly in programmes of language training. Programme development has also been limited by our lack of knowledge of the functional development of skills. Much is known about motor development, for example, and many precise and interesting observations have been made, but all too often they have been on isolated motor achievements which have little relevance to the overall development of the sort of skills which may be important to the severely retarded child.

Kevin Connolly's paper is therefore particularly important as it demands that we take a fresh look at the development of skills in children and relate them to the feedback the child should normally receive and which would facilitate his learning.

I would like to briefly review the development of feeding in children, as I understand it, and try to look at some of the snags which may arise when we try to relate our knowledge of the normal development of this skill to that of the severely retarded child delayed in the development of motor skills. Babies of a few weeks of age often rest a hand on their bottle while being fed. Gradually the hands are brought in front of the infant's face and he begins to look at them. At about 2 weeks of age, and sometimes earlier, he starts to put the fingers of one hand to his mouth and begins to suck his fingers. At about 4 months he recognizes the bottle and at 5–6 months holds it in both hands. He can then reach out and grasp and will take a rusk to his mouth, suck it and quickly drop it. Some children at 8–9 months will guide their mother's hand when she is feeding them with a spoon, and at 9 months will hold their own bottle. They will also be able to finger-feed and eat semi-solid food from a spoon and are beginning to make the sideways movements of the jaw necessary for chewing. At about this time the child will often snatch at the spoon but will only use it to bang on the table or plunge it in the food and lick it. By 15 months he can grasp the spoon with his whole hand and feed himself for short periods, but in a clumsy way.

The retarded child may have difficulty over any of these stages for a number of reasons: –

(1) In the early stages he may be visually impaired or suffer from a lack of visual attention. Thus, the blind child is particularly likely to have difficulties over weaning and will have come to rely on tactile reinforcement.

(2) The child with a spastic type of cerebral palsy or with simple motor delay may show persistence of primitive reflexes and fail to lose the grasp reflex at an appropriate stage or develop a persistent sucking reflex which will interfere with spoon feeding. The reflex may be stimulated by touching of the lips or face with the spoon as surplus food is removed.

(3) The hypotonic child or the child with simple motor delay may have difficulty in grasping a spoon handle and fail to release or fail to grip a handle which is too thin.

In an earlier paper, Connolly (1975) noted the use of a pincer grip as a disadvantageous type for spoon holding before a palmar grasp which is more appropriate. We normally expect, as in his example of holding a pencil, that the skill will develop in the opposite direction and perhaps in this case the child has to unlearn a pincer grip which he has been busy practising in order to hold a pencil.

These are just a few examples of some of the ways in which I think we should be looking at the relationship between the analysis of normal development of skills and the development of programmes to promote these in handicapped children.

REFERENCE

CONNOLLY, K. (1975) The growth of skill. In *Child Alive* (Lewin, R., ed.). Maurice Temple Smith, London

Communication, Language, and Behaviour Modification

WILLIAM YULE and MICHAEL BERGER

*Department of Psychology, University of London Institute of Psychiatry, and
Department of Educational Psychology and Child Development,
University of London Institute of Education*

Some years ago at a conference on the language of the mentally retarded (Schie-felbusch 1972), Baer was asked if he could 'indiscriminately pick children' and, using operant techniques, get them to produce rule-governed speech, albeit of a simple type. His reply was "Let me have up to 200 hours and I'll spot you nine out of ten" (Discussion following Baer, Guess and Sherman 1972).

There can be little doubt that in general, the results of behaviour modification studies in a variety of settings have been 'overwhelmingly encouraging' (Kazdin 1973b). Despite methodological shortcomings (Kazdin 1973a; Yule, Berger and Howlin 1975), the value of behavioural techniques in the development and modification of speech has been affirmed by a number of reviewers (Hartung 1970; Yule and Berger 1972; Yule et al. 1975; Garcia and de Haven 1974). Our purpose in this paper is to highlight some of the broader issues as well as the specific problems in the application of behavioural techniques aimed at fostering the speech and language development of the mentally retarded. In focusing on the problems we in no way wish to detract from what has been achieved to date. Our concern is to produce a realistic appraisal, and, we hope, stimulate further research into techniques for helping the severely retarded and others with similar problems.

One problem, which we presumably share with many others working in applied settings, is to try and come to terms with the ever-increasing literature which in one way or another is relevant to our therapeutic endeavours. The 'academic' or 'pure' researcher can concentrate on his speciality; the applied worker cannot. Anyone working with children, for instance, ought to have a good grasp of neuropsychology, psychometrics, research design, family and group dynamics, therapeutic dynamics, therapeutic principles and techniques, child development, developmental psycholinguistics, etc. Obviously few people, if any, can encompass such diversity. They have therefore to get some secure base and from there venture out into other areas which are relatively unknown to them. Our base is behaviour modification. We have interpreted our brief for this conference to be an examination of behavioural approaches to speech and language problems, with special reference to the severely handicapped child. This must inevitably take us into the realms of developmental psycholinguistics.

Those of you who, like ourselves, cannot claim to be fully conversant with the surface and deep structures of psycholinguistics, will readily understand our problems. We must therefore apologize in advance if our transformations have not penetrated to the proper depth.

THE CURRENT SITUATION

The recent accomplishments, as well as some of the limitations of operant techniques in the establishment and generalization of 'language' have been reviewed by Garcia and de Haven (1974) as well as ourselves (Yule et al. 1975). The main conclusions are summarized below.

The role of reinforcement

There is evidence to the effect that some verbal behaviour is controlled by its immediate consequences.

Imitation

Operant speech-training procedures have always included imitation training. This has involved the imitation of motor acts as well as speech. The evidence to date suggests that while there may be generalization within a class of behaviours, each has to be trained separately for this to occur. That is, preliminary motor imitation training does not lead to generalized vocal imitation. As yet, we do not know if vocal imitation is facilitated in any way by motor training.

Functional speech

Labelling and question-and-answer responses have been achieved using operant procedures. There is little evidence that functional speech generalizes beyond the immediate training setting.

Generative response class

This concept, a relatively recent addition to the operant vocabulary, refers to verbal (and other) behaviours which show evidence of what psycholinguists might call 'rule usage'. A number of studies (Guess et al. 1968; Baer and Guess 1971; Baer et al. 1972) have shown the generative use of plural endings, verb and adjectival inflections following training in the use of only a few responses of each type. Studies have employed both productive and receptive speech-training procedures and the small numbers of subjects involved have produced evidence that they learned the rules that were trained. In one study (Guess and Baer 1973), only one of the four severely retarded subjects generalized from receptive training (plural ending 'es') to productive testing.

Generalized speech usage

There is very limited evidence that the child's accomplishments within the therapeutic setting generalize beyond the confines of the setting. Garcia and de Haven (1974) point out that for this to occur, other therapists need to work with the children in other settings.

SOME GENERAL PROBLEMS

The conflict between operant psychology and psycholinguistics is deep-rooted. Until the publication of Chomsky's *Syntactic Structures* in 1957, American linguistics was dominated by the ideas of Leonard Bloomfield (Palermo 1970a; Lyons 1970). Particularly in his later writings Bloomfield had assimilated the philosophy of behaviourism, and according to some authorities was even more radical in his approach than his behaviourist contemporaries (Lyons 1970, p. 31). Interestingly, Chomsky was both a pupil and colleague of one of the important proponents of 'Bloomfeldian' linguistics. The 'paradigm shift' (Kuhn 1970) initiated by Chomsky was, among other things, a reaction against the philosophy of behaviourism. His well-known critique of Skinner's *Verbal Behaviour* (Chomsky 1959) was not simply a rejection of a behaviourist's attempt to account for the phenomena of language. It was also a rejection of the philosophy of behaviourism.

Among the practitioners of behaviour modification is a substantial group who reject the extremes of operant psychology. Bandura (1969, pp. 127–128), for example, is strongly critical of functional behaviourists who have little sympathy for concepts which might entail mediational determinants in behaviour. Such determinants are assigned a major role in Bandura's exposition of the social learning theory position. Both operant and social learning adherents have also been criticized for their disregard of important psychometric principles in their studies (Wiggins 1973, p. 364). To these criticisms we must add the failure of at least some practitioners to take cognizance of the contributions of experimental psychologists such as O'Connor and Hermelin (O'Connor 1970). The extent to which behaviour modification practitioners have to take account of the criticisms of others is of course a problem which will have to be resolved empirically. The position we adopt is that until otherwise demonstrated, our approach has to be broadly based. The applied setting presents a variety of problems for the practitioner. Such problems are unlikely to be resolved by a rigid adherence to operant psychology.

OPERANT TRAINING, COGNITION AND LANGUAGE

Of particular interest in the Garcia and de Haven review is the introduction of the 'generative response class'. It represents one of operant psychology's concessions to contemporary psycholinguistics. In one of the first studies to make this concession, the authors (Guess et al. 1968) noted that "... it is true that the roles of differential reinforcement and imitative stimulus control in the acquisition of generative morphology and syntax largely remain to be demonstrated." A series of studies ensued, the outcomes of which were summarized above (*Generative Response Class;* see also Yule et al. 1975). Their potential importance for us lies in the fact that all the subjects were severely subnormal, and Baer's assertion that given 200 hours of operant training, 90% of the severely retarded can achieve rule-governed speech. What he has not emphasized is that this has been accomplished in a fairly narrow group of individuals and that the numbers involved have been small. Table 1 illustrates this point.

TABLE 1

Examples of recent operant language studies

Authors	Year	N	Age range (Years)	Aspects taught
Guess et al.	1968	1	10*	Plural morpheme
Baer and Guess	1971	3	7–13	Comparatives and superlatives
Twardosz and Baer	1973	2	16	Asking questions
Baer and Guess	1973	4	11–16	Verbs to nouns
Garcia	1974	2	12 and 18	Three-word sentences
Striefel and Wetherby	1973	1	11	Response to instructions
Garcia, Guess and Byrnes	1973	1	10*	Singular and plural declarative sentence
Guess and Baer	1973	4	11–21	Receptive and productive plurals

* May be the same subject.

Although not an exhaustive list, the studies included in Table 1 illustrate two main points. First, the number of subjects is small. Secondly, nearly all the subjects were of advanced chronological age. Most normal children by the age of 3–4 years show all the features which have been trained in these severely retarded subjects. Given that even in the severely retarded, mental age can increase with increasing chronological age, the outcomes of the studies in Table 1 permit several interpretations. Unfortunately, the published reports, apart from stating that the subjects were severely retarded (or mongols), make no reference to mental age. One interpretation of the data is that operant training instilled language skills in these individuals. This interpretation is implicit in the write-up of those studies. An alternative interpretation is that the operant procedures enabled these individuals to show what skills they already possessed or were capable of. In many instances, the therapists had to spend substantial amounts of time getting their subjects prepared for focused language training. It is therefore possible that as they became more amenable, the subjects were able to show the linguistic skills they were already capable of and not that operant training had instilled such skills in them. There is a strong parallel between this hypothesis and the studies of sign-language training in chimpanzees (Gardner and Gardner 1969). Simply stated, the chimpanzees had the competence: the task of the researcher was to externalize this in a way that the

38

researcher could understand. The rapid acquisition of certain linguistic junctions in a group of aphasic children taught a sign language adds weight to the latter hypothesis (Hughes 1972, see below).

The role of 'mental age' (level of cognitive development) is being increasingly emphasized in the literature on language acquisition (O'Connor 1970; Bloom 1972; Slobin 1973b; Cromer 1974).

McNeill (1970) identifies two aspects of this relationship. The first is what he calls the problem of 'cognition and language' which needs to be differentiated from the second, the problem of 'language and cognition', the question of the influence of language on thought. The former problem, according to McNeill, has not been widely recognized, although a number of recent papers have discussed it. Slobin (1973b) for example has stated that "the pacesetter in linguistic growth is the child's cognitive growth, as opposed to an autonomous linguistic development which can then reflect back on cognition." Although this issue could readily descend into a 'chicken-or-egg' debate, there is some evidence that the development of cognitive capacities predetermines the use of some linguistic forms.

Cromer (1974) has drawn together much of the evidence relating to the view that early language development depends, at least to some extent, on the child's cognitive development. As he states, the child "brings certain meanings to the task of language acquisition, and these affect even his very first words." Cromer's general conclusion is presented in terms of the 'weak form' of the cognitive hypothesis, namely "... we are able to understand and productively use particular linguistic structures only when our cognitive abilities enable us to do so." Cromer appears to suggest some form of 'overlap hypothesis' in the sense that following cognitive changes, the child uses his already available language forms to express the new ideas and relationships and also "rapidly acquires new forms of expression which he lacked until that time."

In his examination of the data from studies of language acquisition in somewhat older children, Cromer also finds evidence that certain forms of language acquisition are constrained by complexities that are a function of the specific language being acquired. In effect, the child has the meanings but the language he is learning inhibits their grammatical expression. It appears that before other linguistic changes emerge, they require the development of much more complex cognitive structures.

SEMANTICS

Like the grammars they study, the interests of psycholinguists have undergone a series of transformations over the past decade. The focus on taxonomy moved to a focus on transformational grammar and the development of syntax. More recently, there has been an increased emphasis on semantics. The concern now is not only with surface structure and transformations but with semantic structure and semantic intent (Slobin 1973a).

In the early 1960s, the phenomenon of 'telegraphic utterances' was described and was considered to be an important aspect of language development. It was also observed that adults responding to telegraphic utterances 'expanded' such utterances into grammatically correct sentences. At this time, the 'pivot–open class' constructions were described. Subsequent investigations have suggested that the latter is a phenomenon much less general than originally expected, a consequence perhaps of the small number of subjects observed in these studies. The relationship between telegraphic utterances and expansions has become clarified, mainly due to the work of Bloom and Schlesinger (Brown 1970; Bloom 1972). It now appears that "children really did intend certain aspects of the meanings attributed to them by adult expansions." The phenomenon of importance was that before adult-type syntax emerged in their utterances, children produced two one-word utterances in close succession. The order of the words varied and semantic interpretation appeared to be a function only of the context and any simultaneous behaviour. Brown (1970) regards such two-word utterances as the first sentences in child speech. He has classified them into two major categories (*Operations of Reference* and *Relations*) with a number of specific forms in each. These categories cover a substantial proportion of two-word utterances. What is special about them is that the contiguity of the words suggested semantic intent. That is, they were not simply words in chance proximity but were related to each other cognitively; they were *constructions* intended by the children and appropriate in the context in which they were produced.

The question naturally arises as to the status of single-word utterances. 'Holophrastic speech', according to McNeill (1970) refers to the possibility that the first single-word utterances are expressions of complex ideas. They are complex in the sense that they can be linked with actions, express emotional states and frequently but not inevitably name things (McNeill 1970). Some can be purely expressive. These characteristics should not, according to Bloom (1972), be taken to imply that the child has a knowledge of linguistic structure. In her studies of the speech of young children Bloom identified a group of words "which had identifiable semantic intent in relation to some aspect of the child's experience." Some of these words then began to acquire different meanings (i.e. were used in different ways). Bloom, incidentally, regards her observations as evidence that children are aware of "relational aspects of their experience before they are able to code such experience linguistically." The learning of linguistic structures would, in her view, depend on the prior development of certain conceptual structures.

It is unfortunate that developmental psycholinguistics has not, to our knowledge, encompassed gesture. Bloom's records for example show that her child said 'mama', pointed to and looked at an object associated with her mother. Anyone who observes pre-speech normal children will recognize that some of their gestures (as well as babble) have semantic intent and can be understood in the context of their occurrence. Given the complexities of phonation (Ferguson 1973) it is perhaps not surprising that crude motor acts, including babble, may be the first indications of semantic structures and intention in the pre-speaking child. The 8- to 9-month-old baby who stretches out his arms, babbles, and bounces up and down while trying to reach an object is communicating something. Parents usually understand and respond appropriately. Perhaps psycho-linguists should do likewise.

On the assumption that current psycholinguistic characterizations of language development do not share the fate of pivot–open class constructions, the recent research now gives a much clearer conception of language development. As yet it is difficult to know where it begins, if such a point exists. Perhaps it begins in the undifferentiated motor acts (including vocalizations) which then become increasingly differentiated into gesture forms and sound patterns which are distinguishable by an observer who 'knows' the child. These early features become even more distinct to the point that they are understandable within a culture wider than the immediate family. That is, the gestures (e.g. bye-bye wave) and the words are of culturally acceptable forms. More words and gestures are added and combined with variable word order (the first two-word sentences) leading to the emergence of adult grammar. This at least is how we see things at present. Obviously, much of what we say is conjectural. But one point we wish to emphasize is that young babies (before the emergence of what we arbitrarily have decided to accept as words) may be communicating. Our problem is that we have not yet learned how to understand them. Parents, as we noted above, usually do.

IMPLICATIONS

There are many practical implications in the foregoing excursion into psycho-linguistics.

If we can accept the evidence for the primacy of cognitive development, then assessment of cognitive functioning becomes very important. On the basis of an appropriate assessment it may be possible to decide whether to proceed immediately into language training (and at what level to begin), or to focus some or all of the time on fostering the development of cognitive skills. Adequate assessment may require the use of behaviour modification procedures to overcome behavioural difficulties which can interfere with assessment (e.g. tantrums). In carrying out various forms of assessment, care has also to be taken that the associated handicaps of the retarded individual (visual, auditory, motor) are not masking his cognitive achievements. We have discussed these and related issues in a previous paper (Berger and Yule 1972).

In addition to traditional assessment procedures, use should be made of tech-niques which aid the investigation of attentional and short-term memory difficulties. Such procedures have been described by Hermelin and O'Connor (O'Connor 1970). Operant techniques have been used to help reduce the effect of some of the associated handicaps prior to speech training. Such techniques may be of use in attempts to provide an adequate basis for cognitive 'training'. With regard to cognitive training, it is necessary to question the value of cog-nitive stimulation if it is to take the form of stimulus bombardment. If the child has problems in maintaining attention, what we consider to be a stimulating environment may well be 'blooming and buzzing' confusion for him. The most appropriate environment might well be the bare windowless room into which 'enrichment' is introduced gradually and carefully.

As we are not yet certain of which cognitive functions are necessary for particular linguistic skills we can only suggest the use of published work on cognitive development as a guide. Proper cognitive assessment may also be useful in helping to decide on what to teach. If the child has the concept of 'plurality', it will be helpful to teach plural endings in speech. Once we have a clear idea of what we are looking for, operant procedures may be very helpful in assessment. Such procedures are available for assessing what sounds can be heard (Bricker and Bricker 1969). We see no reason why they could not be used to test for the attainment of concepts not only in the severely handicapped, but in pre-speech children as well.

It might be argued here that functional target assessments or functional analysis are all that is needed. There are several reasons for not being so restrictive. Functional assessments appear to lack generalizability and they entail observational procedures which are problematic (Wiggins 1973).

Given that some of the first communications may be context-bound, any assessment of current accomplishments must cover the many environments of the individual. For various reasons, we may not see them in the consulting room. What we cannot observe in the classroom we may observe in the home. Much greater reliance must be placed on the observations of parents, siblings and caretakers in the initial stages of our investigations. We also have to be very careful to ensure that when we ask about the child's language, we are not understood as referring simply to speech. We have to rely on questions such as "How do you know when he wants to go to the toilet?" or "How do you know that he wants a biscuit?" Obviously, the reliability of such observations will need to be checked. We need to both look and listen.

Some years ago, we suggested as others have done (Bricker 1972) that the teaching of gesture might be a better way of initiating communication than trying to establish speech (Yule and Berger 1972). Mittler (1973) also suggested that use should be made of gesture, although his suggestions had a more limited scope. The undeniable success of behaviour modifiers in training motor imitation indicates that we have the techniques. Unfortunately, attempts are then made to try and develop speech. Although various gestural systems are available (e.g. Levitt 1970) perhaps we should consider the use of those gestures which are used by the deaf. The power of combined operant techniques and the American Sign Language has been amply demonstrated by the Gardners (Gardner and Gardner 1969) in their work with the chimpanzee Washoe. One also needs to recognize that imitation skills are complex; simpler systems could therefore be used. Premack (1970), also working with a chimpanzee has developed an approach which only involves the manipulation of plastic tokens. His work could be usefully adopted in attempts to instigate communication in the severely retarded. Hughes (1972), in an unpublished study (see Cromer 1974), reports the successful use of Premack's technique with aphasic children of average non-verbal IQ. These children "rapidly acquired all the functions taught" (Cromer 1974), including names for objects, verbs, negation, questions, etc.

One of the important tasks for behaviour modification is to come to terms with semantics and semantic intent. It is not sufficient to show that within-class or between-situation generalization takes place, even though these are important. The central issue here is the nature of the differences between the subnormal or autistic child and a normal child who produce identical words or strings of words in the same order; or the child and chimpanzee who respectively produce words or signs in close succession. This is the problem that confronted Brown (1970) in his analysis of the signs learned by Washoe (Gardner and Gardner 1969).

In discussing the first sentences of children, Brown states: "There was, in the child's speech, something to suggest that they intended these relations. This same 'something', the aspect of child speech that justified the attribution to them of certain relational meanings, turns out to be missing from the linguistic performance of an important comparison case: the home-raised chimpanzee named Washoe." Brown's problem with Washoe is the same as our ultimate problem in language training, irrespective of whether or not we use operant procedures. At some stage we have to consider whether the child has been taught a language that is appropriate for his developmental level. Brown's 1970 paper is very useful in this respect. Unfortunately, the criteria he proposes and his reasons for proposing them would require much more space than we have at our disposal here. The reader is therefore referred to the original. Our main purpose is to draw attention to the semantic aspect of language and to suggest that more attention should be paid to it in the future.

The criticisms of operant-produced 'speech-language' which have centred around the question of the isomorphisms between such trained skills and 'true' language (Yule and Berger 1972; Yule et al. 1975) have been very important in helping to moderate the claims of operant psychologists. The explicit and implicit challenges have led to such important studies as those of response class (even though they have their limitations), so that the conflict has been fruitful. For various reasons, we should not allow the criticisms of the psycholinguists to inhibit our attempts to establish communication skills in the severely retarded. Whether or not such skills turn out to be isomorphic with language depends very much on how psycholinguists resolve their problems over the definition of language. Their understanding of 'language' changes as their discipline evolves, and no doubt will change more as they move even further backwards along the developmental sequence.

THE CONTENT OF PROGRAMMES

As we have argued before (Yule et al. 1975), our approach to treating children with language deficits is a clinical psychological one – i.e., we attempt to apply empirically based knowledge from the general field of child development to the particular problems presented. This means that when devising programmes for language-retarded children, one must draw heavily on the rapidly expanding body of published work in developmental psycholinguistics to guide one in selecting appropriate target behaviours in an appropriate sequence.

This strategy assumes that most retarded children with language problems are showing *delayed* language rather than *deviant* language. That is, it assumes that if there is a normal sequence of language development then mentally retarded children will probably develop language skills in the same sequence, but at a slower rate. As Miller and Yoder (1972a) conclude from their review of the evidence, this appears to be the most likely hypothesis on the basis of present evidence. They therefore counsel that: "The content for language training for retarded children should be taken from the data available on language development in normal children, and this content should be taught in the same sequence that it is acquired in the normal child."

We agree that in the present state of our knowledge, this is probably the most efficient strategy to follow. However, we emphasize that although the *content* of training should parallel that of the normal sequence of acquisition, the *method* of training need not. It is irrelevant for present purposes to discuss whether normal children acquire language through operant training. All that need be noted is that operant programmes have shown considerable success in teaching language to retarded children.

Some recently published programmes illustrate the ways in which behaviour modifiers have used psycholinguistic literature to guide the content of their programmes.

Bricker (1972) presents a detailed flow diagram of the major steps in his carefully-thought-out programme. An early and vitally important stage is to establish the child's hearing level. Then, after training in receptive vocabulary, verbal imitation is established before simple labelling or naming is trained. Finally, sentences are trained using information on morphological and syntactical inflections to guide the trainer. A similar sequence of stages has been proposed by Williams (1973), although the sub-units are not described in such great detail.

Sailor, Guess and Baer (1973) propose another closely similar training programme. They conceptualize the training in three major stages. Stage I involves getting a good description and assessment of the child's current level of functioning, as well as training him to attend. Stage II involves training in imitation, and Stage III moves on to functional speech and language training. This last stage has no less than 61 different steps—each step being a sub-programme in its own right.

Gray and Ryan (1973) describe a similarly complex programme. They present a core of 13 programmes to teach basic skills and simple sentences; a further 10 programmes to teach some important morphological, inflection and syntactical structures; and a final 18 programmes to teach what they regard as more advanced language skills. Only a few of their programmes are presented in great detail. For example, a programme to teach the use of the verb *is* in a simple sentence such as 'The boy is happy' consists of 22 steps in training during which prompts are systematically faded and an attempt is made to encourage the child to use such sentences spontaneously. Throughout this programme, the emphasis is on training particular *sentence forms*, and not just single sentences. Thus, a different picture with a different content is presented on each trial. This approach

44

is much more sophisticated than in most of the studies we reviewed a few years ago (Yule and Berger 1972).

As we have noted earlier, the early psycholinguists' attempts to describe a child's first grammar did so in terms of a two-word structure which was termed Pivot and Open Class. This was based on statistical counts of relative word frequencies, and the concept caught on widely before it had been tested on many cases. Early on, many people suggested that the Pivot and Open Class structure might be taught to language deficient children (Yule and Berger 1972; Mittler 1973; Jeffree, Wheldall and Mittler 1973). In fact, the programme referred to earlier (Bricker 1972) provides details of a complex sub-programme to train this simple structure.

Bloom (1970 and 1972) is highly critical of the notion of the Pivot and Open Class structure. She presents an alternative analysis of early two-word utterances which takes into account the semantic intent of the child. She argues that children's earliest 'sentences' represent a reduction of a more complex underlying syntactical structure, and should be understood as such.

Miller and Yoder (1972b) develop some of Bloom's ideas and have presented an outline programme for training syntax. They emphasize that the words and syntactical structures trained must have clear functional relevance to the child in his natural environment. Relational terms such as 'more', 'no', and 'stop' are trained early along with labels. Word strings are trained as an intermediate step between single word utterances and two word phrases. Then the three forms of two-word phrases described by Bloom – Verb/Object, Subject/Object and Subject/Verb – are separately targeted.

This latter paper is discussed to highlight the problem that applied scientists have in keeping up with the literature. Like most of the earlier programmes mentioned, it represents more a statement about the authors' current conceptual framework than a description of an empirically evaluated treatment package. As long as this is clearly understood, then such detailed descriptions can be important sources of ideas for the applied worker.

Doubtless, this latest analysis of children's earliest grammars will be refined before the present paper is published. By then, numerous children will have been subjected to programmes based on Bloom's analysis. In our present state of knowledge, this is not necessarily a bad thing, provided the outcome of training is adequately evaluated. In fact, as Tizard pointed out in his Presidential Address to the British Society for the Study of Mental Subnormality (Tizard 1972), "... it is through a proper consideration of practical issues that social science is most likely to make theoretical advances during the present century."

Tizard went on to say that he is "... inclined to agree with Karl Popper (1961) that a technological approach to the social sciences 'imposes a discipline on our speculative inclinations' (which, especially in the field of sociology proper, are likely to lead us into the region of metaphysics); for it forces us to submit our theories to definite standards, such as standards of clarity and practical testability. As Popper points out, 'this emphasis upon the practical technological approach does not mean that any of the theoretical problems that may arise from the analysis of practical problems should be excluded. On the contrary

45

... the technological approach is likely to prove fruitful in giving rise to significant problems of a purely theoretical kind'."

It seems to us that Popper is likely to approve of the behaviour modification or applied behavioural analysis approach to significant problems (although we have been unable to find anything in print which says so). If for 'sociology' in the above quotation we insert 'psycholinguistics', we can better appreciate that the relationship between psycholinguistics and behaviour modification need not be as one-way as we have hitherto been arguing. Behaviour modifiers are in a good position to test out hypotheses based on psycholinguistic speculation. Where the tests are carried out with retarded subjects, the findings may be generalized to that population even though they may not be relevant to answering fundamental questions regarding language development in normal children.

Thus, the studies seeking to train Pivot and Open Class structures may be based on an invalid premise, but nevertheless they may prove valuable in training that behaviour in retarded children. Jeffree, Wheldall and Mittler's (1973) exploratory study with two Down's syndrome boys demonstrates that with great ingenuity it is possible to teach such children at least some two-word structures, and that such learning can generalize. If future attempts at training two-word structures in retarded children can show that the Pivot and Open Class structure is easier (or more difficult) than the different types of structures claimed by Bloom, then we may be in a position to re-examine the assumption that retarded children develop speech in a manner that is only quantitatively different from normal children. This is only one example of how applied research can relate back to 'pure' research.

To return to the question of content. The programmes cited earlier differ greatly in the detail of what they actually train at any one point, and how they train it. For instance, Gray and Ryan (1973) state that the therapist should always present a perfect model sentence—such as 'The ball is red'—even though they do not expect the child to reproduce the definite article. By contrast, Miller and Yoder (1972b) state that it is important that adults should "reduce their syntax to telegraphic speech whenever possible when talking to the child."

This disagreement on strategy is fundamental. It is often suggested that when a child is having difficulty with language, the adults should talk to him in simpler sentences at a level which he can comprehend. It is our impression that this advice is often given, but the practice is rarely evaluated directly. It is based on the assumption that comprehension precedes production, and the experimental evidence on this point is equivocal (Yule et al. 1975). Although we ourselves have given this advice, we recognize the danger that limiting the language models presented to the child may inhibit his development of more complex syntactical forms.

Of course, there is some evidence that mothers of retarded children already present simplified language models (Buium, Rynders and Turnure 1974; Jeffree and Cashdan 1971), but whether this is cause or effect is not clear. However, it seems to us that there is a real difference between adults adjusting the complexity of their language intuitively, and adjusting their language output in a controlled

46

systematic way such that important structures are highlighted and redundant content is omitted. This question is clearly capable of empirical investigation.

To pursue it a little further, Palermo (1970b) notes that there is a close relationship between the morpheme-length-of-utterance and the appearance of rules of negatives and interrogatives. Does this imply that an analysis of MLU should be made, and that adults should then confine themselves to modelling structures which are likely to be produced at that time? Herriot (1970) notes that "... a sentence with a phrase added to the subject is more difficult to deal with than one with the same material tagged onto the predicate." Slobin (1966) reports that negative sentences are more difficult for young children to deal with than were passive sentences. And at a simpler level, Palermo (1970b) reminds us that it is easier for a young child to produce 'The cat is being chased' than to produce 'The cat is being chased by the dog'.

We are not in a position to draw together all such observations and empirical findings which bear upon the question of sentence complexity and its relation to ease of production in both normal and retarded children. What we are arguing is that there is information and many ideas in the psycholinguistic literature, and it should soon be incorporated in language-training programmes. At the very least, where such information is ignored, it should be by a deliberate decision to exclude the finding from consideration. As more and more behaviour modifiers turn their attention to training language, they should not have to rediscover the rules of phonology, morphology, syntax and semantics anew on each child.

As an approximation to a specification of the content of a language programme, we suggest the following:

1. *Sounds*

If you are teaching a child with few or no sounds, learn which sounds are normally easiest. For example, Bricker (1967) groups sounds in five groupings from easiest (*b*, *w*, *m*, *t* and *d*) to the most difficult (*th*, *v*, *y*). Obviously one is guided both by this knowledge and by careful observations of the child in deciding both where to start and how long to persevere.

2. *Nouns*

Teach singulars before plurals, and teach nouns before verbs and adjectives.

3. *Verbs*

Teach present tense before past tense. Notice that when children do learn past tense, they tend to learn the most frequent irregular inflections first (e.g. was, ran). When they do learn the regular inflection (mov*ed*, point*ed*) they often overgeneralize and use nonsense words such as runned, breaked (Palermo and Eberhart 1968; Ervin 1964). When teaching inflections for the past tense, note that the markers | -t | and | -d | are more easily learned than | -əd |. Presumably, if you want to teach a rule-governed past-tense behaviour you should concentrate initially on examples of the former kind.

4. *Adjectives*

Fenn (1972) cites Palermo and other workers in the field to demonstrate that the use of 'opposites' increase with age. Thus, she argues that young children should not be trained to respond to opposites at an early stage in training. And yet, how many of us have spent hours with retarded children saying "Give me a *little* doll. Good. Now, give me the *big* doll." Certainly, the big/little discrimination is taught as step 46 by Sailor et al. (1973). We should always remember that because a discrimination is simple for adults, it need not be so for any children, let alone mentally retarded children.

5. *Questions*

Remember that work has been carried out on WH questions (Brown 1968). On the whole, 'what' is easier than 'where' and both are easier than 'when'.

Many other points to guide the selection of contents are to be found in Palermo (1970b).

SOME PARTICULAR PROBLEMS

Data collection

All behaviour modifiers would agree that good, reliable, valid data are the keystones to successful treatment. Insofar as one can select a sensitive index of change, one can feed back results into the therapeutic system. Interventions producing progress can be strengthened; those that produce no progress are altered. The problem in language development programmes is to select relevant indices.

At a simple level, it appears to be very easy. If a child is being taught to say the label 'ball' every time a ball is displayed, the therapist can merely note down whether a sufficiently close approximation was produced. With skill, the therapist can note whether a prompt was delivered or not. But is it really as easy as this?

Where only one label is being targeted at a time, it is probably possible for the therapist to note and code every response. But where different labels are being worked on, and the therapist has to put down one object and present the next, recording becomes more problematical. A second adult present to record or to present the materials helps, but this immediately makes the treatment session much more expensive.

At some stages, where many trials on few exemplars are being conducted, some form of prepared coding sheet may be helpful. Gray and Ryan (1973) recommend the use of a simple coding system. Answers are scored *right*, *wrong* or *no response*, and a sequence of ten consecutive correct responses is taken to indicate mastery of that particular step in the programme. This sounds easy to use, but it presents difficulties in practice. The major disadvantage is that where an error is made, one does not record the quality of the error. This means that if the child is learning an incorrect rule, this might not be noticed. Errors are often more informative than successes. In passing, it should also be noted that no clear rationale is given for applying the criterion of ten consecutive correct responses to every stage, and even more worryingly, so few trials beyond ten appear to have been needed in their studies that results were often presented as percentages on very small denominators.

In theory, all sessions could be audio-taped. However, the resulting transcription and analysis are often so time-consuming as to make this an uneconomic option, at least within a service setting. For example, in our own studies of the speech of mothers of autistic children, *three* hours of transcription were needed for every hour of language interaction recorded (Howlin, Cantwell et al. 1973). Although this is essential for experimental purposes, easier methods must be found to gather good data in clinical settings.

The above examples have all assumed a level of pre-arranged task presentation which is not often met, at least in our clinical experience. Although the therapist may have intended working for 20 minutes on one particular word or structure, if the child spontaneously uses a different structure which is new in his repertoire, or if the child's attention cannot be held for the intended time and a different stimulus has to be introduced, many therapists will be flexible enough to follow the child's lead. The greater the degree of flexibility, the more difficult the recording task.

In summary, it seems to us that there are no simple ways of gathering data during language training. Mechanical aids may help, but the more complex the apparatus, the less likely it is that such aids can be used in the more naturalistic treatment sessions. We must examine more critically different ways of collecting good data in experimental settings, and then adapt these methods for use in the clinic. Such a development has recently taken place in behaviour modification in the classroom; laboratory-based techniques both of modification and recording have been successfully simplified and adapted for use in ordinary large classrooms by the teachers themselves (Hall 1971). Priority should be given to a parallel development in language training.

The relationship between assessments

Most published accounts of therapeutic gains in behavioural language problems appear to be in terms of changes on criterion measures, such as the number of labels used, rather than in terms of changes on normative measures, such as improved score on a standardized test of language function (Yule and Berger 1972; Garcia and de Haven 1974). This reflects the bias of practitioners of an experimental analysis of behaviour, but it makes it difficult to comment on whether demonstrated gains are clinically (or developmentally) valuable.

While we accept that in one sense one cannot put a value on teaching a previously mute child a socially relevant vocabulary of a dozen words to indicate bodily needs, it must be recognized that this real achievement may not be very great when considered against what is normal for a child of that age. Developmental psycholinguists point out that normal children develop almost all the syntactical structures to be found in adult speech between the ages of 2 and 4 years. Compared with this achievement, the gains reported in most programmes of language therapy are modest indeed. We suggest that it is important to explore the relationship between the statistical significance and the clinical significance of gains made during treatment.

Such an exploration is important for two reasons. First, gains on criterion tests need to be viewed against the perspective of normal development. An increase of five words may be functionally important for the individual, but the cost of attaining it may be too high. More constructively, if such a gain is seen in a wider context, therapists may be motivated to use their energies and ingenuity to achieve even better results.

Secondly, we have long been critical of most published accounts of behavioural language therapy on the grounds that insufficient detail is given in describing the children given treatment (Yule and Berger, 1972). The accounts typically do not report the children's mental or language ages. We argue that such information is potentially valuable on two counts: (*a*) it may provide indicators of where to begin therapy; (*b*) it may provide evidence of which sort of children benefit most from which sort of treatment programme. Clearly, if both normative and detailed criterion-referenced data were available, both tasks ought to be easier accomplished. This latter point is partially recognized by Sailor et al. (1973) when they note that one target of future language-treatment researches should include "... the possibility that existing behaviour of the language-deficient child might serve as predictive variables for the selection of the best training techniques for that child ... ." Thus, the use of both normative and criterion measures should assist in achieving this goal of prescriptive language teaching.

A further point which requires comment, but cannot be elaborated for lack of space, concerns the question of the validity of assessments. Too often, assessments are made solely in the treatment setting. The assumption is made that if the child shows that he has mastered a skill in that setting, he will be using that skill in other settings. All the recent literature in behaviour modifications calls this assumption into question. Behaviour is much more situation-specific than most of us like to admit, and language behaviour is no exception.

Two errors can be made. First, just because a child uses a language structure in the treatment setting is no guarantee that he will use it, say, at home. Generalization has to be worked for, not merely assumed. Secondly, there is no guarantee that language structures shown at home will be demonstrated in the clinic. Dever's (1970) study is a cautionary example. He showed that retarded children's performance on the Berko Test of morphological inflections bore little relationship to the presence of these speech forms in free play. Behaviour modifiers must constantly be reminded that no matter how reliable an observation may be, other evidence must be provided of its validity. We suggest that if both criterion measures and normative measures are taken, the validity of experimentation in language training will be greatly enhanced.

Appropriate research designs

There are two crucial questions in evaluating the efficacy of a programme of treatment, and each requires a different type of evidence to provide adequate answers. The questions are: (*a*) Can the therapist demonstrate that any observed changes are caused by his intervention? This generally requires that an appropriate single-case research design has been incorporated in the treatment. And (*b*) Is the therapeutic gain greater than expected, either on the basis of maturation or on the basis of a different form of treatment? This is essentially a question about the comparative effects of different types of treatment and generally requires that a comparison of groups has been undertaken. Both sorts of questions need to be asked in language training.

For present purposes, however, we would like to focus on the question of single-case research designs and their use of language training. It is increasingly being recognized that there is an intimate interaction between the behaviour being targeted and the research design necessary to demonstrate that the behaviour has been brought under experimental control (Yule 1974). There are now several review articles dealing with single-case designs (Wolf and Risley 1971; Birnbrauer, Peterson and Solnick 1974), but none has focused on the problem of demonstrating experimental control over a skill during the rapidly accelerating acquisition phase.

Reversal designs are patently inappropriate during language training. They are more suited to demonstrating that the frequency of occurrence of a previously acquired motor skill can be brought under stimulus or reinforcement control. The simple AB (or baseline–treatment) design is probably more appropriate to training new verbal behaviour. The problem here is in deciding how great an inflection must occur at or after the point in the graph at which treatment commenced before 'real' change is accepted. Logically, on considering only one targeted behaviour, it is difficult to ascribe any change to the treatment. However, multiple-baseline designs across different verbal responses (effectively successive or occasionally simultaneous replications within the one subject) provide greater evidence that change is related to treatment rather than chance.

However, the problem with applying a multiple-baseline design to language responses is that the baselines may not be functionally independent. We have argued earlier that behaviour theorists are increasingly discussing the concept of *response classes* within the field of language behaviour. Where such response classes exist, training of one exemplar will produce changes in the probability of the production (or comprehension) of another member of the same class. Thus, when one baseline count is altered by direct intervention, the other will alter vicariously and in parallel. There will then be little evidence that changes occur *only* when the first exemplar is targeted. This is a complex issue, and cannot be pursued further here. It is sufficient for present purposes to note that the possible existence of response classes in language behaviour – that is, the existence of rule-governed behaviour – greatly complicates the problem of providing satisfactory evidence that language is under experimental control. Moreover, unless experimenters are scrupulously careful, it may be possible to 'explain away' unexpected results as being examples of interference from response classes.

51

Training parents

It is increasingly being explicitly recognized that language training for the mentally retarded child is a skilled and time-consuming matter (Garcia and de Haven 1974). Once good, reliable programmes of treatment have been developed, it is therefore highly desirable that the training should be undertaken by the child's parents.

Parent training is being discussed more extensively elsewhere in this book. Recent reviews have amply illustrated that training parents to apply behavioural techniques can be an effective means of delivering scarce services to the children (Berkowitz and Graziano 1972; Johnson and Katz 1973). However, there are many unresolved, or at least unexamined, problems in parent training (Yule 1975), and one of these concerns the role of parents in language training.

If one accepts the growing suggestions that parents require as much if not more help in developing shaping skills as in developing reinforcing skills, then it would be surprising to find that parents could shape complex language structures in their children without skilled advice from outside. It is our impression that parents do have particular difficulty in executing language training. In view of all that has gone before in this paper, this is hardly surprising. If experts cannot agree on what to teach, in what order, how can parents be expected to do any better?

Nevertheless, parents should be involved in language training from the outset for reasons other than those of expense. At least in theory, if parents are trained to elicit language in the clinic, they can greatly assist in the problem of generalizing what is learned there into the home. Further, parents are in a better position than therapists to assist in *maintaining* gains over time. In the recent follow-up study of autistic children, Lovaas et al. (1973) found that the greater the extent of parental involvement in training, the more likely were gains to generalize and persist. This is why in our own studies we have laid a greater emphasis on carrying out treatment within the child's own home (Howlin, Marchant et al. 1973).

CONCLUDING REMARKS

In this paper, we have looked at three broad aspects of the interrelationship between developmental psycholinguistics and behavioural programmes for teaching language to retarded children. We have examined some current theoretical issues in the study of developmental psycholinguistics *per se;* we have tried to illustrate how even meagre knowledge in this area can be used to guide us in selecting the content of what should be taught in a language training programme; and we have highlighted some practical problems which emerge in the training of language retarded children. In all these discussions our emphasis has been, of necessity, on problems rather than on solutions. We hope that this orientation will provoke some useful discussion.

Two points need particular emphasis. First, there is very little guidance in the literature on the development of the child's first word. If we are to help profoundly retarded children, much more attention will have to be paid to this developmental milestone. Secondly, and again with the more profoundly retarded in mind, the use of gesture (both in its own right as a form of communication, and in its role in facilitating spoken language) will have to be accorded a more important role in future developments.

Even from this brief review it is obvious that many exciting concepts are currently being discussed. What is urgently needed are many more well-executed empirical studies to sort out the viable concepts from the more speculative.

REFERENCES

BAER, D.M. and GUESS, D. (1971) Receptive training of adjectival inflections in mental retardates. *J. Appl. Behav. Anal. 4*, 129–139

BAER, D.M. and GUESS, D. (1973) Teaching productive noun suffixes to severely retarded children. *Amer. J. Ment. Defic. 77*, 498–505

BAER, D.M., GUESS, D. and SHERMAN, J.A. (1972) Adventures in simplistic grammar. In Schiefelbusch, R.L. (1972), *op.cit.*, pp. 93–105

BANDURA, A. (1969) *Principles of Behavior Modification*. Holt, Rinehart and Winston, New York

BERGER, M. and YULE, W. (1972) Cognitive assessment in young children with language delay. In *The Child with Delayed Speech* (Rutter, M. and Martin, J.A.M., eds.), pp. 120–135. (Clinics in Developmental Medicine no. 43) Spastics International Medical Publications/ Heinemann, London

BERKOWITZ, B.P. and GRAZIANO, A.M. (1972) Training parents as behaviour therapists: a review. *Behav. Res. Ther. 10*, 297–317

BIRNBRAUER, J.S., PETERSON, C.R. and SOLNICK, J.V. (1974) Design and interpretation of studies of single subjects. *Am. J. Ment. Defic. 79*, 191–203.

BLOOM, L. (1970) *Language Development: Form and Function in Emerging Grammar*. M.I.T. Press, Cambridge

BLOOM, L. (1972) Semantic features in language development. In *Language of the Mentally Retarded* (Schiefelbusch, R.L., ed.), pp.18–33. University Park Press, Baltimore

BRICKER, W.A. (1967) Errors in the echoic behaviour of pre-school children. *J. Speech Hear. Res. 10*, 67–76

BRICKER, W.A. (1972) A systematic approach to language training. In *Language of the Mentally Retarded*. (Schiefelbusch, R.L., ed.), pp. 75–92. University Park Press, Baltimore

BRICKER, W.A. and BRICKER, D.D. (1969) A programmed approach to operant audiometry for low functioning children. *J. Speech Hear. Dis. 34*, 312–320

BROWN, R. (1968) The development of wh questions in child speech. *J. Verb. Learn. Verb. Behav. 7*, 279–290

BROWN, R. (1970) The first sentences of child and chimpanzee. In *Psycholinguistics: Selected Papers* (Brown, R., ed.). Free Press, New York

BUIUM, N., RYNDERS, J. and TURNURE, J. (1974) Early maternal linguistic environment of normal and Down's syndrome language learning children. *Am. J. Ment. Defic. 79*, 52–58

CHOMSKY, N. (1959) Review of 'Verbal Behavior' by B.F. Skinner. *Language, 35*, 26–58.

CROMER, R.F. (1974) The development of language and cognition: the cognition hypothesis. In *New Perspectives in Child Development* (Foss, B., ed.). Penguin Books, Harmondsworth, Middx

DEVER, R.B. (1970) A comparison of the results of a revised version of Berko's Test of Morphology with the free speech of mentally retarded children. Unpub. PhD thesis, Wisconsin, and paper in press

ERVIN, S.M. (1964) Imitation and structural change in children's language. In *New Directions in the Study of Language* (Lenneberg, E.H., ed.). M.I.T. Press, Cambridge, Mass.

FENN, G. (1972) The development of syntax in a group of severely subnormal children. Unpub. PhD thesis, Cambridge

FERGUSON, C.A. (1973) Phonology. Introduction to Part One. In Ferguson, C.A. and Slobin, D.I. (eds.), *op.cit.* pp. 1–3

FERGUSON, C.A. and SLOBIN, D.I. (eds.) (1973) *Studies of Child Language Development.* Holt, Rinehart and Winston, New York

GARCIA, E. (1974) The training and generalization of a conversational speech form in non-verbal retardates. *J. Appl. Behav. Anal. 7,* 137–149

GARCIA, E. and DE HAVEN, E.D. (1974) Use of operant techniques in the establishment and generalization of language: a review and analysis. *Am. J. Ment. Defic. 79,* 169–178

GARCIA, E., GUESS, D. and BYRNES, J. (1973) Development of syntax in a retarded girl using procedures of imitation, reinforcement, and modelling. *J. Appl. Behav. Anal. 6,* 299–310

GARDNER, R.A. and GARDNER, B.T. (1969) Teaching sign language to a chimpanzee. *Science 165,* 644–672

GRAY, B.B. and RYAN, B.P. (1973) *A Language Program for the Non-Language Child.* Research Press, Champaign, Ill.

GUESS, D. and BAER, D.M. (1973) An analysis of individual differences in generalization between receptive and productive language in retarded children. *J. Appl. Behav. Anal. 6,* 311–329

GUESS, D., SAILOR, W., RUTHERFORD, G. and BAER, D.M. (1968) An experimental analysis of linguistic development. *J. Appl. Behav. Anal. 1,* 297–306

HALL, R.V. (1971) *Managing Behavior.* H. and H. Enterprises, Lawrence, Kansas

HARTUNG, J.R. (1970) A review of procedures to increase verbal imitation skills and functional speech in autistic children. *J. Speech Hear. Dis. 35,* 203–217

HERRIOT, P. (1970) *An Introduction to the Psychology of Language.* Methuen, London

HOWLIN, P., CANTWELL, D., MARCHANT, R., BERGER, M. and RUTTER, M. (1973) Analysing mothers' speech to young autistic children: a methodological study. *J. Abnorm. Child Psychol. 1,* 317–339

HOWLIN, P., MARCHANT, RUTTER, M., BERGER, M., HERSOV, L. and YULE, W. (1973) A home-based approach to the treatment of autistic children. *J. Aut. Child. Schiz. 2,* 308–336

JEFFREE, D.M. and CASHDAN, A. (1971) Severely subnormal children and their parents: an experiment in language improvement. *Br. J. Educ. Psychol. 41,* 184–194

JEFFREE, D., WHELDALL, K. and MITTLER, P. (1973) Facilitating two word utterances in two Down's syndrome boys. *Am. J. Ment. Defic. 78,* 117–122

JOHNSON, C.A. and KATZ, R.C. (1973) Using parents as change agents for their children: a review. *J. Child Psychol. Psychiat. 14,* 181–200

KAZDIN, A.E. (1973a) Methodological and assessment considerations in evaluating reinforcement programs in applied settings. *J. Appl. Behav. Anal. 6,* 517–531

KAZDIN, A.E. (1973b) Issues in behavior modification with mentally retarded persons. *Am. J. Ment. Defic. 78,* 134–140

KUHN, T.S. (1970) *The Structure of Scientific Revolutions.* 2nd ed. University of Chicago Press, Chicago

LEVITT, L.M. (1970) *A Method of Communication for Non-speaking Severely Subnormal Children.* Spastics Society, London

LOVAAS, O.I., KOEGEL, R., SIMMONS, J.Q. and LONG, J.S. (1973) Some generalization and follow-up measures on autistic children in behavior therapy. *J. Appl. Behav. Anal. 6,* 131–166

LYONS, J. (1970) *Chomsky.* Fontana/Collins, London

MCNEILL, D. (1970) The development of language. In *Carmichael's Manual of Child Psychology* (Mussen, P., ed.), pp. 1061–1161. Wiley, New York

MILLER, J.F. and YODER, D.E. (1972a) On developing the context for a language teaching program. *Ment. Retard. 10* (2), 9–11

MILLER, J.F. and YODER, D.E. (1972b) A syntax teaching program. In *Language Intervention with the Retarded* (McLean, J.E., Yoder, D.E. and Schiefelbusch, R.L., eds.), pp.191–211. University Park Press, Baltimore

MITTLER, P. (1973) The teaching of language. In *Mental Retardation and Behavioural Research* (Clarke, A.D.B. and Clarke, A.M., eds.), pp.199–212. Churchill Livingstone, Edinburgh

54

O'Connor, N. (1970) Speech and thought in the retarded. In *Proceedings of the Second Congress of the International Association for the Scientific Study of Mental Deficiency* (Primrose, D. A. A., ed.), pp. 23–29. Swets & Zeitlinger, Amsterdam

Palermo, D. S. (1970a) Research on language acquisition: do we know where we are going? In *Life-Span Developmental Psychology* (Goulet, L. R. and Baltes, P. B., eds.). Academic Press, New York

Palermo, D. S. (1970b) Language acquisition. In *Experimental Child Psychology* (Reese, H.W. and Lipsitt, L.P., eds.). Academic Press, New York

Palermo, D. S. and Eberhart, V. L. (1968) On the learning of morphological rules: an experimental analogy. *J. Verb. Learn. Verb. Behav. 7*, 337–344

Popper, K. R. (1961) *The Poverty of Historicism.* Routledge & Kegan Paul, London

Premack, D. A. (1970) A functional analysis of language. *J. Exp. Anal. Behav. 14*, 107–125

Sailor, W., Guess, D. and Baer, D. M. (1973) Functional language for verbally deficient children: an experimental program. *Ment. Retard. 11* (3), 27–35

Schiefelbusch, R. L. (ed.) (1972) *Language of the Mentally Retarded.* University Park Press, Baltimore

Slobin, D. I. (1966) Grammatical transformations and sentence comprehension in childhood and adulthood. *J. Verb. Learn. Verb. Behav. 5*, 219–227

Slobin, D. I. (1973a) Grammar: introduction to Part Two. In Ferguson, C. A. and Slobin, D. I. (eds.), *op cit.*, pp. 169–173

Slobin, D. I. (1973b) Cognitive prerequisites for the development of grammar. In Ferguson, C. A. and Slobin, D. I (eds.), *op. cit.*

Striefel, S. and Wetherby, B. (1973) Instruction-following behavior of a retarded child and its controlling stimuli. *J. Appl. Behav. Anal. 6*, 663–670

Tizard, J. (1972) Research into services for the mentally handicapped: science and policy issues. *Br. J. Ment. Subnorm. 18*, 6–17

Twardosz, S. and Baer, D. M. (1973) Training two severely retarded adolescents to ask questions. *J. Appl. Behav. Anal. 6*, 655–661

Wiggins, J. S. (1973) *Personality and Prediction: the Principles of Personality Assessment.* Addison-Wesley, Reading, Mass.

Williams, C. (1973) An experimental approach to language development with severely retarded children. *Behav. Mod. Newsletter* (4), 3–7

Wolf, M. M. and Risley, T. R. (1971) Reinforcement: applied research. In *The Nature of Reinforcement* (Glaser, R., ed.). Academic Press, New York

Yule, W. (1974) Single case studies methodology in the evaluation of therapeutic intervention. Paper read to the 9th International Study Group on Child Neurology and Cerebral Palsy, Oxford, Sept. 1974

Yule, W. (1975) Training parents in child management. *J. Ass. Educ. Psychol.* (in press)

Yule, W. and Berger, M. (1972) Behaviour modification principles and speech delay. In *The Child with Delayed Speech* (Rutter, M. L. and Martin, J. A. M., eds.), pp. 204–219. Spastics International Medical Publications/Heinemann, London

Yule, W., Berger, M. and Howlin, P. (1975) Language deficit and behaviour modification. In *Language, Cognitive Deficits and Retardation* (O'Connor, N., ed.), pp. 209–223. Butterworths, London

ACKNOWLEDGEMENT

In collaboration with Dr L. Hersov and Professor M. Rutter, the authors are in receipt of a generous grant from the Department of Health and Social Security to evaluate the effects of behaviour modification techniques in the comprehensive treatment of autistic children. We would like to thank these colleagues and Mrs Patricia Howlin, Mrs Rosemary Hemsley and Mrs Daphne Holbrook for their many helpful discussions of the issues raised in this paper.

Commentary

PETER MITTLER

TEACHING A FIRST LANGUAGE

Yule and Berger's paper richly reflects the achievements and promise of recent work on the behavioural approach to language teaching, but equally reveals the awesome complexities of the enterprise. We can now afford to be optimistic both about the amount of progress that has already been made and about the potential developments that lie within our reach. We already have the knowledge to try to teach language and communication skills to non-verbal and non-communicating individuals; the need now is to disseminate this knowledge in a form which is intelligible and relevant to practitioners such as teachers, nurses and above all parents, and persuade those who control resources to institute training programmes to translate our knowledge into practice for the benefit of the retarded people to whom we are in the last analysis accountable.

But the fact that an effective teaching technology is now within our grasp should not blind us to the problems which remain to be tackled and to the vast areas about which we are woefully ignorant. Research and practice therefore need to develop in close association with one another. Indeed, one of the more positive aspects of recent work in this field is the convergence of theoretical and applied interests which makes nonsense of the once fashionable dichotomy between 'pure' and 'applied' research. It is to the credit of the behaviourist movement that this polarity can now be seen to be artificial and in certain contexts meaningless.

How far are we prepared to go?

The first general problem that I want to raise concerns the relationship of behavioural language teaching programmes to the teaching curriculum in general and to other approaches to language teaching in particular. Do we see behavioural methods merely as one of several alternatives to language teaching or are we already in a position confidently to recommend their adoption as the method of choice? This is a question which everyone must answer for himself, but it seems relevant to remind ourselves that other approaches already exist, and are being increasingly developed. The most obvious examples are the Peabody Language Development Kit P (Dunn, Horton and Smith 1968); the DISTAR Language I (Engelmann, Osborn and Engelmann 1969); the Bereiter and Engelmann (1966) programmes, *Concept 7–9* (White, Norris and Worsley 1972); the Scott-Foresman Kit (Monroe 1970); the Gahagan and Gahagan (1970) programme, Conn 1971, Hutt 1973, Lea 1970, Fenn 1973 and 1975, and *Jim's People* (Thomas, Gaskin and Herriot 1973, 1974). The last two of these were designed specifically with the needs of the mentally handicapped in mind, but all of them have been used in ESNS schools. Although we have no empirical data enabling us to compare the effectiveness of any of these methods with one another or with any given behavioural programme, we should not be under any illusion that only behaviourists have made or are likely to make any significant contribution to systematic language teaching. The schemes listed here are merely examples of published and commercially available 'kits'; no mention has been made of the work of individual teachers who have devised their own methods but who do not favour the kit approach. Most of the published programmes can be described as formal and systematic insofar as they rely on task analysis, and on the prescription of lessons to teach specific language skills either within the lesson or in the outside environment, but none of them makes systematic use of reinforcement theory or principles.

The relationship of behavioural methods to the rest of the curriculum is particularly complex in the field of language teaching, since language is necessarily used by everyone in the child's environment in their own way; it is far from easy to create a totally consistent language environment for a single child or for a group of children, even if this were thought to be educationally desirable.

Language teaching repeatedly presents us with this dilemma, and Yule and Berger's paper provides many examples of the special problems which arise. Is it possible to teach the child to generalize what he has learned in the one-to-one situation to the natural environment without involving other adults? It is difficult enough to teach parents to adopt a systematic teaching strategy, but can we ensure that other adults and siblings do not undermine their work? Can we expect residential care staff and hospital nurses to play a full part in maintaining the child's behaviour? Such problems are particularly relevant now that we are beginning to develop technologies for teaching generative response classes.

Similar difficulties arise in deciding how far one has to follow a tightly prescribed programme, and how far it is permissible to follow the leads given by the child. The authors of flow diagrams and procedural lattices rarely specify how they actually use them; indeed, we are at this stage lamentably short of detailed case studies which allow us to follow the exact procedures in detail, and to learn exactly what was achieved inside and outside the training situation. This is partly bound up with problems of recording which are well described in the paper: can you teach and record at the same time? If it is hard enough to do this when following a tightly prescribed programme, how much harder is it to record and evaluate the departures from the programme which arise from the child's own spontaneous interventions and interests?

In teaching language to a non-verbal child we must largely prescribe the path that he should follow; we need to abandon a particular set of assumptions or procedures if they manifestly do not work, though we might differ about the length of time that should elapse before part or all of a training programme is abandoned.

It is also relevant to ask oneself how long and to what stage of language development one can continue to maintain a systematic behavioural approach. Can we assume that one of its main strengths lies in getting the individual started on the first stages but that sooner or later he becomes an 'autonomous learner' who finds language learning an intrinsically rewarding experience and therefore needs less assistance from the programme planners?

Somehow or other we have to build into our programmes the possibility of the individual making choices and exercising increasing degrees of responsibility for his own behaviour and development. Operant psychology even provides us with at least part of the technology of doing so by means of gradually exposing the individual to increasing degrees of choice.

In this connection, we are beginning to pay more attention to the way in which language is used in the various natural environments in which handicapped people live and the kind of demands which the community makes on them. We should at least aim to help them to achieve minimum levels of communication in a variety of settings, but also be on the lookout for ways in which their linguistic competence can be stretched to the utmost. Perhaps this is not a task which the behaviour modifier need tackle directly, but his advice on goals and settings should be available. For example, we know very little about normal adult conversational strategies to handicapped children and the extent to which our language is appropriate or understood. A few studies suggest that parents and teachers tend to overuse the 'what's that?' strategy, thus reinforcing single-word noun responses, possibly for an unnecessarily long period. The questions that we ask, the stories that we tell, the commands we give and in general the linguistic demands that we make on children in the course of ordinary activities all constitute an essential part of the general language environment which we rarely study or take into account in planning language programmes (Mittler 1975).

What do we teach?

Yule and Berger's paper is a most useful contribution to the problem of the source of the curriculum. How do you decide what you are doing to teach the child and where do you start? They suggest that developmental psycholinguistics is potentially a powerful curriculum source, but rightly remind us that the emphasis has now shifted from syntax to semantics and meaning.* Yule and Berger urge us to study both cognitive psychology and developmental psycholinguistics in an effort to derive a framework for curriculum development, but indicate that the search may need to extend more widely than this. Three areas might be singled out for special mention.

In the first place, we need to return to the earliest beginnings of language development, and to consider teaching the elements of language skills long before the child is ready to speak. So far we have been urging the importance of assessing and remediating receptive skills at the level of the holophrase and the two-word utterance, and have reported some modest successes in this direction (Jeffree, Wheldall and Mittler 1973). However, it is now clear that receptive processes can be studied long before this. Morse (1974) and Eimas (1974) have shown that at as early as two months normal infants are able to discriminate

---

* Since preparing their paper, even fuller documentation of developments in this field has now appeared in an exhaustive compilation of conference papers (Schiefelbusch and Lloyd 1974). This volume promises to provide a rich source of suggestions on ways in which psycholinguistics can be harnessed to the service of language teaching.

between different kinds of speech sounds, though discrimination between non-speech auditory stimuli is not achieved until much later. Some years earlier, Friedlander (1970) made a strong plea for the study of receptive processes in normal and speech-delayed infants, but the therapeutic implications of the few experimental studies in this field have not yet been fully appreciated.

Secondly, we would do well to look at the relationship between cognitive and linguistic development from a remedial point of view, and put on one side for a while the theoretical problems that beset this complex relationship (Cromer 1974). Yule and Berger seem to equate cognitive development with mental age, though the rest of their paper reflects an awareness of the mismatch between them. It is not just a question of the level of cognitive development which a child needs to acquire either receptive or expressive skills, but more a question of the way in which he interacts with his immediate environment, and the kind of meanings which it comes to acquire for him. Here, as they point out, the notion of semantic intent is particularly important, though it would be useful to have some guidance on how this concept can be operationally studied and taught – either from an operant or a cognitive standpoint.

Thirdly, they are right to stress the importance of non-verbal systems of communication. The severely handicapped child who may never develop expressive abilities needs an alternative medium of communication—if only with the intention of ultimately replacing it with more advanced or more natural forms of communication. We can distinguish here between 'natural' non-verbal systems that may already be in the child's repertoire and artificial systems which we can try to teach him to use—e.g. plastic or visual languages. In the first group we find a wide range of behaviours such as smiling, arm-reaching, pointing and gesture which may yield their own 'grammar' and which may have a certain communicative consistency. In the second category the work of the Premacks and the Gardners is now well known; its implications for language teaching in our field have been repeatedly advocated but not very actively pursued (Premack and Premack 1974). Avis Dickinson (1974), one of our students in Manchester, has been laying the foundations for such an approach by a series of experimental studies on labelling and classification using wooden shapes, following the paradigm originally developed by Heidbreder (1948) and others, but there may be more promise in the use of visual media, as reported by Moores (1974), since these are less artificial and situation-specific and more easily communicable to others in the environment.

The contribution of experimental psychology

The work of the Premacks provides a powerful example of the educational implications of experimental work originally carried out in the animal or psychological laboratory. However, as Yule and Berger emphasize, there is already a considerable body of experimental work in retardation which could be used to assess the cognitive skills relevant to language learning. The work of O'Connor and Hermelin (1963, 1970), Zeaman and House (1963) and Ellis (1963, 1970) might be adapted in at least three different ways. In the first place,

Baumeister (1968) has suggested certain general educational principles which follow from their work; secondly, a study of their experiments suggests a number of relatively simple methods of experimentally investigating a single child in respect of his ability to cluster or organize incoming material, store and retrieve material for later recall, impose patterns or extract regular features from patterned stimuli (Frith 1971). These techniques are within reach of the educational or clinical psychologist in the field, and need not be seen as the prerogative of the specialized research worker.

Experimental methods are also particularly important in the detailed assessment of cognitive level which should be the base of any intervention programme. It is not, of course, just a question of establishing the mental age or IQ of the child, though even this information may not be entirely irrelevant. More pertinent to the design of a teaching objective is the establishment of the child's level of object permanence, his ability to achieve simple and complex discriminations in both auditory and visual modalities, and his ability to organize, retain and generalize learned material.

Finally, experimental methods can be devised to assess cognitive correlates of certain linguistic skills—e.g. rule usage, plurality, concepts of past, present and future, directionality etc.

Task analysis

The immediate objective of any teaching programme surely lies in the selection of target behaviours. It is in this respect that behavioural approaches have made considerable progress in recent years. The identification of what is to be taught is a complex process, and it is doubtful whether behaviour modification can *by itself* provide a specification of all the relevant language skills that need to be taught. Ideally, we require a detailed knowledge of the stages and processes of both normal and delayed language development and a thorough knowledge of both theoretical and empirical changes taking place in cognitive psychology and developmental psycholinguistics. Yule and Berger's paper is important because it looks far beyond the immediate frontiers of behaviour modification and considers in some detail how a knowledge of these and other fields can be used to inform the content of language-teaching programmes. Thus, they attempt to reconcile two previously contrasted positions—developmental delay versus deficit dichotomy (e.g. Herriot 1973)—by emphasizing that "whilst the *content* of training should parallel that of the normal sequence of acquisition, the *method* of training need not." This is an important bridging statement: not all behaviourists would agree with such an eclectic position although its authors do state that behaviour modification is the secure base from which they venture to explore less familiar territory. It goes without saying that knowledge derived from other disciplines needs to be adapted and interpreted in the light of the objectives of any teaching programme and the needs of handicapped children. It is hard to believe that anyone would now force a child to progress step by step up or along a procedural lattice merely because it was based on normal development or psycholinguistic research; on the other hand it has to be admitted that in the first flush of enthusiasm behaviour modifiers were not always as interested in the relevance of what was taught as in their success in teaching it. The essence of more recent approaches seems to lie in a careful consideration of the task analysis procedures.

If this is a fair description of recent developments, how vital is systematic reinforcement and appropriate scheduling in language teaching? Perhaps this must remain an open question for the time being, but it is relevant to point out that reinforcement may not play as central a role in language teaching as it does in other areas – e.g. attention training. There is evidence that parents and other non-skilled therapists find systematic reinforcement difficult, especially when they need to move to variable ratio schedules; on the other hand they learn shaping, prompting, fading and imitation procedures relatively well and take readily to the notion of task analysis if it is carefully explained and taught (O'Dell 1974; Cunningham, this volume, p. 175; Mitchell 1975). Behaviour modifiers are now appreciating that some people, including parents, object to an over-emphasis on reinforcement, and do not like having to dispense reinforcements to children on schedule and to command.

It is clear that a systematic approach to teaching of a first language has been outlined by means of the behavioural approach, and that impressive progress has already been made in teaching severely handicapped children the elements of their own language. But much work remains to be done in relating possibilities for further progress to the child's wider needs as a developing individual in the setting of his family, his school and the wider community.

REFERENCES

BAUMEISTER, A.A. (1968) Learning abilities of the mentally retarded. *Mental Retardation: Appraisal, Education, Rehabilitation* (Baumeister, A.A., ed.), pp. 181–211. University of London Press

BEREITER, C. and ENGELMANN, S. (1966) *Teaching Disadvantaged Children in the Preschool.* Prentice-Hall, Englewood Cliffs, NJ

CONN, P. (1971) *Remedial Syntax.* Invalid Children's Aid Association, London

CROMER, R. (1974) The development of language and cognition. In *New Perspectives in Child Development* (Foss, B., ed.), pp. 184–252. Penguin Books, Harmondsworth, Middx

DICKINSON, A. (1974) A visual response mode for investigating aspects of class concepts for ESN(S) children. Paper presented to Annual Conference, Educational Section, British Psychological Society, Edinburgh, September 1974

DUNN, L.M., HORTON, K.B. and SMITH, J.O. (1968) *Peabody Language Development Kits. Manual for Level#P.* American Guidance Service, Minnesota

EIMAS, P.D. (1974) Linguistic processing of speech by young infants. In *Language Perspectives – Acquisition, Retardation and Interventions* (Schiefelbusch, R.L. and Lloyd, L.L., eds). University Park Press, Baltimore

ELLIS, N.R. (1963) The stimulus trace and behavioral inadequacy. In *Handbook of Mental Deficiency* (Ellis, N.R., ed.), pp. 134–158. McGraw-Hill, New York

ELLIS, N.R. (1970) Memory processes in retardates and normals. In *International Review of Mental Retardation.* Vol. 4 (Ellis, N.R., ed.), pp. 1–32. Academic Press, New York

ENGELMANN, S., OSBORN, J. and ENGELMANN, T. (1969 *DISTAR Language I.* Science Research Associates, Chicago.

FENN, G. (1973) The development of syntax in a group of severely subnormal children. Unpublished Ph.D. dissertation, University of Cambridge

FENN, G. (1975) Against verbal enrichment. In *Language and Communication in the Mentally Handicapped* (Berray, P.B., ed.). Arnold, London (in press)

FRIEDLANDER, B.Z. (1970) Receptive language development in infancy: issues and problems. *Merrill-Palmer Quart. Behav. Devel. 16*, 7–51

FRITH, U. (1971) Spontaneous patterns produced by autistic, normal and subnormal children. In *Infantile Autism: Concepts, Characteristics and Treatment* (Rutter, M., ed.), pp. 113–131. Churchill Livingstone, Edinburgh.

GAHAGAN, D.M. and GAHAGAN, G.A. (1970) *Talk Reform: Explorations in Language for Infant School Children.* Routledge and Kegan Paul, London

HEIDBREDER, E. (1948) The attainment of concepts: exploratory experiments on conceptualisation at perceptual levels. *J. Psychol. 26*, 193-216

HERMELIN, B. and O'CONNOR, N. (1970) *Psychological Experiments with Autistic Children.* Pergamon, Oxford

HERRIOT, P. (1973) Assumptions underlying the use of psychological models in subnormality research. In *Mental Retardation and Behavioural Research* (Clarke, A.D.B. and Clarke, A., eds.), pp. 153–165. Churchill Livingstone, Edinburgh/Williams & Wilkins, Baltimore

HUTT, E. (1973) *Systematic Sequential Instruction.* Invalid Children's Aid Association, London

JEFFREE, D.M., WHELDALL, K. and MITTLER, P. (1973) The facilitation of two-word utterances in two Down's syndrome boys. *Am. J. Ment. Defic. 78*, 117–122

LEA, J. (1970) *The Colour Pattern Scheme.* Moorhouse School, Oxted, Surrey

MITTLER, P. (1975) Assessment for language learning. In *Language and Communication in the Mentally Handicapped* (Berry, P.B., ed.). Arnold, London (in press)

MITCHELL, D.R. (1975) Parent–child interaction. In *Language and Communication in the Mentally Handicapped* (Berry, P.B., ed.). Arnold, London (in press)

MONROE, M. (1970) *Scott Foresman Language Activities Kit.* Scott Foresman, Glenview, Illinois

MOORES, D.F. (1974) Non-vocal systems of verbal behavior. In Schiefelbusch, R.L. and Lloyd, L.L. (eds.), *op. cit.*

MORSE, P.A. (1974) Infant speech perceptions: a preliminary model and review of the literature. In Schiefelbusch, R.L. and Lloyd, L.L. (eds.), *op.cit.*

O'CONNOR, N. and HERMELIN, B. (1963) *Speech and Thought in Severe Subnormality.* Pergamon, Oxford

O'DELL, S. (1974) Training parents in behavior modification: a review. *Psychol. Bull. 81*, 418–433

PREMACK, D. and PREMACK, A. (1974) Teaching visual language to apes and language-deficient persons. In Schiefelbusch, R.L. and Lloyd, L.L. (eds.), *op. cit.*

SCHIEFELBUSCH, R.L. and LLOYD, L.L. (eds.) (1974) *Language Perspectives–Acquisition, Retardation and Intervention.* Macmillan, London/University Park Press, Baltimore

THOMAS, B., GASKIN, S. and HERRIOT, P. (1973/1974) *Jim's People (Sets 1, 2 and 3).* Hart Davis Educational, St. Albans, Herts

WHITE, J., NORRIS, R.A. and WORSLEY, F.J. (1972) *Concept 7–9.* Arnold, Leeds

ZEAMAN, D. and HOUSE, B.J. (1963) The role of attention in retardate discrimination learning. In *Handbook of Mental Deficiency* (Ellis, N.R., ed.), pp. 159–221. McGraw-Hill, New York

Discussion

Yule: I believe one must alter a language programme quite drastically if one is working with an unusual child who uses some parts of the language expressively but who refuses to put them together into appropriate conventional forms. I disagree with Gray and Ryan's (1971) instructions which require you to clearly enunciate perfect examples such as "The boy is happy" and "The boy is sitting" every time, even when you know that the child utterly rejects the definite article or the verb 'to be'. When I said "The boy is sitting" to one child he responded immediately "sitting on the green chair", which startled and delighted me (the boy uses complex adverbial phrases, but refuses to say 'is' and refused to say the subject in a sentence until recently). But Gray and Ryan's programme says that I should have regarded that response as an error, because that's not what I was working on in that session. I can't accept that as correct.

Berger: I'm also very concerned about these attempts to impose formalized speech on children when nobody really speaks like that.

Kushlick: What was the consequence to the child of not being able to speak in formal sentences?

Yule: The very important consequence that neither his mother nor his teachers recognized that he *can* communicate very well, if unconventionally, and in consequence underrated his intelligence grossly. They therefore continued trying to teach him things at a very low and uninteresting level. The other consequence was that we were unable to get him transferred from an SSN children's centre to the ESN school which I think he could cope with.

Walker: Will you allow me a slightly critical comment? I think your paper gives an impressive array of connections between psycholinguistic and behaviour-modification ideas. But are they going to be helpful in practice? I wondered this particularly when you discussed the standard issue of competence and performance and also with respect to semantic intent. The virtue of behaviour modification is surely that you can stand aside from philosophical questions of semantic intent. I mean, how are we ever going to decide whether a child has semantic intent unless we examine his performance or see how well he can be trained to put words together? I think it would be a tragedy if people involved in practical work were to get side-tracked into wondering whether there is or is not semantic intent.

Yule: It's true that one must guard against being seduced by every new theory, but I do think semantic intent has practical connotations. Elizabeth Barton says (p. 213) that she plugged away endlessly at 'cup' and 'shoe' with an autistic girl, without much result until she made the concrete connections between the objects and names. Once placed in context, the verbal learning was made much easier.

Mittler: The other aspect of this is in relation to the holophrase. In general the shift from syntax to semantics in psycholinguistics has been pretty productive, not just for psycholinguistics but for us, because it's enabled us to think out what the child is communicating with his one single word. Before a child has got to the two-word utterance stage, there is a whole range of meanings you can help him to produce – just by means of a single word – by giving him different patterns of intonation, for example. In addition, you can ask him questions which require only a one-word response, but that one word can be a noun, a verb, a class of objects and so on. When the child is developing so slowly that it takes 4 or 5 years to go from one-word to two-word utterances, you can cling to semantics in order to try to enlarge what he's able to talk about. Now you don't have to buy the theory about intentionality any more than you have to buy the competence/performance theory. If the idea can be transposed into the behaviour modification field it's operational, and this is its strength.

Berger: There is another point we were trying to get across in the paper: the difference between the autistic child who will echo a phrase mechanically and the 'normal' child who produces phrases in a particular way which gives a certain quality to them. Within the behavioural framework such qualitative things are not significant, but in our own understanding of the development of language I think they are. This quality is lacking in behaviour modification language programmes. It's related, as is the question of intent, to the question "Does behaviour modification produce speech or language?"

Carr: Peter Mittler was suggesting teaching retarded children to use single words in a variety of ways to convey different meanings. Do you know of any examples of this happening spontaneously with retarded children, as of course we know it does with normal ones?

Mittler: No, but it has not been looked for systematically. We need to do longitudinal studies of a few subnormal children similar to those which Roger Brown produced on Adam, Eve and Sarah, except that we can now use video as well as tape recorders. Gordon Wells is collecting data on normal children from 9 months to 5 years, using a tape recorder in the home which is automatically switched on at a pre-set time each day. We need to do the same thing with retarded children. My guess is that they *don't* use the one word in different ways, in the classical holophrase manner, or at least not as effectively as normal children, but that they could be taught to do so.

Yule: I would be sceptical of simply collecting audiotapes. I think you need to be able to see the child and his context to be able to judge just what it is he is saying, or trying to convey.

Jones: I can give Janet Carr an example: one of our subnormal children at Meldreth was using the single word 'me' to mean "I need help" or "I want food" or "Give me something". In fact, we have trained her *out* of this and into four-word utterances in the space of one term by refusing to discriminate her needs without further verbal indicators!

Kiernan: One rather dispiriting thing about psycholinguistics, and indeed about many contributions from study of the normal child, is that it tends to tell you what is likely to be unsuccessful, and it's probably a good thing that workers on the practical level disregard this conclusion and go right ahead and try it. We've just heard a good example: the literature would have led one to believe that Malcolm Jones' pupil would stick at one-word utterances for years, but her teachers just made up their minds that she wouldn't, and she didn't! My second point is that Joe Carrier and Jennie Hughes, extending Premack's work, were avowedly non-psycholinguistic and in my opinion their work is going to be a lot more productive than what has been coming from psycholinguistics up to now.

Mittler: I can't agree that psycholinguistics is depressing and negative, and I think Chris Kiernan's comment is unnecessarily pessimistic. I believe with Bill Bricker that the psycholinguists' work should be a challenge, not an epitaph. Even if Lenneberg and Chomsky are right when they say that part of the language-acquisition device is fully governed by biological maturation, we can still say "To hell with it, we'll teach language acquisition." To use a rather contentious analogy, even if Cyril Burt and Jensen and Eysenck really could prove that 80% of the variance of intelligence is due to genetic factors, that doesn't mean that we shouldn't try to develop the intelligence that's there.

Berger: I think that going into the psycholinguistics literature in fact gives you a feeling of hope, not depression, with some otherwise hopeless children, because it sensitizes you to signs of language you wouldn't otherwise look for. In our paper we have stressed the notion of communicating through gesture, not only speech: looking at gesture from a psycholinguistic viewpoint provides very useful feedback to those of us working with the retarded. I don't think the psycholinguists' findings are dampening at all: quite the contrary.

Yule: The main contribution of psycholinguistics is a conceptual framework within which we can gather data to test hypotheses and to feed back to the psycholinguists, who are not in my opinion getting hard enought data but who are providing new bases from which to work.

P. Williams: Language is to me a subject *par excellence* in which you have to consider the child's whole environment and modify the behaviour of those around him unless you are willing to risk teaching him something which is going to be extinguished when he returns to his usual surroundings. The people around the child have become used to his not being a contributor to the verbal bath which surrounds most of us. Thus it is essential to change their expectations in order to enhance the individual work being done with the child.

The Development of Social Behaviour

RITA R. JORDAN and C. A. SAUNDERS

Thomas Coram Research Unit, Institute of Education, University of London

ABSTRACT

This paper concentrates on two aspects of social behaviour: social responsiveness and imitation. It attempts to delineate the actual behaviours implied by the term 'social responsiveness' and to discuss ways in which they can be developed. Particular reference is made to the difficulties involved in establishing social stimuli as secondary reinforcers, and this is discussed in relation to research.

The way in which the cue functions of social stimuli vary in relation to the different use of such stimuli in the general environment, and the implications of this in using social stimuli as reinforcers, is discussed. The importance of distinguishing between contingency and reliable contiguity of reinforcement arises from this discussion.

The training of imitative behaviour is considered as a critical development, since effective imitation facilitates incidental learning within the natural environment as well as training methods used in teaching.

I INTRODUCTION

If we were to take as a guide to the behaviour that might be considered 'social' those suggested by Anderson and Messick (1974) as necessary for social competence, we would find few behaviours to exclude from this category. We intend, therefore, to avoid the issue of definition and make no attempt at a comprehensive coverage of social behaviour and its development. Instead we will focus on some of the behaviours that we consider important in this area, examine some of the confusion that surrounds them and, by clarifying the component and prerequisite behaviours, go on to consider ways in which two at least of these behaviours might be developed. Where we have chosen to neglect a topic, as for example communication, there is obviously no implication as to its importance in social behaviour; we have chosen topics where we have been or are engaged in research where we feel there is a need for fresh examination and further investigation. In particular we will focus on two main topics – social responsiveness and imitation.

II SOCIAL RESPONSIVENESS — A COMPLEX DEFINITION

Perusal of published work might lead one to suppose that it would be a simple matter to decide whether or not a child is socially responsive; one can observe his behaviour in social situations or ask adults who come into contact with him. But what behaviour exactly should we observe or ask about? If a child smiles when he is approached and shows signs of enjoying physical contact with others he might well be judged as socially responsive. Yet his failure to work for social rewards or initiate social contacts might lead to a negative view of his social responsiveness. Clearly, we will need to be more precise in describing the kinds of socially responsive behaviours he exhibits and those he does not, if we are going to use this information in a training programme.

It is convenient to break down social responsiveness into four different kinds of behaviour:

i) Appropriate social responses to social stimuli. This is not the same as working for social rewards, as will be seen later, but implies reactions to social stimuli as 'releasers' of social responses or as discriminative stimuli for those responses, according to the theory underlying this link. Initially the responses to social stimuli may simply be responses, but the interactionist nature of social situations leads to the responses coming in turn to serve as social stimuli for the behaviour of others; finally the child learns to initiate such situations.

ii) Cooperation. At its simplest this implies allowing control of behaviour by others, but at another level it involves reciprocal relationships and includes actions of sharing and non-competitiveness.

iii) Response to commands. The commands are not necessarily verbal commands, but obedience to complex commands does imply comprehension of some language system even if it is gestural. Imitation may be used as an initial step in developing response to commands, but it is neither a sufficient nor a necessary condition for response to commands via a language system.

iv) Behaviour in many different situations which is under control of social reinforcers.

III APPROPRIATE SOCIAL RESPONSES TO SOCIAL STIMULI

Appropriate social responses are important for the mentally handicapped since they are crucial factors in maintaining the behaviour of the givers of social stimuli to the individual and so help to determine the social acceptability of the individual. Work with infants has shown that these behaviours develop early in the non-handicapped individual, who is apparently 'programmed' to respond selectively to a range of stimuli consistent with social stimuli (Haith 1966; Rheingold, Gewirtz and Ross 1959; Schaffer and Emerson 1974; Spears 1963). For various reasons, this sequence does not always develop in mentally handicapped individuals and social stimulation may produce no response in them or may produce responses only after training.

However, the practical details of this training suggest problems of theory as well as practice. Doubt has recently been cast on the extent to which the relationship between an operant and a reinforcer is dependent solely on their relative positions within the reinforcement hierarchy of the individual; the suggestion has been made that reinforcement/response compatibility is crucial if one is to obtain the successful results which have been reported and from which many of the principles of operant work have been developed (Seligman 1970). This has not yet filtered through into the practice of behaviour modification techniques with the mentally handicapped; obviously, however, lack of such compatibility may be a factor when difficulties are experienced in establishing effective operant programmes. If, for example, social responses are to be trained by the use of material reinforcers there may be problems in competing out other responses elicited by these reinforcers. Training a child to turn his head when his name is called can be successful with edible reinforcers, but head-turning is an appropriate response to feeding as well as a social response. It may be more difficult, for example, to train 'hugging' to the stimulus of out-stretched arms, using food as a reward. We shall return to this problem later.

Once the social behaviour has developed to the point where the child is initiating social interactions, we are dealing with attention seeking. Inappropriate behaviours in this activity (such as versions of coercive behaviour described by Patterson and Reid (1970), where one partner in a social interaction is receiving aversive stimuli which nevertheless provoke reactions that serve as positive reinforcers for the other partner) may need to be extinguished. For reasons of economy as well as humanity, one must try to train more appropriate responses while one extinguishes this behaviour—not that it is an easy circle to break, even with a two pronged attack, for coercive actions demand reaction in ways one can ignore only with great difficulty. It may prove necessary to prevent such actions physically until alternatives have been effectively trained, and then gradually fade out the prompts to this enforced response control.

IV COOPERATION

The recent finding of Madsen and Connor (1973) [that mental retardates exhibited more cooperative and less competitive behaviour than non-handicapped children is an interesting one, although it is open to many interpretations. One explanation is that in the particular 'mini-culture' of the handicapped individual, normal reinforcements for competitive behaviour that are prevalent in our culture do not operate. This does raise the question for those who see 'normalization' as the only appropriate goal for the education of the mentally handicapped and suggests that other criteria should at least be considered.

However, cooperation is more than the obverse of competitiveness. There have been simple and effective programmes for training some aspects of cooperation such as cooperative play through ball rolling (Van Eck 1972, unpublished). This involves training a child, through prompting, to roll a ball to an adult and then fading the prompts; once two children have been trained in this way they can be prompted to roll the ball to each other. Maintenance of this behaviour may depend on extrinsic reinforcement, at least occasionally, although the aim would be to 'compensate' each child for alternating loss of the ball by social rewards from the child receiving it. Thus effective cooperation programmes depend for their maintenance on the participants being able to emit and respond to appropriate social stimuli so they need not rely on material reinforcement.

One element in cooperation is the existence of a common 'goal' for the participants, otherwise the situation becomes indistinguishable from a control/ dependency situation. Much practical intervention with the mentally handicapped begins with the acquisition of control over their behaviour by the interventionist. Situations in which the individual is exerting control over the 'trainer' are generally regarded as 'problems' to which solutions must be found. Obviously, there will be situations during training or teaching where the control must rest with the teacher or trainer if the training is to be effective, but there are dangers in extrapolating from this condition to the complete environment of the individual. One may actually be eliminating a powerful motivating factor from the child's environment if he is never allowed control over the significant adults around him and such relationships may also make genuine cooperative behaviour impossible.

Thus, a necessary step in training cooperative behaviour may be to allow at least some consistent experience of control of the other's behaviour even if clear discriminative stimuli are used to 'mark off' this time from other times when the trainer needs to re-establish control. Other aspects of cooperative behaviour, such as sharing, will need prior training of delay of reinforcement and the substitution of other rewards—preferably social ones intrinsic in the act of sharing.

V RESPONSE TO COMMANDS

If an individual is to respond to commands he must not only comprehend the command, but have been reinforced sufficiently for compliance that commands have become discriminative stimuli for obedience. In practice the establishment of control in this manner is relatively easy with a single person who is an effective reinforcer in the individual's environment, but it may be difficult to isolate this person-specific cue from the gestural or verbal cues in order that the latter can serve as discriminative stimuli whoever employs them. Perhaps this is after all a desirable constraint on a situation where indiscriminate manipulation by others is not necessarily a goal.

VI RESPONSE TO SOCIAL STIMULI AS GENERALIZED REINFORCERS

This aspect of social responsiveness is the one most frequently used in behaviour modification programmes with the mentally handicapped, and one often inferred from other aspects. It may, however, be an independent response class, and it is here that the distinction between social stimuli as discriminative stimuli and as reinforcers needs to be made. The situation can be illustrated from the work we are engaged in at the moment. A particular child is considered as 'socially responsive' because of his clear social responses to social stimuli and the fact that he spends a lot of his time eliciting social behaviour by seeking eye contact and smiling. A training programme is therefore devised using social rewards, but it is not successful because the response to be trained is not a social response. The child, instead of attending to the task, spends his time in the session seeking social reward by using his repertoire of previously rewarded social behavours. When he is prompted to perform the task and rewarded with social stimuli these only elicit more of the child's social responses. It is difficult to break into this chain except by the use of alternative reinforcement. So social responsiveness in one situation may not be a good predictor of social responsiveness in another when different responses are wanted.

This again raises the question of reinforcement/response compatibility and whether in fact it is always desirable to use social stimuli as reinforcers. Obviously, social stimuli are tremendously useful reinforcers in that they are readily available, are easy to administer and fit readily into a 'normal' framework. But in some circumstances it may be necessary to 'compete out' the social responses of the individual produced by the social reinforcement, and this may well not be in the long-term interests of the child if there is generalization outside the training situation. Perhaps we should reconsider the use of social reinforcers for all responses. Manipulative tasks, for example, might be more appropriately reinforced by intrinsic reinforcers, and we should look more at ways of training skills that encourage effective intrinsic motivation.

It remains doubtful that the development of intrinsic reinforcers will be possible for all skills or all individuals, and social reinforcement control will often be a desirable goal. Hall and Broden (1967), Redd and Birnbrauer (1969), Baer and Sherman (1964) and Baer and Wolf (1970) have all shown that it is possible to use social reinforcement effectively with mentally handicapped children, but there will be some behaviours and some children for whom the effectiveness of social reinforcement will need to be developed. One way in which this may be done reflects the theoretical view of the nature of social reinforcement as a secondary reinforcer.

VII SOCIAL REINFORCEMENT AS A SECONDARY REINFORCER

Social reinforcement is still traditionally regarded as a form of secondary reinforcement—deriving its effectiveness as a reinforcer from association with primary reinforcers. Since the publication of Premack's ideas (1965), however, this has been seen to be a simplistic view. If primary reinforcement is empirically defined and all stimuli are potential reinforcers (and probably actual reinforcers) of at least one operant, then the notion of a neutral stimulus, which acquires a reinforcing function through association with a primary reinforcer, has no meaning. But when we consider a particular individual and a particular operant, then the stimulus following contiguously that operant, and which affects the probability of its recurrence, might be said to be a primary reinforcer, at least at that time; whereas a stimulus which, under the same conditions of contiguity, does not initially affect the operant's probability of recurrence, and then by association with the primary reinforcer comes to have the same effect (or at least an effect in the same direction) as the primary reinforcer, might be called a secondary reinforcer.

Although the notion of behavioural control by secondary reinforcers is much used as an explanation of the maintenance of behaviour patterns separated from established reinforcers, it has proved much more difficult to demonstrate the long-term effectiveness of secondary reinforcers in controlling behaviour. The assessment of secondary reinforcers, however, has most often been carried out under conditions of extinction for the reinforcers from which it was held to derive its effectiveness. Thus, although it has been established that a stimulus not able to reinforce an operant can acquire a reinforcing function by being paired with an effective reinforcer, it has also been shown that this acquired reinforcing function diminishes rapidly in the absence of the effective stimulus. A situation more closely paralleling that found outside laboratory situations would be to assess the effectiveness of a secondary reinforcer when it was still being paired with an effective reinforcer from time to time; the problem with such a procedure is to distinguish the effects on behaviour of the secondary reinforcer from that of the primary reinforcer.

One method that has been developed to overcome this problem is the use of concurrent schedules of reinforcement to separate the function of the two stimuli. Zimmerman (1969), Zimmerman and Hanford (1967) and Zimmerman, Hanford and Brown (1967) have undertaken a series of experiments using this procedure and using key pecking in pigeons as the operant. Their work showed that low rate of responding could be maintained for the conditioned reinforcer even when pairing of the conditioned and unconditioned reinforcer were minimal and if the pairings were moderately frequent the conditioned reinforcer remained effective over an indefinite period.

There have been attempts to enhance the reinforcing properties of a stimulus with children as subjects, but the results have been equivocal. There has been one successful application of Zimmerman and Hanford's techniques to the area of social reinforcement with handicapped children by Lovaas, Gilbert, Kinder, Rubenstein, Schaeffer and Simmons (1966). They paired 'good' with food in one schedule and were able to turn it into a functional and durable reinforcer for lever-pressing in another schedule, but there were only two subjects, and the occasional use of tactile stimuli made interpretation of the results difficult.

In 1973 one of us (Jordan 1973, unpublished) undertook a small study which attempted to replicate Zimmerman and Hanford's study but used social reinforcement as the conditioned reinforcement and four pre-school handicapped children as the subjects. The results were in the direction that would support Zimmerman and Hanford's results but showed variations, no doubt due in part to failure to control the situation adequately. The study was useful, however, in highlighting for the author some of the difficulties in attempting to establish social reinforcement as an effective reinforcer.

VIII DIFFICULTIES IN THE USE OF SOCIAL REINFORCEMENT

The above study was conducted with children in an environment where there was a lot of non-contingent social stimulation available to the children. This may have had straight satiation effects, and this is always a likely disadvantage in 'good' environments. The effect may also be difficult to produce in situations where the training situation increases the 'response cost' of the reinforcement, so that stimuli that are freely given in the general environment now have to be 'worked for'. The training environment becomes a discriminative stimulus for this response cost and thus comes to function overall as a negative reinforcer of training behaviour (Premack 1965).

Added to this will be the loss of cue function of social stimuli that are given non contingently in the environment. Paris and Cairns (1972) found that positive social stimuli were used far less contingently on the children's behaviour than negative social stimuli in a classroom, and this was reflected in the relative effectiveness of these stimuli as positive or negative reinforcers of behaviour. This imbalance in the contingent use of positive and negative reinforcers was supported by the small study referred to above, but the methodology employed does not allow confidence in the results. We are at present considering ways of repeating these measurements more efficiently.

A further problem in the use of social stimuli as effective reinforcers lies in the apparent need for contingent use of such stimuli. Contingency implies that the reinforcer occurs only if the response occurs. The reinforcer may or may not be contiguous to the response, but absolute contingency means that it never occurs independently of it. Contingency itself has frequently been asserted as a necessary condition for the establishment of *any* effective reinforcer; it has even been suggested that it is the contingency itself which makes for effective reinforcement regardless of the stimulus used (Cairns 1970), although this is not generally supported. That contingency is important seems to be confirmed by the work of Baer and Sherman (1964) and of Redd and Birnbrauer (1969) with handicapped children, but these studies do not distinguish between contingency and reliable contiguity. Davis and Hubbard (1972) have attempted to demonstrate with rats, for example, that reliable contiguity is a sufficient and necessary condition for the relationship between response and reinforcement, rather than contingency. This may seem to be hairsplitting about terms, but it is an important issue in social reinforcement. If contingency is an important requirement, this would be a further disincentive to the use of social reinforcers for non-social tasks, since the non-contingent use of such stimuli in the general environment of the child would need to be severely curtailed, if not eliminated. But if reliable contiguity is sufficient, programmes of training are not liable to disruption by the normal social intercourse of the day. It is obviously difficult to test the situation of contingent but not contiguous reinforcement under conditions that could maintain behaviour, but the parallel situation (as in Zimmerman and Hanford's study) where there is contiguous but not contingent reinforcement needs to be clearly established for children.

Little has been said about the establishment of social stimuli as negative reinforcers, apart from Paris and Cairns' finding that it tends to be a more effective reinforcer anyway because of its more contingent use in the general environment. However, there are situations where verbal punishment is the most appropriate form of social control (in danger situations, for example) and its effectiveness as such needs to be established. Much of what was said about social stimuli is applicable to both positive and negative reinforcement, but there are added difficulties in using a conditioning procedure to enhance the effectiveness of a negative reinforcer. The drawbacks of physical punishment using any form of pain have been extensively debated (Ulrich and Craine 1964; Ulrich, Wolff and Azrin 1964) and much the same caution may apply to the use of Time Out (Azrin, Hutchinson and Hake 1966). It may be that physical control (a prompted self-control) will prove the most effective way of establishing 'no' as an inhibitor, plus the training of competing behaviours where appropriate.

Parallel to the behaviours concerned in social responsiveness are behaviours that are dependent on the behaviour of other individuals but need not involve interaction with the individuals concerned. These are imitative behaviours.

IX IMITATION: PROBLEMS OF BEHAVIOURAL DEFINITION

Imitation is a term which covers a wide variety of behaviours and hence has opened itself to much controversy. One of the main issues is the problem of determining the distinction between matched response behaviour and observational learning. From a behaviourist viewpoint one would have to suggest that imitative behaviour is a function of the individual's acquiring discriminative stimulus control over matched responses, which implies acquisition through conventional learning processes (Gewirtz 1971). The opposite view holds that this explanation accounts only partly for imitative behaviours. The discrepancy lies in its apparent inability to account for, among other things, the acquisition of new behaviours when neither subject nor model receives reinforcement and when there is extensive delay between model and response. This approach has necessitated the postulation of cognitive mediating functions and the assumption that observational learning is a 'built-in' acquisition process. In the normal child this process would function without the preliminary conditioning of the response dimension of imitation.

X DEVELOPING IMITATIVE BEHAVIOUR

However, when one is faced with the problem of children who demonstrate little or no imitative behaviour the relevance of this issue diminishes somewhat. Many studies of 'normal' children have shown that specific imitative responses can be trained, maintained and weakened through the use of extrinsic reinforcement (Flanders 1968). Furthermore, there is ample evidence to suggest that one can establish imitation as a functional response class in non-imitative children. Baer, Peterson and Sherman (1967) showed that over a training period in which 130 simple imitative responses were taught, the probability of the child's matching correctly on the first presentation rose from very low to almost 100%. Four points emerge from this study:

(1) That imitative behaviour could be trained, and effectively maintained on a variable-ratio schedule of reinforcement.

(2) That extinction took place if there was a delay of 30 seconds between response and reinforcement, and if the delayed reinforcement was not made contingent upon correct responses.

(3) That spontaneous recovery occurred if immediate and contingent reinforcement, albeit on a variable-reinforcement schedule, was reintroduced.

(4) That there was a good generalization from reinforced to non-reinforced tasks.

XI GENERALIZED IMITATION

The generalizability of the behaviour appears to be the most critical of these findings with respect to the mentally handicapped. It is clearly important that skills trained within a tightly controlled teaching situation should be generalizable to other settings. Also it is important in a class of behaviours such as imitation that stimulus control should not be confined to the trainer, since much of the relevance of imitative behaviour is in its value for incidental learning within the natural environment. Work by Saunders and Kiernan (1975) (unpublished) has demonstrated effective generalization of non-reinforced tasks along both these dimensions. However, generalization seemed to be affected by the tester, with maximal transfer to trainer, less transfer to non-trainer but familiar person, and least transfer to unfamiliar person. The setting had no statistically significant effect on transfer. Thus it is clear that adult models for imitation become distinct discriminative stimuli.

Substantial evidence supports the notion that generalization from reinforced to non-reinforced trials is not due to the child's failure to discriminate between these two situations. Peterson (1968) demonstrated that generalization was good only when non-reinforced trials were interspersed between reinforced trials. If non-reinforced trials were introduced in blocks, response to these models was weakened. Steinman (1970) demonstrated that children who were given a choice of responding to either consistently reinforced or consistently non-reinforced models produced little matching of the non-reinforced models.

A fourth variable affecting generalization is response topography. Garcia, Baer and Firestone (1971) distinguished between gross and fine motor movements. Their work suggests that generalization from reinforced to non-reinforced tasks in the same topographical class was greater than generalization from reinforced tasks in one class to non-reinforced tasks in the other class. Evidence from the Kiernan and Saunders study is inconclusive in this respect. The distinctions made in this study were between gross and fine motor responses, and object- and body-orientated responses. The data produced no statistically significant interaction between training in one class of responses and transfer along that dimension in the non-reinforced responses. This may, however, be accounted for by constraints imposed by the experimental design. The non-reinforced probe sets consisted of only eight tasks – two for each of the four topographical classes – and these could not be balanced for complexity along other discriminative variable dimensions.

75

From the above we can conclude that it is possible to train non-imitative children to imitate and that this trained behaviour is generalizable to other people, other settings and different topographical dimensions. It is significant that this generalization occurs despite the fact that the adult model, the potential for extrinsic reinforcement, and topographical class of the response are all clearly discriminative features affecting the probability of a matched response. It seems probable that during imitation training the child is not only taught to observe an adult model, but also that the stimulus class of behavioural similarity takes on a positive reinforcing function.

XII CONCLUSIONS

The aim of applying behaviour modification techniques to severely retarded children should include not only the training of skills in which the children are deficient but also the identification of the necessary environmental conditions to maintain those skills in the natural setting. The imitation studies reported show that generalization of imitative behaviour occurred across settings and models and may then be possible to maintain in most natural settings with occasional reinforcement; the major constraint on the situation would be the availability of good models in these settings.

Other aspects of social behaviour should prove self-maintaining once all the members of reciprocating relationships have acquired appropriate social skills. The difficulties arise in maintaining social stimuli as reinforcers for appropriate social responses and keeping their role as generalized trans-situational reinforcers. In many cases these two aims may be in conflict.

REFERENCES

ANDERSON, S. and MESSICK, S. (1974) Social competency in young children. *Devel. Psychol.* 10, 282–293

AZRIN, H., HUTCHINSON, R.R. and HAKE, D.F. (1966) Extinction-induced aggression. *J. Exp. Anal. Behav. 9*, 191–204

BAER, D.M., PETERSON, R.F. and SHERMAN, J.A. (1967) The development of imitation by reinforcing behavioral similarity to a model. *J. Exp. Anal. Behav. 10*, 405–416

BAER, D.M. and SHERMAN, J.A. (1964) Reinforcement control of generalized imitation in young children. *J. Exp. Child Psychol. 1*, 37–49

BAER, D.M. and WOLF, M.M. (1970) Recent examples of behavior modification in pre-school settings. In *Behavior Modification in Clinical Psychology* (Neuringer, C. and Michael, J.L., eds.), pp. 10–25. Appleton-Century-Crofts, New York

CAIRNS, R.B. (1970) Meaning and attention as determinants of social reinforcer effectiveness. *Child Devel. 41*, 1067–1082

DAVIS, H. and HUBBARD, J. (1972) An analysis of superstitious behavior in the rat. *Behaviour 43*, 1–12

FLANDERS, J.P. (1968) A review of research on imitative behaviour. *Psychol. Bull. 69*, 316–337

GARCIA, E., BAER, D.M. and FIRESTONE, I. (1971) The development of generalized imitation within topographically determined boundaries. *J. Appl. Behav. Anal. 4*, 101–112

GEWIRTZ, J.L. (1971) Conditional responding as a paradigm for observational imitative learning and vicarious reinforcement. In *Advances in Child Development and Behavior, Vol. 6* (Lipsitt, L.P. *et al.*, eds.), pp. 274–304. Academic Press, New York

HAITH, M.M. (1966) The response of the human newborn to visual movement. *J. Exp. Child Psychol. 3*, 235–243

HALL, R.V. and BRODEN, M. (1967) Behaviour changes in brain injured children through social reinforcement. *J. Exp. Child Psychol. 5*, 463–479

JORDAN, R.R. (1973) Unpublished Master's thesis, University of London, Institute of Education

LOVAAS, I., FREITAG, G., KINDER, M.I., RUBENSTEIN, R.D., SCHAEFFER, B. and SIMMONS, J.Q. (1966) Establishment of social reinforcers in two schizophrenic children on the basis of food. *J. Exp. Child Psychol. 4*, 109–125

MADSEN, M.C. and CONNOR, C. (1973) Cooperative and competitive behaviour in retarded and nonretarded children at two ages. *Child Devel. 44*, 175–178

PARIS, S.G. and CAIRNS, R.B. (1972) An experimental and ethological analysis of social reinforcement with retarded children. *Child Devel. 43*, 717–729

PATTERSON, G.R. and REID, J.B. (1970) Reciprocity and coercion: two facets of social systems. In *Behavior Modification in Clinical Psychology* (Neuringer, C. and Michael, J.L., eds.), pp. 133–177. Appleton-Century-Crofts, New York

PETERSON, R.F. (1968) Some experiments on the organisation of a class of imitative behaviors. *J. Appl. Behav. Anal. 1*, 225–235

PREMACK, D. (1965) Reinforcement theory. In *Nebraska Symposium on Motivation* (Levine, D., ed.), pp.123–188. University of Nebraska Press, Lincoln

REDD, W.H. and BIRNBRAUER, J.S. (1969) Adults as discriminative stimuli for different reinforcement contingencies with retarded children. *J. Exp. Child Psychol. 7*, 440–447

RHEINGOLD, H.L., GEWIRTZ, J.L. and ROSS, H.W. (1959) Social conditioning of vocalizations in the infant. *J. Comp. Physiol. Psychol. 52*, 68–73

SCHAFFER, H.R. (1971) *The Growth of Sociability*. Penguin Books, Harmondsworth, Middx.

SCHAFFER, H.R. and EMERSON, P.E. (1964) Patterns of response to physical contact in early human development. *J. Child Psychol. Psychiat. 5*, 1–13

SELIGMAN, M.E.P. (1970) On the generality of the laws of learning. *Psychol. Rev. 77*, 406–418

SPEARS, W.C. (1963) The assessment of visual discrimination and preferences in the human infant. (Abstract only) *Dissert. Abstr. 23*, 2998

STEINMAN, W.M. (1970) The social control of generalized imitation. *J. Appl. Behav. Anal. 3*, 159–167

ULRICH, R.E. and CRAINE, W.H. (1964) Behavior: persistence of shock-induced aggression. *Science 143*, 971–973

ULRICH, R.E., WOLFF, P.C. and AZRIN, N.H. (1964) Shock as an elicitor of intra- and interspecies fighting behavior. *Animal Behav. 12*, 14–15

VAN ECK, O. (1972) Unpublished Master's thesis, University of London, Institute of Education

ZIMMERMAN, D.W. (1969) Patterns of responding in a chained schedule altered by conditional reinforcement. *Psychonom. Science 16*, 120–122

ZIMMERMAN, J. and HANFORD, P.V. (1967) Differential effects of extinction on behaviors maintained by concurrent schedules of primary and conditioned reinforcement. *Psychonom. Science 8*, 103–104

ZIMMERMAN, J., HANFORD, P.V. and BROWN, W. (1967) Effects of conditioned reinforcement frequency in an intermittent free-feeding situation. *J. Exp. Anal. Behav. 10*, 331–340

Commentary

MARIA CALLIAS

This very interesting paper draws our attention to important but largely neglected aspects of the social behaviour of severely retarded children. Although the question of defining social behaviour has been sidestepped, a useful distinction has been made between social behaviour as an area of developing competence and skill in relating to people on the one hand, and the use of social stimuli as reinforcers for developing a wide variety of skills on the other. This distinction serves as a valuable reminder that there is a difference between a content area of development and the use of techniques to bring about changes in behaviour when these present as clinical problems. I should like to discuss these two aspects separately.

Our knowledge of the development of social competence of severely retarded children lags far behind that of other areas such as cognitive ability, self-help skills and language. From our general observations, we are well aware of the wide range of individual differences in social behaviour. Some children do not seem to discriminate people as a separate class of 'objects', others respond in conventional but possibly less complex ways than normal children while a few will interact in ways that reveal astute social awareness but do so in ways that distress or irritate other people. As Jordan and Saunders point out, the child's social responsiveness is likely to be a crucial factor in determining and maintaining the way adults relate to him. Sociability is thus as important for retarded children as it is for others and is a content area that we should consider more frequently when we select target skills in programmes designed to increase competence. As this paper shows, most energy has so far been directed towards developing only a small, though very significant aspect of social behaviour, namely attention to and imitation of others. Imitation skills are considered mainly in their role as prerequisites for training language and other practical skills or as skills in their own right rather than in relation to the part they play in social development.

Obviously, the importance of imitation in all skills development is not disputed but it does seem time to move on to consider a wider range of social behaviour and interactions.

Our limited knowledge of the course of social development in retarded children and the factors which influence it clearly needs to be extended. The rapidly growing body of knowledge on normal children, and particularly infants, provides useful guidelines and a base from which to begin answering some important questions. These include questions about, first, the nature of social development such as whether it follows essentially the same sequence as that of normal children (e.g. Schaffer 1971) albeit at a slower pace, or a different one; second, the contribution of the individual characteristics of the child himself to the process of socialization (e.g. Schaffer 1971; Richards 1974); and third, the role of the social environment itself.

At this stage, it seems to me that awareness of the course of the various aspects of normal social development provides a useful background for planning intervention programmes in social skills. It can serve to alert us to relevant behaviours to consider when carrying out an initial analysis of a child's social skills, and to provide a rough guide in the selection of a suitable sequence of goals in training. How useful this strategy will be in practice or in the long term remains an open question.

I found some of the issues and problems raised in this paper about reinforce-

78

ment particularly thought-provoking, as they challenge us to reconsider our current approach to the selection of reinforcers in clinical and educational settings. The view that reinforcement/response compatibility may be crucial for successful outcome in modification programmes with human subjects certainly requires investigation. To use reinforcers that are related to responses seems conceptually sound and certainly simpler in practice if such a reinforcer is in fact available for the particular child. However, numerous studies, including those on imitation training quoted in this paper, demonstrate that successful results can be obtained with the use of a wide variety of reinforcers which are not specifically response-related. Similarly, in our clinical work we have found that unusual or material reinforcers have often been essential because of the extremely limited range of stimuli that some children find reinforcing. In training sessions we have not found it to be an insuperable problem to use these reinforcers, paired with seemingly neutral social stimuli, and to use prompts for graded training to elicit responses.

Although the secondary reinforcement theory of social responsiveness does not account at all adequately for normal social development (e.g. Schaffer 1971), we have found, again in a clinical setting, that pairing social stimuli with potent reinforcers has often facilitated social responsiveness in the child, and it has then been possible to use social reinforcement in some learning situations. There have also been instances where it has not been possible to fade out non-social reinforcement. In Jordan and Saunders' discussion on the extent to which it is possible to establish and then use social reinforcement, it seems to me that problems arise from their decision to avoid the issues of definition of social phenomena, and that in fact some clarification of their use of the term 'social reinforcement' is necessary. Some investigators use the term to indicate a whole class of social responses, including (for example) verbal and non-verbal signs of approval in words, smiles, cuddling or stroking, whereas others restrict the term to a specific act, for example, saying "good boy" or "good girl." It seems necessary to establish whether these two extremes of 'social reinforcement' are comparable or not in terms of their effectiveness as reinforcers.

The discussion of difficulties encountered in using social reinforcement in training sessions is useful and alerts us to the important differences between working in a laboratory and in a naturalistic setting. The issue of contiguous versus contingent use of social reinforcement is interesting. In an applied setting, I feel that this can be resolved to some extent without depriving the child of social stimulation generally but by trying to create a different kind of contrast effect between training session and other times where it is necessary to have special training sessions. This could be done by compromising and introducing additional potent reinforcers during the training period. Alternatively, there is some evidence to suggest that fairly short periods of 'deprivation' lasting about 20 minutes can enhance the reinforcement value of social attention (see Gewirtz 1972). It may be relatively easy to time training sessions so that they follow periods of quiet play or rest. These difficulties with the use of a particular 'reinforcer' raise the problem of definition of reinforcement once again and are a reminder that it should not be assumed that any specific stimulus or event, social or otherwise, has necessarily identical reinforcing properties for a group of children, or indeed for any one child at different times. It emphasizes the need for flexibility in selective reinforcers, and for choosing on the basis of a detailed assessment of the child's reinforcement history. Some of the issues raised in relation to social reinforcement, e.g. satiation effects and control of reinforcers, are ones that need to be considered with the use of any reinforcer.

The question of whether it is desirable or suitable to use social stimuli as reinforcers for a variety of responses is an interesting one. To some extent the choice of reinforcers will be dictated by the setting in which training takes place and by the availability of other relatively convenient reinforcers. In home and school settings, several factors may influence the selection of reinforcement. For example, it may be possible for some parents or teachers to consider the possibility of using other reinforcers, social reinforcement may be the one most readily available and easiest for the adult to control and dispense, and third, in a natural setting the problem is often that the contingencies for social reinforcement need to be altered rather than that social reinforcement needs to be introduced, e.g. in cases where social reinforcement may be maintaining disruptive behaviour.

The suggestion is made that we should attempt to make more use of intrinsic reinforcers and find ways of training skills that encourage intrinsic reinforcement. I wholeheartedly agree with the hope that children will at some time derive intrinsic pleasure from their new skills, but we cannot assume that this will always be possible. The need for extrinsic reinforcement at any time usually arises because intrinsic interest is lacking. Clinical observations suggest that in the course of operant training some children do develop an intrinsic interest in new skills, or that these skills are maintained by naturally occurring reinforcers. The conditions under which external reinforcement is essential or becomes unnecessary in training or maintaining new skills, including social ones, are still unclear and merit attention.

It is worth noting that most of the issues and questions raised in this paper arise out of a shift from the confines of a laboratory setting to the child's own environment. The development of social behaviour becomes a topic of interest in its own right, the need to take account of the influence of general environmental variables on individual training sessions becomes evident and the factors affecting generalization and maintenance of new learning become very important. This paper has gone a long way towards indicating important problems that require further thought and investigation.

REFERENCES

GEWIRTZ, J.L. (1972) Some contextual determinants of stimulus potency. In *Recent Trends in Social Learning Theory* (Parker, R.D., ed.). Academic Press, New York

RICHARDS, M.P.M. (1974) Introduction. In *The Integration of the Child into a Social World* (Richards, M.P.M., ed.). C.U.P., London

SCHAFFER, H.R. (1971) *The Growth of Sociability*. Penguin Books, Harmondsworth, Middx.

Discussion

Jordan: Just one point on social reinforcement. I don't believe it's humanely permissible to use deprivation to strengthen the effectiveness of social reinforcers. Quite apart from anything else, the effect on the care staff would be devastating.

Carr: Is it in fact necessary? We know that deprivation strengthens food as a reinforcer, but is there any evidence that the same applies to social reinforcers?

Harzem: I doubt very much that the analogy with food deprivation holds. If a mother withholds approval from her child, that does not make approval more effective as a reinforcer.

Jordan: Another problem with social reinforcement, which I haven't begun to solve, arises where it is not closely matched to the behaviour you want to elicit. Only too often, social reinforcement elicits social responses, and what can you do but compete them out? And if that extinction generalizes, what does that do to the child's general social behaviour?

Kiernan: Do you mean there is an innate incompatibility, in the terms used by Garcia *et al.* (1971)?

Yule: Well, is there any good evidence of such a thing, because if you go along that road you're going to have to deny the validity of Premack's system of selecting the child's preferred behaviours and using them as a reinforcer for other behaviours, and I don't think anyone will do that.

Harzem: Surely the social response and the desired behaviour are rarely physically incompatible.

Mittler: Even when they're not, the social response can really slow a training session down. Some children are so elated by loud and enthusiastic praise that they go prancing round the room for 10 minutes, during which time you can't work with them.

This brings me to another problem of social reinforcement. What do you do about the paradoxical use of speech in the natural environment? Here we all are, saying "Good boy" constantly as a positive reinforcer of behaviour, whereas the usual idiomatic phrase is "*Don't* do that, there's a good boy." Does anyone use the thumbs-up sign as a general primary reinforcer instead?

Jordan: No, but we have used a clap.

Mittler: That can be too infectious, and start the whole class clapping, whereas a thumbs-up sign, perhaps coupled with a broad grin, is essentially a private signal between you and the child.

Carr: Once you start a child clapping it may be difficult to get him to stop.

Jordan: I am also worried about the artificiality of the environment with which we surround the children. Are we justified in making all the adults behave in a specialized way because we want to use something as a reinforcer? Shouldn't we rather be making the child tolerant to the negative use of "Good boy," for instance, and in general to the wide variation in meanings in everyday life?

Mittler: Well, of course, you must start in the formal, artificial setting with everything clear-cut and consistent, only fading the prompts gradually to enable the child to tolerate the chaotic system in which most of us operate.

Walker: You say you don't want to use Time Out. Is this because it would make you less effective as a socially reinforcing person?

Jordan: Yes, especially as I have experience of becoming an aversive stimulus even without Time Out for at least two children after many weeks of daily training sessions.

Yule: Patterson's work with antisocial children (Patterson 1973; Patterson *et al.* 1973) showed that Time Out had to be inserted before the children could be reinforced by the normal everyday responses of parents or teachers.

81

Mittler: Time Out is surely Time Out from positive social reinforcement.

Yule: Just so. This result means that the reinforcers had not been identified, but were present in the modest praise which was potentiated as a reinforcer by the 2–5 minutes of isolation.

Kiernan: There is a difference here between children in hospital, who seem starved of social contact, and—as we have seen—children in a family and community who can afford not to respond to a smile and praise from Rita Jordan. This variable has not, to my knowledge, been investigated systematically.

Hogg: There is a little evidence to support that: Bijou and Oblinger (1960) found that the number of trials to extinction in a ball-dropping response was far greater for institutionalized retarded children than for three different groups of normal children, amongst whom there were also differences in extinction rate that could be predicted from the relative richness of their environment. Zigler (1973) has also provided information on this point.

Mittler: A notice at the entrance to a children's ward at a certain hospital warned visitors to take no notice of children who came up to them. It soon became clear that there was a programme in effect to extinguish inappropriate approach behaviours, but it certainly didn't reinforce the visitors' approach behaviours to the handicapped, and it brought home to me how difficult it is sometimes to reconcile your actions as a behaviour modifier with your sensitivity as a human being.

REFERENCES

BIJOU, S.W. and OBLINGER, B. (1960) Responses of normal and retarded children as a function of the experimental situation. *Psychol. Rep. 6*, 447–454

GARCIA, E., BAER, D.M. and FIRESTONE, I. (1971) The development of generalized imitation with topographically determined boundaries. *J. Appl. Behav. Anal. 4*, 101–112

PATTERSON, G.R. (1973) Reprogramming the families of aggressive boys. In *Behaviour Modification in Education* (Thoresen, C.E., ed.), 72nd Yearbook of the National Society for the Study of Education, Chicago. Univ. Chicago Press, Chicago

PATTERSON, G.R., COBB, J.A. and RAY, R.S (1973) A social engineering technology for retraining the families of aggressive boys. In *Issue and Trends in Behavior Therapy* (Adams, H.E. and Unikel, I.P., eds.). Charles C. Thomas, Springfield, Ill.

ZIGLER, E. (1973) The retarded child as a whole person. In *The Experimental Psychology of Mental Retardation* (Routh, D.K., ed.), pp. 231–322. Aldine, Chicago

Methodology of Behaviour Modification

C.C. KIERNAN

Thomas Coram Research Unit, University of London, Institute of Education

ABSTRACT

Most designs and techniques used in behaviour modification have been inherited from laboratory animal research, along with orientating attitudes to operational definition and statistical analysis. It is argued that the application of behaviour modification to service problems necessitates a rapprochement with other traditions of experimental design. In particular, intergroup comparison procedures and observational and questionnaire techniques are needed to clarify the effects of behaviour modification.

TRADITIONAL METHODOLOGY

Initial attempts at application of behaviour modification were traditionally attempts to modify the behaviour of 'the worst case in the institution'. For these cases the conceptual framework offered by functional analysis and own-control designs allowed the highly individual quality of behaviour to emerge and to be analysed and modified. For treatment purposes the methodology fitted extremely well. In addition, behaviour modification showed that experimentation in the natural environment was feasible, if not easy. The combined impact of these factors brought behaviour modification into prominence. Not only did the theoretical approach work, but the methodology allowed a very clear picture of the results to be presented both to professionals and to the lay public.

During the mid to late sixties, the methods of treatment and of research on treatment continued to develop. Demonstrated applications of an increasingly wide range of behaviours established the value of the approach in psychiatric, educational and rehabilitation settings (Gardner 1971; Kiernan 1974a). Methods used in research on treatment continued to centre on the basic reversal, multiple-baseline and probe procedures, with some extension through inclusion of rather simple observational techniques (Baer, Wolf and Risley 1968; Bijou, Peterson and Ault 1968).

The strengths and weaknesses of reversal procedures are well established. In its simplest form 'reversal' involves the demonstration of a stable baseline and the application of a treatment. If a change in consequence can be shown to result in a corresponding change in behaviour an effect may be claimed. Given a long and stable baseline and a substantial and long-lasting shift in behaviour, the simple reversal procedure is often impressive in itself. In our experience practitioners often happily accept such demonstrations, perhaps because they are unaware of possible alternative treatment effects or because their experience leads them to regard other explanations as implausible.

From a research viewpoint simple reversal or baseline-treatment designs are inadequate because of the possible confounding of treatment effects with uncontrolled variables (Campbell and Stanley 1963). Full reversal designs (baseline-treatment-extinction) overcome some of these problems. In particular, the possible coincidence of another variable changing simultaneously with onset of treatment may well introduce several changes in the situation, only one of which is highlighted by the theory. There may be an increase in the amount of attention given, in quality of general response by teachers and in general structuring of the environment as well as programmed changes relating to delivery of contingent reinforcement.

The effects of some of the treatment-correlated variables may be eliminated by tighter controls within the single-reversal design. An additional strategy is to make use of systematic replication procedures (Sidman 1960). In systematic replication the same basic manipulations are repeated in different settings in which correlated variables are allowed to change or will be different simply in the nature of things. Sidman points out that if an effect is retained over several settings differing in several ways, the active agent can be validly inferred. In practice, systematic replication may take the form of demonstration of basic effects across situations. For example, repeated demonstrations that contingent positive social reinforcement affects behaviour across settings, behaviours, agents and recipients lead to ready acceptance of its effectiveness as such rather than as a correlate of increased generalized attention.

The second application of systematic replication is through multiple reversal, in which there are several consecutive baseline and treatment sessions. This technique allows for similar variation on 'non-critical' variables across settings and people. If used ingeniously multiple reversal should allow successive elimination of different hypotheses to explain behaviour change. One can conceive of a situation in which there are several alternative explanations for a basic effect, each one of which could be tested within a single experiment by systematically modifying the treatment situation to test each in turn. Such sophisticated use is rare: application in operant audiometry represents the closest approximation to the full use of multiple reversal. More commonly, the technique is used to eliminate historical and maturational variables as contenders for the explanation of effects.

The disadvantages of reversal and multiple-reversal designs are also well known. Reversal may be undesirable on ethical grounds, for instance when head-banging has been eliminated. Alternatively, the behaviour may not be reversible. Responses which have been established by contrived reward may be trapped by natural contingencies (Baer and Wolf 1970): the child who is taught appropriate use of 'yes' and 'no' is likely to be so heavily reinforced by naturally occurring contingencies as to render this behaviour very difficult to reverse, and once independent feeding and toileting have been established, powerful positive natural consequences come into play. Secondly, the subject himself may 'take over'. We have recently observed a child who was systematically restrained at the beginning of a sequence which built up to severe self-mutilation. The restraint prevented self-mutilation. After a time the child would *request* restraint at the beginning of the sequence, i.e. he used the imposed punishment procedure to control his own behaviour. Self-control in the form of self-reward and self-punishment is not rare, even in more profoundly retarded children; clearly, it represents a limitation on reversibility. Thirdly, some behaviour may not be reversible for physiological or anatomical reasons. It seems unlikely that once maladaptive reflexes have been eliminated in physiotherapy they can be re-established.

Multiple-baseline designs were developed largely to avoid the drawbacks of reversal procedures. The requirement of the multiple-baseline procedure is that the behaviour should be analysable into several limited-response classes each one of which can be dealt with on a programme. Thus, a play programme might involve repeated observation of play with a group of six toys. An initial baseline phase would involve observation of play with all six toys. In the first training period, appropriate play with toy A would be rewarded, baseline conditions being maintained for the rest. Change would be expected to occur *only* in relation to Toy A. Play with other toys would be identical to baseline play. The second training phase would involve reward for appropriate play with both A and B, baseline for the rest; the third would involve A, B, C and so on. At each stage it would be expected that changes would occur only where reward was delivered, other play remaining at baseline.

Multiple-baseline procedures can be used to answer the same questions as the multiple-reversal procedure. It would be possible to arrange a multiple-baseline procedure in such a way that each new training phase used a slightly different application of the same general principle. There is no reason why different successive phases should not each employ a different positive reinforcer, and hence demonstrate the general principle of the effectiveness of rewards through systemative replication. This use of the procedure provides an answer to the question 'what precisely is critical in controlling the behaviour?'

Multiple-baseline procedures generally stress a different but related question. They are clearly adapted to showing whether an effect is specific to the behaviour being reinforced or whether reinforcement has non-specific effects. Clear demonstrations through the multiple-baseline approach would establish this specificity. Instances where effects are not clear-cut and where treatment effects generalize across two or more defined responses reveal two important assumptions underlying the approach.

The first assumption is that the response classes identified are independent (or can be rapidly discriminated in training). For instance, if we were to assume that each of our toys involved a different response class from the others we could hope to achieve a pure multiple-baseline demonstration. Clearly this assumption will be very questionable in most cases. Direct generalization of trained responses from one toy to another may occur in the form of new manipulative responses. Or there may be a functional dependence. Barton, Guess, Garcia and Baer (1970) found that decrease in the use of fingers in a feeding programme led to increase in the messy use of the spoon. Or there may be negative contrast effects such that decreases in behaviour in certain segments of the session may give rise to increases in others.

The second assumption made by the multiple-baseline design is related. It is that the order or sequence in which the teaching or elimination of responses is either known or unimportant. So it would be assumed that in teaching visual tracking it was either self-evident or irrelevant whether horizontal, vertical or circular tracking was taught first. On the other hand it might be assumed that attention training ('look at this') was a necessary first stage in training. In the Barton et al. (1970) study an apparent increase in responsiveness to the contingency (Time Out) occurred across phases of the study. This may have reflected a general increase in contingency awareness. In fact it seems quite likely that most situations will cause one or another of these effects to appear. The problem is familiar from published work on the transfer of training (cf. Deese and Hulse 1967).

Given these restrictions on the clarity of multiple-baseline procedures it is not surprising that good examples of its use are rare.

The qualifications concerning reversal and multiple-baseline techniques must not be taken too far. These are valuable and powerful techniques for demonstrating within-subject effects. Furthermore, a great deal of useful information on the structure of behaviour can be gained from the 'problem' instances. Multiple-baseline procedures throw up hypotheses concerning interrelations of response classes and cumulative effects. This means that the techniques are doing their job. In fact what is to be regretted is that the techniques are customarily used in a way which restricts their value. For example, the use of multiple reversal with systematically varied conditions in each of the treatment phases represents an obviously powerful procedure which appears to be missing from applied research.

Probe procedures have a special place in the assessment of behaviour change. As initially formulated, the probe is a single trial of generalization. Usually, non-reinforced test trials on generalization displays are interspersed in Variable Ratio schedules. As developed, the procedure may involve direct translation of this technique into the applied field or the use of observational or questionnaire procedure becomes identical with more traditional pre- and post-test procedures.

The traditional methodological armamentarium of the behaviour modifier is complemented by procedures related to particular types of treatment. These include generalized procedures like Time Out and Differential Reinforcement of Other (DRO) behaviour, as well as more specialized procedures for developing particular responses patterns, for example self-control (Thoresen and Mahoney (1974). This aspect of methodology is more effectively dealt with in papers covering particular areas. We will confine our attention to methods of assessing treatment effects.

APPLIED METHODOLOGY

Two significant questions arise from the extension of use of behavioural techniques to applied settings. First, how can we evaluate their effectiveness? And secondly, what are the most effective sequences for use in training particular skills? Behaviour modification offers the means of changing behaviour, but gives no indication of what behaviour can be changed and in what sequence components of a target behaviour should be changed. The behaviour modifier needs to import new methods in order to cope with hese problems.

Evaluation of change in practical settings

The evaluation of change in practical settings raises several issues. Those considered here reflect basic problems of assessment, problems of evaluating packages, and problems concerned with the purpose of evaluation.

Functional analysis As defined and operated in its full form, functional analysis represents a means whereby antecedents and consequents of behaviour are analysed and isolated experimentally as they affect an individual's behaviour (Kiernan 1973). It is the natural technique of assessment derived from the operant model. The full analysis, by definition, involves experimentation in order to identify antecedents and consequences. As a result, the analysis of a single behaviour may take a lot of time.

The fate of functional analysis in applied settings reflects the differences between methodology for treatment and methodology for research on treatment. In practice, full-scale functional analysis appears to be necessary only when other more approximate methods fail. Most workers appear to rely on a combination of two strategies. The first involves a gross analysis based on general observations of likely setting and discriminative stimuli and reinforcing events. This analysis is then followed by tentative experimental modifications in conditions, which may result in immediate change. These modifications are likely to involve the second strategy, the attempt to override the influence of existing discriminative, setting and reinforcing stimuli by shifting the individual to new settings, highlighting new high-potency discriminative stimuli and using known reinforcers which are potentially more powerful than existing reinforcers.

The combination of these two strategies attempts to cut through existing functional relations rather than analyse them. Another assessment strategy offers itself under circumstances where skills are being trained. This is the use of generalized assessment procedures which place the individual in some sort of educational network. These macro-assessment procedures are familiar in lattice form (Bricker 1972; Jones and Kiernan 1973) (see Figure 1). They serve to substitute for full functional analysis.

These three strategies represent first-line approaches to assessment. In practice it is only when these strategies fail that recourse is made to full-scale functional analysis.

The technique of overriding raises significant research questions. Is it as

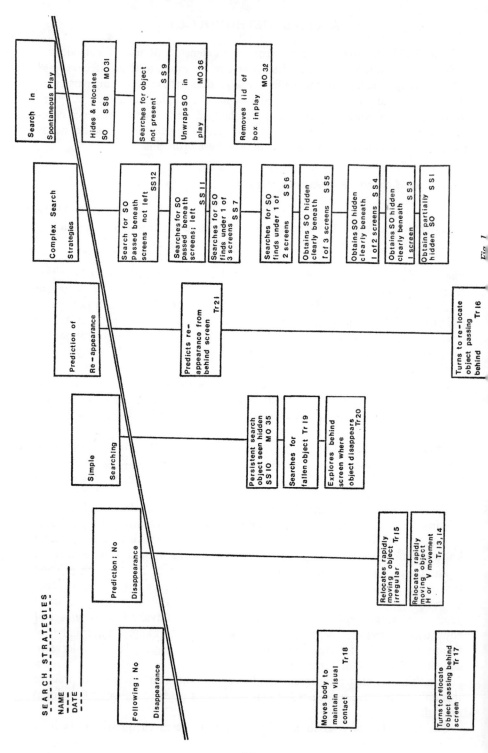

Fig 1

effective in treatment as the methods that are more obviously based on theory? Its use is partly predicated on the need to save time in treatment. From the methodological viewpoint its apparently successful use is backed by general laws. If a behaviour is not being reinforced at all, reinforcement may obviously change its frequency. It does not take a full-scale functional analysis to establish this. At a less obvious theoretical level we can ask 'Under what circumstances does overriding work?' Are the characteristics of behaviours which can be changed in this way predicted by operant theory, or do new principles have to be developed to handle some phenomena? For example, do high-rate self-orientated operants, like rocking or posturing in autistic individuals, behave in the same way as low-rate operants?

Techniques need to be viewed both as tools for direct analysis and for producing new hypotheses when they do not work as planned. The shift in the form of functional analysis is typical of the changes brought about in methodology by application to treatment. The shift from research to treatment requires a simplification of procedures which raises both direct and indirect research questions.

Demonstration of the effectiveness of packages. The application of any new treatment in schools, hospitals or the community has effects at all levels of the relevant organization. The introduction of operant techniques into a hospital will potentially affect patients, nurses, paramedical and medical personnel, administrators, relatives and the general public, and possibly the design, equipment and furnishing of the hospital. This would be true for any new procedure but is especially the case with operant techniques because of the clear implications which the operant approach has for the organizational framework of the institution and the provision of material resources. Many studies show that operant programmes cannot be run successfully on an extensive scale without adequate organizational development and adequate material resources. For example, the adequate operation of a behaviour modification programme in a school appears to depend critically on the provision of a timetable which allows teachers to have individual teaching sessions with children and an agreed job description for a teacher requiring that she does sessions on a regular basis. If these organizational requirements are not met, reaching is likely to be patchy, progress delayed, and the overall effectiveness of the programme jeopardized.

It follows that any programme claiming to demonstrate the effectiveness of a procedure needs at least to describe the organizational setting required for its successful implementation. In studies on the effectiveness of treatment many questions need to be considered (Kiernan 1974b; Kiernan, Wright and Hawks 1973). These questions range from small, specific changes to the impact of programmes on the community. It is impossible for every intervention study to cover every question, but many studies have implications for several levels and fail to document changes at these levels. The whole range of questions needs to be considered in relation to the methodology of research on treatment. We can list some of these questions as follows:

(1) Can the behaviour of the handicapped individual be changed by experts

in behaviour modification in ideal settings? This is the fundamental question of modifiability which leads to the case study approach. As stated, it assumes ideal organizational and material back-up.

(2) Can the behaviour of the handicapped individual be changed by teachers, nurses, parents, etc., in ideal settings? Does it take special skills to use the techniques or can any suitably trained individual do it? If so, what is the best form of training?

(3) Can the behaviour be changed by experts under *existing* material and organizational conditions? Is the existing material environment rich enough to support a programme run by experts? And is the organizational framework adequate? Can a system be run with an organizational framework of shifts, where decisions are taken by teams and where ordering of materials is centrally organized? Answers to these questions take us away from traditional designs to the development of techniques for examining the 'quality' of environmental provision (Doke and Risley 1972) and to the use of techniques for the analysis of decision making developed by organizational and occupational psychologists (French and Bell 1973).

(4) Can behaviour be changed by nurses, parents, teachers, etc., under existing or improved material and organizational conditions?

(5) *Is* behaviour changed by nurses, parents, teachers etc., under existing or improved material and organizational conditions?

Questions 4 and 5 go together, but the difference between them is critical. It is quite likely that behaviour could be changed when a project is on a research footing but not when the procedures pass into practice. For example, in the development of programme materials stress is usually placed on the adequacy of coverage and programming of teaching for particular skills. The Parsons, Kansas Research Centre programmes involve careful analysis and programming of skills such as ironing and hair-rolling (J. Lent, personal communication). The programmes are designed for use by attendants with moderately retarded girls and have been carefully standardized on this basis. This answers the 'can' question. The 'do' question is a more significant service question. Do the attendants use the programmes under existing service conditions or is there a need for changed service conditions to ensure their use? And if the service conditions are changed, what happens to job satisfaction?

The same considerations apply to the general use of operant techniques. Parents, nurses or teachers may be given skills and provided with an adequate setting in which to use them, but they may not do so. Such considerations have of course led to the use of records and accountability systems in order to ensure implementation.

These points are important for research. It is necessary to demonstrate not only that behaviour can be changed but that it is changed, and by the methods which are supposedly being used. It is also necessary to document the material and organizational changes which enhance the effectiveness of the programme. At least four types of data need to be collected:

(i) Data on specific changes occurring as a result of carefully maintained operant-based programmes. This is the traditional data base.

(ii) Data derived from observation of change agents which can demonstrate the agent's generalized use of techniques. This may include records of sessions and probes completed by parents, teachers, nurses, etc.

(iii) Data from probes, which may be in the form of diaries, interviews, formal tests, etc., which demonstrate the generalized effect of programmes on children.

(iv) Data drawn from interviews, formalized schedules, attitude scales, institution records, etc., which relate to the changes in material provision and organizational framework: needed to accommodate the project. For example staffing records, daily timetables and the Child Management Schedule (King, Raynes and Tizard 1970) were used by Kiernan, Wright and Hawks (1973) in an attempt to log data in relation to a ward-wide operant programme.

It also follows that there is a need to demonstrate the effectiveness and value of the 'new' package as opposed to existing packages. This immediately involves the establishment of control groups and a substantial break with tradition in the employment of between-group statistics. This in turn brings a whole series of difficulties, one or two of which will be noted later.

We have referred to programmes as packages because any programme has *several* elements, each one of which is important. One traditional objection from operant workers to the use of Fisherian statistics has been that important differences between packages can be drowned by the use of Fisherian statistics. And yet we need to compare programmes. The dilemma can only be avoided by the concurrent use of several techniques which will fill out an adequate picture.

The evaluation of a programme requires another substantial divergence from traditional practice. An educational programme needs to be considered in relation to its cognitive, motor and emotional effects both where it is taught and in the home, public places, etc. This requirement presents a substantial methodological challenge which can only be met by extension of procedures to the use of diary, questionnaire and other non-traditional procedures.

(v) What is the impact of the behaviour modification programme on the institution? Hospitals, schools and communities may accept or reject new techniques. For example 'reformed' wards in a hospital system may be further developed, tolerated, or dismantled. What happens depends partly on the attention which the initiators of change pay to the need to foster acceptance within the existing framework. To this extent the methodological skills of the behaviour modifier need to be extended to include those of the agent of organizational change (French and Bell 1973). In addition, changes of attitudes and of institutional goals, etc. need to be analysed and recorded if a full picture is to be presented. One important final implication is that programmes have to be followed up in order to assess the reasons for their survival or non-survival.

The prospect presented by the analysis just presented is daunting. It is, however, inevitable that the application of behaviour modification in an institution will have effects at several different levels, each one of which will potentially affect overall success. No research project could attempt to accurately measure and control all the factors involved. The best that can be attempted in evaluation is:

(1) A focusing on particular levels of interest with full recording at these

levels, e.g. traditional operant methodology plus observations and question-naires.

(2) Generalized documentation of other factors, for example, the natural history of the project from the organizational viewpoint and observations arising from the experience of the project which cannot be fully documented but which represent informed opinion.

(3) Combination of (1) and (2) and integration into a coherent picture related to the theoretical base of the programme.

Methodology for whom? In the previous section the argument suggested an extension of operant methodology in order to include other techniques and facilitate communication. The type of communication which will be effective depends on the audience. The simple assumption that communication will be assured if control groups are used and various methods employed to trace the changes is clearly untrue.

Many 'consumers' are not interested in scientific niceties. Parents, teachers and nurses are often prepared to accept simple demonstrations of baseline–treatment changes as evidence of effectiveness of procedures. The use of reversal designs may be strongly resisted. If motivation is to be maintained, goals need to be set and feedback provided. But recording procedures need to be an integral part of the overall programme design, for example a trial-by-trial record as opposed to a formal record taken at the end of a session. Probe trials need to be 'sold' and may have to be brief or administered under supervision.

The general question is, do we need a new methodology for teachers, parents, nurses and others who will use the techniques? Such a methodology would serve the purpose of providing feedback and setting goals, but would be carefully tailored to these needs rather than involving each teacher in a quasi-research project. As with functional analysis, great sophistication may not be needed for the attainment of treatment aims.

The assumption that control groups and Fisherian statistics will ensure com-munication is clearly wrong for another reason. Control-group methodology has the inherent danger that spurious conclusions based on averages may be reached. Agencies may claim an interest in 'average data' because of the desire to deliver the best overall service. The distinction between averaged data and optimized conditions is not always made. A service is interested in producing the best possible solution for a given cost in order to use resources optimally. In this respect medians and quartile deviates may be more appropriate than averages.

The adoption of control-group methods and Fisherian statistics carries with it the requirement that the audience should be informed as to the limitations of the methods. This need is highlighted by the question of follow-up. The evalua-tion of non-operant treatments normally employs treatment and non-treatment follow-up phases. This design cannot be accepted, as an operant approach predicts either persistence of behaviour if natural contingencies take over from experimental contingencies or extinction if they do not, or change in the behaviour brought about by new shaping. One must investigate the follow-up conditions to reach a valid assessment in an operant framework.

Control-group methodology also raises all the problems concerned with the initial selection of groups. This topic has been exhaustively argued elsewhere, especially in terms of the appropriateness of mental-age or chronological-age matching. From a behaviour modification viewpoint the type of conclusion reached by Baumeister (1967) seems appropriate. Baumeister argues for the use of multiple-factor designs where particular behavioural characteristics are isolated and correlated with experimental variables. It is clear that at least the behaviour modifier will tend to match subjects or balance groups according to particular *behaviours* rather than on global measures. The use of multi-factorial analysis may well allow more sensitive assessments of change, although to date scaling requirements for appropriate use of such analysis seem to be beyond our technical competence.

The adoption of control groups solves some problems but brings others in its train. Additional measures need to be taken, over and above those normally required by the control-group approach. The audience for the research needs to be educated into seeing the reasons for the approach adopted. We cannot simply map non-operant designs into operant theory. An adequate synthesis of the two needs to be made.

Scaling and the planning of sequences to be used in training

We return finally to the question 'What are the most efficient sequences for use in training particular skills?' If there are two ways of breaking down and teaching a skill, one will presumably be more efficient than the other if all the other factors are equal. It is clear from work on toilet training that some procedures are more effective than others (Azrin and Foxx 1971).

The question of sequences reflects back on the previous discussion of overall evaluation. Different operant programmes will not be homogeneous in this respect. So 'Evaluation' of 'an operant programme' overall without taking into account the characteristics of individual components will be rather like weighing shopping bags at the check-out counters of Sainsbury's and Tesco's in the hope of finding out whether Sainsbury's or Tesco's is the better supermarket.

The ideal sequence of steps in a programme would consist of a series of critical behaviours each one necessary for the acquisition of the target behaviour and each one in its 'correct position' with respect to others. These sequences would represent scales along which an individual could be assessed. Such sequences have been gleaned from several sources. Some have resulted from analyses of the functional requirements of settings and target behaviours (e.g. for self-help skills). Others have derived from a logical analysis of target behaviours. Carrier (1974) describes a language training programme based purely on a logical and systems analysis of communication. Other programmes derive from consideration of developmental norms. This approach is really rather a poor basis for programming. Normative scales do not set out to isolate critical behaviours (Jones and Kiernan 1973). There is no reason why normal development should not be improved on and it is in many ways illogical (Carrier 1974). Finally, some programmes are based on theory, in particular Piagetian theory. Other theories could clearly be used, especially those implicit in existing treatment procedures like physiotherapy.

Each of the scales represented by these different sequences constitutes a theory concerning the steps necessary for teaching a skill. Given this, one sequence may be tested against another in order to isolate the most effective sequences. This mammoth job has not yet been seriously undertaken. The methodology for such a venture is already established in work on programmed learning and in some work more within the behaviour modification tradition (Bijou 1968; Sidman and Stoddard 1966).

A closely related scaling problem emerges in overall evaluation of operant programmes. The value of a programme to an agency will depend at least in part on the standards required by the agency. In toilet training a programme may have two goals: habit training, in which the individual performs appropriately at a set time and place and without accidents elsewhere, or independent toileting in which the person takes himself to the toilet as need requires. In a large institution where block treatment is in use, habit training may be the desired goals and independent toileting may add little to the value of the programme. At home, habit training may be of little help and only independent toileting will be of value. Again, in a general communication programme getting the child to stand still when told 'stop' may be of little value to a ward staff member in a hospital, but may be a matter of life and death if the child lives at home and has a tendency to run away in heavy traffic when out shopping with his mother.

The general point is that different people in different settings will scale the importance of behaviour differently. Consequently it is unlikely that meaningful scales can be constructed for evaluation across settings. This problem reflects the contrast between behavioural as against statistical significance (Badia, Haber and Runyon 1970). The problem is similar to the control-group problem. All that can be done to tackle both problems is to insist on as full a description as possible of the *actual* changes brought about in addition to the levels of statistical significance. The consumer is then left in a position to judge whether the changes in behaviour observed are significant to him.

CONCLUSIONS

This paper discussed the value of traditional operant methodology and the need to modify and extend this methodology in evaluation of operant-based programmes. In particular, techniques from conventional control-group methods and statistics need to be imported, along with procedures designed to assess the broad impact of operant procedures. The extended techniques bring their own problems and increase the need to carefully plan, document and report research projects in behaviour modification.

REFERENCES

AZRIN, N.H. and FOXX, R.M. (9171) A rapid method of toilet training the institutionalized retarded. *J. Appl. Behav. Anal. 4*, 89–99

BADIA, P., HABER, A. and RUNYON, R.P. (1970) *Research Problems in Psychology.* Addison-Wesley, Reading, Mass.

BAER, D.M. and WOLF, M.M. (1970) The entry into natural communities of reinforcement. In *Control of Human Behaviour. Vol. 2: From Cure to Prevention* (Ulrich, R., Stachnik, T. and Mabry, J., eds.). Scott Foresman, Glenview, Illinois

BAER, D.M., WOLF, M.M. and RISLEY, T.R. (1968) Some current dimensions of applied behavioural analysis. *J. Appl. Behav. Anal. 1*, 91–100

BARTON, E.S., GUESS, D., GARCIA, E. and BAER, D.M. (1970) Improvement of retardates' mealtime behaviors by timeout procedures using multiple baseline techniques. *J. Appl. Behav. Anal. 3*, 77–84

BAUMEISTER, A.A. (1967) Problems in comparative studies of mental retardates and normals. *Am. J. Ment. Defic. 71*, 869–875

BIJOU, S.W. (1968) Studies in the experimental development of left–right concepts in retarded children using fading techniques. In *International Review of Research in Mental Retardation, Vol 3* (Ellis, N.R., ed), pp. 66–96. Academic Press, New York

BIJOU, S.W., PETERSON, R.F. and AULT, M.H. (1968) A method to integrate descriptive and experimental field studies at the level of data and empirical concepts. *J. Appl. Behav. Anal. 1*, 175–191

BRICKER, W.A. (1972) A systematic approach to language training. In *The Language of the Mentally Retarded* (Schiefelbusch, R.L., ed.), pp. 75–85. University Park Press, Baltimore

CAMPBELL, D.T. and STANLEY, J.C. (1963) Experimental and quasi-experimental designs for research. In *Handbook of Research on Teaching* (Gage, N.L., ed.). Rand-McNally, New York

CARRIER, J.K. (1973) *Application of Functional Analysis and a Non Speech Response Mode to Teaching Language*. Kansas Centre for Research in Mental Retardation and Human Development, Parsons, Kansas

DEESE, J. and HULSE, S.H. (1967) *The Psychology of Learning*. 3rd ed. McGraw-Hill, New York

DOKE, L.A. and RISLEY, T.R. (1972) The organisation of day-care environments: required versus optional activities. *J. Appl. Behav. Anal. 5*, 405–420

FRENCH, W.L. and BELL, C.H. (1973) *Organisation Development*. Prentice-Hall, Englewood Cliffs, New Jersey

GARDNER, W.I. (1971) *Behaviour Modification in Mental Retardation*. Aldine-Atherton, Chicago (University of London Press, 1972)

JONES, M.C. and KIERNAN, C.C. (1975) The development of a teaching oriented assessment battery for the profoundly retarded. In *Proc. 3rd. Intl. Cong. I.A.S.S.M.D.* (Primrose, D.A., ed.), pp. 241–248. Polish Medical Publications, Warsaw

KIERNAN, C.C. (1973) Functional analysis. In *Assessment for Learning in the Mentally Handicapped* (Mittler, P., ed.), pp. 263–283. Churchill Livingstone, Edinburgh

KIERNAN, C.C. (1974a) Behaviour modification. In *Mental Deficiency: the Changing Outlook*. 3rd ed. (Clarke, A.M. and Clarke, A.D.B., eds.), pp. 729–803. Methuen, London

KIERNAN, C.C. (1947b) Application of behaviour modification in the ward situation. In *Experiments in the Rehabilitation of the Mentally Handicapped* (Gunzburg, H.C., ed.), pp. 93–109. Butterworths, London

KIERNAN, C.C., WRIGHT, E.C. and HAWKS, G. (1975) The ward wide application of operant training techniques. In *Proc. 3rd. Intl. Cong. I.A.S.S.M.D.* (Primrose, D.A., ed.) pp. 235–240. Polish Medical Publications, Warsaw

KING, R.D., RAYNES, N.V. and TIZARD, J. (1971) *Patterns of Residential Care*. Routledge & Kegan Paul, London

SIDMAN, M. (1960) *Tactics of Scientific Research: Evaluating Experimental Data in Psychology*. Basic Books, New York

SIDMAN, M. and STODDARD, L.T. (1966) Programmed perception and learning for retarded children. In *International Review of Research in Mental Retardation Vol. 2* (Ellis, N.R., ed.), pp. 151–208. Academic Press, New York

THORESEN, C.R. and MAHONEY, M.J. (1974) *Behavioral Self-Control*. Holt Rinehart & Winston, New York

Commentary

MICHAEL BERGER

Journal papers reporting the outcome of behaviour modification studies persistently maintain an image of precision and control. Little is conveyed of the political and personal problems which precede the implementation of a programme and surround it while it is being implemented, and only recently has it emerged (Clarke et al. 1972) that yet other problems arise when attempts are made to sustain a programme in the institution or at home.

The world of the journal paper and the world of the institution are two separate realities. It is the recognition of this other world, and the problems it poses for behaviour modification that I find most important and stimulating in Dr Kiernan's paper. Applied research in behaviour modification has to come to terms with institution wards full of uncontrolled and often uncontrollable variables, administrative hierarchies, personal relationships, financial restrictions, bureaucracy, and of course, the unfortunate inmates. Treatment evaluation in such a context is very complex indeed, and we must thank Dr Kiernan for confronting us both with the problems and with some tactics for coping with them.

Treatment evaluation in complex settings must of necessity entail some form of compromise. Dr Kiernan's paper makes this clear. What needs to be asked however, is "What is to be compromised?" Before this question can be answered, we need a statement of what, as psychologists, we see as the 'ideal' evaluation. Once this has been specified, the nature of any compromise will be explicit.

The task of setting up an 'ideal' evaluation can be facilitated by casting the problem within an analysis-of-variance framework, without at this stage suggesting that analysis of variance is the appropriate procedure for data analysis. If we do this, then the important question takes the form "How much of the treatment outcome variance (or, depending on the criteria, outcome variances) can be accounted for by various determinants?" In setting up such a model, we are immediately confronted by the traditional operant orientation which directs all its attention to situational or environmental determinants in behaviour. On the basis of this model, we can set up an analysis-of-variance equation as follows:

$$V_c = V_t + V_e$$

where V_c is outcome variance, V_t is treatment variance, and V_e is the error component.

While much of behaviour modification adheres to the 'environmentalist' orientation, Dr Walker's paper (p. 119) shows that our animal laboratory colleagues no longer subject themselves to such constraints. It is also interesting to note that this model has, until recently, been the characteristic expression found in child development research and in functional psychology generally. It is the familiar undergraduate conception of behaviour, i.e. $V_c = f(V_t)$. More recently-however, it has come to be appreciated that such an approach is inappropriately

96

one-sided. The more complete view is one which recognizes that the individual is an equally important determinant of what happens to him (Bell 1974). Hence, the variance equation must now take the form:

$$V_c = V_0 + V_{0t} + V_t + V_e$$

where V_0 is the proportion of variance attributable to the characteristics of those being treated—individual difference variables, genetic, constitutional factors, etc., and V_{0t} is the interaction term.

What Dr Kiernan has suggested in his paper is that we subdivide V_c and V_t in the first equation. That is, we not only consider the procedures used but monitor the institutional, therapist and other environmental components in addition to the target behaviours. Outcome is then a function of these. In effect, he has suggested a multivariate expansion of V_t and V_c. I would add that we need to introduce V_0 into our conceptualization and recognize that it too is multivariate.

Once we have specified these components, we are in a position to decide which we are to monitor and what form such monitoring has to take. One of the important implications of an extension of monitoring is that behaviour modifiers can no longer confine themselves to their standard measures of response frequency and the like. They will have to come to terms with current psychometrics and the principles which underlie the design, use, and interpretation of these techniques.

The strength of my argument depends on a demonstration that all outcome variance is not simply a function of environmental variance. This is an empirical question and I certainly don't have the evidence to enable me to support my position. But then, neither do the others. We cannot rely on journal papers to settle the issue. They can only give us some grounds for optimism. But in case anyone thinks my point irrelevant, let me cite one case which has been reported in print.

In their book on behaviour modification in child treatment, Browning and Stover (1971) present a candid and detailed account of their attempts at imitative speech training in a severely handicapped girl. They state: "After a total of 152,914 trials and uncounted hours of training, we had not taught Heidi to imitate the names of her family reliably."

The goal was six names. Their eventual hypothesis was that her failure to learn was due to a retention deficit. This was not tested. They next decided to try and teach her sign language. Unfortunately, details are not provided but they did manage to train her to point to things she wanted, and to get someone to lead her to where she wanted to go.

The behaviour modification commitment to evaluation is one of its most valuable characteristics. In the past this commitment has expressed itself in a somewhat oversimplified way. However, if evaluation is to be taken seriously, then we must be prepared to spend more time on deciding how best to accomplish it. Once we have delineated the multitude of variables that must be taken into account, we will be able to undertake a more realistic evaluation of what behaviour modification has to offer. Such an evaluation will, as its second task, have to reconsider the question of what type of research design is most appropriate for the evaluation problem. This question has been considered by Dr Kiernan and I simply wish to endorse his conclusions.

The Browning and Stover (1971) case leads me to consider a further issue in Dr Kiernan's paper. This is the role of functional analysis in applied settings. As it comes across in his paper, functional analysis is regarded as a last-resort technique of the frustrated behaviour modifier. I would suggest that it is merely another tool and should be seen as such. Functional analysis is one type of what O'Leary (1972) calls target assessment. It is the form of assessment most commonly associated with behaviour modification practice, although, as Dr Kiernan points out, 'overriding' is commonly used in conjunction with a partial functional assessment. The point at issue here is whether or not the traditional operant approach to assessment is sufficient. Our experience, and the experience of others—exemplified by the Browning and Stover case—would suggest not. Assessment may well require the use of diagnostic procedures not in the operant armamentarium and practitioners will have to familiarize themselves with these.

Dr Kiernan's experiences in applied settings, as these are reflected in this paper, also lead on to a third major problem, that of training new generations of therapists who may wish to use behaviour modification techniques. Teaching which encompasses only the principles of behaviour modification will be inadequate. If, as Dr Kiernan suggests, account has to be taken of the social and psychological context in which a programme has to be implemented, then it becomes essential to include other topics in the training of therapists. What form such training should then take cannot be detailed here, but some of the things it should include can be stated at this point. In addition to a genera grounding in psychometrics, therapists will need to know about the structure and social organization of institutions, the way in which administrative practices become institutionalized, and the ways in which institutionalized practices can themselves be changed. Particular attention will also need to be given to the general quality of care offered to the inmates (King et al. 1971) and to ways providing adequate, if not optimal, psychological care: the latter would include techniques for fostering language development and play.

For this discussion, I have selected three of the many issues in Dr Kiernan's paper, mainly because I consider them to be fundamental problems of general importance for behaviour modification. Experience in applied settings suggests that behaviour modification practices require some re-orientation. Dr Kiernan's paper provides the stimulus and I hope that practitioners will respond.

REFERENCES

BELL, R.Q. (1974) Contributions of human infants to caregiving and social interaction. In *The Effect of the Infant on its Caregiver* (Lewis, M. and Rosenblum, L.A., eds.). Wiley, New York

BROWNING, R.M. and STOVER, D.O. (1971) *Behaviour Modification in Child Treatment.* Aldine-Atherton, Chicago

CLARK, F.W., EVANS, D.R. and HAMERLYNCK, L.A. (eds.) (1972) Introduction to *Implementing Behavioural Programs for Schools and Clinics.* Research Press, Champaign, Illinois

KING, R.D., RAYNES, N.V. and TIZARD, J. (1971) *Patterns of Residential Care.* Routledge and Kegan Paul, London

O'LEARY, D.K. (1972) The assessment of psychopathology in children. In *Psychopathological Disorders of Childhood* (Quay, H.C. and Werry, J.S., eds.). Wiley, New York

Discussion

P. Williams: We are postulating here, as we do rather glibly in many meetings of this sort, that organizational change is needed in order to enable modification programmes to work. Now if we acknowledge the great complexities—exemplified in this study group—of working with a single child, the mind boggles at the thought of extending from the single subject to a whole organizational system. Our only hope of making the transition lies in beginning to work quite intensively on the people immediately surrounding the child, namely the nurses or parents. In the *experimental* situation, a reinforcer or contingent event for the child is also a reinforcer or contingent for the experimenter's behaviour—but it is overridden by external events or reinforcers because the experimenter is independently supported in his role of behaviour modifier. This may not be true for a nurse, mother or teacher and I think that in training them not to cuddle the child when he screams, for example—behaviour which is *not* immediately reinforced—one must be very careful about altering the antecedents and consequences of their behaviour. What is needed is a functional analysis of the effect of a behaviour modification programme on the nurse or mother rather than only on the child.

Kushlick: I'm not so sure. Even when those of us who are concerned with the best care of mentally retarded children (or of deprived children or of the elderly) are convinced that what is going to affect their lives most is the way an institution is run or a decision at the Department of Health or the Treasury, the important thing is to stay with the subjects and continue to observe what is happening to them. What you need for this task is some quantitative indicator of their behaviour. Whatmore and Durward in our group have used the proportion of disruptive, inappropriate, neutral and appropriate behaviours (previously defined and characterized) as this indicator. In Kansas, Doke and Risley (1972) have devised a scale of *level of engagement* in the activity provided or being taught. The higher the proportion of time for which the subjects are actually engaged in the activity in question, the better—whether from the educational, social, or plain commonsense humanitarian view. When one has such a measure, if it is reliable and stable, one can begin to judge the effects of organizational changes on the degree of engagement of the residents and the ranges of engaging activities in which residents participate.

Barton: Two unrelated points, the first concerning reversal designs. I have an uneasy feeling that a reversal is just a probe session. Wouldn't it be useful to use reversal as a probe, to check on generalization?

Kiernan: In practice, this is how it's done. But most people don't want to reverse for just one session.

Barton: Secondly, I agree that it's difficult to get good programmes carried out on the ward until you've got staff stability. Unfortunately, an awful lot of our wards depend on student nurses as their main ward manpower, and until this changes, and they are used as they should be, as supernumeraries, much of our work will be negated.

Kiernan: This really gets to the heart of the problem. Although what you've just pointed out seems self-evident, perhaps we shall have to produce research results which prove the point before anything is done about it. A study along the lines Albert Kushlick has just described may be necessary, in which turnover of staff is the independent variable. We have some indirect evidence from the F6 study at Queen Mary's, Carshalton. As the number of staff increased, self-help skills continued to improve, but the socialization index of the children's interaction with staff and other adults actually went down. This is another reminder that one should build into one's research projects measures of things other than what one is working on directly.

Yule: However, looking at a broad spectrum of factors is not enough: they have to include the right, the important ones. Two rude reminders of this are provided in the fifth Banff Symposium on Evaluating Large-Scale Programs of Intervention (Davidson *et al.* 1974). In the first example, geriatric patients were moved out from institutions into well-staffed group homes, apparently a great improvement all round; but behaviour evaluation showed that after a while the old folk had lost many of their self-help skills. In the second example, it was arranged that social workers visited old people in a geriatric hospital daily. At first, everything seemed to be going fine, there was more contact with individuals and so on. But after 1 or 2 years they discovered the death rate was three times as great in the active-intervention group as in a control group.

Kushlick: Although that was a good study—one of the few controlled studies of domiciliary care—I'm not sure that mortality is a valid measure of success. More of those receiving domiciliary care were institutionalized, and mortality was highest among people institutionalized from both experimental and control groups. It may have been that they were institutionalized more frequently because they were more seriously ill: it is not clear in the paper whether or not this was so. Engagement level of people living at home appears to be a more relevant measure of effectiveness than mortality. We have found, for example, among old people living at home, that when the health visitor goes in and gives lots of advice and makes arrangements for others to visit, the home help goes in to do the cleaning and the district nurse to give the injections, and so on, the old people may begin just to sit around and wait for the next knock on the door. Their level of engaged activity appears to go down. This decrease can be detected before it would be possible to detect any loss of self-help skills.

Corbett: We found that one of the things which reduced staff–child interaction was the increasing number of meetings we were having to discuss programming and training! One has to be careful and quite sophisticated in this organizational aspect, otherwise you can increase staff, training and programming and end up reducing the most important thing: interaction with the child.

Tizard: I've been thinking about what Paul Williams said at the beginning of this discussion, and concluded that I don't agree with his solution of moving out stepwise from the experimenter–child interaction to the total organization. Like most people here, I suppose, I started out in this field working on the application of laboratory work in a service setting, in the expectation that this would eventually change the organization in which I was working. After a period of increasing disillusionment with that approach, I've begun tunnelling in from the other end and am convinced that the form of organization is what's important. You don't need to do functional analysis of every little interaction. You have to determine the factors which facilitate or militate against a pattern of care continuing, and I think our methods for determining those factors and the magnitude of their effects are becoming increasingly sophisticated.

REFERENCES

DAVIDSON, P.O., CLARK, F.W. and HAMERLYNCK, L.A. (eds.) (1974) *Evaluation of Behavioral Programs in Community, Residential and School Settings.* Research Press, Champaign, Illinois

DOKE, L.A. and RISLEY, T.R. (1972) The organization of day-care environments: required vs. optional activities. *J. Appl. Behav. Anal.* **5**, 405–420

Comment

C. C. KIERNAN

The next two papers largely concern research on infra-human organisms. Their inclusion in a discussion of behaviour modification with the mentally handicapped is unusual and requires special comment.

The bases of behaviour modification were laid by research on lower organisms. There has, however, been a gradual separation of human and infra-human research to the extent that workers in the applied human field have separate journals, attend separate conferences and pay little attention to developments in the infra-human field. To a large extent this separation is inevitable and without adverse consequences. But it is as well to rehearse the values of animal research and to point out that total separation almost certainly works against the best development of both applied and pure research.

The old concept of infra-human research as providing a clear model for human behaviour needs to be substantially qualified. Human beings are not chimpanzees, rhesus monkeys, rats, pigeons or geese. Many of the behaviours of infra-human organisms reflect the ecological niches in which their behaviour has evolved.

Powerful inferences can, however, be drawn from the responses developed in the context of particular patterns of antecedent, behaviour and consequences at one phylogenetic level and applied to other levels. Research on animals into the operation of reinforcers in reward learning and punishment and the development of stimulus control has proved of clear value in building a model of human behaviour (Honig 1966). Infra-human research can act as a test-bed for hypotheses which cannot be examined in Man for ethical reasons. Currently, animal research is concentrating on some issues which parallel human work, where it contributes concepts for use in applied work and a range of alternative explanations to be considered. This point is illustrated by the concept of reinforcement, discussed by Harzem and by Walker. In a looser way animal work can represent a valuable general stimulus to thought, without having any direct bearing on particular cases. A new view of existing concepts can lead to a relaxing of stereotyped ways of thinking.

The rigour of animal research and conceptualization can have valuable corrective influence in the applied field, where there is always a temptation towards poor recording and loose inference. Again, the demonstration of what animals can learn often jerks the researcher into realizing the degree to which failures to change behaviour are *our failures to teach adequately* rather than the failure of the organism. For instance the fact that Premack can teach a chimpanzee a language is humbling in the context of our inability to teach the same to many children whose brains, though damaged, almost certainly still have greater capacity than that of the chimpanzee (Premack and Premack 1974).

A final, associated, point. Most researchers working with infra-human organisms develop a high respect for their subjects. They see them as immensely complex and fascinating creatures who have their own individuality and will to live and develop. The animal researcher coming to work in the field of handicap does not in general 'over-simplify' his problems. The feelings of respect for the organism and the challenge of his behaviour are simply enhanced. Certainly the sensitive animal researcher is unlikely to underestimate his handicapped subjects or to treat them as automata.

REFERENCES

HONIG, W. K. (ed.) (1966) *Operant Behaviour: Areas of Research and Application.* McGraw-Hill, New York

PREMACK, D. and PREMACK, A.J. (1974) Teaching visual language to apes and language deficient persons. In *Language Perspectives—Acquisition, Retardation and Intervention* (Schiefelbusch, R.L. and Lloyd, L.L., eds.). University Park Press, Baltimore

Reinforcers and the Problem of Reinforcement

PETER HARZEM

Department of Psychology, University College of North Wales, Bangor

Amongst the various forms of treatment of behaviour disorders, and of ways of helping retarded persons, the cluster of techniques which has come to be known as behaviour modification has a unique characteristic. This is that behaviour modification is entirely founded upon the findings of *experimental* investigations of behaviour. Behaviour modification derives both its conceptual basis and its technology from the studies of operant responding known, pointedly enough, as the *experimental analysis of behaviour*. Without such a basis it would be yet another pragmatic approach, subject equally to their disadvantages—and advantages. There would remain the age old problem of how to choose between these approaches without resorting merely to assertion and counter-assertion; a form of exchange that has long bedevilled especially the area in which behaviour modification is expected to make a major contribution.

Despite this, the relationship between behaviour modification and experimental research appears not to be entirely happy. There remains the feeling that the practical worker resorts to common sense in almost all he does with or for his patients, and that experimental research continues along its largely irrelevant path untouched by the problems of the ward and the clinic. Several contributors to the previous study groups in this series (cf. Mittler 1973; Clarke and Clarke 1973) have expressed their concern in this regard, and some have even asserted that much of the research that is done is *in principle* inapplicable (e.g. Ryan 1973).

Like most extreme views, the last-mentioned is mistaken. Any finding that enhances our understanding of behaviour must, in principle, contribute to the technology of treating behaviour. It is also the case, however, that some lines of research may be trivial, or remote from the practical problems that have to be faced here and now. And this, unfortunately, seems to be true of much operant research.

The difficulty arises largely because there is a fundamental divergence between the traditional interests of operant psychology and the kind of phenomena with which behaviour modification has to be concerned. Traditionally, the experimental analysis of behaviour has taken as its basic measure the rate at which a simple manipulative response, the *operant*, occurs. Skinner (1966) has argued, for example, that the "rate of responding is especially relevant to the principal task of a scientific analysis". Almost all of operant research has been concerned with the analysis of variables which affect the rate of responding. The development or shaping of the operant response itself is usually considered to be a part of the preparation for the experiment, an incidental requirement. In behaviour modification, on the other hand, the rate at which a simple response will be repeated is seldom an important question. What is wanted is not to affect the subject's behaviour so that he dresses himself frequently, or that he eats at ever-increasing rates, but rather to shape relatively complex patterns of response to occur in correct sequence, and in only the appropriate situations. Many such patterns of behaviour with which the behaviour modifier is concerned are appropriately emitted only once, or a few times, per day. Even in self-feeding, where taking a filled spoon to the mouth resembles the paradigm case of repeatedly emitting an operant, other, less often emitted, responses are involved such as sitting at the table and holding the spoon.

For behaviour modification, what is particularly relevant is to investigate in detail the variables which affect the shaping of responses, and the variables that contribute to the durability of complex sequences of responses even though they are emitted infrequently. However, as early as 1960 Sidman had declared his satisfaction that the experimental analysis of behaviour had progressed beyond studying the acquisition of a simple response. As it turns out, it was especially unfortunate for operant research to leave behind, so early in its development, the investigation of acquisition processes. This is an area of research especially important for behaviour modification, and at present it remains unexplored.

An even more fundamental issue for behaviour modification arises from the questions of what constitutes a reinforcing stimulus, and what are the ways in which such a stimulus affects behaviour. Reinforcement is undoubtedly the basis phenomenon in the study of operant behaviour, and yet surprisingly little is known about the process itself. It has been discussed as a conceptual problem, and some have maintained that it is a circular notion, and therefore invalid (cf. Gibson 1960). This is a false argument, and we need not be concerned with it here. Let it suffice to point out that reinforcement is a term that entails a relation, and consequently its definition must include reference to the response to which it is related (cf. Hocutt 1967). To ask that reinforcement be defined without referring to a response is like asking that, say, the term *husband* be defined without reference to a wife.

It is, nevertheless, true that in operant research reinforcement has been taken for granted. In animal experiments food is the almost universally used reinforcer, with food deprivation as the setting operation to ensure its effectiveness. The question of what else might serve as reinforcer (not 'conditioned reinforcer') is seldom considered. Is it necessary, for example, to conduct with all reinforcers a setting operation? Is satiation observable whatever the reinforcer? Are all reinforcing stimuli, given that they have been shown to be reinforcers, equally effective? These kinds of questions appear especially relevant to behaviour modification, and with regard to them experimental research has had, in the past, little to say.

Faced with a wide gap between his own interests and the orientation of laboratory research, the behaviour modifier is apt to assume that the relationship between his work and laboratory research is through the most general of principles, namely, that reinforcement strengthens behaviour (and its corollary, that withdrawal of reinforcement weakens behaviour). But such a general assertion is by no means a discovery of operant psychology, nor is it a property of experimental psychology. The principle of reward, in its simplest form, has been known for centuries. Some of the very early accounts of human affairs describe the subtle ways in which the conduct of man was affected by reward and punishment. Later examples of it are abundant in literature, and include descriptions of practices that might now be termed conditioning. Mowrer (1960) has quoted the story, for example, by the 17th century Spanish playwright Lope de Vega, of how the hero was able to train a horde of pestilent cats to run away at the sound of his coughing. Even the term reinforcement is not new in its application in this context. To take just one example, George Eliot wrote "... I was so crude a member of the congregation that my nurse found it necessary to provide for the reinforcement of my devotional patience by smuggling bread-and-butter into the sacred edifice" (*Scenes of Clerical Life*, 1857).

In fact, the relationships entailed in reinforcement are far more complex than a simple principle of reward (or the law of effect) would imply. Some of the effects of a reinforcing stimulus are quite contrary to commonsense expectation. And analyses of these relationships are likely to prove pertinent and applicable in behaviour modification, especially in those frequently observed situations where the subject's behaviour corresponds little to what might be expected on a commonsense basis. Although much of laboratory research has, in the past, proceeded along lines unrelated to the direct interests of applied work, there have recently been developments which appear more relevant. For example, there is growing research interest in the suggestion that acquisition of a response and its maintenance may not both depend on the same factors. A contingent relationship between a response and reinforcement may be more important for the acquisition of a response than for the subsequent maintenance of that response. Moreover, it seems that the same reinforcer may affect different responses differently (see Staddon 1976a, b). As yet the evidence on these and other related possibilities is small and it will not be reviewed here. However, in the remainder of the paper I will present, by way of example, some experimental findings obtained in my laboratory along these lines.

In operant research little consideration is usually given to the possibility that different individuals of the same species may respond differently under identical conditions. With regard to animal research there is ample justification for this, as in most cases not only members of the same species but also different species show little variation in their performance on the same schedule of reinforcement (cf. Skinner 1968). Even in published work on animals, however, there are notable exceptions. For example, pigeons perform poorly on schedules that require spacing of single responses in time (Reynolds 1964), and more recent evidence shows that there are important differences in the response patterns of rats and pigeons (Harzem and Lowe 1974; cf. Staddon 1974). As every behaviour modifier knows, humans constitute a special case with regard to inter-subject variability, although there is little in operant research concerning the factors that affect these variations. It is usually supposed that either different pathology or different personal histories contribute to the variations. However, these are post hoc explanations, and they are over-general.

There have been some experimental demonstrations that conditioning history affects human performance (e.g. Weiner 1964). However, adult human subjects show considerable inter-subject variation in their operant response patterns, without any explicitly programmed history of conditioning. Moreover, this is the case even with individuals very closely matched in age, sex, home background, and intellectual abilities and performance (Harzem 1975). Fig. 1 shows cumulative records obtained from five sixth-form pupils under identical con-

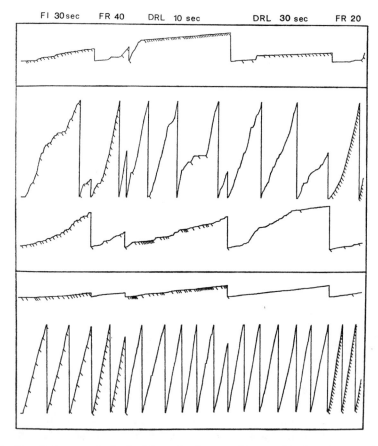

Fig. 1. Cumulative records obtained from five human subjects under the same experimental conditions. The subjects were sixth-formers matched with regard to age, sex, background, subjects studied, and future plans. In the experimental session five different schedules of reinforcement (FI 30 sec, FR 40, DRL 10 sec, DRL 30 sec, and FR 20) were presented consecutively, in that order, without any accompanying stimulus change, and reinforcement consisted of scoring, registered on a counter.

ditions. There were 52 subjects in this experiment, and the cumulative records shown here are typical of the performance of all of them. The subjects responded on a telegraph key, to score on an electromechanical counter placed in front of them. In a single 50-minute session five different schedules of reinforcement were presented consecutively, without any accompanying stimulus change. The schedules were fixed-interval (FI) 30 sec, fixed-ratio (FR) 40, differential-reinforcement-of-low-rate (DRL) 10 sec, DRL 30 sec, and FR 20, in that order.

The response patterns under these conditions showed wide variation, but more importantly the variation was not haphazard. The patterns fell into one of the following three distinct categories: (i) adjustment of responding with reference to each schedule in operation; (ii) variation in responding without adjusting to the schedules; or (iii) responding at a steady rate throughout the experimental session regardless of the schedule in operation. Moreover the subjects in the latter two categories responded either at a high rate or at a low rate, there being no intermediate rates. Thus it seems that although human responding shows wide variation, there are orderly effects in these variations. It is, therefore, a mistake to explain away these differences by reference to, say, the past history of the subject. In the study described here, the response patterns were found to be related to the intellectual achievements and abilities of the subjects, despite the fact that the subjects were selected so that they differed little in these respects. In particular, the least able were in the group showing response variability without adjusting to the schedule in operation.

Just as considerable inter-subject variability occurs with human subjects, the same subject may respond differently under similar conditions. Behaviour modifiers know well the phenomenon where the same subject may change in his behaviour from day to day. In some cases it is, of course, possible to point to particular events in the daily life of the individual as possible causes of such variation. On the other hand it is also possible that the stimuli used by the behaviour modifier may contribute to the variation.

Most studies of behaviour modification procedures have used as reinforcers some combination of verbal approval ('social reinforcement') and food. Spradlin and Girardeau (1966) have noted, however, that "social reinforcers will only work with selected children, and even then their effects may be limited or unpredictable." Moreover, the efficacy of two reinforcers, presented together, is not always predictable from their effects when presented separately (cf. Woods 1974). With vegetative retardate subjects, Rice and McDaniel (1966) and Rice (1968) have found that the effectiveness of the reinforcers used were unpredictably variable. However, few studies have compared the reinforcing efficacy of different stimuli, and those which are available have been confined to few stimuli (e.g. Altman, Talkington and Cleland 1971; Hollis 1965; Hopkins 1968; Logan, Kinsinger, Shelton and Brown 1971; Watson, Lawson and Sanders 1965).

Fig. 2 shows the results of a study with two severely retarded adults, comparing the effectiveness of different events as reinforcers (Harzem and Damon 1975). The responses studied were imitations of simple motor movements. The reinforcing stimuli were similar to those normally available in the subjects'

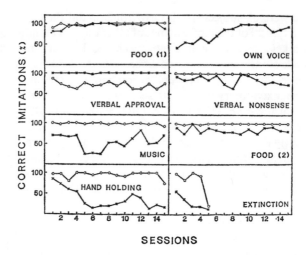

Fig. 2. Correct imitative responses of two severely retarded adults, shown as a percentage of modelled responses. Circles and crosses represent the data for Subjects 1 and 2 respectively. Own voice was used only with Subject 2. The level at which imitative behaviour was maintained varied with the stimulus used as reinforcer, the effect being more marked with one of the subjects.

environment, and differed in the extent to which they may be considered 'social'.

With each reinforcer the performance of Subject 1 was relatively stable. Although this subject maintained a steady level of performance with every reinforcer, the level varied with different reinforcers; it was low with verbal approval, and always at 100% with verbal nonsense. In extinction this subject's performance remained at a high level for four sessions and declined abruptly in the fifth sessions. The performance of Subject 2 differed considerably from that of Subject 1. The highest percentage of correct imitations emitted by Subject 2 was with verbal approval. With this reinforcer Subject 2 performed at a higher level than Subject 1, while with all the other reinforcers used Subject 1's performance was at a higher level. In general the behaviour of Subject 2 was more variable. This subject's percentage of correct imitations gradually declined when handholding was the reinforcer, and gradually increased when her own voice was the reinforcer. In extinction the decline in her performance was gradual. For both subjects the two verbal reinforcers maintained correct imitation at a high level, and there was some bias in favour of verbal nonsense. The series were long enough so that any novelty effect of verbal nonsense was likely to have been lost.

Different levels of performance were achieved by the same subject with different stimuli. It seems that stability of responding may be established at a level lower than the optimal, and conversely that the establishment of stable performance is not necessarily indicative that the performance is at its highest possible level. Moreover, the most commonly used reinforcers such as food and verbal approval do not appear necessarily to provide the optimal levels of performance. Whatever the explanation for the differences in the efficacy of stimuli used as reinforcers, the factors that affect such variability should be investigated, as analyses of these relations will have important implications for behaviour modification.

Traditionally it has been assumed that a reinforcing stimulus relates to the response on which it is contingent, along the lines that might be expected on a commonsense basis. To some extent, this is supported by the early findings that a positive relationship exists between the magnitude of reinforcement and the rate or speed of response (Crespi 1942; Guttman 1953; Zeaman 1949). Generally, the shifts in the rate of responding produced by changing the magnitude have been attributed by most theorists to concomitant changes in motivation (cf. Bartoshuk 1971). However, the relationships involved are more complex than previously thought (cf. Bolles and Moot 1972; Kling and Schrier 1971). Recent evidence suggests that greater magnitude of reinforcement, apart from having motivational effects, may also depress responding immediately after it occurs. For example, Staddon (1970) found that on FI schedules longer durations of reinforcer availability resulted in longer post-reinforcement pauses. One explanation of this is that increasing the magnitude of reinforcement enhances its discriminative effect, and consequently the performance improves in precision (Di Lollo, Ensminger and Notterman 1965; Notterman and Mintz 1965). On FI schedules the occurrence of longer post-reinforcement pauses is taken to indicate greater precision, since extra responses in the course of the fixed interval do not affect reinforcement. However, in a recent series of experiments we have found that increasing the magnitude of reinforcement results in longer post-reinforcement pauses even in those schedules where the longer pauses reduce the frequency of reinforcement (Lowe, Davey and Harzem 1974). These results, obtained with rats, are summarized in Fig. 3, which shows that the duration of the post-reinforcement pause was an increasing function of reinforcer magnitude, not only on the FI schedule, but also on FR and response-initiated FI (tandem FR 1 FI) schedules. In the latter two schedules the longer the post-reinforcement pause, the less frequent were the reinforcements obtained by the subject. It appears, therefore, that the reinforcer has an inhibiting after-

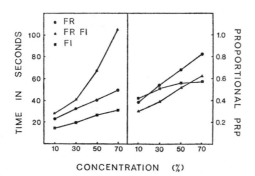

Fig. 3. Duration of the post-reinforcement pause as a function of the concentration of the reinforcer used, with rat subjects. In all three schedules used (FR, response initiated FI, and FI) the greater the magnitude of reinforcement, the longer was the pause. (Reproduced, by permission, from J. Exp. Anal. Behav. 1974, 22, 553–560)

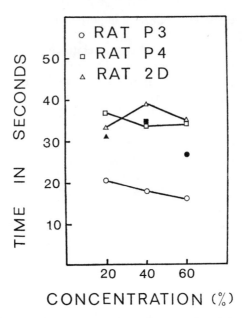

Fig. 4. Duration of post-reinforcement pauses as a function of reinforcer concentration. Each data point was obtained after the establishment of response stability. Unconnected points show re-determination data.

effect; that is, an effect that is present regardless of whether it results in optimal performance with reference to reinforcement.

Moreover, this inhibiting after-effect of a reinforcer depends upon the context in which the reinforcer is presented. We found that the effect was observed when two reinforcer magnitudes were contrasted closely in time but not when the subjects were trained on an FI schedule until stable performance was established separately with each reinforcer (Harzem, Lowe and Davey 1975a). Fig. 4 shows that reinforcer concentration did not systematically affect the mean duration of post-reinforcement pauses in the stability conditions. In Fig. 5 the post-reinforcement pauses are compared between the last three sessions on one concentration and the first three sessions on the next concentration. When the concentrations were contrasted in close succession, in eight of the nine cases the duration of the post-reinforcement pause increased with reinforcer concentration.

Of course, in addition to having inhibiting effects a reinforcer may also function as a discriminative stimulus. In fact, individual reinforcements (as well as single non-reinforced responses) control with remarkable accuracy the duration of the pause following their occurrence. This was shown in an experiment by Harzem, Lowe and Davey (1975b) where a complex schedule was devised, requiring temporal spacing of individual responses. According to this schedule, as in conventional DRL schedules, a response was reinforced only if it was separated from the response before it by an interval longer than a specified minimum duration. This duration was specified separately depending on

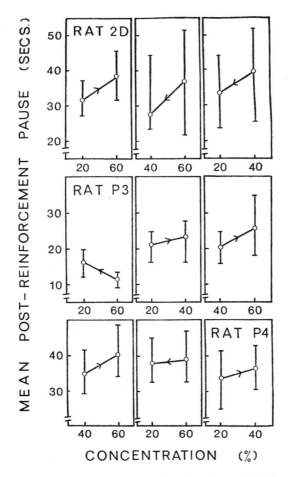

Fig. 5. The relationship between the magnitude of reinforcement and the duration of the post-reinforcement pause, with three different rat subjects. The data points are from the last three sessions with one concentration and the first three sessions on a different concentration. Arrows show the direction of change. The magnitude-effect was observed only when different magnitudes of reinforcement were contrasted closely in time.

whether the preceding response was a reinforced response or a non-reinforced response. For example, in the two-component DRL 20 sec–40 sec schedule, if the event starting an IRT was reinforcement, then, provided that a minimum duration of 20 seconds elapsed, the next response was reinforced. However, after a non-reinforced response, the minimum IRT required was 40 seconds.

Fig. 6 shows sequences of individual IRTs with several different parameters of the two-component DRL schedule. In every case the duration of an IRT depended on whether that IRT was initiated by a reinforced or a non-reinforced response, matching the appropriate component in operation. For example, in the top left section an IRT is shown exceeding the minimum IRT criterion, and therefore being terminated by reinforcement. The next IRT was just short of the

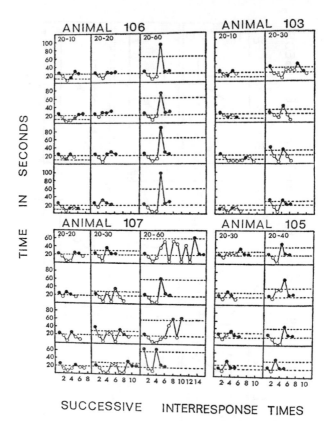

Fig. 6. Successive individual IRTs, obtained from four rats on two-component DRL schedules. The duration of an IRT was controlled by whether the event initiating that IRT was a reinforced (filled circles) or a non-reinforced (open circles) response. The figures with hyphens show, in seconds, the parameters of the schedule in operation. Horizontal dotted lines indicate the minimum IRT criteria above which a response was reinforced. (Reproduced, by permission, from J. Exp. Anal. Behav. 1975, 24, 33–42)

criterion and consequently the response terminating it was not reinforced. This non-reinforced response resulted in switching of the criterion to 10 seconds. The next IRT was very short, indicating a response burst, a characteristic of responding on DRL schedules. This was followed by an IRT which met the 10-second criterion, and the response was reinforced. Reinforcement switched the criterion to 20 seconds, and the next IRT met this criterion. This very close control of behaviour was a characteristic of individual reinforcements, and not an averaged effect, attributable to variables such as the frequency of reinforcement.

SUMMARY

The evidence presented in this paper shows that considerable inter-subject variability occurs in the operant performance of humans. This variability is not merely random, however, but manifests orderly effects which should be investigated in detail. Moreover, human subjects do not respond in the same way with different reinforcing stimuli, even when the schedule of reinforcement and other conditions are the same. Establishment of a stable response pattern with a given reinforcer does not necessarily indicate that optimal performance has been achieved.

Animal experiments indicate that a reinforcing stimulus, in addition to its traditionally known function of strengthening or maintaining the strength of a response, has other effects. One of these is the inhibition of responding immediately after the occurrence of reinforcement. Another is that a reinforcer may acquire the properties of a discriminative stimulus, controlling the behaviour that follows its presentation.

Much remains to be discovered about reinforcers, and the effects of reinforcement. At present it seems reasonable to suppose that investigations of this kind are relevant to behaviour modification, and that this relevance will become more evident as research progresses. Perhaps the most important outcome of all this would be a consistent increase in the interaction of laboratory research and application, so that each might influence the problems and practices of the other.

REFERENCES

ALTMAN, R., TALKINGTON, L.W. and CLELAND, C.C. (1971) Effects of novelty on verbal reinforcement effectiveness with retardates. *Psychol. Rec. 21*, 529–532

BARTOSHUK, A.K. (1971) Motivation. In *Experimental Psychology* 3rd ed. (Kling, J.W. and Riggs, L.A., eds.), pp. 793–845. Holt, Rinehart & Winston, New York

BOLLES, R.C. and MOOT, S.A. (1972) Derived motives. *Ann. Rev. Psychol. 23*, 51–72

CLARKE, A.D.B. and CLARKE, A.M. (eds.) (1973) *Mental Retardation and Behavioural Research.* Churchill Livingstone, Edinburgh

CRESPI, L. (1942) Quantitative variation of incentive and performance in the white rat. *Am. J. Psychol. 15*, 467–517

DI LOLLO, V., ENSMINGER, W.D. and NOTTERMAN, J.M. (1965) Response force as a function of amount of reinforcement. *J. Psychol. 70*, 27–31

GIBSON, J.J. (1960) The concept of stimulus in psychology. *Am. Psychol 15*, 694–703

GUTTMAN, N. (1953) Operant conditioning, extinction, and periodic reinforcement in relation to concentration of sucrose used as reinforcing agent. *J. Exp. Psychol. 46*, 213–224

HARZEM, P. (1975) Operant response patterns and intellectual performance of sixth-form pupils. Paper read to the Annual Conference of the Experimental Psychology Society, 1975

HARZEM, P. and DAMON, S.D. (1975) Relative efficacy of reinforcers in the maintenance of imitation and generalized imitation. (unpublished manuscript)

HARZEM, P. and LOWE, C.F. (1975) A comparative study of fixed-interval performance with rats and pigeons. *Psychol. Rec.* 1975 (in press)

HARZEM, P., LOWE, C.F. and DAVEY, G.C.L. (1975a) After-effects of reinforcement magnitude: dependence upon context. *Quart. J. Exp. Psychol.* (in press)

HARZEM, P., LOWE, C.F. and DAVEY, G.C.L. (1975b) Two-component schedules of differential-reinforcement-of-low-rate. *J. Exp. Anal. Behav. 24*, 33–42

HOCUTT, M. (1967) On the alleged circularity of Skinner's concept of stimulus. *Psychol. Rev. 74*, 530–532

HOLLIS, J. (1965) The effects of social and nonsocial stimuli on the behaviors of profoundly retarded children. *Am. J. Ment. Defic. 69*, 755–789

HOPKINS, B.L. (1968) Effects of candy and social reinforcement, instructions and reinforcement learning on the modification and maintenance of smiling. *J. Appl. Behav. Anal. 1*, 121–129

113

KLING, J.W. and SCHRIER, A.M. (1971) Positive reinforcement. In *Experimental Psychology*, 3rd ed. (King, J.W. and Riggs, L.A., eds.), pp. 615–689. Holt, Rinehart and Winston, New York

LOGAN, D.L., KINSINGER, J., SHELTON, G. and BROWN, J.M. (1971) Use of multiple reinforcers in a rehabilitation setting. *Ment. Retard. 9*, 3–6

LOWE, C.F., DAVEY, G.C.L. and HARZEM, P. (1974) Effects of reinforcement magnitude on interval and ratio schedules. *J. Exp. Anal. Behav. 22*, 553–560

MITTLER, P. ed. (1973) *Assessment for Learning in the Mentally Handicapped*. Churchill Livingstone, Edinburgh

MOWRER, O.H. (1960) *Learning Theory and Behavior*. Wiley, New York

NOTTERMAN, J.M. and MINTZ, D.E. (1965) *Dynamics of Response*. Pp. 204–212. Wiley, New York

REYNOLDS, G.S. (1964) Temporally spaced responding by pigeons: development and effects of deprivation and extinction. *J. Exp. Anal. Behav. 7*, 415–421

RICE, H.K. (1968) Operant behavior in vegetative patients. III: Methodological considerations. *Psychol. Rec. 18*, 297–302

RICE, H.K. and MCDANIEL, M.W. (1966) Operant behavior in vegetative patients. *Psychol. Rec. 16*, 279–281

RYAN, J. (1973) Scientific research and individual variation. In *Mental Retardation and Behavioural Research*. (Clarke, A.D.B. and Clarke, A.M., eds.), pp. 23–30. Churchill Livingstone, Edinburgh

SIDMAN, M. (1960) *Tactics of Scientific Research*. Basic Books, New York

SKINNER, B.F. (1966) Operant behavior. In *Operant Behavior: Areas of Research and Application* (Honig, W.K., ed.), pp.15–16. Appleton-Century-Crofts, New York

SKINNER, B.F. (1968) *The Technology of Teaching*. Appleton-Century-Crofts, New York

SPRADLIN, J.E. and GIRARDEAU, F.L. (1966) The behavior of moderately and severely retarded persons. In *International Review of Research in Mental Retardation* Vol.1. (Ellis, N.R., ed), pp. 257–298. Academic Press, New York

STADDON, J.E.R. (1970) Effect of reinforcement duration on fixed-interval responding. *J. Exp. Anal. Behav. 13*, 9–11

STADDON, J.E.R. (1974) Temporal control, attention and memory. *Psychol. Rev. 8*, 375–391

STADDON, J.E.R. (1976a) Schedule-induced behavior. In *Handbook of Operant Behavior* (Honig, W.K. and Staddon, J.E.R., eds.). Prentice Hall, Englewood Cliffs, NJ (in press)

STADDON, J.E.R. (1976b) Learning and adaptation. In *Handbook of Learning and Cognitive Processes* (Estes, W.K., ed.) (in press)

WATSON, L.S. JR., LAWSON, R. and SANDERS, C. (1965) Reinforcement preferences of severely mentally retarded children in a generalized reinforcement context. Paper presented to the annual convention of the American Psychological Association, Chicago, 1965

WEINER, H. (1964) Conditioning history and human fixed-interval performance. *J. Exp. Anal Behav. 7*, 383–385

WOODS, P.A. (1974) Schedule effects in the operant behaviour of the severely subnormal. *Bull. Br. Psychol. Soc. 27*, 188 (abstract)

ZEAMAN, D. (1949) Response latency as a function of the amount of reinforcement. *J. Exp. Psychol. 39*, 466–483

Commentary

JAMES HOGG

The inclusion of Peter Harzem's paper in this Study Group is both welcome and significant. His contribution indicates that there are workers in the main-stream of operant psychology who are attempting to relate the conceptual and technical framework in which they carry out their research to the field of

114

behaviour modification. As someone else has put it, the Journal of the Experimental Analysis of Behavior (JEAB) is still on speaking terms with the Journal of Applied Behavior Analysis (JABA).

The paper addresses itself to the general question of the relation between operant psychology, or the experimental analysis of behaviour (TEAB), and behaviour modification. It deals with this relation partly through a discussion of the specific issue of reinforcement. The way in which Harzem deals with the specific issue is in fact determined by his view of the general relation. I should like to put forward a somewhat different interpretation of this general relation. Briefly, Harzem suggests that behaviour modification is 'entirely founded' on TEAB both conceptually and technically. While behaviour modification ultimately owes its existence to TEAB, it is also informed to a significant extent by a variety of other procedures. Among these we may mention systems analysis, techniques of curriculum development, and formal observational procedures. In addition, behaviour modification's frame of reference includes many elements that are extrinsic to TEAB. These can briefly be subsumed under the heading of criteria of social value. These are distinct from and additional to the scientific criteria (also admittedly social) that might inform a paper in JEAB.

Thus, the constituents of behaviour modification and its frame of reference are wider and more complex than is the case with laboratory-orientated TEAB. Before any attempt to produce TEAB analyses of the problems of behaviour modification is made, the way in which the two frames of reference and their respective contents are related must be defined in detail. The two cannot be simply linked by pointing to the fact that there are concepts and operations common to them. The question of whether a laboratory study is 'in principle' relevant to behaviour modification or not begs the issue and is unanswerable without an understanding of the overall relation. Harzem, in fact, makes an interesting contribution to such an analysis in his discussion of the 'traditional interests' and phenomena with which the two approaches are respectively concerned. However, I disagreee with Harzem's assertion that the question of what constitutes a reinforcing stimulus is actually more fundamental than this analysis. What he appears to do is to move from a fundamental conceptual analysis, i.e. what are the phenomena with which the two approaches are concerned and how are and should they be related, to an empirical question which can only be raised, or should only be raised, following a more detailed conceptual analysis.

There seems, therefore, to be a discontinuity in the paper which leaves me uncertain as to why Harzem considers the studies he describes as relevant to the 'problem of reinforcement' in behaviour modification. This is not to say that the studies are uninteresting or, within the more restricted TEAB framework, unilluminating. However, there is nothing that convinces me that "it seems reasonable to suppose that investigations of this kind are relevant to behaviour modification." Thus, his study of inter-subject variation when subjects are exposed to the same conditions is an experimental confirmation of what is already clear from many behaviour modification studies. As an experimental finding in its own right it is of interest. It is not clear, however, in what way the finding could inform practice. The same comments are equally applicable to the experimental demonstration of reinforcer effectiveness. Neither study actually addresses itself to the problem of reinforcement in behaviour modification settings; rather, they are experimental demonstrations of known, but poorly documented phenomena. The discussion of animal experiments should certainly sensitize behaviour modifiers to other reinforcement effects than the strengthening or maintenance of responding. Again, however, they do not appear to pose or address themselves to the typical reinforcement problems of the behaviour modifier, problems such as the maintenance of reinforcer effectiveness, manageability of reinforcer delivery, compatibility of response and presentation of reinforcer, and so on.

Interaction between laboratory and field studies requires more than the hope that the investigation of common concepts will lead to cross-fertilization. Kiernan (1973) has argued for what would amount to a formal programmatic approach to such integration. Peter Harzem's paper must be regarded as a step towards this goal, one with which I am sure he is in sympathy. The critical points made here should not be taken to devalue his contribution towards Kiernan's suggestion, which itself merits exhaustive discussion. Another Study Group—perhaps?

REFERENCE

KIERNAN, C. (1973) The sacred and the profane: the relationship between pure and applied behaviour analysis. Paper presented to the Experimental Analysis of Behaviour Group, Cambridge, April 1973

Discussion

Connolly: Why were you surprised at the variability of responses?

Harzem: I wasn't surprised: I am just pointing out that these are the first hard data, to my knowledge, on variability of human operant responding and of differences in the effectiveness of different reinforcers. It seems that there is a whole range of things which can act as reinforcers, and I begin to question whether it is useful to divide stimuli into reinforcers, conditioned reinforcers, and non-reinforcers.

Walker: In your summary you said that a reinforcer can reinforce, inhibit, or act as a learned discriminative cue. You didn't mention that some reinforcers make subjects elated or depressed, so that a fourth function is to pre-set a whole range of emotional responses that may not be learned.

Harzem: Isn't that discriminative?

Walker: I think you have to distinguish between the discriminative cue learned on spaced responding schedules, and pre-set available responses (where reinforcers change the emotional state of the subject) that are less susceptible to the same kind of learning variables.

Harzem: Discriminitive functions are open to empirical investigation irrespective of whether they have been learned in that particular context, have been learned in the past, or have been there all the time.

Jordan: I was struck by the pausing as a part of the third function. Could that not be another part of the function of reinforcers as a discriminative stimulus?

Harzem: I think it is a combination of effects. Let me define my terms. If you get a situation in which presentation of the stimulus stops responding whereas the optimal behaviour for being reinforced is to respond, I think it reasonable to call that inhibition. If on the other hand the discriminative stimulus signals in the direction of pausing, and pausing is also optimal for getting reinforcement, it's reasonable to call that a discriminative effect.

Hogg: I endorse Steve Walker's point about the fourth function. As you know, there are now analyses of emotional behaviour in which a stimulus which has served as a reinforcing stimulus in an operant paradigm functions effectively as a stimulus in a classical conditioning paradigm, the resulting behaviour being described as 'emotional'. These effects may be—to use your term—elating, or they may be suppressing. It may be a long time before we can use that information in a setting with mentally handicapped people, but if we think that emotional tone and atmosphere are important, this may be one direction in which we can move on an operant basis. But we must recognize that reinforcers have emotional significance in their own right. I mean, a parent's picking up and kissing his child quite gratuitously must be a crucial factor in establishing the emotional atmosphere in which the child develops, and may determine the effectiveness of kissing as a reinforcer on other occasions.

Harzem: The form that an emotional or social reinforcer takes can also determine behavioural response. One of our very severely retarded adults has a special relationship with one of the nurses, who accompanies her encouraging remark "Oh good girl, Josie" with a playful thump on the arm. So 'good girl' has become a discriminative stimulus for a playful thump, and if in the experimental room you say to the subject "Oh, good girl!", she is likely to hit out at you. Perhaps analysing emotional relationships in some detail would give us more explanations of behaviour, especially of the kind of behaviour that seems bizarre. And it's the relationship we have to look at, not just isolated behaviour on the part of a subject, isolated from its context, i.e. from its discriminative control.

Current Laboratory Analyses of Behaviour and Behaviour Modification

S. F. WALKER

Department of Psychology, Birkbeck College, London

ABSTRACT

Recent laboratory research on operant conditioning and theoretical analyses of animal behaviour do not support the strict environmentalism of traditional behaviourists. Species-specific factors in operant conditioning paradigms are again coming to the fore, and responses formerly treated as typical or arbitrary have been found to be special cases. For example, key pecking by pigeons is exceptionally compatible with some types of positive reinforcement, but highly incompatible with negative reinforcement. The results of training procedures using reinforcement probably depend on the degree of compatibility between responses, stimuli, and the type of reinforcer to a much greater extent than has previously been acknowledged. Other factors which contribute to variability in the effectiveness of reinforcers include damage to brain structures, interactions between different kinds of reinforcers, previous experience with a particular reinforcer, and associations between primary and secondary reinforcers. The selection of stimuli, responses and reinforcers should therefore receive more attention in behaviour modification, and individual differences in sensitivity to particular reinforcers or procedures should be taken into account.

Since the bulk of this paper is about research on animal behaviour, I shall begin with a few remarks about the relationship of such research to the practical application of behaviour modification.

First, one should acknowledge that, on the face of it, laboratory exercises with rats or pigeons (the most common subjects) are a very unlikely source of useful information about what could or should be done in training or therapy for people. It would not be sensible to undertake behavioural research on animals with the clear goal of solving practical human problems. Whatever the field of research, the path from laboratory studies to socially or economically useful outcomes is usually circuitous and unreliable. In this case there is the added disadvantage that to a greater or lesser extent—depending on personal viewpoints—animal behaviour is simply a different kettle of fish.

It is therefore quite remarkable that the analysis of animal behaviour has in fact played an important part in the development of ideas and techniques involved in behaviour modification. It may be an oversimplification to say that "The foundation of behavioural technology was established in the animal laboratory" (Ulrich, Stachnik and Mabry 1970), and Watson (1928, p. 109) may have overestimated the flexibility of the medical profession in predicting that "A large number of basal problems in method and technique in psychiatry and analysis can be worked out in the animal field." But in both the Skinnerian and Hullian ambits it is demonstrable that fundamental psychological research with animals provided great impetus for new thinking about human problems and a sizeable body of serviceable concepts and methods.

There is no guarantee, of course, that further experimentation on animal behaviour will provide any additional impetus or insight for workers in applied fields (Yates 1970, p. 402). For the purpose of mitigating criticism of behaviour modification (e.g. Breger and McGaugh 1965) it might be wisest to consolidate practical successes in the applied field and say as little as possible about their historical connection with animal research. But in view of the salutary influence that animal behaviour research has already had in the origins of behaviour modification, it seems reasonable at least to make an occasional survey of current research with the hope of abstracting ideas or techniques which could be applicable in man.

This paper attempts a fairly narrow survey by selecting research findings which bear on two main issues—constitutional influences on learning and changes in reinforcer effectiveness—in both of which the initial analyses of animal behaviour produced powerful generalizations which influenced the growth of behaviour modification.

CONSTITUTIONAL INFLUENCES ON LEARNING

The behaviourist emphasis on the overwhelming effect of interactions with the environment on human behaviour can be dated back to Watson's famous claim that he would be able to determine which profession a healthy infant would eventually enter if he was allowed completed control of its upbringing and surroundings (Watson 1930). Since he was arguing against Galton's view that whether one became a doctor or a criminal was decided entirely by constitutional factors it was surely a reasonable point to make. But within the behaviourist tradition there grew up environmental analyses of a much finer grain, especially as applied to mental retardation and disorder, which are rather less reasonable. Whereas Watson was content to say that lack of self-care skills could be a consequence of being 'born without certain brain equipment' (Watson 1928, p. 31) later writers, assiduously avoiding reference to non-behavioural factors, have kept *all* deficiencies and malfunctions at a behavioural level. An example is Kantor's explanation of the whole range of mental retardation: "the basic principle is the failure of the individual to build up response equipment to certain things. There is failure to coordinate certain stimulus–response functions" (Kantor 1959, p. 176, quoted in Bijou 1963). Bijou's list of organismic factors in retardation contains only three categories: impairment of response equipment; restriction of environmental stimuli; inadequacy of the appearance or behaviour of the retarded person for eliciting proper social reactions from others. This is a very restricted list which deliberately excludes any trait or capacity concepts, even of the type 'native ability to form stimulus–response connections' or 'native sensitivity to reinforcement'.

Bijou's concern is to avoid reducing psychological variables to biological terms by using a system in which only behaviour–environment interactions are studied or mentioned, while any biological factors are strictly left for the biologists. This approach has merit, in so far as it bypasses the undoubted conceptual and practical problems which seem inevitable when nature–behaviour–nurture interactions are considered, even when very careful quantification is attempted, as in the case of IQ measures (Clarke 1965). The scheme obviously springs from the success of the Skinnerian analysis of animal behaviour, which makes a point of leaving out physiology and such obvious constitutional factors as the species of the animal studied and the biological function of the behaviour being analysed (Skinner 1938).

However, much recent work has cast doubt on this approach to animal behaviour, mainly because constitutional factors have a marked effect on how easily a response is learned, even under standard training conditions (Seligman 1970; Hinde and Stevenson-Hinde 1973; Seligman and Hager 1972). The behaviourist tradition, both in research strategy and in the application of research findings, has been that all behaviours may be regarded as equally susceptible to modification by interaction with the environment. Pavlov says in introducing his work on conditioning that "It is obvious that the reflex activity of any effector organ can be chosen for the purpose of this investigation, since signalling stimuli can get linked up with any of the inborn reflexes" (Pavlov 1927, p. 17). Skinner accorded even less attention to the particularity of operants: "The general topography of operant behaviour is not important, because most if not all specific operants are conditioned. I suggest that the dynamic properties of operant behaviour may be studied with a single reflex (or at least only as many as are needed to ensure the general applicability of the results)" (Skinner 1938, pp. 45–46). Hull, though following Pavlov in using 'unlearned stimulus–response connections' as his starting point did not qualify his general postulates about learning by reference to the response involved, except to say that incentive learning is more rapid than habit learning (Hull 1952). These attitudes have become incorporated into the assumptions, implicit or explicit, of behaviour modifiers. One finds the notion that all behaviours, usual or unusual, have arisen because of the same kind of environmental variables, and that by sufficiently prolonged or intensive application of methods of conditioning and reinforcement one target behaviour may be shaped as easily as any other (Bijou 1963; Ferster 1961; Lovaas, Schaffer and Simmons 1965). Self-destructive, ritualistic or asocial behaviours must have arisen from unusual combinations of circumstances affecting social, environmental and internal reinforcement. If these reinforcers can be cut off from the unwanted behaviour and applied with additional rewards to other target behaviours, we can expect the unwanted behaviours to disappear and the new ones to supplant them (Ferster 1961; Lovaas and Simmons 1969; Hall and Broden 1967). For the strict environmentalist, the only constraints on this process lie in the available degree of control over the environment and the time span of the procedures.

As applied in practice, this kind of principle can be accepted as a fertile and helpful rule of thumb, to be judged by its results. But its underpinning in the animal laboratory now has to be qualified in a number of ways. Much evidence shows that all responses are not learned equally easily, and that all stimuli do not link up equally well with a response. This is in itself not too surprising. However, the observation that one response, but not another, is easily learned with food reinforcement has led to attacks on the response-reinforcement principle (Bindra 1974), and on the feasibility of any widely applicable law of learning (Seligman 1970).

I believe it is fortunate for reinforcement theorists, rather than unfortunate, that the type of reinforcement seems to determine which responses are most readily learned, or 'highly prepared' (Seligman 1970). In any event, the main research findings can be classified according to whether positive or negative reinforcement is involved, and according to whether response-learning or stimulus-learning is the outcome.

Compatibility of stimuli with negative reinforcers

Establishing an association between a negative reinforcer and a neutral stimulus which signals it is a basic operation in classical conditioning. Pavlov and his contemporaries studied the 'defence' reflex of a dog salivating to a sound, when the sound signalled that acid was about to be put in the dog's mouth; and the reflex of a dog bending its leg to a signal preceding an electric shock. A similar kind of association is observed by means of operant techniques based on that of Estes and Skinner (1941) in which ongoing operant responding ceases during the signal for electric foot-shocks. The association of a stimulus with negative reinforcement is assumed to exist when it is supposed that the stimulus can evoke an emotional reaction, labelled 'fear' or 'anxiety', which has separate effects on behaviour (e.g. Mowrer 1960).

Another method for looking at the learned association between a stimulus and negative reinforcement is to pair the ingestion of a food or fluid with an aversive event and measure the amount by which an animal reduces its intake after this experience. By this means Garcia and Koelling (1966) discovered that the quality of an aversive stimulus determines the kind of 'neutral' stimulus which will best serve as a signal for it. In their series of experiments thirsty rats were allowed to drink from a metered source in an experimental box. The conditioning was brought about by flavouring the water and using external cues of lights and sounds to accompany drinking, which was succeeded by unpleasant events: either electric foot-shock, or intestinal distress caused by X-rays or lithium chloride poisoning. Subsequent tests showed that taste reduced intake after sickness, but that audiovisual cues reduced intake after electric shocks. The internal unpleasantness was associated with attendant tastes, but the external unpleasantness was associated with the external cues. In other words, taste and audiovisual cues are not equivalent stimuli for associations with the two kinds of negative reinforcer.

However, animals are not rigidly programmed in a way which allows only for links between stimuli and compatible reinforcers. Best, Best and Mickley (1973) found that rats made ill in a black compartment avoided that compartment in later tests, provided that they were not given the more powerful signal of drinking flavoured water in the compartment. Also, the compatibility of taste with sickness depends on the species of animal, since visual cues appear to have priority over taste cues in some birds (Wilcoxon, Dragoin and Kral 1971).

The effect of stimulus compatibility on associations with negative reinforcers is not limited to the selection of the most compatible stimulus from a collection of stimuli surrounding the reinforcer. Very long intervals between illness and an associated taste can be used, compared to the intervals needed for associations of external stimuli with electric shock. Garcia, Ervin and Koelling (1966) and Revusky (1968) demonstrated that the maximum effective interval between taste and illness is a matter of hours, whereas the effective interval between audiovisual cues and shock must be measured in seconds (Kimble 1967). Garcia, McGowan and Green (1972) have argued convincingly that this discrepancy is due to an underlying difference in the action of the central nervous system for the two types of sensory input, rather than to peripheral factors such as aftertastes or regurgitation.

Compatibility of stimuli with positive reinforcers

It seems probable that stimulus–reinforcer compatibility affects links between stimuli and positive as well as negative reinforcers, although there is less experimental evidence here. The research example is again the association of oral cues with internal post-ingestion states. Although Rozin and Kalat (1971) have suggested that the main mechanism in diet selection is rejection of foods whose consumption is concomitant with ill-health, there is also evidence of positive preferences for tastes which have been followed by beneficial aftereffects. Thiamine deficient rats given vitamin B injections increase their preference for the flavour of water drunk prior to the injections (Garcia, Ervin, York and Koelling 1967; Zahorik and Maier, 1969). Similarly, Booth and Simson (1971) and Holman (1969) found increased preferences for odours and tastes associated with relief from protein or general diet deficiencies.

Injection of glucose can become linked with postural cues (Coppock and Chambers 1954) and milk delivered via a stomach fistula can reinforce T-maze reactions (Miller and Kessen 1952). But the long time intervals between taste and odour cues and their beneficial after-effects suggested that oral stimuli are more compatible than external cues with sensations of nutritional well-being.

If these stimulus compatibility effects were confined to diet regulation in rats there might be little need to worry about them in the context of behaviour modification. But many kinds of stimulus–response compatibility effects are known to exist for both animals and man (Downey and Harrison 1972; Fitts and Biederman 1965; Shulman and McConkie 1973; McCormick 1970). This should prepare one for the possibility that with any reinforcer (whether it is related to task completion or to nutritional or social factors) certain combinations of stimuli, responses and the reinforcer are more effective than others.

Compatibility of responses with negative reinforcers

Bolles (1970) has put forward strong arguments for connecting the efficiency with which a response may be modified by negative reinforcement to the similarity of the response to the 'species-specific defence reactions' elicited by the reinforcer. This is not a novel concept; Guthrie (1934) pointed out that a dog will learn to jump forward more readily to escape a slap if the slap is applied to its behind rather than its nose. More data are now available to support the position that in both escape and avoidance learning, the behaviour elicited by the reinforcer is an important variable in determining how fast, if at all, a particular response is learned. For rats, it appears that in some environments (such as a running wheel, shuttlebox, or alley) running is a high priority response when the reinforcer is electric shock (Bolles 1969). The strength of the relation between peripheral pain and 'running away' can be gauged from the result that, once having learned to run to avoid shock, rats will persist in the 'vicious circle' behaviour of unnecessarily running over a shocking grid (Brown 1969). This unnecessary running may even reappear after it has died out under no-shock conditions, when shock is reintroduced in an alley, but not in the start box in which the rat could stay (Melvin and Smith 1967).

In enclosures such as an operant conditioning box, 'running away' is restricted and passivity or 'freezing' becomes a strong feature of the behaviour of rats subjected to painful shock. For instance, Brener and Gosling (1970) used an ultrasonic device to measure rats' activity in a small box and compared the learning of immobility and activity as avoidance responses. They found that immobility was learned much better. When shocks are used to condition lever pressing in a box, prolonged freezing while holding the lever down is often observed (Meyer, Cho and Wesemann 1960; Davis, Hirschorn and Hurwitz 1973). This, like running, can take the form of 'vicious circle' behaviour, when punishment for continued lever holding extends it, with the animal enduring many unnecessary shocks (Migler 1963).

Although punishment with additional shocks sometimes adds vigour to such shock-compatible responses as freezing or running, there is now general agreement that punishment is a powerful factor in the long-term suppression or elimination of positively reinforced activities (Campbell and Church 1969; Azrin and Holz 1966). Direct emotional or motor responses of fear and withdrawal are undoubtedly often involved in this suppression, but in some situations it is clear that systematic choices are related to the balance of positive and negative outcomes (Logan 1969; Rachlin and Herrnstein 1969).

However, a separate category of actions which are highly compatible with negative reinforcers is aggressive behaviour. Several reports suggest that electric shocks elicit aggressive behaviour (attack, biting, aggressive posture, etc.) when

124

there is an object present at which the responses may be directed (e.g. Ulrich and Craine 1964; Ulrich, Wolff and Azrin 1964). The attacked object may be another animal of the same or different species or an ill-defined substitute like a stuffed doll or rubber ball. The effect is not specific to shocks, but may be observed with relatively weak aversive stimuli such as absence of scheduled positive reinforcement (Azrin, Hutchinson and Hake 1966). This type of aggression is not simply a matter of reflex motor patterns, since animals will work to obtain an object to be aggressive towards (Azrin, Hutchinson and McLaughlin 1965) as they will when aggression results from direct stimulation of appropriate brain sites (Roberts and Kiess 1964).

The tendency of aversive stimuli to elicit aggression in social situations, and the facilitating effects of punishment on aversively motivated behaviours, support Skinner's consistently expressed misgivings about the practical value of negative reinforcers (Skinner 1953, 1972).

Compatibility of responses with positive reinforcers

The main response of interest in this section is the pigeon's key peck. A pigeon directing a peck to a distinctive disc at head-level for the delivery of grain at the hopper below has probably been the most frequently studied situation in operant conditioning since the publication of *Schedules of Reinforcement* (Ferster and Skinner 1957). Pecking has been the major 'single reflex' used to investigate 'the dynamic properties of operant behaviour' (Skinner 1938). It appears now that any generalizations based on this response will have to be re-evaluated, because it is anything but an arbitrary response in a food-reinforced behaviour.

Hernnstein and Loveland (1972) have pointed out that one special feature of the key peck is that it is extremely incompatible with electric shock. But while pigeons can be trained to key peck to escape or avoid shock only with great difficulty and by highly specialized procedures (Rachlin and Hineline 1967) they will key peck in a variety of circumstances which include food deliveries, even when key pecking actually prevents food delivery. There is a case for saying both that key pecking is preselected against by shock, because of interference from shock-elicited behaviour, and that key pecking is positively preselected by grain deliveries.

The first step in the experimental re-examination of the influence of food reinforcers on the key peck was the discovery of the procedure termed 'auto-shaping' (Brown and Jenkins 1968). In this method, the illumination of the pecking disc is made the signal for unconditional or 'free' food deliveries. The pairing of the key-light with food appears to be a sufficient condition for making pigeons peck the disc and is actually quicker and simpler than the traditional method of shaping the key peck by giving contingent reinforcement for successive approximations to the required response. So powerful is this peck-eliciting factor that key pecking persists even if pecking the lit key eliminates food delivery on that cycle (Williams and Williams 1969). The latter finding is reminiscent of the 'omission' procedure used to test for the independence of classical conditioning from reward and punishment effects, and some have characterized autoshaping as a genuine classical conditioning procedure, with the key peck being a 'directed' version of a Pavlovian response (Moore 1973; Jenkins 1973). It is true that the procedures are virtually identical, with a conditioned stimulus signalling the unconditioned stimulus, causing a response to be shifted from the unconditioned stimulus to the signal. The classical conditioning account is made even more plausible by the fact that the details of the autoshaped peck follow the variations produced by substituting drinking for eating as the original response (beak open for food and closed for water (Jenkins 1973).

But the results discussed above concerning associations between stimuli and reinforcers prompt the conclusion that such associations do not follow a universal and standard set of rules. The additional procedures investigated by Herrnstein and Loveland (1972) indicated that, although reflexive responses may be one element of behaviour under autoshaping procedures, they do not tell the whole story behind the compatibility of pecking with positive reinforcement. In Herrnstein and Loveland's experiments, pigeons experienced cycles of changes in key illumination with a variety of different consequences attached to pecks at the key. It was confirmed that pecking is reduced but not extinguished when pecks prevent food delivery. Complete absence of pecking was found only when no food at all was given in the Skinner box and when pecking produced no change in illumination. If pecking merely turned out all lights, this was sufficient to maintain a low level of pecking when food was absent, but a substantial level when food was delivered at a completely unrelated point in the cycle. There are several reports that illumination changes can function as tangible, if weak, reinforcers for rat bar pressing (Lockard 1963; Kiernan 1969) and Herrnstein and Loveland suggest that stimulus change is a weak reinforcer for pigeons' key pecking, but becomes a much stronger reinforcer when juxtaposed with food deliveries. One might say that pecking is an investigative response for the pigeon, when there is something around worth investigating. That would be going too far, but pecking clearly interacts with experimental conditions in a way different from head raising, treadle pressing, wing flapping, or some arbitrary movement.

It is important to know, of course, if autoshaping is unique to the pigeon, and also whether it works with responses which are not such a common part of the repertoire as pecking is for the pigeon. No attempts seem to have been made to autoshape other behaviours in the pigeon, but approach to and manipulation of the signal for reward may be a general phenomenon. Rats tend to chew a light paired with food delivery (Moore 1973) and press levers under a modified autoshaping procedure (Powell, Saunders and Thompson 1968). Autoshaping has been found in fish and in birds other than the pigeon (Squier 1969; Gardner 1969). Most promising results have been obtained with monkeys and dogs, both of which press a lever if a light in the lever signals reinforcement delivery. They also choose the correct lever out of three available if only one of the levers is lit as the signal (Sidman and Fletcher 1968; Smith and Smith 1972). Beissel (1972) reported autoshaping of lever pressing in mental retardates.

126

Autoshaping can thus be regarded as an additional technique for modifying behaviour with positive reinforcement, in the same category as the external prompting or guiding of the correct response, which may be quicker than gradual shaping. In the same way, the special relationships of some responses to some reinforcers can be regarded as an addition to our knowledge about what can be done with positive reinforcement, rather than a restriction on the applicability of reinforcement principles. Stevenson-Hinde (1973) has analysed her results concerning the limited behaviours that may be reinforced by playing back their song to chaffinches, and has also discussed Shettleworth's findings on the weakness of food reinforcement for scratching and washing responses in hamsters (Shettleworth 1973), along with autoshaping and the findings mentioned in previous sections of this paper. Her conclusion is that it is less constructive to say that some responses are more highly 'prepared' than others (Seligman 1970) than it is to search for order and principles in the variety of results.

Conclusions

Naturally the details of the constraints on learning in various animals have little direct import for applied work with humans. The fact that scratching and washing are controlled by specialized reinforcers in rodents does not mean that self-care behaviours cannot be brought under the control of social approval or extrinsic reward in children. But it may be useful to use the animal data to emphasize the importance of particular stimulus-response-reinforcer combinations. The decisions concerning which response to reinforce, or which stimulus to present for one individual under one set of motivating circumstances, are not arbitrary, but are likely to be crucial to the outcome of a behaviour-modification procedure. It is better to make the reward fit the performance than to 'make the punishment fit the crime', in view of the problems encountered with negative reinforcement.

It is conceivable that more definite strategies might also be gleaned from the data. Perhaps the optimum method of encouraging children to wash is not to give food reinforcement for particular washing movements. Increasing the importance of 'being clean', perhaps by making this a signal for greater personal comfort, might sometimes be a quicker way of generating cleaning behaviours. If that were so, it would be consistent both with common practice and with some authors' stress on intrinsic rather than extrinsic reinforcers for long lasting effects (Staats 1968, pp. 520–540). But the thrust of recent basic research on constraints in learning is to give more weight to careful selection of procedures, and less support to assumptions about the functional equivalence of arbitrarily chosen behaviours than has been manifested in previous analyses.

CHANGES IN REINFORCER EFFECTIVENESS

The question of the adequacy of reinforcers has been raised in the theory of behaviour modification mainly in the sense that deficiencies in reinforcement may be diagnosed as the cause of behavioural inadequacies. 'Inadequate reinforcement history' is a cry often heard from behaviourists searching the environment for the roots of retardation. Under this heading, it is usually the sketchiness of the history rather than the weakness of properly scheduled reinforcers which is referred to. "A child may fail to be exposed to the physical and social stimulation ordinarily provided children in the culture" (Bijou 1963) and this could obviously impose limitations on the child's behavioural repertoire. A less extreme insufficiency of history is the case of intermittent reinforcement, where it is assumed that the usual reinforcers are present, but are not applied often enough to sustain normal behaviours. Ferster (1961) has stressed that infrequent reinforcement produces weak behaviour, especially in the early stages of learning, even though long exposure to intermittent reinforcement after learning is known to increase the persistence of behaviour after reinforcement has stopped altogether.

It is only the presence or absence of reinforcers, and not their quality or effectiveness, which matters in the cases of intermittent reinforcement and complete lack of exposure to reinforcers. Less weight has been given to the possibility of an inadequate reinforcement history caused by weakness or unreliability of a properly scheduled reinforcer. Perhaps that is partly because of a reluctance to consider physiological variables, since weakness or ineffectiveness of scheduled reinforcers could be related to the impairment of reinforcement mechanisms by, for instance, damage to known reinforcement pathways in the brain. However, at the behavioural level, the reinforcing stimulus, though present, may be of inadequate intensity or quality; parental attention might be given often enough, but not well enough. The failure of reinforcing stimuli has in fact been emphasized as a characteristic of childhood autism and psychoses by Ferster (1961), Leff (1968) and Lovaas et al. (1965), and the lack of available effective reinforcers can be a stumbling block for the implementation of behaviour modification procedures with psychotic or severely retarded patients (Allyon and Azrin 1968).

Ferster's paper is an extensive and influential account of how rare combinations of circumstances in upbringing might engender autistic behaviours. The reactions of the child to normal and abnormal sources of reward are hypothesized to be a major aspect of the syndrome. Small changes in physical sensation appear to be very pleasurable to the autistic child, since activities like water splashing and dirt smearing are prominent. Ferster supposes that this is not because of strong reinforcement, but because weak reinforcers can be easily and continuously produced by these activities, and there is a lack of alternative reinforcers. Although tantrums and self-destructive acts are said to be maintained because of their effects on the onlooker, a very noticeable feature of the autistic child's everyday behaviour is that conditioned, delayed or generalized reinforcers seem almost totally without power.

Ferster follows Skinner's analysis (Skinner 1953), in which the behaviour of normal children is described in terms of sequences of responses that are maintained by conditioned reinforcers which serve to fill the gap between most behaviour and its ultimate consequence. Going through a door into another room to get a toy to bring back to show to someone else involves a chain of behaviours, with separate parts being reinforced by progress to the next bit of the chain.

Opening a door will provide conditioned reinforcement only if one wishes to go through it, but the most important kind of conditioned reinforcer is a generalized one, which works in the absence of any particular precondition. Smiles, attention and expressions of approval by the parent are examples, insofar as their effect is independent of particular 'deprivation states' of the child.

Another important generalized reinforcer identified by Skinner (1953), Ferster (1961) and Leff (1968) is control of the environment. It is supposed that individual acts of control of the environment are associated with the receipt of a wide range of reinforcers, and thus any control of the environment becomes reinforcing.

In Ferster's analysis, failure to develop these conditioned and generalized reinforcers is a critical factor in the creation of autistic behaviour. The failure is attributed not directly to constitutional factors but to an accumulation of faults in child–parent interaction. A low level of activity by the child prevents the development of conditioned reinforcers and "A limited development of simple conditioned reinforcers in turn prevents the development of a generalized reinforcer... Without parental generalized reinforcement, educational processes and positive parental control are all but impossible" (Ferster 1961, p. 449).

In summary, analysis of the concept of reinforcement in behaviour modification contexts has concentrated on the possibility that behaviour problems are caused by insufficient exposure to positive reinforcers with emphasis on consequent failure in the development of conditioned and generalized reinforcers. Less consideration has been given to the implications of variation in the effectiveness of reinforcers that are delivered either in the history of the individual or in modification procedures. The issues of variation in reinforcer effectiveness and the development of conditioned reinforcers are examined below in the context of basic research with animals.

Primary reinforcers: variation in effectiveness

Traditionally, the effectiveness of a primary reinforcer is seen as a constant factor in behaviour change, which is highly predictable if the state of deprivation of the organism and the physical properties of the reinforcer are known (Skinner 1938; Hull 1952). A small number of deprivation states and corresponding primary reinforcers could be used to account for a wide range of behaviours if it were assumed that their basic reinforcing effect transfers to accompanying neutral stimuli, which thus acquire conditioned reinforcing powers. However, several strands of research, including those already discussed, have led to rather more involved theories of how primary reinforcement works (e.g. Glickman and Schiff 1967; Bindra 1968, 1974). Without entering into theoretical speculation, it is possible to examine briefly two aspects of work on primary reinforcement: (i) the physiological bases of reinforcement and (ii) behavioural studies pointing to a multiplicity of 'primary reinforcers' and inconsistencies in their effectiveness.

Physiological bases of reinforcement.   Although the physiological evidence does not provide definite and agreed conclusions, the fact that something is known about the brain mechanisms involved in reinforcement makes it increasingly difficult to ignore the possibility that there may be interactions between behavioural and physiological factors. The simplest result perhaps is that which shows that small lesions in particular areas of the hypothalamus can completely change the way in which food acts as a reinforcer (Teitelbaum and Epstein 1962; Nisbett 1972). If the lateral hypothalamus is damaged, rats may starve rather than eat or drink. If they are fed artificially, they may eventually eat and drink enough to stay alive. In this condition, they show very little interest in eating, but access to food may paradoxically still act as a reinforcer, even if they eat little of it (Devenport and Balagura 1971). On the other hand, rats with damage to the ventromedial hypothalamus overeat and become fat, but refuse to eat unpalatable food, and will sometimes not work to obtain food which they eat readily if it is freely available. However, there is some evidence that particular reinforcement schedules will produce high levels of food-reinforced behaviour in these rats (Wampler 1973). These results suggest that food used as a reinforcer normally has a combination of behavioural effects, and that observed peculiarities about the way an individual is affected by food reinforcement may be connected with central nervous system factors, in which case special sequences of reinforcement procedure may be necessary to maximize the behavioural effectiveness of the reinforcer.

Such conclusions are confirmed, for other reinforcers as well as food, by studies of reinforcement by electrical stimulation of the brain. To the extent that this corresponds to more natural reinforcement, the results suggest that receipt of a reinforcer involves more than the incrementing of antecedent response strengths. Animals will work systematically for the stimulation of certain brain areas, but the receipt of stimulation may render additional behaviours reinforcing. For some sites, rats will work for stimulation but will also eat when stimulated; for others, they will work for stimulation but will copulate in response to the electrical stimulus. In both cases a goal object needs to be present to release the additional behaviour, and the animals will perform separate responses to obtain the goal object (Valenstein, Cox and Katolewski 1970; Caggiula 1970).

One interpretation of these results is that they indicate a physiological basis for the connection between particular responses and reinforcers discussed above, although there is some evidence that the link between a particular site of brain stimulation and a response elicited from that site is flexible, and depends on previous experiences (Valenstein *et al.* 1970). The main aspect of the brain stimulation results which is relevant here is that the receipt of the reinforcer alters the effectiveness of other reinforcers.

This theme, that the effectiveness of a reinforcer cannot be estimated simply in terms of its corresponding deprivation state but depends on experience with alternative or previous reinforcers, is reflected in the behavioural data discussed below.

Behavioural evidence of interaction between reinforcers. There is not a great deal of evidence suggesting interactions between reinforcers, but the vast majority of experiments with animals utilize only a single reinforcer and take the effectiveness of the reinforcer for granted. However, Verplanck and Hayes (1953) showed that there is considerable interaction between food and water reinforcement if both are used concurrently, and a wider range of interactions is indicated by the phenomenon which Segal (1972) has termed 'emotional induction'. This term covers a variety of cases where spaced presentations of one reinforcer give rise to behaviour appropriate to an alternative reinforcer, irrespective of the deprivation level for this alternative. In a typical example, spaced presentation of small amounts of food eventually leads to bouts of drinking following food presentation which are far in excess of the drinking necessary to maintain a metabolically adequate water intake (Falk 1961).

Research has since shown that this is not an isolated effect of eating dry food on drinking water (Segal 1972; Falk 1972). Many other behaviours, apart from drinking, can be induced by spaced presentations of food. Eating or gnawing of inappropriate objects ('pica') has been observed in monkeys and rats (Falk 1972; Laties, Weiss, Clark and Reynolds 1965) and 'air drinking' and wheel running in rats (Mendelson and Chillag 1970; Levitsky and Collier 1968). Which behaviour appears depends mainly on what is available; water drinking appears if water is available, paper shredding and chewing if paper is available, and so on. Wheel running takes place if a wheel is available, but if water and a running wheel are available, drinking and running appear. If dilute alcohol instead of water is presented high levels of alcohol ingestion develop (Hawkins, Schrot, Githens and Everett 1972). As noted previously, periodic brief shocks are likely to induce aggression towards another animal, but eating or copulation may also be evoked by shocks if food or receptive females are available (for male rats: Caggiula and Eibergen 1969).

These behaviours have been classified as 'schedule-induced' and 'adjunctive' and 'displacement activities' (Gilbert and Keehn 1972). But an alternative interpretation of the phenomena, which points to more general implications, is that 'adjunctive' behaviours appear because they are reinforcing, having been made reinforcing by the presentations of the initially scheduled reinforcer. It is not, of course, advisable to say that a behaviour is reinforcing merely because it happens, although the frequency of a behaviour can be an index of its power to reinforce other behaviours (Premack 1965). But the few tests which have been made all show that 'adjunctive' behaviour is capable of reinforcing other behaviour (Falk 1966; Falk 1972). In the case of schedule-induced polydipsia, where excessive drinking occurs between food presentation, rats will press a lever on fixed-ratio schedules to obtain small amounts of water. Azrin et al. (1965) have shown that animals will work to obtain objects to attack after they have been shocked. The work of Hawkins *et al.* (1972) suggests that schedule-induced alcohol drinking becomes independently rewarding.

In some, if not all cases, therefore, 'adjunctive' or 'schedule-induced' behaviours have motivational properties. This, together with the motivating effects of brain stimulation, make it difficult to sustain the distinction between a small number of independent primary reinforcers and a much larger number of secondary reinforcers. There appear to be large numbers of activities and sensations that have some degree of 'wired-in' reinforcing power, with the effectiveness of any reinforcer being heavily dependent on its context in a sequence of other reinforcers. The presentation of strong reinforcers such as food and shock not only affect the behaviour reinforced but may induce adjunctive behaviours, or as has been suggested here, change the reinforcing properties of other activities.

One should be alert to the possibility, therefore, that similar relationships may hold in practical situations with human subjects. The effectiveness of food or approval as reinforcers may be bound up with their context in the stream of other reinforcing events. And the regular presentation of a reinforcer in a behaviour modification procedure may change the reinforcement value of activities other than the target response. For instance, it might be that spaced presentations of food given when a child correctly names a picture will make shouting, jumping, or some other non-target activity more rewarding. If so, it could be helpful to bear this fact in mind when designing or evaluating the procedure.

Behavioural evidence for interaction within one reinforcer.   Crespi (1942) claimed to have found elation and depression in rats as a result of changes in reward size. His rats ran much faster for a given reinforcer if it represented an increase of the usual reinforcer than if the previously experienced reinforcers had been bigger. Subsequent research has confirmed that rats run more slowly to a given amount of food if they have been accustomed to a larger amount, but has thrown doubt on the reliability of the increase in response strength obtained by prior training on a small reward (Spence 1956; Walker 1969). Recently, however, both types of effect have been observed when brain stimulation or sugar solutions are used as reinforcers for non-deprived rats (Panksepp and Trowill 1970, 1971). When a rat can obtain two values of a reinforcer concurrently, for responses on different levers, it can be shown that the rate of response for a given reinforcer size is inversely related to the size of the alternative (Walker and Hurwitz 1971).

A similar kind of effect, known as 'behavioural contrast', has been repeatedly demonstrated with pigeons since it was reported by Reynolds (1961). In this case the contrast is between two frequencies of reinforcer rather than between two reinforcer sizes. If pigeons receive grain about once every three minutes, for instance, they will peck much faster if this condition is alternated with a condition in which the reinforcer is only given once every 10 minutes. Although theoretically this phenomenon has nothing to do with rest or fatigue, it looks as though more intensive behaviour is produced when periods of standard reinforcement are interspersed with periods of sparse reinforcement which sustain little responding. Cliffe, Gathercole and Epling (1974) have recently recommended that this principle be applied in behaviour modification.

Unfortunately, the Reynolds type of behavioural contrast is one of the

132

phenomena which have to be re-evaluated in the light of the special status of the key-peck response in pigeons. No behavioural contrast appears in pigeons if the response is not key pecking (Hemmes 1973; Westbrook 1973; Keller 1974; Redford and Perkins 1974) and it is also likely that the customary visual stimuli are more conducive to the original result than auditory stimuli (Lo Lordo, McMillan and Riley 1974).

Despite these restrictions on the generality of behavioural contrast in pigeons, behavioural contrast and Crespi effects have been reported for retarded human subjects (O'Brien 1968; Claridge and O'Connor 1957). If due regard is paid to response factors, it is possible to suggest principles of practical interest.

The main principle, which does not violate common sense, is that the effectiveness of a reinforcer depends on previous and concurrent experience of that reinforcer. It is impossible to be definite about all the interactions which may happen, but the 'contrast' type of effect, where the subject overreacts to a change in reinforcement conditions, is one thing to look out for. These cases have been successfully analysed by connecting the effectiveness of a reinforcer to its *relative* value rather than its actual value, the relative value being determined by comparison with the other sizes or densities of the reinforcer which have been experienced (Herrnstein 1970, 1971). But it should not be forgotten that under some circumstances the opposite of contrast occurs, when the subject *under*-reacts to a change in reinforcement conditions and adjusts gradually to the new level of reinforcement or remains permanently anchored to the original conditions (Reynolds 1963; Hurwitz, Walker, Salmon and Packham 1965).

Secondary reinforcers

It has been asserted above that it is unrealistic to restrict the concept of primary or 'unconditioned' reinforcers to a short list of nutrients and comforts. Many sensations and activities work as reinforcers without an explicit history of pairing with food, water or sex. However, this is not to say that originally unreinforcing stimuli or responses cannot acquire reinforcing powers through association with known reinforcers, and recent research has in fact widened the range of such kinds of association.

Control of the environment. The idea put forward by Skinner (1953) and Ferster (1961) was that reinforcing properties accrue to any kind of control of the environment because controlling the environment is normally a means of access to many kinds of reinforcer. There has never been much evidence for this kind of process in the animal laboratory, except insofar as primates persist in solving puzzles, become more adept at handling sticks and boxes after using them to obtain food, and show improvement when solving a series of problems (Harlow, Blazek and McClearn 1956; Birch 1945; Harlow 1949). An additional line of evidence has arisen, though, which shows the negative effect of lack of control of the environment, and is therefore pertinent to Ferster's discussion of the failure to develop this generalized reinforcer.

The finding is that giving dogs a period of inescapable electric shock results in their failing to learn a subsequent shuttle-box avoidance task (Seligman and Maier 1967). Maier, Seligman and Solomon (1969) present a series of experiments on this 'learned helplessness' and conclude that there is a genuine form of learning taking place, rather than some artifact such as emotional exhaustion. Thus, inescapable shocks may diminish the reinforcement value of interacting with the environment in the same way that successful problem solving may enhance the secondary reinforcement value of problem solving attempts.

Increases in the secondary reinforcing value of task attempts may have contributed to the transfer of training found in imbeciles by Clarke and Blakemore (1961) and Clarke and Cookson (1962), since the subjects were always rewarded and praised for attempting the task and Clarke and Clarke (1965, p. 381) note that this aspect of the procedure seemed to maximize transfer.

Therefore, although we still lack detailed evidence concerning how the secondary reinforcement value of 'controlling the environment' varies with the degree of reward or punishment it gains, it seems necessary to take into account the possible cumulative effects of success or failure on this general response class.

Types of association between primary and secondary reinforcers. The simplest procedure likely to increase the reinforcing value of an event is pairing it with a known reinforcer. The original Hullian theory (Hull 1943) was that a forward pairing, with a known reinforcer following a neutral event, always increased the value of the neutral event. Alternatives to this idea were along the lines that only fairly vivid or functional pairings would do. According to Dinsmoor's suggestion (Dinsmoor 1950), only a neutral stimulus which becomes a discriminative stimulus (calling for some response) will be able to acquire effectiveness from a following reinforcer. Egger and Miller (1962) also showed that just pairing things in time was not enough, since stimuli close in time to a reinforcer are not effectively conditioned if they are not good signals (when they occur some of the time without the reinforcer, or when some other stimulus gives earlier information).

On these grounds, manipulable tokens would be expected to work very well as conditioned reinforcers, if they combine the factors of calling for a response and being a reliable index of reward. Usually tokens require a number of responses to do with collecting them and exchanging them for the back up reinforcers, and are good guides to reward if the exchange system operates properly. It has sometimes been found in practice that the manipulability of tokens can be a drawback if they are lost, lent or stolen in social situations, and that the manipulability of tokens is therefore best restricted (O'Leary and Drabman 1971). When such restrictions are necessary, it is obviously advisable to retain as much of the discriminative and signalling functions as possible.

Recent work on second-order schedules with animals can be interpreted as suggesting that, if the discriminative and signalling functions of a stimulus are strong enough, it may acquire reinforcing properties even if it is never actually paired with the known reinforcer.

Second-order schedules. The initial experiments by Kelleher on second-order schedules (Kelleher 1966) set a pattern for later research. He gave a brief light flash instead of the usual reinforcer on a fixed interval schedule. Only when 30 fixed intervals were completed was food presented along with the light flash. The important point is that typical fixed interval responding was maintained throughout the cycle of 30. Leaving out the light flashes resulted in a much lower response rate, with none of the typical speeding-up of response rate within each fixed interval component. This demonstrates the effectiveness of the light flash as a conditioned reinforcer, able to sustain behaviour at a far remove from the known food reinforcers. Findley and Brady (1965) had previously shown that giving light flashes as 'subgoals' helped the performance of extremely large fixed ratios (4,000 and 120,000 responses) in chimpanzees. But much more limited amounts of behaviour had been maintained in chained schedules with pigeons (Kelleher and Gollub 1962), where a continuous key-light changed in colour when individual fixed intervals were completed, so that the stimuli remote from food reinforcement were dissimilar to those closer.

Kelleher's results with second-order schedules are of interest chiefly because they add to the procedures devised by D. W. Zimmerman (1957) and J. Zimmerman (1969) which provide clear demonstrations of how stimuli that did not start off as reinforcers come to provide a powerful source of motivation for behaviours they are contingent upon.

But Herrnstein and Loveland's (1972) suggestion of special interactions between lights, food and key pecking in the pigeon should alert us to the possibility of some unexpected features arising in procedures which involve these three elements. Such an unexpected feature is indeed supplied by the work of Neuringer and Chung (1967) and Stubbs (1971). In the former, it was found that blackouts given for pecking on a fixed-interval schedule had a 'quasi-reinforcing' effect even if blackouts were never paired with food or any other known reinforcer. Stubbs (1971) used several second-order schedules and studied the effects of a brief change in key lighting. He confirmed that the brief stimulus functioned as a reinforcer even when not paired in any way with food, and also that the major factor determining whether or not the brief stimulus acted as a reinforcer was whether there was a systematic relationship between it and the food reinforcer. If the brief stimulus was not paired with food, but also did not occur at any fixed time before food delivery, its effects on the shape of responding were minimal. Stubbs and Cohen (1972) again found that if the brief stimulus came on a fixed time before food delivery, whether or not it was actually paired with food was unimportant.

Thus, at least with the pigeon's key peck, a fixed relation between a brief stimulus and food may be substituted for the simple pairing operation as a method of giving extra behavioural effects to the brief stimulus. Perhaps in human behaviour there are also relationships between stimuli and reinforcers, other than pairing, which allow a stimulus to mimic some of the characteristics of the reinforcer. But this should not be taken to diminish the importance of pairing. In second-order schedules where other time parameters are variable, pairing may be critical (de Lorge 1971) and there is no doubt that pairing with

135

important stimuli is a very rapid way to change stimulus values for children (e.g. Parker and Rugel 1973; Nunnally, Stevens and Hall 1965).

GENERAL CONCLUSIONS

In the first section some doubt was thrown on the predictability of the results of applying a reliable reinforcer to an arbitrary response. In the next section it may seem as though the tenor of the discussion throws additional doubt on the possibility of finding a reliable reinforcer in the first place, especially in the context of the well-attested heterogeneity of biological and behavioural deficiencies in the severely retarded (Penrose 1963; Hilliard and Kirman 1965). A more optimistic view is that the theoretical basis of behaviour modification can only be strengthened, and its practical resources widened, if limiting factors, complex nature–nurture interactions, and special cases are all taken into account. One of the many virtues of operant methodology is that it is particularly well suited to allowing for individual differences in rate of learning, sensitivity to reinforcement, or response and stimulus preferences.

Further, it does not seem necessary to regard any attempts at categorization as foredoomed. Whether or not Ferster was right in attributing the autistic syndrome to environmental misadventures (cf. White 1974) his approach would lend itself to studies of the kinds of reinforcers that do or do not work with autistic children, and what kinds of cues or responses are most compatible with the reinforcers. Different sets of recommendations might be feasible for other large diagnostic areas, such as Down's syndrome. It has been suggested that autistic children are especially responsive to sounds (Hermelin and O'Connor 1968) and that Down's syndrome may include lack of visual preferences from an early age (Miranda and Fantz 1973). Naturally, differences between individuals would have to have first priority whatever more general guidelines might be possible.

But the discovery of the importance of species differences in operant paradigms in the animal laboratory and the continuing extension of basic knowledge about the physiological variables involved in reinforcement make it difficult to support the strategy of ignoring the possibility of interactions between biological factors and behavioural processes (Bijou 1963). Moreover, in purely behavioural terms, it appears that it is difficult to isolate a single behavioural process of reinforcement from the overall experience and constitutional predilections of an experimental animal. Further investigation of apparently capricious behaviour changes and spasmodic variations in reinforcer effectiveness might therefore be worthwhile in the real world of behaviour modification.

REFERENCES

ALLYON, T. and AZRIN, N.H. (1968) *The Token Economy*. Appleton-Century-Crofts, New York

AZRIN N.H. and HOLZ, W.C. (1966) Punishment. In *Operant Behavior: Areas of Research and Application* (Honig, W.K., ed.), pp. 380–447. Appleton-Century-Crofts, New York

AZRIN N.H., HUTCHINSON, R.R. and HAKE, D.F. (1966) Extinction-induced aggression. *J. Exp. Anal. Behav.* 9, 191–204

AZRIN, N.H., HUTCHINSON, R.R. and McLAUGHLIN, R. (1965) The opportunity for aggression as an operant reinforcer during aversive stimulation. *J. Exp. Anal. Behav.* 8, 171–180

BEISSEL, G.F. (1972) Autoshaping of lever pressing in mental retardates. Unpublished doctoral dissertation, University of Mississippi

BEST, P.J., BEST, M.R. and MICKLEY, G.A. (1973) Conditioned aversion to distinct environmental stimuli resulting from gastrointestinal distress. *J. Comp. Physiol. Psychol.* 85, 250–257

BIJOU, S.W. (1963) Theory and research in mental (developmental) retardation. *Psychol. Rec.* 13, 95–110

BINDRA, D. (1968) Neuropsychological interpretation of the effects of drive and incentive-motivation on general activity and instrumental behavior. *Psychol. Rev.* 75, 1–22

BINDRA, D. (1974) A motivational view of learning, performance, and behavior modification. *Psychol. Rev.* 81, 199–213

BIRCH, H.G. (1945) The relation of previous experience to problem solving. *J. Physiol. Comp. Psychol.* 38, 367–383

BOLLES, R.C. (1969) Avoidance and escape learning: simultaneous acquisition of different responses. *J. Comp. Physiol. Psychol.* 68, 355–358

BOLLES, R.C. (1970) Species-specific defense responses and avoidance learning. *Psychol. Rev.* 77, 32–48

BOOTH, D.A. and SIMSON, P.C. (1971) Food preferences acquired by association with variations in amino acid nutrition. *Quart. J. Exp. Psychol.* 23, 135–145

BREGER, L. and McGAUGH, J.L. (1965) Critique and reformulation of 'learning-theory' approaches to psychotherapy and neurosis. *Psychol. Bull.* 63, 338–358

BRENER, J.M. and GOESLING, W.J. (1970) Avoidance conditioning of activity and immobility in rats. *J. Comp. Physiol. Psychol.* 70, 276–280

BROWN, J.S. (1969) in *Punishment and Aversive Behavior* (Campbell, B.A. and Church. R.M., eds.), pp. 467–514. Appleton-Century-Crofts, New York. *The Century Psychology* series

BROWN, P.L. and JENKINS, H.M. (1968) Auto-shaping of the pigeon's key-peck. *J. Exp. Anal. Behav.* 11, 1–8

CAGGIULA, A.R. (1970) Analysis of the copulation-reward properties of posterior hypothalamic stimulation in male rats. *J. Comp. Physiol. Psychol.* 70, 399–412

GAGGIULA, A.R. and EIBERGEN, R. (1969) Copulation of virgin male rats evoked by painful peripheral stimulation. *J. Comp. Physiol. Psychol.* 69, 414–419

CAMPBELL, B.A. and CHURCH, R.M. (1969) *Punishment and Aversive Behavior*. Appleton-Century-Crofts, New York

CLARIDGE, G.S. and O'CONNOR, N. (1957) The relation between incentive, personality type and improvement in the performance of imbeciles. *J. Ment. Defic. Res.* 1, 16–25

CLARKE, A.D.B. (1965) In *Mental Deficiency*, 2nd. ed. (Clarke, A.M. and Clarke, A.D.B., eds.), pp. 92–137. Methuen, London

CLARKE, A.D.B. and BLAKEMORE, C.D. (1961) Age and perceptual-motor transfer in imbeciles. *Br. J. Psychol.* 52, 125–131

CLARKE, A.D.B. and CLARKE, A.M. (1965) In *Mental Deficiency*, 2nd ed. (Clarke, A.M. and Clarke, A.D.B., eds.), pp. 356–384. Methuen, London

CLARKE, A.D.B. and COOKSON, M. (1962) Perceptual-motor transfer in imbeciles: a second series of experiments. *Br. J. Psychol.* 53, 321–330

CLIFFE, M.J., GATHERCOLE, C. and EPLING, W.F. (1974) Some implications of the experimental analysis of behaviour for behaviour modification. *Bull. Br. Psychol. Soc.* 27, 390–397

COPPOCK, A.W. and CHAMBERS, R.M. (1954) Reinforcement of positive position preference by automatic injection of glucose. *J. Comp. Physiol. Psychol.* 47, 355–358

CRESPI, L.P. (1942) Quantitative variation of incentive and performance in the white rat. *Amer. J. Psychol.* 55, 467–517

DAVIS, H., HIRSCHORN, P. and HURWITZ, H.M. (1973) Lever holding behaviour during a leverlift shock escape procedure. *Anim. Learn. Behav.* 1, 215–218

DE LORGE, J. (1971) The effects of brief stimuli presented under a multiple schedule of second-order schedules. *J. Exp. Anal. Behav.* 15, 19–25

DEVENPORT, L.D. and BALAGURA, S. (1971) Lateral hypothalamus: re-evaluation of function in food motivated behavior. *Science, 172*, 744–746

DINSMOOR, J.A. (1950) A quantitative comparison of the discriminative and reinforcing functions of a stimulus. *J. Exp. Psychol. 40*, 458–472

DOWNEY, P. and HARRISON, J.M. (1972) Control of responding by location of auditory stimuli: role of differential and non-differential reinforcement. *J. Exp. Anal. Behav., 18*, 453–463

EGGER, M.D. and MILLER, N.E. (1926) Secondary reinforcement in rats as a function of information value and reliability of the stimulus. *J. Exp. Psychol. 64*, 97–104

ESTES, W.K. and SKINNER, B.F. (1941) Some quantitative properties of anxiety. *J. Exp. Psychol. 29*, 390–400

FALK, J.L. (1961) Production of polydipsia in normal rats by an intermittent food schedule. *Science, 133*, 195–196

FALK, J.L. (1966) The motivational properties of schedule-induced polydipsia. *J. Exp. Anal. Behav. 9*, 19–25

FALK, J.L. (1972) In *Schedule Effects: Drugs, Drinking and Aggression*. (Gilbert, R. and Keehn, J.D., eds), pp. 148–173. University of Toronto Press, Toronto

FERSTER, C.B. (1961) Positive reinforcement and behavioral deficits of autistic children. *Child Develop. 32*, 437–456

FERSTER, C.B. and SKINNER, B.F. (1957) *Schedules of Reinforcement*. Appleton-Century-Crofts, New York.

FINDLEY, J.D. and BRADY, J.V. (1965) Facilitation of large ratio performance by use of conditioned reinforcement. *J. Exp. Anal. Behav. 8*, 125–129

FITTS, P.M. and BIEDERMAN, I. (1965) S-R compatibility and information reduction. *J. Exp. Psychol. 69*, 408–412

GARCIA, J., ERVIN, F.R. and KOELLING, R.A. (1966) Learning with prolonged delay of reinforcement. *Psychonom. Sci. 5*, 121–122

GARCIA, J., ERVIN, F.R., YORKE, C.H. and KOELLING, R.A. (1967) Conditioning with delayed vitamin injection. *Science, 155*, 716–718

GARCIA, J. and KOELLING, R.A. (1966) Relation of cue to consequence in avoidance learning. *Psychonom. Sci. 4*, 123–124

GARCIA, J., McGOWAN, B.K. and GREEN, K.F. (1972) In *Biological Boundaries of Learning* (Seligman, M.E.P. and Hager, J.L., eds.). Appleton-Century-Crofts, New York

GARDNER, W.M. (1969) Auto-shaping in bobwhite quail. *J. Exp. Anal. Behav. 12*, 279–281

GILBERT, R. and KEEHN, J.D. (eds.) (1972) *Schedule Effects: Drugs, Drinking and Aggression*. University of Toronto Press, Toronto

GLICKMAN, S.E. and SCHIFF, B.B. (1967) A biological theory of reinforcement. *Psychol. Rev. 74*, 81–109

GUTHRIE, E.R. (1934) Reward and punishment. *Psychol. Rev. 41*, 450–460

HALL, R.V. and BRODEN, M. (1967) Behavior changes in brain-injured children through social reinforcement. *J. Exp. Child Psychol. 5*, 463–479

HARLOW, H.F. (1949) The formation of learning sets. *Psychol. Rev. 56*, 51–65

HARLOW, H.F., BLAZEK, N.C. and McCLEARN, G.E. (1956) Manipulative motivation in the infant rhesus monkey. *J. Comp. Physiol. Psychol. 49*, 444–448

HAWKINS, J.D., SCHROT, J.F., GITHENS, S.H. and EVERETT, D.H. (1972) in *Schedule Effects: Drugs, Drinking and Aggression* (Gilbert, R. and Keehn, J.D., eds.), pp. 95–128. University of Toronto Press, Toronto

HEMMES, N.S. (1973) Behavioral contrast in pigeons depends upon the operant. *J. Comp. Physiol. Psychol. 85*, 171–178

HERMELIN, B. and O'CONNOR, N. (1968) Measures of occipital alpha rhythm in normal, subnormal and autistic children. *Brit. J. Psychiatr. 114*, 603–610

HERRNSTEIN, R.J. (1970) On the law of effect. *J. Exp. Anal. Behav. 13*, 243–266

HERRNSTEIN, R.J. (1971) Quantitative hedonism. *J. Psychiat. Res. 8*, 399–412

HERRNSTEIN, R.J. and LOVELAND, D.H. (1972) Food-avoidance in hungry pigeons, and other perplexities. *J. Exp. Anal. Behav. 18*, 369–383

HILLIARD, L.T. and KIRMAN, B.H. (1965) *Mental Deficiency*, 2nd ed. Churchill, London

138

HINDE, R.A. and STEVENSON-HINDE, J. (eds.) (1973) *Constraints on Learning*. Academic Press, New York

HOLMAN, G.L. (1969) The intragastric reinforcement effect. *J. Comp. Physiol. Psychol. 69*, 432–441

HULL, C.L. (1943) *Principles of Behavior*. Appleton-Century-Crofts, New York

HULL, C.L. (1952) *A Behavior System*. Yale University Press, New Haven

HURWITZ, H.M.B., WALKER, S.F., SALMON, E.A. and PACKHAM, D. (1965) The effects of two sucrose solutions on rate of response under a fixed ratio schedule. *Psychol. Rec. 15*, 145–150

JENKINS, H.M. (1973) In *Constraints on Learning* (Hinde, R.A. and Stevenson-Hinde, J., eds.), pp. 189–206. Academic Press, New York

KANTOR, J.R. (1959) *Interbehavioral Psychology*, 2nd ed. Principia Press, Bloomington, Indiana

KELLEHER, R.T. (1966) Conditioned reinforcement in second-order schedules. *J. Exp. Anal. Behav. 9*, 475–485

KELLEHER, R.T. and GOLLUB, L.R. (1962) A review of positive conditioned reinforcement. *J. Exp. Anal. Behav. 5*, 543–597

KELLER, K. (1974) The role of elicited responding in behavioral contrast. *J. Exp. Anal. Behav. 21*, 249–257

KIERNAN, C.C. (1969) *Reward Facilitation and Arousal in Light Onset Reinforcement*. Unpublished Ph.D. thesis, University of London

KIMBLE, G.A. (ed.) (1967) *Foundations of Conditioning and Learning*. Appleton-Century-Crofts, New York

LATIES, V.G., WEISS, B., CLARK, R.L. and REYNOLDS, M.D. (1965) Overt 'mediating' behavior during temporally spaced responding. *J. Exp. Anal. Behav. 8*, 107–116

LEFF, R. (1968) Behavior modification and the psychoses of childhood. *Psychol. Bull. 69*, 396–409

LEVITSKY, D. and COLLIER, G. (1968) Schedule-induced wheel running. *Physiol. and Behav. 3*, 571–573

LOCKARD, R.B. (1963) Some effects of light on the behaviour of rodents. *Psychol. Bull. 60*, 509–529

LOGAN, F.A. (1969) In *Punishment and Aversive Behaviour* (Campbell, B.A. and Church, R.M., eds.), pp. 43–54. Appleton-Century-Crofts, New York

LO LORDO, V.M., MCMILLAN, J.C. and RILEY, A.L. (1974) The effects on food-reinforced pecking and treadle pressing of auditory and visual signals for response independent food. *Learning and Motivation, 5*, 24–41

LOVAAS, O.I., SCHAEFFER, B. and SIMMONS, J.Q. (1965) Building social behavior in autistic children by use of electric shock. *J. Exp. Res. Pers. 1*, 99–109

LOVAAS, O.I. and SIMMONS, J.Q. (1969) Manipulation of self-destruction in three retarded children. *J. Applied Behav. Anal. 2*, 143–157

MCCORMICK, E.J. (1970) *Human Factors Engineering*, 3rd ed. McGraw-Hill, New York

MAIER, S.F., SELIGMAN, M.E.P. and SOLOMON, R.L. (1969) In *Punishment and Aversive Behavior* (Campbell, B.A. and Church, R.M., eds.), pp. 299–342. Appleton-Century-Crofts, New York

MELVIN, K.B. and SMITH, F.H. (1967) Self-punitive avoidance behavior in the rat. *J. Comp. Physiol. Psychol. 63*, 533–535

MENDELSON, J. and CHILLAG, D. (1970) Schedule-induced air licking in rats. *Physiol. and Behav. 5*, 535–537

MEYER, D.R., CHO, C. and WESEMANN, A.F. (1960) On problems of conditioning discriminated lever-press avoidance responses. *Psychol. Rev. 67*, 224–228

MIGLER, B. (1963) Experimental self-punishment and superstitious escape behaviour. *J. Exp. Anal. Behav. 6*, 371–386

MILLER, N.E. and KESSEN, M.L. (1952) Reward effects of food via stomach fistula compared with those of food via mouth. *J. Comp. Physiol. Psychol. 45*, 555–564

MIRANDA, S.B. and FANTZ, R.L. (1973) Visual preferences of Down's syndrome and normal infants. *Child Devel. 44*, 555–561

Moore, R.R. (1973) In *Constraints on Learning* (Hinde, R.A. and Stevenson-Hinde, J., eds), pp.159–188. Academic Press, New York

Mowrer, O.H. (1960) *Learning Theory and Behavior.* Wiley, New York

Neuringer, A.J. and Chung, S.H. (1967) Quasi-reinforcement: control of responding by a percentage-reinforcement schedule. *J. Exp. Anal. Behav. 10,* 45–54

Nisbett, R.E. (1972) Hunger, obesity and the ventromedial hypothalamus. *Psychol. Rev. 79,* 433–453

Nunally, J.C., Stevens, D.A. and Hall, G.F. (1965) Association of neutral objects with rewards: effect on verbal evaluation and eye movements. *J. Exp. Child Psychol. 2,* 44–57

O'Brien, F. (1968) Sequential contrast effects with human subjects. *J. Exp. Anal. Behav. 11,* 537–542

O'Leary, K.D. and Drabman, R.S. (1971) Token reinforcement programs in the classroom. *Psychol. Bull. 75,* 379–398

Panksepp, J. and Trowill, J.A. (1970) Positive incentive contrast with rewarding electrical stimulation of the brain. *J. Comp. Physiol. Psychol. 70,* 358–365

Panksepp, J. and Trowill, J.A. (1971) Positive and negative contrast in licking with shifts in sucrose concentration as a function of food deprivation. *Learning and Motivation, 2,* 49–57

Parker, R.K. and Rugel, R.P. (1973) The conditioning and reversal of reward value. *Child Devel. 44,* 666–669

Pavlov, I.P. (1927) *Conditioned Reflexes.* Dover, New York

Penrose, L.S. (1963) *The Biology of Mental Defect,* 3rd ed. Sidgwick and Jackson, London

Powell, R.W., Saunders, D. and Thompson, W. (1968) Shaping, auto-shaping and observational learning with rats. *Psychon. Sci. 13,* 167–168

Premack, D. (1965) In *Nebraska Symposium on Motivation, 1965* (Jones, M.R. ed.), pp. 123–180. University of Nebraska Press, Lincoln

Rachlin, H. and Herrnstein, R.J. (1969) In *Punishment and Aversive Behaviour* (Campbell, B.A. and Church, R.M., eds.), pp. 83–109. Appleton-Century-Crofts, New York

Rachlin, H. and Hineline, P.N. (1967) Training and maintenance of key pecking in the pigeon by negative reinforcement. *Science, 157,* 954–955

Redford, M.E. and Perkins, C.L. (1974) The role of autopecking in behavioral contrast. *J. Exp. Anal. Behav. 21,* 145–150

Reynolds, G.S. (1961) Behavioral contrast. *J. Exp. Anal. Behav. 4,* 57–71

Reynolds, G.S. (1963) Some limitations on behavioral contrast and induction during successive discrimination. *J. Exp. Anal. Behav. 6,* 131–140

Revuksy, S.H. (1968) Aversion to sucrose produced by contingent X-irradiation: temporal and dosage parameters. *J. Comp. Physiol. Psychol. 65,* 17–22

Roberts, W.W. and Kiess, H.O. (1964) Motivational properties of hypothalamic aggression in cats. *J. Comp. Physiol. Psychol. 58,* 187–193

Rozin, P. and Kalat, J.W. (1971) Specific hungers and poison avoidance as adaptive specializations of learning. *Psychiol. Rev. 78,* 459–486

Segal, E.F. (1972) In *Reinforcement* (Gilbert, R.M. and Millenson, J.R., eds.), pp. 1–34. Academic Press, New York

Seligman, M.E.P. (1970) On the generality of the laws of learning. *Psychol. Rev. 77,* 406–418

Seligman, M.E.P. and Hager, J.L. (eds.) (1972) *Biological Boundaries of Learning.* Appleton-Century-Crofts, New York

Seligman, M.E. and Maier, S.F. (1967) Failure to escape traumatic shock. *J. Exp. Psychol. 74,* 1–9

Shettleworth, S.J. (1973) In *Constraints on Learning* (Hinde, R.A. and Stevenson-Hinde, J., eds.), pp. 243–263. Academic Press, New York

Shulman, H.G. and McConkie, A. (1973) S-R compatibility, response discrimination and response codes in choice reaction time. *J. Exp. Psychol. 98,* 375–378

Sidman, M. and Fletcher, F.G. (1968) A demonstration of auto-shaping with monkeys. *J. Exp. Anal. Behav. 11,* 307–309

Skinner, B.F. (1938) *The Behaviour of Organisms.* Appleton-Century-Crofts, New York

SKINNER, B.F. (1953) *Science and Human Behavior*. MacMillan, New York

SKINNER, B.F. (1972) *Beyond Freedom and Dignity*. Cape, London

SMITH, S.G. and SMITH, W.M. (1972) Auto-shaping: a three-manipulanda technique for dogs. *Psychol. Rec. 22*, 377–380

SPENCE, K.W. (1956) *Behaviour Theory and Conditioning*. Yale University Press, New Haven

SQUIER, L.H. (1969) Autoshaping key responses with fish. *Psychon. Sci. 17*, 177–178

STAATS, A.W. (1968) *Learning, Language, and Cognition*. Holt, Rinehart and Winston, New York

STEVENSON-HINDE, J. (1973) In *Constraints on Learning* (Hinde, R.A. and Stevenson-Hinde, J., eds.), pp. 285–296. Academic Press, New York

STUBBS, D.A. (1971) Second-order schedules and the problem of conditioned reinforcement *J. Exp. Anal. behav. 16*, 289–293

STUBBS, D.A. and COHEN, S.L. (1972) Second-order schedules: comparison of different procedures for scheduling paired and non-paired stimuli. *J. Exp. Anal. Behav. 18*, 403–413

TEITELBAUM, P. and EPSTEIN, A.N. (1962) The lateral hypothalamus syndrome. *Psychol. Rev. 69*, 74–90

ULRICH, R.E. and CRAINE, W.H. (1964) Behavior: persistence of shock-induced aggression. *Science, 143*, 971–973

ULRICH, R., STACHNIK, T. and MABRY, J. (eds.) (1970) *Control of Human Behavior*, Vol. II. Scott, Foresman, Glenview, Ill.

ULRICH, R.E., WOLFF, P.C. and AZRIN, N.H. (1964) Shock as an elicitor of intra- and interspecies fighting behavior. *Anim. Behav. 12*, 14–15

VALENSTEIN, E.S., COX, V.C. and RATOLEWSKI, J.W. (1970) Re-examination of the role of the hypothalamus in motivation. *Psychol. Rev. 77*, 16–31

VERPLANCK, W.S. and HAYES, J.R. (1953) Eating and drinking as a function of maintenance schedule. *J. Comp. physiol. Psychol. 46*, 327–333

WALKER, S.F. (1969) *Parameters of Conditioned Incentive in the Control of Operant Behaviour*. Unpublished PhD thesis, University of London

WALKER, S.F. and HURWITZ, H.M.B. (1971) Effects of relative reinforcer duration on concurrent response rates. *Psychon. Sci. 22*, 45–47

WAMPLER, R.S. (1973) Increased motivation in rats with ventromedial hypothalamic lesions. *J. Comp. physiol. Psychol. 84*, 275–285

WATSON, J.B. (1928) *The Ways of Behaviorism*. Harper, New York

WATSON, J.B. (1930) *Behaviorism*. University of Chicago Press, Chicago

WESTBROOK, R.F. (1973) Failure to obtain positive contrast when pigeons press a bar. *J. Exp. Anal. Behav. 20*, 499–510

WHITE, L. (1974) Organic factors and psychophysiology in childhood schizophrenia. *Psychol. Bull. 81*, 238–255

WILCOXON, H.C., DRAGOIN, W.B. and KRAL, P.A. (1971) Illness-induced aversions in rat and quail: relative salience of visual and gustatory cues. *Science, 171*, 826–828

WILLIAMS, D.R. and WILLIAMS, H. (1969) Auto-maintenance in the pigeon: sustained pecking despite contingent non-reinforcement. *J. Exp. Anal. Behav., 12*, 511–520

YATES, A.J. (1970) *Behavior Therapy*. Wiley, New York

ZAHORIK, D.M. and MAIER, S.F. (1969) Appetitive conditioning with recovery from thiamine deficiency as the unconditioned stimulus. *Psychon. Sci. 17*, 309–310

ZIMMERMAN, D.W. (1957) Durable secondary reinforcement: method and theory. *Psychol. Rev. 64*, 373–383

ZIMMERMAN, J. (1969) In *Conditioned Reinforcement* (Hendry, D.P., ed.), pp. 91–124. Dorsey Press, Homewood, Ill.

Discussion

Walker: It is an interesting idea (p. 101) that one might have a two-way interaction between animal and human work. Things now being done in behaviour modification

141

in humans may well make this possible: it is rather easier to investigate operant effects on cognitive function in people than in animals, and this may well allow one to generalize back to the latter for more detailed work on mechanisms. The work done by the Gardners on language and cognition in chimpanzees (Gardner and Gardner 1971) has certainly been *implicitly* influenced by operant analysis of human cognition. The way in which animal experiments ought to yield results helpful in clinical work is with the problem of the development of reinforcers. Work on this problem has been held back by the thought that because reinforcement is the basic tool in behaviour modification we must assume that it's all right. But everything suggests that in the severely retarded the normal mechanisms of reinforcement are just what are not all right. Any work that could be done, either in the laboratory or directly with the retarded, towards methods of getting new reinforcers to work by behavioural or non-behavioural methods (e.g. the use of drugs) would be most valuable.

Hogg: Would either Chris Kiernan or Steve Walker like to elaborate a bit on this two-way interaction, which sounds all very well in principle but remains for me quite abstract? How could the animal work enable us to decide, for example, what are the basic psychological processes we're interested in? I feel we need in all our work more of a theoretical framework which would help us to specify problem areas to work in.

Walker: My guess would be that animal work to strengthen attention theory and to investigate what are the intellectual abilities involved in attention and in cognitive functioning with respect to object permanence would be fruitful.

Kiernan: For me, the value of new developments in animal work is that they demonstrate experimental rigour, which we can all do with periodic doses of, and stimulate my imagination when I'm getting bogged down in endless variations of procedure. It is also good to be reminded by new animal work just how provisional some of our procedures are. For instance, we all tend to say that we know how to establish conditioned reinforcement, by pairing primary reinforcers with social behaviour and so on, with far greater assurance than would those who are actually doing specialized animal work in that field. Collaboration between workers in the animal and human fields would surely be constructive here.

As for specifying problem areas, I suggest that self-destructive behaviour may be ripe for solution. Although it's a tough problem, there is at least a wealth of hypotheses as to the cause (or causes) which can be worked on.

Corbett: The difficulty about that is that there are no good animal models for it, or at least none that will be useful to the clinician and tell him whether aversion therapy is likely to work, for example.

C. Williams: Isn't that because the animal experimentalists have been concerned with determining the settings in which self-injury will develop, whereas we want to know what the conditions are under which self-destructive behaviour will decrease? Even if I had the luxury of being able to wait until someone arrived at a theory of the aetiology of self-destruction, this wouldn't help me with my practical problem. The models for aetiology and extinction are just not the same.

Harzem: Which is not to say that it will not be useful in the future to know something about the aetiology, of course.

What seems to me a more obvious lack is work on the operant responding of normal children. We seem to want to go straight from the behaviour of (presumably normal) rats and pigeons to the behaviour of retarded children or adults. The literature on the behaviour of normal children on, say, standard schedules of reinforcement is quite astoundingly impoverished.

Mittler: There is a lot of published work on neonates which is very productive and

142

has not yet been applied systematically to profoundly handicapped subjects, who are after all operating at or near the neonatal level. There's enormous potential here: look at the work done in the last 10 years by people in the general Lipsitt tradition (see *Annual Reviews of Psychology*, especially 1972).

Harzem: I agree, but neonates are the only normal human subjects I can think of with whom this work has been done. There is nothing on the operant behaviour of older children, with the exception of the work of Long (Long *et al.* 1958; Long 1962, 1963), which people always quote, as there is nothing else.

Hogg: The trouble with that work is that it was informed entirely by Ferster and Skinner (1957). There isn't much justification for investing a lot of time in work of that kind on fixed-interval schedules with human subjects unless it is in the service of some theoretical concept—for instance, investigating theories of how people make temporal discriminations.

Harzem: What I'm saying is that even though that work wasn't very good, it is all there is. What we should be doing is not to replicate with human subjects the work of Ferster and Skinner using the same schedules, but to do with humans the kind of things Ferster and Skinner set out to do with animals and do it better, as far as possible. I think we would arrive at different conclusions from theirs.

Kushlick: Shouldn't one aim to choose animal problems which will throw light on the kind of human problems that seem insoluble in the natural human environment?

Walker: I don't think so, really: as John Corbett says, good animal models for the human condition are hard to find. I don't think we should worry that animal and human work is not neatly integrated, but just be thankful that so much more has proved transferable than might have been predicted.

Kushlick: It would have been helpful to me to work in surroundings where I could have learned techniques from someone in a nearby laboratory instead of having to pick up what I could just from reading.

Walker: Admittedly, methodology is important. And again, we probably haven't seen nearly the end of the applied implications of the work with Washoe the chimpanzee and Premack's work with primates and dogs (Premack 1972). Finally, much investigation of brain physiology can be done only with animals. Examples of valuable work of this kind are the rehabilitation of animals with certain kinds of brain damage and the correlation of hippocampal lesions with attentional deficit. From the latter work has come the discovery of lots of ways to overcome over-persistence in a hippocampal-lesion animal which should prove illuminating with at least some kinds of autistic subject.

REFERENCES

FERSTER C.B. and SKINNER, B.F. (1957) *Schedules of Reinforcement.* Appleton-Century-Crofts, New York

GARDNER, B.T. and GARDNER, R.A. (1971) Two-way communication with an infant chimpanzee. In *Behavior of Non-human Primates* Vol. 4 (Schrier, A.M. and Stollnitz, F., eds.), pp. 117–184. Academic Press, New York

LONG, E.R. (1962) Additional techniques for producing multiple-schedule control in children. *J. Exp. Anal. Behav.* 5, 443–456

LONG, E.R. (1963) Chained and tandem scheduling in children. *J. Exp. Anal. Behav.* 6, 459–472

LONG, E.R., HAMMACK, J.T., MAY, F. and CAMPBELL, B.J. (1958) Intermittent reinforcement of operant behaviour in children. *J. Exp. Anal. Behav.* 1, 315–339

PREMACK, D. (1972) Two problems in cognition: symbolization, and from icon to phoneme. In *Communication and Affect* (Alloway, T., Krames, L. and Pliner, P., eds.), pp. 51–56. Academic Press, New York

143

II Applications

The contributions in this section discuss existing behaviour modification programmes in various surroundings from home to subnormality hospital.

Two central questions arise in applications in particular settings. First, how suitable is the setting to carry the educational or therapeutic model? A behavioural approach assumed that all antecedents and consequences are potentially powerful in maintaining or changing behaviour. At first sight, therefore, a 'professional' framework allowing 24-hours-a-day monitoring and control appears optimal. In practice, the second question emerges sharply. How adequate is the professional framework provided by a hospital or institution: are there enough adequately-trained staff, and can communication be optimized, or do the institutional requirements dictate the form of the programme, against the best interests of the handicapped?

In the following contributions these factors emerge in various forms and various solutions are implied or suggested. The optimal pattern of health or social service is likely to differ from region to region depending on resources and population. We hope that these discussions open up issues which clarify and make the point that no one system is necessarily optimal. We should also note that the papers tend to emphasize what each contributor feels to be the weaknesses rather than the strengths of some programmes applied in particular contexts.

Behaviour Modification Programmes in a Community Setting

MARIA CALLIAS and JANET CARR

Department of Psychology, Institute of Psychiatry (University of London)

ABSTRACT

This paper presents a review of some aspects of the work done by psychologists at Hilda Lewis House, Croydon, Surrey (England) during 2½ years (1971–1974). Behaviour modification programmes were carried out by psychologists alone, or in conjunction with other professionals, in the children's homes and schools, and in some cases in hostels and institutions. The data are analysed according to characteristics of the child and of the family, the number and type of problems tackled, techniques taught, and success rate achieved. Factors relating to the success or failure of intervention are examined. Since these data are derived from records of clinical work and not from a systematic research project, this raises problems of homogeneity and of evaluation.

Significant findings to emerge included a positive correlation between: success on acceleration targets and intellectual level, good hand function and comprehension level of the child; success on deceleration targets and mobility of the child, marital harmony and small family size; success on both acceleration and deceleration targets and numbers and length of contacts with the family.

Ways to develop this work, in particular the use of group training methods, are discussed. Also examined are criteria for evaluating both training and intervention, and how both could be improved and extended; how long contacts should continue and how they may be concluded; and whether special methods can be developed to supply the needs of different families and situations.

This paper presents a review of work with parents and teachers of severely mentally handicapped children, carried out in a community setting and with the emphasis on behaviour modification methods. The work was not planned as a research project, but individual cases were taken on as problems arose in the course of our clinical work at Hilda Lewis House. We felt it would be worth while to examine and evaluate the work that had been done so far, partly in order to see whether there might be in its disordered depths any answers to the questions that are constantly presenting themselves; and partly to give ourselves a more rational basis on which to structure future work.

The study we are describing arose from our work as clinical psychologists at

Hilda Lewis House, a small 24-bedded in-patient unit for the assessment and treatment of severely subnormal children with additional handicaps. Hilda Lewis House forms part of the Bethlem Royal and Maudsley Hospitals, and like them has special responsibility for the District of Camberwell: three-quarters of the children accepted for in-patient treatment come from Camberwell. Children up to the age of 16 are seen, and all have problems in addition to severe mental retardation, such as epilepsy, cerebral palsy, visual or auditory difficulties, or behavioural problems.

Children may be seen first at an out-patient clinic or on a domiciliary visit for assessment, and this may be followed by various kinds of contact between the child and the unit. He may be admitted as an in-patient, and after discharge followed up at home and at school: he may attend the unit daily, or as an out-patient: or he may not attend the Unit at all, being seen and treated at home or at school or both.

The unit is generously staffed, with doctors, occupational therapists, nurses, teachers, social workers and psychologists. While the child is an in-patient the members of the different professions work as a team on the child's problems. It has always been a part of the Unit policy to involve and inform the parents as much as possible. Early in 1971, we began as part of our clinical work to see the children in their own homes, not in order to treat them there ourselves but in order to help the families to devise and carry out programmes that would help them in the training and management of their children. At the same time we visited schools that the children attended, or in a few cases hostels and institutions, to help with setting up programmes there.

In this paper we have reviewed all the cases in which psychologists have been concerned in working with families and involving them in the child's treatment. We have not included cases in which families have been visited only to gain information, or to give social work support, nor those who were given help by doctors, nurses, teachers, social workers or occupational therapists working on their own (because of the difficulty of collecting the relevant information), although we have included many cases in which we worked with a family in conjunction with a member of one of these disciplines.

All the data we present are retrospective, drawn from our reports written at the time of the interviews. Many of the data are derived from ratings made by ourselves on our own cases, on topics ranging from the quality of a marital relationship to the success of treatment. Inevitably the quality of the data is affected by the fact that they are retrospective and subjective, and our findings can be regarded as only a crude assessment of our work and of the usefulness of the approach. Nevertheless we have found this review an instructive, albeit a chastening, exercise and one which has raised issues which we feel should be examined systematically.

DESCRIPTION OF THE SAMPLE

The sample consists of 37 children, 33 of whom were living at home. 43% were Camberwell children; this rather low proportion is due to the fact that one

TABLE 1

Social class of families

		Social class*				
		I and II	III NM	III M	IV	V
Population						
Total group	No.	9	3	14	6	4
(n = 36)	%	25	8	39	17	11
				47		
Camberwell only	No.	3	7		3	3
(n = 16)	%	19	44		19	19
Camberwell census	%	10	59.7		17.3	13
for 1961						

* n = 36; 1, not known

of us (MC) saw children at an out-patient clinic of whom many (because they were non-Camberwell) were unlikely to be admitted as in-patients to Hilda Lewis House in the near future and for whom family help offered the best chance of treatment. Social class distribution of the whole group of families, and of the families from Camberwell, is shown in Table 1 together with the distribution for the borough of Camberwell (1961 Census). Table 1 shows that both the whole group of families and the Camberwell sub-group were fairly similar in social class composition to that of the borough of Camberwell, but with a higher proportion of class I and II families.

13% of the families were judged to be living in poor housing conditions, while the rest were in good or adequate housing. In 18% of the cases the house had been damaged by the child.

Marital relationships were assessed as between the couple at present in the home: i.e. if the mother had separated from the child's father and re-married, the state of the present couple, and hence presumably of the atmosphere of the household now, was assessed. In 36% of the families there was some discord, severe in 27% of the whole group.

Mental health of the parents was rated on a 3-point scale from psychiatric or social work reports. A rating of 1 indicated no known psychiatric disturbance; 2, mild symptoms (present or past); 3, severe neurotic (usually depressive) or psychotic disorders. Eighteen, or nearly half the sample of families, had some degree of mental disturbance in at least one parent (usually the mother), and this was severe in 4 families.

Just over half the children (19) had been in-patients at Hilda Lewis House at some time, and 7 parents of these 19 had attended the Unit to work with their children. There were 27 boys and 10 girls in the sample, a proportion of nearly 3 to 1, compared with 2:1 found in the whole population of retarded children in Camberwell (Corbett 1973). Half the children were in the 5–10 age range while a fifth were under 5 years old (Table 2). All the children had been tested (on the

149

TABLE 2

Age distribution of children

	under 5 yrs	5 to 10 yrs	11 to 15 yrs	Total
Number	7	18	12	37
%	19	49	32	100

TABLE 3

WHO classification of intelligence

	Category						Total
	1	2	3	4	5	6	
Number	1	1	4	11	14	6	37
%	3	3	11	30	37	16	100

TABLE 4

Physical and sensory handicaps of children

	Adequate		Some handicap	
	No.	%	No.	%
Physical handicap				
Walking	32	86	5	14
Manual skill	27	73	10	27
Sensory handicap				
Vision	30	81	7*	19
Hearing	28	76	9**	24

* includes one child with severe visual handicap
**includes 3 children with no useful hearing
14 children had a variety of other physical handicaps, including 7 with epilepsy.

Bayley, Merrill-Palmer, WISC or Griffiths scales); mental age at the most recent test was converted into a ratio IQ and the children were graded according to the WHO classificatory system. Two-thirds of the children fell into the moderately or severely retarded category, while one-sixth were profoundly retarded (Table 3).

30% of the children were independent or required only a little help with feeding, washing, dressing and toileting; 19% required considerable help; 46% needed much help with most of these activities.

Less than a fifth of the children in our sample had difficulty with walking or with vision (Table 4), but about a quarter had difficulty with controlling their hands or with hearing. The figures for walking and visual handicaps are somewhat lower, and for auditory handicaps rather higher, than those found in the whole population of retarded children in Camberwell (Corbett 1973).

150

TABLE 5

Behavioural handicaps

Problem	Children	
	Number	%
Aggression	11	15
Destructiveness	16	22
Disruptiveness	27	36
Self-injury/stereotypies, rituals	14	19
Miscellaneous, including phobias	6	8

TABLE 6

Number of behavioural handicaps per child

	No. of handicaps						Total
	0	1	2	3	4	5	
No. of children	1	11	11	10	3	1	37
% of children	3	30	30	27	8	3	100

TABLE 7

Comprehension and expressive language abilities of children

	Children	
	No.	%
Comprehension level		
0 No problem	6	15
1 above 2½ yr level	1	8
2 18–30 mths level	12	31
3 Simple commands and gestures	12	31
4 No understanding	6	15
Expressive level		
0 Sentences	5	14
1 Word combinations	7	19
2 Single words	4	11
3 Gestures and <10 words	8	22
4 No expressive ability	13	34

The largest number of behaviour problems fell into the disruptive category, which included tantrums, screaming, teasing and hyperactivity (Table 5). Over half the children had two or three behavioural problems, while one child had five (Table 6).

The children were assessed on a 5-point scale on their ability to comprehend and to use spoken language (results of psychometric tests were used where these had been given). About a sixth of the children did not comprehend language,

TABLE 8

Where parents and children were seen

	Home only	Home and School	Home, School and HLH	School or Institution only	HLH and Home	HLH only	Total
In-patients	8	3	2	2	4	–	19
Out-patients	5	3	3	4	1	2	18

and about a third had no expressive language (Table 7). These figures are very close to those found in Camberwell as a whole (Corbett 1973).

In most cases children and their parents were seen at home, but sometimes they attended Hilda Lewis House so that we could make use of the special facilities available or to permit teaching to take place in neutral surroundings. Some children were seen only at school (visits to children in institutions are included here), and some at home and at school (Table 8). Table 8 shows that most of the children (29/37) were seen at some time at home, while only about half that number (17) were seen at any time at school. The number of contacts was much higher in relation to homes than to schools and institutions (cf. Tables 18 and 19). Altogether, work with parents was a good deal more intensive than was work with schools, mainly because of the different needs of those in the different situations.

THE EFFECTS OF TREATMENT

In this section we have looked at the factors that might affect the outcome of treatment and have tried to relate them to outcome. The factors we have considered fall into four groups:

1. Factors deriving from the child: intellectual level (WHO category), physical and sensory problems, level of language comprehension.

2. Factors deriving from the family: social class, marital discord, mental health of parents, number of siblings.

3. Factors deriving from the nature of the problems tackled, their number and their severity.

4. Factors deriving from aspects of intervention: the number and duration of contacts, and techniques taught.

Each of these factors was separately, and sometimes in combination, related to the outcome of treatment. Outcome was considered separately for acceleration and deceleration targets, and for problems dealt with at home or at school.

Before we present the results it may be appropriate to describe the kinds of problems that were tackled. These came under two headings, acceleration, and deceleration targets.

Acceleration targets

54 problems were tackled at home and 31 at school, grouped under four headings (Table 9).

TABLE 9

Number and percentage of problems tackled at home and school

	Home		School		Total	
	No.	%	No.	%	No.	%
Acceleration problems						
1. Self-help	23	43	8	25	31	36
2. Occupation	11	20	9	28	20	23
3. Communication	11	20	8	25	19	22
4. Miscellaneous	9	17	7	22	16	19
Total	54	100	32	100	86	100
Deceleration problems						
1. Aggression	10	16	6	17	16	16
2. Destructiveness	14	23	9	25	23	24
3. Disruptiveness	25	41	16	44	41	43
4. Self-injury/rituals	8	13	4	11	12	12
5. Miscellaneous	4	7	1	3	5	5
Total	61	100	36	100	97	100

1. Self-help skills: feeding, drinking, dressing and toileting.

2. Occupation: playing with toys, helping in the house.

3. Communication: sign language, sound production and imitation, use of appropriate language.

4. Miscellaneous: a wide variety of individual projects, such as establishing eye contact, increasing attention span and concentration, training in wearing a hearing aid, co-operative social interaction.

Deceleration targets

There were 61 problems tackled at home and 36 at school, grouped under 5 headings (Table 9).

1. Aggression: hitting, pinching, hair pulling, biting.

2. Destructive: throwing, smearing, tearing clothes.

3. Disruptive: tantrums, screaming, teasing, disturbances at night.

4. Self-injury and rituals: head-banging, handslapping, food fads, ritual wearing of clothes.

5. Miscellaneous: panic attacks, school refusal.

The number of acceleration and deceleration targets was very similar, both at home and at school, with 53% of the total in each case being deceleration.

Table 9 shows the number and percentage of each of these problems at home and at school. In general, the proportions of types of problems in each situation are very similar, with the exception of self-help: nearly twice as many self-help targets were tackled at home compared with at school, a difference which might have been expected in view of the different interests and emphases in the two situations. Among the deceleration targets, disruptive problems were the most frequently tackled both at home and at school.

ASSESSMENT OF OUTCOME

We assessed outcome of treatment retrospectively on the basis of our clinical reports. Each of us assessed our own cases, rating each problem tackled on a 5-point scale:
1. Total success
2. Considerable success
3. Fair success
4. Minimal success
5. No change

In view of the small numbers of children and problems involved we grouped categories 1, 2 and 3 into an 'improved' category and 4 and 5 into an 'unimproved' category, and have used these two categories throughout the tables concerned with outcome.

The methods of calculating the chi squares is shown in the Appendix (p. 170). Children in whom the outcome of a problem is not known are included in the totals on which the chi squares are calculated; this was thought preferable to omitting them altogether.

Significance is shown as follows: $*P < 0.05$, $**P < 0.01$, $***P < 0.001$.

RELATIONSHIPS BETWEEN VARIOUS FACTORS AND OUTCOME OF TREATMENT

1. Child characteristics

a. WHO classification

In view of the small numbers involved (see Table 3), categories 1–4 and 5 and 6 have been combined. Intellectual level was positively related to success of outcome for acceleration targets at home, and for home and school combined, although the figures fail to reach significance for school alone, presumably because of small numbers (Table 10). Neither at home nor at school, nor for the two combined, was the relationship between intellectual level and deceleration targets significant. It is interesting (and reassuring) to note that there is a significant association between traditional IQ classification and ability to learn new skills, although intellectual level does not seem to have the same relationship to elimination of behaviour problems.

b. Physical and sensory problems

Outcome was related to presence or absence of physical and sensory handicaps (see Table 4). Partly because there were rather few children with these handicaps the relationships were not significant apart from two: children without

154

TABLE 10

WHO classification and outcome of problems

WHO categories	Outcome								
	Home			School			Total		
	Im-proved	Unim-proved	Not known	Im-proved	Unim-proved	Not known	Im-proved	Unim-proved	Not known
Acceleration									
1–4 (IQ: 36+)	19***	3	0	8	2	1	27***	5	1
5–6 (IQ: 35−)	6	16	10	7	5	7	13	21	17
Deceleration									
1–4	27	10	2	12	5	3	39	15	5
5–6	13	6	3	11	1	3	24	7	6

TABLE 11

Language comprehension and outcome

	Home			School			
	Im-proved	Unim-proved	Not known	Im-proved	Unim-proved	Not known	
Acceleration							
Some comprehension	14**	4	2	9*	1	3	
Little or no comprehension	11	15	8	6	6	7	
Deceleration							
Some comprehension	20	10	2	15*	4	0	
Little or no comprehension	20	6	3	8	2	7	

impairment of hand function did better on acceleration targets ($P < 0.01$) and children without difficulty in walking did better on deceleration targets ($P < 0.05$) both at home. There were no significant differences either at home or at school between children with and without impairment of visual and auditory function.

c. Language comprehension

Table 11 shows the relationship between comprehension level and outcome, with the five categories (Table 7) collapsed into two groups, 'some comprehension' (0, 1 and 2) and 'little or no comprehension' (3 and 4).

Comprehension level was significantly related to outcome for acceleration targets both at home and at school, and for deceleration targets at school. Since comprehension level was significantly related to WHO classification ($P < 0.01$)

155

TABLE 12

Social class and outcome

Social class	Home			School		
	Improved	Unimproved	Not known	Improved	Unimproved	Not known
Acceleration						
Non-manual	13	10	3	6	1	4
Manual	12	9	7	9	6	6
Deceleration						
Non-manual	19	8	1	5	2	3
Manual	21	8	4	18	4	4

TABLE 13

Marital relationship and outcome at home

Marital relationship	Outcome					
	Acceleration			Deceleration		
	Improved	Unimproved	Not known	Improved	Unimproved	Not known
Satisfactory	18	11	8	28*	8	1
Discord	7	8	2	12	8	4

the relationship between comprehension and outcome on acceleration targets was expected, but was quite unexpected in the case of deceleration targets at school.

2. Family characteristics

a. Social class

The figures for social class groups (Table 1) were collapsed into two: non-manual (I, II and III NM) and manual (III M, IV and V). No relationship was found between social class and outcome (Table 12).

b. Marital relationships

Marital discord had no significant effect on acceleration targets, but deceleration targets were significantly better achieved where relationships were satisfactory (Table 13).

c. Mental health

Mental ill-health in parents (usually the mother) was found to have no significant effect on success of outcome.

156

TABLE 14

Number of siblings and outcome of home problems

| | Outcome | | | | | |
| | Acceleration | | | Deceleration | | |
Number of sibs	Improved	Unimproved	Not known	Improved	Unimproved	Not known
0–1	16	13	4	30**	6	2
2+	9	6	6	10	10	3

TABLE 15

Outcome of problems tackled at home and school

| | Home | | | | | | School | | | | | |
| | Improved | | Unim-proved | | Not known | | Improved | | Unim-proved | | Not known | |
Type of problem	No.	%	No.	%	No.	%	No.	%	No.	%	No.	%
Acceleration												
Self-help	12	52	6	26	5	22	2	25	2	25	4	50
Occupation	2	18	7	64	2	18	5	56	2	22	2	22
Communication	5	45	4	36	2	19	3	38	3	38	2	24
Miscellaneous	6	67	2	22	1	11	5	71	0	0	2	29
Deceleration												
Aggression	5	50	5	50	0	0	3	50	1	17	2	33
Destructiveness	8	57	5	36	1	7	5	56	1	11	3	33
Disruptiveness	18	72	4	16	3	12	11	69	3	19	2	13
Self-injury	5	63	2	25	1	12	3	75	1	25	0	0
Miscellaneous	4	100	0	0	0	0	1	100	0	0	0	0

d. Siblings at home

The number of siblings living at home had no significant effect on acceleration targets, but deceleration targets were significantly more often achieved when there were fewer than two siblings living at home (Table 14).

3. Problem variables

a. Type of problem

It seemed possible that certain problems would be easier to deal with than others, so we looked at the success rate in different types of problems (Table 15). In general, acceleration targets were less successfully dealt with at home than were deceleration targets. Targets in the disruptive category had the highest rate of success (apart from the four problems in the Miscellaneous category), while

157

TABLE 16

Average outcome rating per child related to number of problems tackled per child

No. of problems per child	Home		School	
	Improved	Unimproved	Improved	Unimproved
1–3	11	8	5	2
4+	7	2	5	1

TABLE 17

Deceleration problems: severity at outset related to success at outcome

Severity	Home						School					
	Improved		Unim-proved		Not known		Improved		Unim-proved		Not known	
	No.	%	No.	%	No.	%	No.	%	No.	%	No.	%
1 and 2	23	62	9	24	5	14	16	70	1	4	6	26
3	17	71	7	29	0	0	7	54	5	39	1	8

those involving occupation seemed the most difficult. At school the trends were similar, although here occupation does not stand out as the least successfully achieved target.

b. Number of problems for each child

The number of problems in any one child ranged from 1 (four children) to 13 (one child) at home, and 1 (one child) to 8 (one child) at school. In order to see whether problems were better dealt with when they were relatively isolated we calculated the average success rating per problem for children with different numbers of problems. These figures were then combined to produce Table 16. No significant differences were found, possibly because of small numbers, but there was a tendency for those families tackling several problems to deal with them more successfully than those tackling fewer.

The figures for school were too small for comment.

c. Severity of problems

Deceleration targets were rated, on a 3-point scale from 1 (mild) to 3 (severe), as at the beginning of treatment. The severity of the problems was then related to success of outcome (Table 17).

No significant or consistent effect of severity of problem was found on the success of outcome: the more difficult problems were slightly more effectively dealt with at home, while the reverse held at school.

158

TABLE 18

Number and duration of contacts related to outcome at home

	Acceleration						Deceleration					
	Improved		Un-improved		Not known		Improved		Un-improved		Not known	
	No.	%	No.	%	No.	%	No.	%	No.	%	No.	%
Number of contacts												
1–10	10	29	15	43	10	29	20	57	10	29	5	14
11–22	15***	79	4	21	0	0	20*	77	6	23	0	0
Duration of contacts												
0–12 mths	7	25	12	43	9	32	13	46	8	29	7	25
12–43 mths	18***	69	7	27	1	4	27**	82	6	18	0	0

TABLE 19

Number and duration of contacts related to outcome at school

	Acceleration targets						Deceleration targets					
	Improved		Un-improved		Not known		Improved		Un-improved		Not known	
	No.	%	No.	%	No.	%	No.	%	No.	%	No.	%
Number of contacts												
1–2	5	36	2	14	7	50	13	65	0	0	7	36
3–9	10	56	5	28	3	17	10	63	6	37	0	0
Duration of contact												
0–6 mths	4	25	2	12	10	63	10	59	0	0	7	41
7–43 mths	11**	69	5	31	0	0	13	68	6	32	0	0

4. Intervention variables

a. Number and duration of contacts, home

The number of visits made, and the length of time over which they were made, were related to success of outcome for children at home (Table 18). A higher number of visits and contacts over a longer period were significantly associated with a more successful outcome for both acceleration and deceleration targets.

b. Number and duration of contacts, school

Similar calculations to those described in 4a were carried out in relation to problems tackled at school (Table 19). The trends were similar to those shown

TABLE 20

Success with which different techniques were learnt by parents

Technique	Degree of success							
	Good		Medium		Poor		Not known	
	No.	%	No.	%	No.	%	No.	%
1. Reinforcement	8	32	12	48	4	16	1	4
2. Shaping/prompts	7	29	11	46	3	13	3	13
3. Aversive	9	38	10	42	2	8	3	13
4. Desensitization	1	(50)	3	(50)	0	0	0	0
5. Recording	5	39	6	46	2	15	0	0
	30	34	40	45	11	13	7	8

in Table 18; a higher number of contacts and longer contact tended to be associated with a more successful outcome, but a significant association was found only between duration of contact and success on acceleration targets.

c. Techniques taught, and how successfully they were learnt

We wanted to relate the types of techniques that we taught parents (reinforcement, shaping etc.) to their success in dealing with each problem, but this proved impossible because techniques were taught at different times, and several techniques might be taught to cope with any problem. Instead, we rated on a 3-point scale how well we felt the parents had learnt the techniques. The results are shown in Table 20. About a third of each of the techniques was rated as having been well learnt, while about 13% were poorly learnt.

An attempt was made to assess how far parents were able to put the techniques into practice, but apart from a few notable cases the level of application of the techniques seemed indistinguishable from level of learning about them.

DISCUSSION

Child characteristics

One of the most interesting of our findings is that although no association was found between intellectual level (WHO classification) and outcome of treatment on behaviour problems, there was a positive relationship where acceleration targets were concerned. It should be noted that 17 out of 19 successful home acceleration projects carried out in the brighter group (Groups 1–4, Table 10) were on children in WHO category 4, with IQs below 51, and a very similar proportion was found in the school group. IQs above and below 50 have previously been shown to be related to outcome on follow-up of autistic children (Rutter, Greenfeld and Lockyer 1967; De Myer et al. 1974). In the present study the IQ within the group with IQs below 50 was also shown to be related to learning skills. Although differences in abilities have less often been studied

160

within this low IQ group, De Myer (1971) found that children with a mean IQ of 27.4 did less well on a variety of tests including speech, ball play, ring stacking, etc. than did the group of children with a mean IQ of 52.7, while Stephen and Robertson (1970) found that although imbecile children responded well to a 'residential nursery' kind of regime, and children in the borderline group made some progress, idiot children (IQ < 20) showed no change on scales of verbal and non-verbal ability and self-help skills.

These findings suggest that where the problem presented is one of behaviour we may confidently expect a considerable degree of success with behaviour modification methods regardless of the child's intellectual level (6 out of the 13 deceleration successes in the lower WHO categories were in category 6, the profoundly retarded). Where the problem is one of acquiring skills, we may expect considerable success with the brighter group. We emphatically do not believe that it is inappropriate for the more retarded group to attempt learning tasks, or that parents of these children should be discouraged from seeking treatment (De Myer et al. 1974). Rather we believe that, first, both the parents and we as professionals should realize that the process of learning will be likely to be even slower than it is with the brighter group, and prepare ourselves to work with increased patience and persistence; and second, that we should look for greater refinement and ingenuity in our teaching methods with the severely and profoundly retarded group of children. For example, there is scope for improvement in the art of applying operant learning—in particular, in breaking down an activity into sufficiently small steps, and in paying more attention to reinforcement and reinforcement schedules. Of course, if new or more careful teaching methods were devised we might find they worked equally well with the brighter group, but this would be only an added bonus.

Language comprehension levels, which were (not surprisingly) closely related to WHO classification, also correlated positively with success on acceleration targets, and also, in the schools, with success on deceleration targets. The latter finding is difficult to explain, but possibly teachers tended to use a more suitable level of verbal instruction than did parents when dealing with problem behaviours, which enabled the children with better language comprehension to understand and comply with instructions better.

Physical and sensory problems bore rather little relationship to success, although children seen at home had greater success on acceleration targets where there was little impairment in walking, and on deceleration targets where there was less impairment in hand function. The connection in the latter case seems fairly clear, in that children with good hand function might be expected to learn a variety of skills more easily than those without, but why problem behaviours were more easily dealt with in children who could walk is obscure, and inspection of the individual cases concerned does not offer any answers.

It is interesting that difficulties with vision and hearing did not significantly affect the rates of success with either learning or behaviour problems, since subjectively these children often seem difficult to manage. It may be that targets were chosen for these children with these particular handicaps in mind, which might have lessened the degree to which they influenced the outcome.

Family variables

One of the variables thought to have an effect on the ability of parents to profit from teaching in behaviour modification is parental intelligence, usually measured by educational level or social class gradings. In some studies, parents of lower intelligence or educational level have been found less able to use the skills successfully when their training was based primarily on didactic verbal learning of behavioural principles (Salzinger, Feldman and Portnoy 1970; Patterson, Cobb and Ray 1973) but this is not always the case, for in Cunningham and Jeffree's (1971) study the educational level of the parents was not related to success in carrying out treatment of their children. Again, parents with mental health problems have been found more difficult to teach, or have been excluded from this type of work (e.g. Wiltz 1969; Patterson, Jones, Whittier and Wright 1965).

In our study neither social class nor mental health of the parents was related to successful outcome of treatment. Although the number of studies in which these two factors have been considered as variables is too small for comparisons to be made, it seems possible that our results may have been due to the fact that, in common with some other studies (Hirsch and Walder 1969; Mira 1970), we did not require parents to read manuals or to master technical terms, but taught them directly the skills they needed. It seems possible too that our results were influenced by the fact that we did not follow a preconceived or rigidly structured training regime but were flexible and tailored our approach to particular parents' needs. It must be said, too, that we sometimes felt that severe mental health problems, usually depression, had a bad effect on the parent's ability to carry out treatment, although it was not possible to show this statistically. Similarly, our impression was that mental health problems combined with marital difficulties in the same family made treatment almost impossible, but although the trend in the figures supports this view the differences do not reach statistical significance.

Marital discord has been thought to affect parent training and participation in programmes adversely (Patterson, unpublished, 1973) and our study supports this as far as deceleration targets are concerned. A similar situation obtained for size of family: deceleration targets were more successfully achieved where the child had not more than two siblings. The common factors in these two situations, marital discord and a larger family, seem to be an increased likelihood of disruption and distraction in the household, and it is perhaps difficult to see why these should not also affect acceleration targets adversely. It may be that, for acceleration targets, time and place can be found to work relatively uninterruptedly on a task that can be scheduled deliberately, whereas a deceleration problem requires an appropriate response to be given however unexpectedly it may occur, and hence may be more vulnerable to general levels of disturbance in the home. In addition, our evidence on the lack of relationship between number of siblings and the learning of skills supports that of Carr (1975), who found no association between number of siblings and intelligence level in young children with Down's syndrome.

Problem variables

No relationship was found between the severity of deceleration problems at outset and success at outcome. This may be related to another, tentative finding, that in general deceleration targets were more successfully dealt with than were acceleration targets. The reasons for this may be, first, that it is in many ways easier to see when an unpleasant behaviour has been eliminated than to judge how far a desirable behaviour has been acquired, which may make for differences in our assessment of outcome in the two cases; second, it may be that unpleasant behaviours were seen as of highest importance by the families, who may have applied themselves particularly to dealing with these problems, while acceleration targets may have been treated in a more leisurely manner, which might contribute to a real difference in success rates. It is interesting that the lowest rate of success on acceleration targets is on occupation, which has seemed to us a particularly difficult skill to teach, especially to the profoundly retarded child.

Training variables

Our clinical findings are in line with many others previously reported and show that it is possible to train non-psychologists in behaviour modification skills with a fair degree of success. The problem of how this training can be done most effectively and economically is of major importance, especially in a service setting. Several reviewers (O'Dell 1974; Johnson and Katz 1973; Yule 1975) have drawn attention to the wide range of reported types of training and have commented on the lack of an empirical basis for deciding on the most effective way to train parents in any particular circumstances, although there are some tentative suggestions and many beliefs surrounding the subject.

Perhaps the most obvious feature of our training approach is the lack of uniformity in terms of place of training, teaching methods, number and duration of contacts. This was largely due to the clinical context of our work, which meant that families were taken on as their problems arose and not according to a prearranged plan.

Our training of the parents and teachers of the out-patients usually took place in the homes and schools, where the advantages of obtaining direct observational information about the problems in their natural setting, of minimizing the problems of generalizing treatment effects and of inconvenience to families on the whole outweighed the disadvantage of loss of experimental control. As can be seen from Table 8, the decision as to the place of treatment was a flexible one. In particular, when we seemed to be failing in our training, a few families attended Hilda Lewis House for special training sessions in which a one-way screen room and a 'bug in the ear' device or videotape could be used to enable parents to learn to use techniques more effectively. Sometimes it also proved useful to deal with a particular problem in neutral surroundings where the parents were free from distraction and where the problem could be isolated from a highly charged emotional setting. The decision to vary the place of

163

training was based on our clinical evaluation of the situation, but it seems important to look for factors which might suggest from the outset when intensive training would be necessary. This is a problem for consideration in future research.

Our methods of training focused on practical skills and techniques in relation to each parent's individual problems. Principles of behaviour modification were taught only incidentally in most cases, but more explicitly to some parents whose children presented many problems, so that they would be able to generalize application of the principles. Instruction, modelling and direct teaching were frequently used. Manuals or other material were not used—mainly because it was difficult to obtain suitable material for use with English parents—but treatment programmes were sometimes specially written for parents and teachers. Better general manuals for parents of retarded children (e.g. Baldwin, Fredericks and Brodsky 1973) and the development of materials for instructing parents in teaching self-help skills (e.g. Lance and Koch 1973) are becoming available and should be tried out. They could be particularly useful in teaching the fine art of breaking down skills into sufficiently small stages and chaining —an art which seems to us to require considerable teaching effort for its acquisition (although this is not shown in our data).

The question of how much contact is necessary to teach skills to parents is problematic, as it depends on the aims. In most cases the aim was to teach the parents to cope not only with the current problems but to be able to apply their knowledge to prevent new problems arising and to teach the child new skills. Our finding (Table 18) was that more frequent contacts and longer contact related to more favourable outcomes. This raises the question of how decisions should be taken to terminate contact. This may be quite clear with specific problems like phobias, or with mild behaviour problems when the child is making adequate progress in other areas. But in a population such as ours, which is so obviously lacking in fundamental self-help and cognitive skills (p. 150 and Table 7) it often happens that when the most urgent problem has been dealt with parents want to go on to others, hitherto less important but with which they now want help. In addition, we have sometimes found that, after we have stopped visiting parents who seem to be managing successfully, they ask later for further contact about new problems or because a crisis has arisen. Similar difficulty with terminating contact has been found by Howlin et al. (1973) in their home intervention project with parents of autistic children.

There are several possible reasons why parents may feel the need for continued contact. These include the desire to do as much as possible for their child, the need for support in carrying out procedures they are unsure about, and inadequacies in our methods of teaching them. It seems important to try to find out which are salient, so that intervention can be appropriate. In some cases the main continuing need may be for support or general counselling rather than for instruction or even assistance in maintaining treatment intervention. A social worker was actively involved in 30–50% of our cases and we sometimes made joint visits to families. It is not possible to disentangle the effects of this additional contact or intervention on the outcome of the behavioural projects, but it is obviously necessary to try to do so in future if we intend to make the best possible use of our resources. In this connection the relative merits and disadvantages of one professional person carrying out all the treatment intervention needed with any one family (as described by Howlin et al. 1973), compared with sharing the treatment intervention between different professional disciplines, particularly in the case of families with complex problems, also requires investigation.

As our individual approach to training is extremely costly in terms of professional time and it is clear that the demands for intervention far exceed even our comparatively generous resources, we have recently concerned ourselves with alternative methods of teaching behaviour modification to non-psychologists, and particularly with the use of group teaching (e.g. Hall et al. 1972; Patterson *et al.* 1973; Walder *et al.* unpublished, 1967; Cunningham and Jeffree 1971).

Callias and Jenkins (unpublished) carried out a pilot project in 1973 to examine the feasibility of training a group of parents in the principles and application of behaviour modification in a course of 10 meetings. Fifteen well-motivated parents (10 mothers and 5 fathers) of 10 severely mentally handicapped children attended 10 two-hour long evening meetings at Hilda Lewis House. The first 9 meetings were held weekly or fortnightly, and the 10th meeting seven weeks later for follow-up. Principles of behaviour modification were taught (and illustrated by the use of videotape) in the first half-hour of each meeting. This was followed by discussion and supervision of projects that the parents were carrying out independently at home. The children were seen only twice, once for assessment before the course began and again after the ninth meeting to videotape the parents working with their children.

The results of this project were encouraging in that the parents conducted a total of 28 supervised projects and 19 independent projects with a considerable degree of success. Only one parent failed to achieve any change in her child's behaviour in either of her two projects. The group approach seemed to us to have some advantages over exclusively individual teaching in that, first, it provided opportunities for vicarious and incidental learning as parents heard about a wider range of application of principles from the other parents; and, second, they were able to support, encourage and help each other when difficulties arose.

The other form of group training we have undertaken began with the need to provide more systematic training in behaviour modification for staff of all disciplines at Hilda Lewis House. As there is a regular turnover of staff, a system of holding a special training week approximately every six months has evolved. Four courses have been held so far. Each of the five morning sessions of the course consists of a lecture on behaviour modification followed by workshop practice in the application of the principles and techniques. The afternoons are spent on more general topics, including medical and social aspects of mental retardation and an introduction to some relevant aspects of child development. After this introductory course, staff are expected to carry out a small project under supervision in order to consolidate and apply their knowledge. In response to requests for training by people in other settings, students on the two most recent courses have also included nurses from other hospitals, teachers from ESN (severe) schools and two workers from overseas, and in the latest course, a few parents of children seen at Hilda Lewis House. These participants were all enthusiastic and felt they had learnt a great deal. An attempt is being made to devise suitable assessment procedures to evaluate this brief course more objectively.

So far, our experience with groups suggests that this is a potentially useful training method in the community. Of course more research is needed to compare its effectiveness with that of individual intervention, to find out which families would benefit from it most and which families will require more intensive or individual treatment. The question of whether variables such as characteristics of parents need to be taken into account when methods of training are considered requires further research attention.

Methodological considerations

A few reports of programmes aimed at helping a number of families of retarded children, as opposed to reports of intervention with one or two families only, already exist (e.g. Terdal and Buell 1969; Cunningham and Jeffree 1971; Callias and Jenkins, unpublished) but these have usually not reported in sufficient detail on the efficacy of their methods over the whole group. Their research methods, however, far outstrip ours. With all the shortcomings of our reported review before us, we are more than ever compelled to ask how evaluation of intervention may be improved, bearing in mind that it will be done as part of our clinical work and commitment to the community, and not as a specially designed research project. We would like to outline some of the ways in which we would wish to structure future projects, although we are aware of how unambitious these will appear to sophisticated research workers in this field.

Most of the improvements that we feel essential and feasible fall into three main categories: Recording, Goal and Task Definition, and Evaluation.

a. Recording

Although it has always been part of our policy to keep records of the work we do, the present project has made us dismally aware of how inadequate these have been for research purposes. Record-keeping needs to be improved both by ourselves and by the families we work with. In our own work this project has shown us that, if we are to attempt to relate success in treatment to an assortment of demographic and other factors, data on these factors should be collected by us at the beginning of the project: we should not rely, as we did in the present study, on winkling out this information from case notes, an extremely wearisome process with no guarantee of complete information at the end of it. For instance it was often difficult to discover the occupation of the father, and hence the social class rating of the family, from the case notes. Again, we wanted to see whether parental age had any influence on success in treatment but could only occasionally find parental ages recorded. These data, together with data on mental health and marital relationships, siblings, handicaps and psychological test data on the children should be systematically collected and recorded.

Throughout each intervention project, records should be kept of every contact with the family. It may be that some sort of routine record form, to be filled in on every occasion, would be more useful than the reports we write now, especially in ensuring that certain essential facts were not overlooked. Such a form might include information on child and parent health and mood, number of sessions run since the last visit, sessions omitted and reasons for this, targets achieved if any, sessions or interactions observed during that visit, adequacy of application of the techniques—reinforcement, prompting, fading—that were used, and so on. The use of such a record form might also result in our seeing more clearly the needs for further work, in the goals to be set for the child and the learning needs of the parents.

Families also need help in keeping records of what goes on in treatment sessions or occurrences in between contacts with the psychologist. Only about a third of our families kept records at all, and only two kept records that were adequate. Not all of our families were asked to keep records, perhaps because record-keeping was so difficult for the parents, and the records we did ask for were so poor that record-requesting behaviour in us was extinguished. In addition, record-keeping seemed to many parents a pointless chore which they were reluctant to undertake; in fact, where reasonable records have been kept, they have proved a considerable source of encouragement to the parents (see also Brown 1974) and of feedback, and examples of this might be used to spur on other parents. Another barrier to record-keeping appears to lie in the drawing-up of record forms; this difficulty could be overcome if appropriate forms (and a sufficient supply of them to last until the next visit) were given to the parents. Here again standardized all-purpose forms, devised and reproduced in quantity, could be adapted to the needs of the particular parent and problem.

b. Goal and task definition

While the eventual goal of treatment was usually fairly clear ('he should learn to walk along the road with his eyes open', 'he should not throw food or furniture') it was not always made explicit and seldom written down. This, if carried out systematically, would be helpful in keeping the distant target clearly in view. In addition to this we should define intermediate steps between the present position and the final goal so that each intermediate step presents an attainable target from the viewpoint of the previously-achieved target. In this way success on each step, or on a number of steps, would constitute a measure of success that would be an improvement on our present ill-defined ratings. Although this would provide a reasonable method of measuring success in any one programme, or in similar programmes with different children, it would not get over the difficulty posed by the need to compare results of different programmes. There would be problems in comparing successes in, say, a feeding programme with that in a toileting programme, and difficult then to go on to assess the relationship of other factors such as handicap or mental ill-health in the parents to these successes. Nevertheless even if ratings or comparisons had to be made at a later stage the data on which they were based would be less ambiguous than the subjective assessments with which we have worked.

c. Evaluation

We have already suggested that the results of treatment would be better evaluated if careful records of progress were kept throughout a project. In addition it would also be desirable to have ratings and assessments made by a second observer, at the outset and at various stages of treatment, and indeed for a second observer to attend from time to time throughout the project to make reliability checks on the data.

It seems clear that the kind of progress notes that we envisage as forming the basis of our evaluation would be easier to assemble in regard to acceleration targets where teaching sessions could be observed, rather than for deceleration targets where the undesirable behaviour may not be shown when the therapist visits. It seems that there is little alternative here to using records kept by the family, though perhaps different members of the family could contribute to reliability studies of deceleration targets.

The need to demonstrate that behavioural control has been established, and that progress is due to the methods used and not to extraneous variables, is often discussed (Johnson and Katz 1973; Kiernan 1974) and maximum respect is accorded those studies in which a reversal, ABAB, design is used. We are not the first to have found it difficult to persuade parents to abandon a technique which has apparently resulted in much-needed improvement in their child (Yule 1973). Furthermore we question the ethics, in relation to the child, of reversing established contingencies. Working with people who appear to be easily confused, do we have the right to confuse them deliberately? We believe that alternative methods should be used wherever possible, and that a suitable alternative is available in the multiple-baseline design. This may bring up problems of order effects but these can be overcome. We feel that the disadvantages of this method are far less than those involved in a reversal design.

We are aware that follow-up data are conspicuously absent from our review. There are three main reasons for this: first, we lack sufficient information on most of the closed cases; second, many of the cases are still under treatment; and third, many of the difficulties we experienced in evaluating the outcome at termination of treatment (or at present for current cases) are magnified in follow-up and confounded by other events. Contact ended in some cases because of major residential changes, such as institutionalization, which may or may not have been the result of the child's own problems; in others, when goals were satisfactorily achieved; and in some families when parental interest and involvement faded. The information we do have suggests that long-term outcome is variable and not always related to the degree of improvement at the end of treatment. In some families changes have persisted and further improvement has occurred, in others there have been fluctuations, with relapses in behaviour problems; we have not always been able to pinpoint the contingencies for this variability. We have also had one or two cases in which the major improvement achieved by parents with very difficult children has failed to be maintained when therapeutic contact has stopped. This is something to which we would like to pay more careful attention in future work by scheduling regular and systematic follow-up and trying to discover the factors that affect maintenance of treatment effects.

CONCLUSIONS

Despite the obvious shortcomings of our retrospective study, some findings of interest have emerged and we have been able to examine systematically some of our clinical impressions of the effect of our work and of the variables affecting outcome.

There is little doubt that programmes such as ours, involving parents in the treatment of their own children, can be of great value, in economizing on professional time, in producing changes in the child within his natural environment, so minimizing difficulties of generalization, and perhaps above all in giving the parents a sense of personal achievement and of their own contribution to the child's well-being. The question remains as to which of the various techniques that we used are the most suitable for which families. For example, in some families the child may be treated satisfactorily entirely at home, in others it seemed essential for the family to attend Hilda Lewis House for treatment, and in others for the child to be admitted so that the parents were at one and the same time relieved of the day-to-day care of the child, and able to carry out some treatment within the Unit. We wonder how many of our unsuccessful cases might have made better progress if we had visited more frequently or used one of these alternative approaches. We have a suspicion that the particular approach used may depend as much on extraneous administrative factors such as the proximity of the family to the Unit, the ready availability of transport, whether or not the mother is working, or the availability of a bed in Hilda Lewis House, as on more legitimate factors such as the severity of the problem. There is a need for more systematic examination of these factors, to enable us to predict more accurately the most useful approach for individual families.

There is some evidence that working with parents in groups is as effective as, and more economical than, working with them individually, but the evidence is slight and needs substantiating. Probably the reason for this lies in the limited range of treatment alternatives offered. Parents are not offered a choice between group and individual treatment: what they have received was what was available, and no systematic exploration has been made of the advantages of each method. This still awaits the relevant research.

We have suggested ways in which we could improve our evaluation, in particular by collecting comparable data prospectively across cases so that future research generalizations may be more firmly based. Most of the suggestions we have made involve more time being spent on each case, which creates problems in a service setting: nevertheless we have tried to confine our suggestions to those which appear to us feasible in such a context.

APPENDIX

Calculating Chi Squares using Nomographs

The significance of the differences between scores has been calculated throughout by the use of nomographs. These were originally published by Zubin and have been recalculated and adapted by Oppenheim (1966). Oppenheim warns that if one uses the nomograph, "a given difference may be significant at the extremes ... but not in the middle ranges," so that any difference was accepted as significant only if it was significant over the whole range of the nomograph. Thus, with two populations of 42 and 39, 94% and 79% appear to be significantly different at the 5% level; however, if this difference of 15% is moved to the middle of the range, say to 40% and 55% the percentages are not significantly different. In this case the difference between the two original percentages, 94% and 79%, would not be regarded as significant.

REFERENCES

BALDWIN, V. L., FREDERICKS, H. D. B. and BRODSKY, G. (1973) *Isn't it Time He Outgrew This? Or, a Training Programme for Parents of Retarded Children.* Thomas, Springfield, Illinois

BROWN, R. (1974) *One in Seven is Special: Home Training of a Retarded Child.* National Society for Mentally Handicapped Children, London

CALLIAS, M. M. and JENKINS, J. Group training in behaviour modification: a pilot project with parents of severely retarded children. Unpublished

CARR, J. (1975) *Young Children with Down's Syndrome: their Development, Upbringing and Effect on their Families.* Butterworths, London

CORBETT, J. (1973) Neuropsychiatric handicaps in children with severe mental retardation. Paper presented to 3rd meeting of U.K. Paediatric Neurologists, Oxford

CUNNINGHAM, C. C. and JEFFREE, D. M. (1971) *Working with Parents: Developing a Workshop Course for Parents of Young Mentally Handicapped Children.* National Society for Mentally Handicapped Children (North West Region), Manchester/Hester Adrian Research Centre, Manchester

DE MYER, M. K. (1971) Perceptual limitations in autistic children and their relation to social and intellectual deficits. In *Infantile Autism: Concepts, Characteristics and Treatment* (Rutter, M., ed.), pp. 81–96. Churchill Livingstone, Edinburgh

DE MYER, M. K., BARTON, S., ALPERN, G. D., KIMBERLIN, C., ALLEN, J., YANG, E. and STEELE, R. (1974) The measured intelligence of autistic children. *J. Aut. Childh. Schiz.* 4, 42–60

HALL, R. V., AXELROD, S., TYLER, L., GRIEF, E., JONES, F. C. and ROBERTSON, R. (1972) Modification of behavior problems in the home with a parent as observer and experimenter. *J. Appl. Beh. Anal.* 5, 53–65

HIRSCH, I. and WALDER, L. (1969) Training mothers as reinforcement therapists for their own children. *Proceedings of the 77th Annual Convention of the American Psychological Association* 4, 561–562

HOWLIN, P., MARCHANT, R., RUTTER, M., BERGER, M., HERSOV, L., and YULE, W. (1973) A home-based approach to the treatment of autistic children. *J. Aut. Childh. Schiz.* 3, 308–336

JOHNSON, C.A. and KATZ, R.C. (1973) Using parents as change agents for their children: a review. *J. Child Psychol. Psychiat.* *14*, 181–200

KIERNAN, C. (1974) Behaviour modification. In *Mental Deficiency: the Changing Outlook*, 3rd ed. (Clarke, A.M. and Clarke, A.D.B., eds.), pp. 729–803. Methuen, London

LANCE, W.D. and KOCH, A.C. (1973) Parents as teachers: self-help skills for young handicapped children. *Ment. Retard. 11* (3), 3–4

MIRA, M. (1970) Results of a behavior modification training program for parents and teachers. *Behav. Res. Ther. 8*, 309–311

O'DELL, S. (1974) Training parents in behaviour modification: a review. *Psychol. Bull. 81*, 418–433

OPPENHEIM, A.N. (1966) *Questionnaire Design and Attitude Measurement*. Heinemann Educational Books, London

PATTERSON, G.R. (1973) Discussion at Behaviour Modification Workshop, Bangor, N. Wales

PATTERSON, G.R., COBB, J.A. and RAY, R.S. (1973) A social engineering technology for retraining the families of aggressive boys. In *Issues and Trends in Behaviour Therapy* (Adams, H.E. and Unikel, I.P., eds.). Thomas, Springfield, Illinois

PATTERSON, G.R., JONES, R., WHITTIER, J. and WRIGHT, M.A. (1965) A behaviour modification technology for a hyperactive child. *Behav. Res. Ther. 2*, 217–226

RUTTER, M., GREENFELD, D. and LOCKYER, L. (1967) A five to fifteen year follow-up study of infantile psychosis. II. Social and behavioural outcome. *Br. J. Psychiat. 113*, 1183–1199

SALZINGER, K., FELDMAN, R.S. and PORTNOY, S. (1970) Training parents of brain-injured children in the use of operant conditioning procedures. *Behav. Ther. 1*, 4–32

STEPHEN, E. and ROBERTSON, J. (1970) Paper no. 2. In *Residential Care for the Mentally Retarded* (Stephen, E., ed.), pp. 19–24. Pergamon, Oxford

TERDAL, L. and BUELL, J. (1969) Parent education in managing retarded children with behavior deficits and inappropriate behaviors. *Ment. Retard. 7*, (3), 10–13

WALDER, L.O., COHEN, S.I., DASTON, P.G., BREITER, D.E. and HIRSCH, I.S. (1967) Behaviour therapy of children through their parents. Revision of a paper presented at the meetings of the American Psychological Association. Washington, D.C.

WILTZ, N.A. (1969) Modification of behavior through parent participation in a group technique. (Doctoral dissertation, University of Oregon): University Microfilms No. 70–9482, Ann Arbor, Michigan

YULE, W. (1975) Training parents in child management. *J. Ass. Educ. Psychol.* (in press)

Discussion

Tizard: It is difficult for parents to be consistent, and the effort to behave consistently imposes great strain on the family. Shouldn't you encourage them to be strictly consistent for specified periods of the day and allow them to relax at others? Otherwise they will be unable to maintain family life and keep their programmes going.

Cunningham: Many of the parents in the Manchester Workshops rejected the idea of half hours of specific training. They said they couldn't organize their day in such a way as to find that half hour. We then turned more to training the parents to observe their children more accurately so that they were better at spotting ways to help their child as the opportunity arose, e.g. with eating skills when eating was going on, and to be more constructive during play sessions.

Maria Callias touched on the problem of termination when working with parents, and I would just like to emphasize that it is a problem. We have tried to phase ourselves out by progressively lengthening the time between sessions with the parents, but I can't say it's been a howling success.

Evaluation, too, is tricky; many people feel inhibited in working with parents and building a relationship with them if at the same time they have to evaluate what the parents are doing. Empathy between trainer and parent is in our opinion extremely important, and this is rarely mentioned.

Finally, what are the optimal qualities for a parent-trainer? We don't know, except that keeping a low profile is one of them: parents don't warm to a know-it-all 'expert'.

Kushlick: One cause of inconsistency in parents' behaviour could be that goals have been set for the client instead of having the client set his/her own goals. This is desirable not only for democratic or participatory reasons, but because goals set in this way have a much higher likelihood of attainment. Only the parent knows his own domestic situation—what is possible in it and what is not.

One respect in which I think evaluation can be too harsh is when a technique is judged a failure because the target behaviour brought about by that technique in a particular setting does not generalize to others. Bringing it about *at all* is a success. It may be that the teaching practices common in the ESN or ordinary school (e.g. neglecting a child when he is on task and paying attention to him when he is not) weaken behaviours strengthened or maintained in the therapeutic setting. We have to watch this one; perfectly good techniques for attaining limited goals in specific situations are being discredited because the behaviours are lost in settings where the contingencies are reversed.

Mittler: Some of the points that Albert Kushlick has just made basically support Cliff Cunningham's position, which is that specific programmes must be set for the parent within the broad aims of education and of development. If you discuss the broad aims as well as the specific objectives with the parents, so that they know what to look for in language development, social skills, and so on, they can then be allowed to choose the level at which they want to work. Some prefer to work at a general stimulation level, others resent such elementary advice as being told to talk to their child. Cliff Cunningham's approach can be described as a general educational approach, of which behaviour modification may or may not form a part. Parents are encouraged to be opportunists, and this appeals to those who cannot manage to sit down and teach the child for half an hour a day or who are unsympathetic to the idea of doing so. Thus each parent's programme is the one which fits the realistic possibilities in his/her household.

Kiernan: Whom do the parent trainers see as their client: the child or the parent?

Callias: Ultimately, our client is still the child, though we are talking here about working almost exclusively with the parent in order to make the interaction between parent and child more relaxed and fruitful. Although it may be economical and sufficiently useful to take only the changes in the child's behaviour as a measure of success, you are getting only a part of the picture.

The point about parent's expectations within the broad aims of development relates of course *only* to the parents. How much consistency can you expect from parents? The answer is that it varies enormously. One can't generalize, just as parents vary considerably in what they want help with, from those who only ask help with one specific problem, e.g. a phobia, to those who want advice on everything. Sometimes you can help to set the parents' sights higher and sometimes you have to tell them that their expectations are unrealistic. There are no rules about it.

Carr: To take up Jack Tizard's point about allowing parents 'on' and 'off duty' periods. I think this can be done only for Acceleration targets, not for Deceleration ones. Inconsistency in the latter case can make matters worse. Fortunately, behaviours that need to be decelerated or extinguished are usually so disruptive that parents are prepared to exert themselves to be 100% consistent once they see that the behaviour modification technique works. But until it does, until the mother finds that she can stop her child screaming and is thereafter totally devoted to the technique, you have got to insist on consistency for Deceleration targets.

Cunningham: I agree that the techniques the parents must learn for teaching pre-academic skills—shape and size discrimination, dressing skills—are different from those for discouraging unwanted behaviour. The problem we are tackling now is, how do you train parents to be more constructive in play? We don't feel this is yet solved.

To answer Chris Kiernan's question: our clients in the Manchester workshops are unquestionably the parents, since we never see the child or the home, and we judge our success or lack of it solely from parents' statements about increased interest in and activity with the children. The approach can be faulted, but it has one merit: the parents are obliged to report their own observation of the child, and this trains them to observe the child more closely and more systematically.

Parents as Therapists and Educators

CLIFF CUNNINGHAM

Hester Adrian Research Centre, The University, Manchester M13 9PL

ABSTRACT

The training of parents in the use of behaviour modification has met with general success in recent years. Although there is little evaluated research on the nature of parent abilities, attitudes and resources in relation to the type of training, and still less on the generalization and long-term maintenance of training, many parents and therapists are enthusiastic about its widespread application to handicapped children.

Most successfully reported applications deal with emotional disturbances or relatively simple self-help skills. Unfortunately, mentally handicapped children have a permanent learning disability often affecting their whole development. Consequently their parents—who feel a need to help their child themselves—are faced with a wide range of training needs which are constantly arising and altering as the child grows. Merely learning the techniques of behaviour modification and analysis of learning situations is insufficient. They need a planned curriculum of activities to guide their teaching and an ever-available support service providing specific advice on immediate training needs and back-up facilities such as toy libraries and short-term stay.

Several studies have emphasized the need for professionals who establish an empathetic rapport and break down the expert–client/doctor–patient barriers usually associated with such services. They also indicate that parents gain considerably from structured group discussions with other parents of handicapped children and that educational level and social class are not closely related to the ability to learn and apply the techniques.

This paper discusses some of the implications of an educational approach to mental handicap and suggests that behaviour modification may not be the most desirable approach, but should be considered as one of many techniques related to specific needs.

BEHAVIOUR MODIFICATION AND PARENT TRAINING: OVERVIEW

Studies aimed at involving parents in the treatment of their children have mushroomed in recent years. The most common approach has been the application of behaviour modification principles to childhood disorders, as emphasized by the recent publication of several major reviews (Berkowitz and Graziano 1972; Johnson and Katz 1973; Tramontana 1971 and O'Dell 1974). Without exception these reviews conclude that parents can be trained to effectively modify their children's behavioural disorders. Further, the studies empirically demonstrate the functional relationship between child behaviours and parental contingencies (O'Dell 1974) and thus confirm the need to modify such behaviours in the setting in which they occur, i.e. the natural environment (Patterson and Brodsky 1966; O'Leary, O'Leary and Becker 1967; Tharp and Wetzel 1969) where the parent behaviours may well be integrally related to the disorder (Patterson, Littman and Hinsey 1964; Sajwaj 1973).

The reviews are equally united in their criticisms of previous work. They emphasize the lack of controls and evaluation, particularly of the generalization and long-term maintenance of training; the need to identify and define critical training variables such as group discussions, lectures, modelling techniques, reading assignments, etc.; and the need for comparative investigations of programme contents and training techniques in relation to various child disorders and parental variables.

Even with these criticisms the application of behaviour modification to parent training is quickly developing. There has been an outburst of parental guides and manuals (e.g. Patterson 1971; Patterson and Gullion 1971; Ora 1971; McIntire 1970; Madsen and Madsen 1972; Becker 1971; Hall 1971; Valett 1969; Williams and Jaffa 1971; Homme and Tosti 1971; Watson 1973), programmed packages (e.g. Latham 1971; Dickerson, Spellman et al. 1973), multimedia presentations (e.g. Latham and Hofmeister 1973; Karlins 1972), and training programmes for parent groups (e.g. Galloway and Galloway 1972; Benassi and Benassi 1973; Peine and Munro 1970; Patterson, Cobb and Ray 1973; Mash, Lazere, Terdal and Garner 1973; Goodwin and McCormick 1970; Eyeberg and Johnson 1974). O'Dell (1974) highlights one reason for this. He states "Like many applied areas of behaviour modification, parent training is being quickly expanded by the vacuum of need." A second reason is undoubtedly that behaviour modification offers a relatively simple and therefore easily learned therapeutic approach (O'Dell 1974; Tarver and Turner 1974) characterized by a concrete, well-structured framework which can be engineered to produce successful results, and thus learner motivation, relatively easily (Ross 1974). Finally, with two notable exceptions (Herbert et al. 1973; Sajwaj 1973), the published studies emphasize the positive, often dramatic, results of the application. As a result one can understand the enthusiasm of many applications. For example Watson writes on page 1 of his manual (1973):

"The particular behaviour modification technique presented in this book ... has proven to be a highly useful method for developing self help, social-recreational, language, educational and vocational skills in mentally retarded, autistic, emotionally disturbed children and children with other learning disorders ..."
However, it is more difficult to understand his reply to his question on page 2: "What has it (behaviour modification) to do with your daily way of life?" when he states: "The answer is everything." Such enthusiasms must give rise to

176

concern particularly when they relate to the widespread application of as effective a technique as behaviour modification. The more precise and efficient a technique, the more serious will be its misapplication. This misapplication not only refers to the incorrect use of elements within the technique (i.e. the *how*) but to its abuse in application to the child's development (i.e. the *why*)—which must be guided by a philosophy of child rearing, and of family and personal needs.

O'Dell concludes his 1974 review with a clear summary of the problems: "A critical issue is whether the area can remain empirically based. There is a strong tendency for applications of the technology to outstrip the speed with which new approaches can be tested. Many procedures are tenuously extrapolated from behavioural research in very different situations. Also, it is irrelevant whether the technology is behaviourally based as long as it is empirically based ... It would be unwise to assume that parent training should be limited to behaviour modification skills. Research is needed to compare and integrate effective techniques from other areas regardless of their theoretical source." This summary is particularly pertinent when one is considering the training of parents with mentally handicapped children; and our present brief to examine the limitations of behaviour modification when applied to the treatment of mental handicap.

PARENT TRAINING AND MENTAL HANDICAP

Their needs

Although few authors have produced detailed descriptions of parent training variables or evaluations of generalization and long-term maintenance of training, detailed descriptions of the specific child disorders and treatments are given. This is not surprising. Most studies have dealt with relatively specific, easily recognizable behaviour disorders, usually of children who do not have a permanent and severe learning disability. Once the behaviour is extinguished or controlled, the objective is attained. Behaviour modification is well suited to such problems. It emphasizes precise, short-term behavioural objectives and the immediate environmental contingencies. Moreover, it offers a rationale for the treatment of many behavioural disorders: for example, it is frequently argued that the severity and duration of temper tantrums is mainly a result of mothers' attention. Unfortunately, parents of mentally handicapped children are faced with a permanent learning disability which has consequences throughout their child's life. Parents have recognized this for many years. Mrs. Max Murray, for example, eloquently argued their case in 1959 and summed it up thus: "The greatest single need of parents of mentally retarded children is constructive professional counselling at various stages in the child's life which will enable the parents to find answers to their own problems to a reasonably satisfactory degree." (Murray 1959)

Although behaviour modification provides a constructive, easily mastered approach to the training of child behaviour, the permanence and totality of the learning disability limits its applicability and sufficiency for parents of mentally handicapped children. They must be concerned with long-term objectives and sustained treatment. They do not have the solace that after the treatment the child will be normal, a factor which must sustain many parents during difficult behavioural learning procedures demanding constant vigilance and consistency. Thus the essential issues for training parents of mentally handicapped are those presently neglected factors of generalization and long-term maintenance of training and parent variable-training method interaction (Yule 1975). Even more important is the question of what it is the parents will teach once they have mastered the techniques.

Principles, not recipes

In response to the need for training which will generalize across learning situations and relate to the growth of the child, there has been an increasing tendency to teach the principles of behaviour modification rather than merely checking and manipulating the parent in the therapeutic situation. The review by Berkowitz and Graziano clearly describes this trend, and the recent study by Mash and Terdal (1973) confirms its usefulness as a preventative measure in relation to non-deviant behaviour in play situations involving mother–child interactions. Similarly, studies applying prescriptive or precision teaching approaches (e.g. Cunningham and Jeffree 1971; Galloway and Galloway 1972) have emphasized the importance of providing parents with basic principles from which to derive their own teaching situations rather than merely applying 'cookbook' recipes (e.g. Watson 1973).

However, this trend places an increasing responsibility upon the parent almost to the extent of suggesting they be fully trained professionals who after learning the principles can devise their own treatment programmes. But is it feasible to expect parents to devise a variety of well-structured training programmes for their child? We must remember that we are not dealing with a specific disorder but a child who needs help in a diversity of areas ranging from specific skills such as dressing, feeding, and physical exercise to complex areas such as language, play, and problem-solving and including such conceptions as curiosity, self-control, and social relationships and interactions. Further, the elements and emphasis within these areas alter as the child grows and develops, and new aspects will continually arise. Obviously no parent can be expected to cope by himself. We must aim at producing a continual supportive service and a detailed curriculum which parents can understand and relate to their child. However, this is not to imply that we attempt to produce highly specific task-orientated recipes. First, the resources needed to produce such a curriculum are too enormous to be contemplated. Secondly, such programmes would probably be so inflexible they could not cope with the heterogeneity of the mentally handicapped population and the variety of parental abilities and attitudes and home and community resources. Finally, the more specific the teaching recipe the less the need for parent or teachers to be creatively involved in the teaching. The result of this superficial involvement in the learning process reduces the parent/

teacher motivation by placing the main emphasis and responsibility for the teaching results on the expert-programmer. Thus if successful, the expert receives the reward. Let us also not forget that parents do feel the need to do something themselves for their child (Murray 1959).

By training the parents in the principles of structured teaching and behaviour modification and the conception of experimentally applying these to their own child in their home, we are likely to produce a more flexible and more motivated and maintained teaching system. Further, we need to supply outline guides of task structures and subject matter and a continual support service of professionals.

This long-term conception requires us to examine the parents' abilities and attitudes in relation to the training objectives.

Parent variables

The present approach to parent variables has been somewhat traditional. It has described parents in relation to such restricted parameters as social class —which is proving to be an extremely poor predictor of child-rearing patterns and home conditions (Seltzer 1973; Caldwell and Richmond 1970—and educational level.

Several studies have reported that parents who received further education were more able to learn from lectures and reading materials whilst those without needed more demonstrations and discussion. However, educational level did not appear to affect the parents' performance in training their child (Salzinger, Feldman and Portnoy 1970; Cunningham and Jeffree 1975).

It may be profitable both for deciding on training methods and determining parents' needs to examine the less behaviourally orientated published work. Michaels and Schucman (1962), for example, report that parents of lower intellectual groups appear better able to accept the fact of having a retarded child, whilst those of high intelligence—who are apt to place a greater emphasis on intelligence in their own value systems—find this acceptance difficult and may well consider training the child to be a waste of family resources. Such attitudes and conceptions of mental handicap must affect the approach to parent training as well as child management, and more objective investigations are vital (e.g. Wolfensberger and Kurtz 1974; Vurdelja-Maglajlic and Jordan 1974). One observation of Michaels and Schucman (1962), for example, is that of the 'prevalence of denial' where parents of mentally handicapped children frequently maintain that this problem lies only in the area of speech. Wolfensberger and Kurtz (1974) found that while 93% of a sample of parents with mentally handicapped children considered the term 'mental retardation' appropriate generally, only 42% judged it appropriate for their own children.

Similarly, many therapists have noted parental feelings in relation to having a mentally handicapped child. The problems of guilt over cause and feelings of chronic sorrow similar to those associated with bereavement and resentment are documented (e.g. Mowatt 1965; Olshansky 1965; Kanner 1953). Mowatt concluded that these feelings frequently result in parents overprotecting the child,

179

and Schulman and Stern (1959) note that when parents accept their child's handicap they begin to make accurate assessments of the child's developmental levels and abilities. Yule (1975) makes the point that behaviour therapists face an acute difficulty with the feeling of guilt over causes of condition. He states "If you teach parents that by altering their behaviour they will alter their child's behaviour, then it is only a small step for the parents to say therefore they must have caused the problem in the first place." Parents with mentally handicapped children will be similarly affected if we argue that educational training can be effective, especially if they have not attempted any such approaches in the past.

A number of parent courses have emphasized or noted the need to provide parents with the opportunity to discuss issues and feelings not necessarily related to specific training tasks and procedures (Wilson 1971; Kovacs 1971; Labon 1974; Cunningham and Jeffree 1975). However, this is not to suggest that all parents of mentally retarded children are suffering from such intense feelings of guilt, sorrow and resentment that they need specific therapy. The majority appear to feel guilt and frustration over *not doing* something to help their child. Given support services which provide practical techniques for the parent to assist their child, many of these feelings and frustrations appear to diminish (Cunningham and Jeffree 1971, 1975).

Finally, it is worth noting that there is an increasing source of information on parents' feelings, needs and resources in their own published accounts (Buck 1950; Van Houten 1960; Green 1966; Park 1968; Roberts 1968; Van der Hoeven 1968; De Vries-Kruyt 1971; Brown 1974; Wilkes and Wilkes 1974).

Parent motivation

Contingency management. One relatively evaluated area is the use of contingency management in the parent training. To maintain parent attendance, the completion of home assignments, and other parent behaviours, many studies have successfully applied token or monetary reinforcers to the parent (e.g. Peine and Munro 1973; Benassi and Benassi 1973), or made attendance of the group contingent upon the completion of home assignments (Mira 1970; Patterson, Cobb and Ray 1973); others, however, find them unnecessary (e.g. Cunningham and Jeffree 1971; Wilson 1971) except in special cases (Shearer and Shearer 1972), arguing that early success of treatment is the main contributing factor for parent cooperation. Again there is a lack of controlled evaluation; thus the recent paper by Eyeberg and Johnson (1974) using multiple assessment procedures to look at parent training and contingency contracting is most welcome. They found contingency contracting superior on all measures, including parent attitudes and home-based independent ratings. (It should be noted that they found a significant discrepancy between the parent-rated data indicating high success and the home observations of independent raters).

The therapist. Returning to Murray's statement of parent needs, it is clear that many parents of mentally handicapped children are highly motivated and wish to 'find answers to their own problems'. This desire for some independence from professionals is worth careful consideration. Ideally, being a parent demands being critically involved in the child's development, being able to do things for and with the child. Yet parents of severely mentally retarded children are often presented with the view that their child needs 'expert' treatment or that treatment is not possible. With respect to the expert–parent interaction, it is interesting to note that several therapy or parent behavioural programme approaches have emphasized the importance of breaking down such 'expertise barriers' before commencing with training (e.g. Kanner 1953; Cunningham and Jeffree 1975; Shearer and Shearer 1972). Further, the approaches which have least emphasized contingency management (e.g. Cunningham and Jeffree 1971; Wilson 1971; Shearer and Shearer 1972) have all noted the importance of the group leader/tutor. Wilson (1971) concludes that "tutors who were parents and could relate his/her own parent emotions and memories" quickly established an empathy and interaction in the groups. He suggests the best group leader would be "a perceptive parent with a high degree of emotional security and a minimal need for ego-reinforcement."

Parents also seem to gain considerably from small group discussions with parents of other handicapped children (Wilson 1971; Cunningham and Jeffree 1975).

Planned success. It is not surprising that many parents become enthusiastic when presented with the more positive concept associated with behaviourally orientated learning programmes; are often astonished at their child's achievements (O'Leary, O'Leary and Becker 1967); and become increasingly motivated and confident as they successfully change their child's behaviour (Shearer and Shearer 1972). This observed early success certainly appears to act as a reinforcer of parental behaviour and it is of paramount importance in parent training programmes and closely interrelated with the technology of behaviour modification such as precise objectives, careful observation and recording and shaping. However, Eyeberg and Johnson (1974) could not find a relationship between the relative ease or difficulty of the initial problem tackled by the parents and parent satisfaction with the course.

Long-term goals

The most crucial issue in training parents of retarded children is that implied by Murray's demand for 'counselling at various stages in the child's life.' Although the principles of behaviour modification may be applied throughout the child's life, they do not indicate to what they should be applied. It is primarily a technique without content, it does not provide information on what subject matter to include in a task or skill-orientated training programme (Bricker and Bricker 1972), or at what point in a learning hierarchy to include such information. Obviously, parents of mentally handicapped children need such information if they are going to help in the day-to-day treatment of their child. A number of parent programmes have provided information derived from child development scales and checklists (e.g. Shearer and Shearer 1971; Cunningham and Jeffree 1971) and developmental theory (Bricker and Bricker 1972). These programmes have been primarily concerned with the 'pre-school' stage. Apart from some self-help-orientated content matter, the other stages of the child's life are largely neglected, though this is no more than a reflection of the general lack of curricular information in mental handicap.

Task structure. The importance of the task structure is often ignored in applying behaviour modification to mental handicap by those who derive the techniques from courses for parents of emotionally disturbed children. They appear to concentrate on the reinforcement contingencies rather than on task structure. Many training manuals, for example, begin with discussions on reinforcers rather than objectives. In mental handicap the reverse emphasis would appear more important. Filler, Bricker and Smith (1973) empirically demonstrated the importance of systematically structuring the task for the child in comparison to providing positive feedback to current responses. In a match-to-sample task the children of mothers who had been reinforced for structuring the task and cueing behaviours performed significantly better than those of mothers who concentrated on reinforcement. Cunningham and Jeffree (1975) report the complementary observation that task structure and step size appeared to be more critical for parents dealing with 'academic' tasks, whilst conceptions of reinforcement contingencies became critical for tasks related to the child's behavioural disorders. This finding reflects the conception of the learning deficit proposed by Clarke and Clarke (1973). They state that mentally handicapped children suffer from a constitutional deficit which includes "the relative inability to spontaneously structure ordinary life experiences" and to "perceive relationships and make deductions without the interaction of another human agent." Thus structural learning approaches, such as programmed instruction with emphasis on breaking down complex tasks into small, related learning steps and presenting these in controlled situations using prompting procedures to ensure attention to relevant variables, is well suited to the deficit (Cunningham 1973a). Clearly, the integration of these techniques and behaviour modification is necessary and will produce a more applicable training content.

Training or education. Perhaps the most crucial question concerns what we suggest that parents should teach their children. Our present emphasis in the treatment of mental handicap is education rather than training or merely occupying their time (Cunningham 1973b). Thus we should think of parents as co-educators rather than co-therapists, and emphasize the distinction between them. Peters (1967) argues that training is primarily concerned with the acquisition of skills, the mastery of a specific type of performance where little emphasis is placed on the underlying rationale. Thus training is essentially concerned with the means to an end, whilst education is concerned with the application of those means and the purpose or rationale of the end. From this viewpoint, behaviour modification, precision teaching and programmed instruction are primarily training techniques which do not inherently demand that the user questions the rationale of the training. Often this limitation alienates the technique from educational approaches. For example, a recent study by O'Brien, Bugle and Azrin (1972) trained an institutionalized child in 'proper eating behaviours' and found it necessary to apply 'continuous motivational procedures' to maintain the behaviours. They conclude "rarely does maintenance appear necessary with normal children, probably because family members naturally provide maintenance to the children while they eat together in the home." The educator must ask why else would one teach the skills to the child unless they were part of the child's needs?

Education is aimed at the needs of the learner, not those of the parent or attendant. Self-help skills are not taught to relieve the parent or institution of an extra burden of care, but because they are necessary for the development of educationally valid behaviours in the child—his autonomy and integrity. No one really wishes to produce people who automatically dress themselves when there is no personal purpose for this action. Thus the concept of independence, so often associated with the self-help literature, has a different connotation if related to educational aims. As argued elsewhere (Cunningham 1974), it is related to the philosophy that the major goal of contemporary education is the development of 'autonomy based upon reason' (Dearden 1968) and the associated concepts of self-esteem, integrity, and the freedom and responsibilities produced by being independent and deciding, even in part, on one's life-style. From this approach one might expect subtle, if not major, differences in the way self-help skills are taught. For example, one might begin training a dressing skill by encouraging the learner to select the clothes he will wear. During training sessions we might also be more alert to the occurrence of behaviours associated with initiative and exploration than to the specific steps of the learning sequence.

An education-orientated training school

Finally, we might also question whether behaviour modification is an appropriate technique to use in relation to the goals of education. Discovery techniques, for example, are derived from contemporary concepts of education and aim at developing abilities to learn for oneself, systematically exploring the environment, and discovering relationships rather than learning facts, and encourage the child to be responsible for his own learning and decision making. As suggested earlier, highly structured learning techniques aim at reducing the uncertainty and complexity of the task and at gaining control of the learner's behaviours; thus, they reduce the chance of exploratory or autonomous actions (Cunningham 1974). This was emphasized by Skinner (1968) when he wrote "the more successfully the teacher spreads knowledge before the student as *terra cognita*, the fewer the chances to learn to explore the unknown and the less the chance to learn to think."

This line of reasoning does not imply that the content of training for parents of children with severe learning disabilities should involve the type of enriched day-care and home tutoring programmes for culturally deprived children that have largely failed to produce sustained results. These approaches have failed to appreciate the totality and duration of Skeels' (1966) original conception and prototype. Studies which have successfully and empirically demonstrated the effect of structured play and training as distinct from quantity of environmental stimulation per se (e.g. Levenstein and Sunley 1968) also emphasize the need to provide parents with a structured approach to their children and to their own training. Thus, whilst it is essential to recognize the limitations of behaviour modification and develop a more educationally orientated approach for parent training programmes, one should not forget that it is precisely these limitations and the highly structured format of behaviour modification which has made its application to parent training so successful. We need to consider how the various principles and approaches can be interrelated to produce a suitably enriched, yet efficient framework.

This framework brings its own set of problems. Parents cannot be expected to analyse or derive the numerous tasks necessary in a treatment programme. They will need continued support from outside agencies. This support must not only deal with training programme variables, but toy libraries, books of instruction and many other practical necessities such as financial help, short-term stay, transport and advice on family problems. This might come from social work agencies, though these appear already to be failing in the supply of basic needs (Bayley 1973). At the pre-school stage there are few facilities and few professionals available to provide intense home visiting. One recent approach in a rural community has been the training of paraprofessionals, responsible to a professional, who visit a small number of families each week (Shearer and Shearer 1972). The results indicate that paraprofessionals can be used in this service and that they had more success in aiding the development of handicapped pre-school children than a comparison group of professional teachers (Schortinghuis and Frohman 1974). Once the child is attending school, the teaching staff might become involved in supporting the parents' training. Indeed such a school–home link would appear to be crucial in the education of mentally handicapped children (Cunningham and Jeffree 1975; Karnes and Zehrback 1972). Similarly, parent discussion groups based on play-school classes have considerable potential (e.g. Faulkner 1969, 1971).

Finally, although we should be encouraged by the research and findings on parent training we must not forget that there will be many cases when the parent, through family circumstances, cannot be expected to enter into complex, time-consuming training programmes for the child (e.g. Lockett 1972; Tizard and Grad 1961). In stating that parents can help their children, let us not forget that this will only lead to increased anxieties unless we provide the means for them to achieve it.

CONCLUSIONS

It is apparent that a majority of parents with mentally handicapped children want and need guidance in the application of practical ideas and teaching techniques to their children, and that even with the lack of detailed evaluation on many essential aspects it is feasible to involve them in the therapeutic or educational treatment of their children.

The range of involvement is as great as the variety of parents' and childrens' needs and resources. Parents have expressed appreciation of structured group discussion on problems of raising handicapped children and equally have found specific training in behaviour modification techniques most useful. Some preliminary observations from our longitudinal study of Down's syndrome infants even suggests that merely visiting parents regularly and giving general, positive advice as compared with the usual negative, commiserative advice given at this time may have a significant effect on the baby's development in the first year of life. Therefore we must be flexible in considering the type of help and support we offer, remembering that this will alter as the child grows.

Behaviour modification has provided a well-structured, effective approach which not only helps the parent to teach the child but can be relatively easily taught to the parent. However, it is not a sufficient training model for parents faced with teaching the many necessary skills needed by mentally handicapped children. It does not give a total curriculum for deciding priority activities. Secondly, the rigour of the approach and the emphasis on reinforcement may not be suited to the everyday regimes of many households, except for short periods, and may not even be necessary in encouraging the development of many social and cognitive skills. Finally we must question whether highly structured teaching approaches with their emphasis on the reduction of uncertainty and a low error rate, teacher control of the learning situation and inflexible objectives are compatible with contempory conceptions of education.

It is certain that parents will be increasingly involved in the treatment of their handicapped children and that behaviour modification has provided an effective model for involvement and has direct application to many of their needs.

However, we need to examine its function in the wider context of parent participation which must encompass the aims of education, the attitude of our society to mental handicap and personal and community resources.

REFERENCES

BAYLEY, M. (1973) The mentally handicapped and their professional helpers. *Br. J. Soc. Work 3*, 349–363

BECKER, W. C. (1971) *Parents Are Teachers. A Child Management Program.* Research Press, Champaign, Illinois

BENASSI, V. A. and BENASSI, B. J. (1973) An approach to teaching behaviour modification principles to parents. *Rehab. Lit. 34*, 134–136

BERKOWITZ, B. P. and GRAZIANO, A. M. (1973) Training parents as behaviour therapists: a review. *Behav. Res. Therap. 10*, 297–318

BRICKER, D. and BRICKER, W. (1972) *Toddler Research and Intervention Project Report—Year II* (IMRD Behavioural Science Monograph No. 21) Inst. Mental Retardation and Intelligence Development, Nashville, Tennessee

BROWN, R. (1974) *One of Seven is Special: Home Training of a Retarded Child.* Nat. Soc. Mentally Handicapped Children, London

BUCK, P. S. (1951) *The Child Who Never Grew.* Methuen, London

CALDWELL, B. M. and RICHMOND, J. B. (1970) Social class level and stimulation potential of the home. In *The Exceptional Infant. Volume 1: The Normal Infant* (Hellmuth, J., ed.). Brunner/Mazel, New York

CLARKE, A. D. B. and CLARKE, A. M. (1973) Assessment and prediction. In *Assessment for Learning in the Mentally Handicapped* (Mittler, P. J., ed.), pp. 23–47. (Institute for

Research into Mental and Multiple Handicap Study Group 5) Churchill Livingstone, Edinburgh

CUNNINGHAM, C.C. (1973a) Programmed instruction and mental handicap. Paper read at the Third International Congress of the International Association for the Scientific Study of Mental Deficiency, The Hague, 1973

CUNNINGHAM, C.C. (1973b) The application of education technology to mental retardation. *Mental Retardation and Behavioural Research* (Clarke, A.D.B. and Clarke, A.M., eds.) (Institute for Research into Mental Retardation Study Group 4), pp. 113–124. Churchill Livingstone, Edinburgh

CUNNINGHAM, C.C. (1974) The relevance of 'normal' educational theory and practice for the mentally retarded. In *Mental Retardation: Concepts of Education and Research* (Tizard, J., ed.), pp. 47–56. Butterworths, London

CUNNINGHAM, C.C. and JEFFREE, D.M. (1971) *Working With Parents: Developing a Workshop Course for Parents of Young Mentally Handicapped Children.* Nat. Soc. Mentally Handicapped Children (NW Region)/Hester Adrian Research Centre, Manchester

CUNNINGHAM, C.C. and JEFFREE, D.M. (1975) The organisation and structure of parent workshops. *Bull. Br. Psych. Soc.* (in press)

DEARDEN, R.F. (1968) *The Philosophy of Primary Education.* Routledge and Kegan Paul, London

DE VRIES-KRUYT, T. (1971) *Small Ship, Great Sea.* Collins, London

DICKERSON, D., SPELLMAN, C.R., LARSEN, S. and TYLER, L. (1973) Let the cards do the talking—a teacher parent communication program. *Teach. Except. Child. 15,* 170–178

EYEBERG, S.M. and JOHNSON, M.S. (1974) Multiple assessment of behavior modification with families: effects of contingency contracting and order of treated problems. *J. Consult. Clin. Psychol. 42,* 594–606

FAULKNER, R.E. (1969) Opportunity class for handicapped children. *Forward Trends 13,* 85–88

FAULKNER, R.E. (1971) Opportunity classes: study of a group of voluntary, integrated nursery classes for handicapped and normal children. *Comm. Med. 126,* 213–217

FILLER, J., BRICKER, W. and SMITH, R. (1973) Modification of material teaching style: the effects of task arrangement on the match-to-sample performance of delayed children. In *Infant, Toddler and Pre-School Research and Intervention Projects. Report—Year III.* (Bricker, D. and Bricker, W., eds.). Inst. Mental Retardation and Intelligence Development, Nashville, Tennessee

GALLOWAY, C. and GALLOWAY, K.C. (1972) Parents' classes in precise behavior management. *Teach. Except. Child. 14,* 120–128

GOODWIN, D. and MCCORMICK, J. (1970) Video-tape feedback and behavior rehearsal in group training of parents in behavior modification techniques: an experimental evaluation. Paper presented at meeting of Western Psychological Association, April 1970

GREEN, M. (1966) *Elizabeth.* Hodder and Stoughton, London

HALL, R.V. (1971) *Behaviour Management Series, Part I, II, III.* H & H Enterprises, Merrian, Kansas

HERBERT, E.N., PINKSTON, E.M., HAYDEN, M.L., SAJWAJ, T., PINKSTON, S., CORDUA, G. and JACKSON, C. (1973) Adverse effects of differential parental attention. *J. Appl. Behav. Anal. 6,* 15–30

HOMME, L. and TOSTI, D. (1971) *Behavioral Technology: Motivation and Contingency Management.* Individual Learning Systems, San Rafael, Calif.

JOHNSON, C.A. and KATZ, R.C. (1973) Using parents as change agents for their children: a review. *J. Child Psychol. Psychiat. 14,* 181–200

KANNER, L. (1953) Parents' feelings about retarded children. *Am. J. Ment. Defic. 57,* 375–383

KARLINS, M. (1972) *Teaching Retarded Persons.* 14 television programs presented by Minnesota Department of Public Welfare, Centennial Building, 658 Cedar Street, St. Paul, Minnesota 55101

KARNES, M.B. and ZEHRBACK, R.R. (1972) Flexibility in getting parents involved in the school. *Teach. Except. Child. 14,* (5), 6–19

Kovacs, M. (1971) *Report of Parents Group Dicussions. Hamilton–Niagara "Model Community Services" Project.* West Lincoln and District Assoc. Mentally Retarded, PO Box 277, Grimsby, Ontario

Labon, D. (1974) Handicapped children – their parents and their teachers. *Forward Trends, 17*, 97–103

Latham, G. (1971) *Parent Training Program.* Packet available from Department of Special Education, Utah State University, Logan, Utah

Latham, G. and Hofmeister, A. (1973) A mediated training program for parents of the preschool mentally retarded. *Except. Child. 39*, 472–473

Levenstin, P. and Sunley, R. (1968) Stimulation of verbal interaction between disadvantaged mothers and children. *Am. J. Orthopsychiat. 38*, 116–121

Lockett, J. (1972) My son John. *Nurs. Tim. 68*, 867–871

McIntire, R.W. (1970) *For Love of Children.* CRM Books, Los Angeles, California

Madsen, C.K. and Madsen, C.H. Jnr. (1972) *Parents Children Discipline: A Positive Approach.* Allyn and Bacon, Boston

Mash, E.J., Lazere, R.L., Terdal, L. and Garner, A.M. (1973) Modification of mother–child interactions: a modeling approach for groups. *Child Study J. 4*, 131–143

Mash, E.J. and Terdal, L. (1973) Modification of mother–child interactions: playing with children. *Ment. Retard. 11*, (5), 44–49

Michaels, J. and Schucman, H. (1962) Observations on the psychodynamics of parents of retarded children. *Am. J. Ment. Defic. 66*, 568–573

Mira, M. (1970) Results of a behavior modification training program for parents and teachers. *Behav. Res. Ther. 8*, 309–311

Mowatt, M.H. (1965) Emotional conflicts of handicapped young adults and their mothers. *Cerebral Palsy J. 26*, (4), 6–8

Murray, M.A. (1959) Needs of parents of mentally handicapped children. *Am. J. Ment. Defic. 63*, 1078–1088

O'Brien, F., Bugle, C. and Azrin, N.H. (1972) Training and maintaining a retarded child's proper eating. *J. Appl. Behav. Anal. 5*, 67–72

O'Dell, S. (1974) Training parents in behaviour modification: a review. *Psychol. Bull. 81*, 418–433

O'Leary, K.D., O'Leary, S. and Becker, W.C. (1967) Modification of a deviant sibling interaction pattern in the home. *Behav. Res. 5*, 113–120

Olshansky, S. (1965) Chronic sorrow: a response to having a mentally defective child. In *Social Work With Families* (Younghusband, E., ed.). Allen and Unwin, London

Ora, J. (1971) *Instruction Pamphlet for Parents of Oppositional Children. Regional Intervention Project for Preschools and Parents.* George Peabody College, Nashville, Tennessee

Park, C.C. (1968) *The Siege.* Smythe, Gerrard's Cross

Patterson, G.R. (1971) *Families: Applications of Social Learning To Family Life.* Research Press, Champaign, Illinois

Patterson, G.R. and Brodsky, G.D. (1966) A behavior modification program for a child with multiple problem behaviors. *J. Child Psychol. Psychiat. 7*, 277–295

Patterson, G.R., Cobb, J.A. and Rar, R.A. (1973) A social engineering technology for retraining aggressive boys. In *Issues and Trends in Behavior Therapy* (Adams, H.E. and Unikel, I.P., eds.). Thomas, Springfield, Illinois

Patterson, G.R. and Gullion, M.E. (1971) *Living With Children.* Research Press, Champaign, Illinois

Patterson, G.R., Littman, R.A. and Hinsey, W.C. (1964) Parental effectiveness as reinforcers in the laboratory and its relation to child rearing practices and adjustment in the classroom. *J. Person. 32*, 180–189

Peine, H.A. and Munro, C. (1970) *Treating Parents Using Lecture–Demonstration Procedures and a Contingency Managed Program.* (Unpublished manuscript). Bureau of Educational Research, University of Utah

Peine, H.A. and Munro, B.C. (1973) Behavioural management of parent training programs. *Psychol. Rec. 73*, 459–466

Peters, R.S. (ed.) (1967) *The Concept of Education.* Routledge and Kegan Paul, London

ROBERTS, N. (1968) *David.* John Knox Press, Richmond, Va

ROSS, A.L. (1974) Combining behavior modification and group work techniques in a day treatment centre. *Child Welfare 53*, 435–444

SAJWAJ, T. (1973) Difficulties in the use of behavioral techniques by parents in changing child behavior: guides to success. *J. Nerv. Ment. Dis. 156*, 395–403

SALZINGER, K., FELDMAN, R.S. and PORTNOY, S. (1970) Training parents of brain-injured children in the use of operant conditioning procedures. *Behav. Therap. 11*, 4–32

SCHORTINGHUIS, E. and FROHMAN, A. (1974) A comparison of paraprofessional and professional success with preschool children. *J. Learn. Dis. 7*, 245–247

SCHULMAN, J.L. and STERN, S. (1959) Parents' estimates of the intelligence of retarded children. *Amer. J. Ment. Defic. 63*, 696

SELTZER, R.J. (1973) The disadvantaged child and cognitive development in the early years. *Merrill-Palmer Quart. Behav. Devel. 19*, 241–252

SHEARER, M.S. and SHEARER, D.E. (1972) The Portage Project: a model for early childhood education. *Except. Child. 39*, 210–217

SKEELS, H.M. (1966) Adult status of children with contrasting early life experiences. *Monographs of the Soc. for Research in Child Development, 31*, serial no. 105

SKINNER, B.F. (1968) *The Technology of Teaching.* Appleton-Century-Crofts, New York

TARVER, R.N. and TURNER, A.J. (1974) Behavior modification techniques for families with behavioral problems. *Am. J. Nurs. 74*, 282

THARP, R.G. and WETZEL, R.J. (1969) *Behavior Modification in the Natural Environment.* Academic Press, New York

TIZARD, J. and GRAD, J.C. (1961) *The Mentally Handicapped and Their Families.* Oxford University Press, London

TRAMONTANA, J. (1971) A review of research on behavior modification in the home and school. *Educ. Tech. 11*, 61–64

VAN DER HOEVEN, J. (1968) *Slant-Eyed Angel.* Smythe, Gerrard's Cross

VAN HOUTEN, N. (1960) *Bartje, My Son.* Hodder & Stoughton, London

VALLETT, R.E. (1969) *Modifying Children's Behavior: A Guide for Parents and Professionals.* Fearon, Palo Alto, Calif.

VURDELJA-MAGLAJLIC, D. and JORDAN, J.E. (1974) Attitude behaviors toward retardation of mothers of retarded and non-retarded in four nations. *Training Sch. Bull. (Vinel) 71*, 17–29

WATSON, L.S. (1973) *Child Behaviour Modification: A Manual for Teachers, Nurses and Parents.* Pergamon, Oxford

WILKES, J. and WILKES, E. (1974) *Bernard: Bringing Up Our Mongol Son.* Routledge and Kegan Paul, London

WILLIAMS, J.L. and JAFFA, E.B. (1971) *Ice Cream, Poker Chips and Very Goods: A Behavior Modification Manual for Parents.* Maryland Book Exchange, College Park, Md

WILSON, L. (1971) Group therapy for parents of handicapped children. *Rehab. Lit. 32*, 332–335

WOLFENSBERGER, W. and KURTZ, R.A. (1974) Use of retardation-related diagnostic and descriptive labels by parents of retarded children. *J. Spec. Educ. 8*, 131–142

YULE, W. (1975) Teaching psychological principles to non-psychologists: training parents in child management. *J. Ass. Educ. Psychol.* (in press)

Commentary

WILLIAM YULE

Cliff Cunningham has succinctly presented an overview of the state of the art in training parents as therapists and educators. Whilst acknowledging the apparent success of behaviour modification approaches, he rightly questions whether the published papers sufficiently describe cases in which the parents are *not* helped in their endeavours to help their own children. Now that the first wave of success stories has been acknowledged, all those professionally involved with the families of the mentally handicapped must address themselves to the problem of which families, with which sort of child presenting, with which sort of difficulty, can best be helped by training the parents to be co-therapists.

In opening the discussion, I would like to focus on two major areas raised in the paper: the question of the content of what to teach; and some problems in training parents.

THE CONTENT OF TRAINING PROGRAMMES

It is apparent from his paper that Cliff Cunningham is not at all comfortable with the view that what he does in his parent-training workshops could be called 'behaviour modification'. He is at pains to differentiate 'training' from 'education', and calls on educational philosophers to support his view that behaviour modification is merely training without regard to the goals of such training. If the hallmark of education is that it is a process which does "inherently demand that the user questions the rationale of the training," then I wonder what it is that many teachers spend their days doing in schools. It certainly isn't education in that particular sense.

The point at issue is how does one decide on what to teach: the content of the curriculum. I cannot agree that educational principles (whatever they may be —and there was precious little agreement on that when I worked at an Institute of Education) guide one in selecting an appropriate content any more than behavioural principles do. I accept the point that in behaviour modification, as in any other intervention approach, one must separate techniques from goals and examine both critically. Educational philosophers may be useful in helping others to clarify woolly concepts, but when it comes to deciding on goals, they are forced to make value judgements like the rest of us lesser mortals.

If anything, following the advise of educators can lead into even more peculiar areas than those that Cunningham is concerned about. Take the example of 'learning by discovery'—that post-Plowden catch word which has been uncritically accepted by so many schools. It is doubtful if such methods are advantageous to all children irrespective of ability and background. As Van der Eyken (1967) points out, the children whom Susan Isaacs worked with at her experimental school in the 1920s had an average IQ of 131. To apply methods which worked with bright children to all other children in the educational system is surely to end up denying the individual needs of individual children, and thereby to fail to meet those needs.

Cunningham quotes the conclusion of the Clarkes that mentally handicapped children suffer from "the relative inability to spontaneously structure ordinary life experiences." If this is so, how will the mentally handicapped fare in schools where 'learning by discovery' is the method of teaching derived from accepted educational principles?

The problems of deciding on content and form of training are not confined to behaviour modification, but are universal wherever one person takes responsibility for intervening in the life of another. Surely it matters little whether the 'intervener' is labelled an educator, a therapist or a trainer, provided he exercises his expertise in a responsible manner. Responsibility implies always asking whether one is justified in intervening, and considering what value the goal has for both the individual and society.

SOME PROBLEMS IN TRAINING PARENTS

Elsewhere (Yule 1975) I have considered in greater detail some of the many problems which exist in training parents as co-therapists. Since this Study Group is expected to examine issues and problems, I would like to recapitulate some of these.

Cunningham has raised the question of how much responsibility parents should have in formulating training programmes. It is clear from published studies that the aim of most parent-trainers is to make the parents as self-reliant as possible—but the parameters of possibility have been little investigated. At the present time, professionals do not know enough to be able to hand over total responsibility for treatment to parents. However, the aim is sound in that parents are potentially the best therapists available in terms of being an economic, continuous treatment resource; parental involvement should minimize the problems of generalizing treatment gains from the clinic to the natural environment; parents should be able to facilitate the maintenance of therapeutic gains; parents should be able to prevent later problems developing; and finally, parents may even be more effective therapists than professionals, who have only fleeting contact with the child. These are all potential gains from parent training. Empirical studies are urgently required to test the validity of such claims.

Advances made in behavioural treatments have come about in large part because of the application of good techniques of measurement and evaluation to relevant problems. Due care has to be paid to the reliability and the validity of the data gathered, as well as to the experimental design employed to demonstrate that intervention is having the desired effect (or not, as the case may be). If we are to argue that parent training offers an important way to deliver services, then we have to acknowledge that a number of technical problems relating to data collection and experimental design have to be tackled. Until these are solved, it will be difficult to gather convincing evidence that parent training is really an effective therapeutic tool.

Even with limited experience, it is already obvious that some problems frequently arise in training parents. Some of them arise within the context of the family, and it is as well to remember that one is dealing with a mentally handicapped child in a family setting, and not just in isolation. Thus, the question of training fathers as well as mothers must be examined. Too many studies report on training mothers alone, and it is unclear whether fathers present any special problems apart from their absence at work. Brothers and sisters must not be forgotten. At present, studies do not indicate clearly when siblings should be incorporated in programmes and when they should be left out. This is a crucial decision which most parents will want guidance on.

Parents have particular difficulties with some aspects of training programmes. For example, parents are often very concerned that they may have caused the problem behaviour in their child. Behaviour therapists face a particularly acute aspect of this universal difficulty. If you teach parents that by altering their behaviour they will alter their child's behaviour, it is only a small step for the parents to conclude that they must have caused the problem in the first place. Even if this conclusion is not expressed openly by the parents, it is probably as well to discuss it openly at an early stage. Behaviour modifiers should not avoid discussing parental feelings of guilt.

Therapists need to be sensitive also to parental feelings of inadequacy. It is all too easy for the expert to produce dramatic changes in a child's repertoire, only to find that the very rapidity of change has reinforced the mother's view that she was pretty ineffective not to be able to do it herself. Child treatment should be a collaborative effort between parent and therapist, with the latter playing an increasingly advisory role.

Earlier, I pointed out that good-quality data are the keys to an effective technology of change. Insufficient attention has been paid to the problem of how best to train parents to gather and present data. Most introductory parent manuals reduce the complexities of observation to a minimum, and herein lies the secret. Parents can gather good data if the recording procedures are simplified. It is claimed that they will persist in data collection if the data demonstrate desirable change. But persuading parents to gather data is still an art, and again empirical studies are needed to get this on to a firmer scientific footing.

In my opinion, one of the greatest difficulties that parents have is with the principles of shaping. Early texts over-emphasized the contingency–management aspect of behaviour change. Structuring the stimulus and of the S–R connection has been under-emphasized by comparison.

Parents may understand the principle of reinforcing successive approximations, at least at an intellectual level. When it comes to practice, they may display the grudging attitude of "I will not reinforce him for doing that—*he should do it anyway*". Again, they may feel that progress is so good that they will skip a few steps in a carefully graded programme, with consequent difficulties.

And this really brings my opening remarks full circle. The difficulties in shaping have to do, in part, with analysing the targeted behaviours into component parts. Selecting the targets and performing such task analysis form a complex set of skills. At present, few professionals have such skills at a highly developed level, but once the principles are understood by parents, they can be applied in very imaginative ways. Thus, in a slightly different sense, I am arguing that the content of programmes is crucial, and many more studies need to be undertaken to improve the service we can offer handicapped children through the parents.

Re-reading these comments, it may seem that I am not enthusiastic about parent training. This would be a false impression to leave. In my view, training parents as co-therapists is one of the most exciting shifts in therapeutic practice in recent years. I firmly believe that the technology is sufficiently advanced to warrant putting parent training on a firmer service-commitment basis. The big problem is implementing this in such a way that the children benefit and do not suffer from ill-thought-out packages mechanically applied by poorly trained therapists. There is an acute shortage of psychologists skilled in applying behaviour modification to the problems of the mentally handicapped (Kiernan and Woodford 1975). This Study Group can indicate what can be achieved, and equally importantly it should point out areas which should yield rich dividends when properly investigated.

REFERENCES

KIERNAN, C.C. and WOODFORD, F.P. (1975) Training and reorganization for behaviour modification in hospital and community settings. *Br. Ass. Behavioural Psychotherapy Bull. 3*, 31–34

VAN DER EYKEN,W. (1967) *The Pre-School Years.* Penguin Books, Harmondsworth, Middx.

YULE,W. (1975) Teaching psychological principles to non-psychologists: 2. Training parents in child management. *J. Ass. Educ. Psychol.* (in press)

Discussion

Cunningham: A problem I would like to emphasize is the difficulty that parents have in relating to schools and the whole educational system, after they have become part of a behaviour modification programme. The same is true of involvement in any intensive programme, such as the Doman–Delacato system. I don't know the answer to this one.

I didn't mean that behaviour modification does not have relevance throughout a child's life. I meant that it does not, in and of itself, provide a background of educational goals constantly adapted to changing circumstances and stages of development.

Corbett: I am grateful that Cliff Cunningham has pointed out the difficulties of getting unselected parents to participate in programmes, in contrast to the self-selected volunteer parents who are reported on in the literature. One often has to be exceedingly sensitive to the existence of quite brittle family dynamics, which are maintained in certain cases for good but not obvious reasons.

I am worried too about people going into homes to do research projects and then pulling out, without getting members of the support system (health visitors, social workers, and so on) involved with the project. Most people find it too complicated and cumbersome to bring them in, but I think that intervening and then pulling out is potentially even more dangerous here than in institutions, where it is bad enough in that it disturbs the stability of long-term care. There are one or two reports from the U.S.A. that involve non-psychologists in the parent training, but surprisingly few. I wonder why?

Jordan: One reason is that the traditional staff of support services are often discriminative stimuli for negative feelings in the parents.

Cunningham: It's not fair to generalize, but several of my parents have indeed complained that the social workers who came to see them seemed to be unable to be honest about the handicap and were simply embarrassed during their infrequent visits. Secondly, parents of a Down's syndrome baby may need most support at 9–12 months, when the differences between this baby and others begins to be marked, and this is just the time at which the support services tend to have dropped out. Thirdly, I wonder whether the support services could ever provide the kind of treatment we're talking about; I don't think they could.

Kushlick: If there are 100 mentally handicapped children for each population of 100,000 and 12 or 13 social workers, of whom only one has any experience with mental handicap, what hope have you of involving support services in any real way?

Tizard: Well, only a proportion of those children who are at home need constant monitoring and shaping and so forth. Perhaps it's not so impossible a task.

Corbett: Let's face it, people pull out because they have nothing to offer, which is the same reason that doctors pull out. Social workers are not evil or lazy or any other of the reasons you could think of for neglecting these families; they are embarrassed because they have nothing to offer. Involving them in a programme would provide them with something.

Cunningham: Which is of course why behaviour modification has caught on.

Hogg: Azrin and Foxx have a toileting programme which can be completed in a few hours. They argue that it is more economical to send in a training team to apply it than to waste time training the parents to do so. What do you think?

Cunningham: Only with toileting has it been claimed that such a brief programme can be successful. I agree, however, that in the majority of cases it is probably wasteful to try to train parents in all the niceties and rigour of behaviour modification. For a serious behaviour disorder you need a highly competent behaviour modifier working with the parent, but in many cases it is sufficient to convey concepts of structured play to the parents. The kind of support service you need then might be provided by paraprofessionals, related to the professionals as in the Portage Project (Shearer and Shearer 1972).

Kiernan: What type of person do you see performing as paraprofessionals in this country?

Cunningham: Married women with grown-up children of their own, students, volunteers. Parents of older mentally handicapped children can be very supportive too. The Portage paraprofessionals all had college education and experience in working with children. They were also given new training (Schortinghuis and Frohman 1974).

Yule: We must not leave the impression that there was a high proportion of paraprofessionals in the Portage Project. In fact, there were three special-education teachers and only four paraprofessionals. Also, I am not all that impressed by the results. The pre-school children had an average IQ of 75 and their development gain in the 8-month project was 13 months instead of the 6 naively expected by the authors. Shearer and Shearer stated that 91% of the prescriptions they gave were carried out successfully, but without stating how difficult the prescriptions were for the children.

Kushlick: The programme and the prescriptions in that project are excellent; the published report does not do the material justice.

Yule: I am prepared to accept that; we intend to get hold of the prescriptions.

Berger: I would like to raise a question, partly related to our own home-based project on autism and partly to the possibility of using paraprofessionals. Emotional and family-relationship problems arise in these families which the paraprofessional is simply not going to be able to cope with. Can we risk sending behaviour modifiers in to tackle behavioural problems and then expose the family to a psychologist with perhaps a different point of view to sort out the other problems? Or must the behaviour modifier be trained to the point of being able to handle the other problems?

REFERENCES

SCHORTINGHUIS, N. and FROHMAN, A. (1974) A comparison of paraprofessional and professional success with pre-school children. *J. Learn. Dis.* 7, 245–247

SHEARER, M.S. and SHEARER, D.E. (1972) The Portage Project: a model for early childhood education. *Except. Children* 39, 210–217

Parent–School Collaboration

C. A. SAUNDERS, RITA R. JORDAN and C. C. KIERNAN

Thomas Coram Research Unit, Institute of Education, University of London

Central to the behavioural approach to retarded development is the proposition that behaviour is a function of the total environment. Central to the modification of behaviour is the proposition that it can most effectively be changed if antecedents and consequents are modified to enhance behavioural development. The historical development of behaviour modification has shown a gradual increase in the extent of practical commitment to this proposition, with an increase in the number of 'total' programmes in institutions and, latterly, an increase in attempts to train parents and to provide coordinated home–school programmes. In this paper we will argue that the model of parent–school collaboration is potentially ideal but that there are problems in the model which may easily be underrated and which can seriously undercut its viability unless determined attempts are made to complement existing services.

THE HORNSEY INTERVENTION PROJECT (H.I.P.)

The discussion here will be based on experience with the Hornsey Intervention Project (H.I.P.). We shall try to expose problems for discussion, emphasizing that much of what we say is impressionistic and unbacked by statistical evidence.

The Hornsey Intervention Project is a DHSS-funded investigation in a pre-school for mentally and multiply handicapped children, drawn from a wide catchment area in North London. Their fees are paid by local authorities and there is no evidence of selective class bias in the school population. Of the 50 or so children on the school roll at any one time, we have been particularly concerned with 24 whose age range is 2–6 years. Allowing for testing difficulties all except one would be classified as severely handicapped; the exception, as moderately handicapped.

The design of the project involves a comparison of the 24 Centre children with controls who are receiving the usual variety of local authority provision. The 24 children were divided into two balanced groups. For one group, the Parent–School group, we dealt with both the parents and schoolteachers in planning and developing the child's programme. With the other group, the School Only group, we worked only with teachers.

Two characteristics of the parents need to be emphasized. In general, children in the Centre do not arrive because of parental pressure, so the parents do not represent a 'pressure group'. Secondly, the parents are roughly representative of all social classes. Differences estimated by teachers in the level of expected co-operation were balanced out between the Parent–School and School Only groups. So, unlike many other studies of this type in which volunteer parents have been employed, we have used an unselected sample. We feel that if estimates of service needs or the value of services are to be made it is important that these estimates are not biased by volunteer effects.

All the teachers in the Centre were trained in behaviour modification techniques by the H.I.P. team in an individual teaching programme (Kiernan and Riddick 1973; Riddick and Kiernan 1973). After training, teachers were given advice and supervision. Some required a minimal amount, others a lot more.

Parents received an initial individual interview followed by six group sessions in which operant procedures and problem behaviours were discussed. At the same time the H.I.P. team visited parents at home and helped to establish programmes. The general policy was to involve parents to the maximum extent. Continued efforts were made to contact and visit parents who appeared reluctant or who did not maintain programmes in order to encourage them to participate. There were no additional 'rewards' or 'penalties' provided.

In adopting this approach, we hoped to find out whether it was possible to break down intitial resistances and shape collaborative behaviour in the parents. Although the numbers of parents are small our suggestions are based on intensive experience. Discussions with other workers who have tried to institute parent programmes both within and outside an operant framework suggest that the problems we have met have not been unique.

THE MODEL FOR TEACHING

The project, and to a large extent the Centre, has adopted a general organizational framework which reflects the operant model. The basic assumptions which have acted as a guide to this organisation are:

(1) *Some behaviour will be extremely difficult to modify under normal classroom or home conditions.* This includes aspects of self-help skills, play or language behaviour. It is expected that individual sessions in specially engineered environments will allow the initiation of new responses.

(2) *Once behaviour is established in a special setting it is necessary to ensure adequate generalization to other settings.* This may require the rearrangement of classroom and/or home settings. New materials may need to be provided and new regimes of general maintenance developed to reinforce generalized responses. What is provided will depend largely on the behaviour in question. If the child is being trained in simple play skills, the provision of a rich stimulating environment in which his new behaviours are continuously elicited and reinforced will be ideal. If, on the other hand, a language-training programme is

196

being developed the 'trapping' of new skills by naturally occurring contingencies requires careful communication between the person who is running the session and others who interact with the child.

(3) *Provision of the opportunity for observation and development of new operants.* There is no reason why emphasis should not be placed on the element in the operant model concerned with the development of new operants. It is well recognized that behaviour is a resultant of a set of contingencies and the initial and developing behaviour of an individual. Schedules do not determine behaviour, they set the occasion for it. The child in a teaching environment is an active agent who partly moulds that environment. A third necessary element within the operant model as it applies to education should therefore be the observation of the child's behaviour in order to identify new developments in behaviour and to clarify the impact of programmes as their effects generalize to other settings. To do this they need training in observation and in assessing the behaviour of the child in relation to the development of behaviour at a general level. Teachers or parents need to be able to interact with the child in a fairly free but monitored situation, and to feed back any information they gain into the child's programme. This may be built into a programme more formally by allowing times when the child dictates the format of interaction.

In practice, we have found it necessary to schedule individual sessions in a half-hour timetable. Within the Centre each teacher is assigned three children (although she may also deal with others) and it is her responsibility to complete daily sessions with the children. The timetable covers maintenance activities, toileting, and feeding, all of which are done by the teachers. Parents have access to teachers and they in turn can call for advice on medical, nursing, physiotherapy and speech therapy services, most of which are available in the Centre. The members of the project team were available at a ratio of one psychologist to eight children for advice and guidance on programmes.

Programmes were established on the basis of a broad-spectrum Behaviour Assessment Battery (Jones and Kiernan 1974; Kiernan and Jones 1974), and discussions with staff on existing programmes and priorities. The initial programme meeting took account also of any audiometric and other assessments which had been completed on the child and on the child's medical condition.

On the parent side advice from teachers, physiotherapists and members of the H.I.P. team was available on request. As already mentioned the H.I.P. team visited the home to advise and guide on programmes and to provide general support and counselling. A social worker attached to the Centre also visited the home. At the request of the parents the children could be screened by a medical consultant. The Centre has a Parent Teacher Association and a Toy Library to which parents have access.

THE STRENGTHS OF THE MODEL

The main strength of the teaching model outlined above is that it could, potentially, provide effective intervention from an early age. This intervention would include comprehensive assessment and programming and care in home and school settings. In practice the Centre deals only with children over two years old, but there seems no reason why the model should not extend to younger children. Much current work is of course attempting this.

Three particular benefits accrue from the model. First, the input to programmes can be multi-disciplinary. Secondly, the level of material provision can be adequate to the child's educational needs in the school and, through lending systems for toys and other equipment, in the home also. Thirdly, parents can be provided with specific training on teaching, general advice on management, information and guidance on services, advocacy, support, general education on child rearing and time off from dealing with the handicapped child in order to cope better with the needs of the non-handicapped siblings.

Ten of the twelve sets of parents attended at least some of the group training sessions and six attended them all; some fathers as well as mothers attended. Certain problems brought up by the parents at these meetings met ready solutions. For instance, one child had developed the habit of spitting out her food in spite of persistent scolding. We suggested to the parents that rather than using ineffective punishment, they should try to ignore this behaviour, and turn their attention to her younger sister whenever spitting occurred. They had considerable success using this method. The spitting was significantly reduced within a fortnight.

Advice at this level, taken up and used successfully, often formed the basis of more substantial training programmes. Of the seven sets of parents who carried out programmes, four showed themselves capable of running multi-stage programmes and keeping records of the progress made during each session. These ranged from an imitation training programme to the training of self-help skills such as feeding and walking.

Even when parents failed to run programmes, they still often saw the intervention as valuable. Home visits took on a general supportive function. They were also an opportunity to put the parents in touch with services such as the Toy Libraries and help them apply for grants to which they were entitled. Finally the model overcomes a problem with Parent Only programmes in which the teacher deals with the parent without working with the child and, occasionally, without even seeing the child—as in the Manchester workshops run by Jeffree and Cunningham. In this framework the extent to which the child benefits will be a direct function of the parents' initial motivation to attend and on the ability of the parents to acquire new skills rapidly or to interpret advice. The child whose parents fail to attend, learn slowly or fail to persist in programmes will be severely penalized. The Parent–School collaboration model avoids this problem.

As we have already argued, the model offers a theoretically ideal educational model. The model can potentially meet the changing needs of parents and children with the speed necessary to prevent problems getting out of hand and to provide effective habilitation.

Our experience with a small but intensely researched group shows that seven out of twelve parents in an unselected group could run adequate programmes.

From this experience we would suggest that parent–school collaboration could make a useful contribution to the child's education.

PROBLEMS WITH THE MODEL

Although our general conclusions are positive we would share the conclusions reached by workers in the normal school system. Parent–school collaboration can be valuable but can be difficult to achieve (Craft, Raynor and Cohen 1972).

Parents

We have already referred to the fact that our sample of parents was not a volunteer group. We presumably included parents who, for various reasons, might not have volunteered. Three groups of possible problems can be isolated, relating to motivation, lack of time and lack of skills.

Motivation.   Several types of parental reaction to handicap have been recorded (Fuchs 1974). On the one hand there is a denial that the child is handicapped, on the other the claim that nothing can be done. We did not find the first problem, but three of the parents showed the second attitude. Parents had rational arguments as to why specific programming was unnecessary. These were parents of multiply handicapped children for whom the idea of remediation had been replaced by the goal of keeping the child happy.

A further aspect of the problem of motivation appeared with two parents. They were able to accept that something should be done for the child but unable to relate what was done in the short run to the long-term consequences for their child. This was particularly a problem with parents of passive children showing little or no physical abnormality. Endearing and dependent characteristics are not incompatible with the image of the normal pre-school child, and parents may have great difficulty in mobilizing themselves for intensive work at an early age. They may become motivated only after their child has begun to develop more obviously abnormal behaviour patterns, when effective training may be more difficult. G. Freeman (1973, unpublished) found that parents of two young Down's syndrome children showed a clear intellectual grasp of their possible further problems but persistent failure in translating that knowledge into current action.

Motivation to participate in the child's education can also be affected by social or environmental constraints which lie outside the control of the adviser. For instance one of the mothers in our project was undergoing treatment in a psychiatric hospital. She continued to receive out-patient treatment throughout the course of the year, but this proved inadequate and she was re-admitted. Home visits took on a supportive function for this mother, who had little opportunity for working with the child. A second family was living in such cramped and overcrowded conditions that even though the mother was potentially an effective trainer, she was never able to implement any of the suggested techniques. A third mother had recently been widowed and used home visits to overcome a feeling of isolation.

Time. Programmes can only be expected to work adequately if they are implemented consistently, and for this to happen parents must find time to work with their children individually. However, free time is not always available. In three of the twelve families both parents were in full-time employment and a fourth mother worked part-time. This factor, coupled with the demands of other siblings, limited the opportunity for sessions. It also placed constraints on the type of sessions run: prolonged feeding sessions before and after the family's meal were very inconvenient and a high-frequency toileting schedule difficult to maintain.

Jean Fuchs (1974) interviewed 25 families of handicapped school children, all of whom had siblings. She found that although most of the families coped well with the handicapped child and his presence did not adversely affect siblings, the parents clearly could not take on additional training commitments outside school hours. None of the parents used free time for teaching. The general tendency was to attempt normalization of the child's environment to the greatest possible degree.

Cooperation. We found that some parents were more willing to be placed in a teaching situation than others. It was possible with some to set up training sessions in the home and demonstrate the application of techniques such as prompt and fade. Some were keen to try out these skills under supervision while others might be very willing to discuss a particular problem, but extremely reluctant to work with the child under supervision. This represented the major difference between working with teachers in the school and parents in the home. In the school there is an assumed obligation for the teacher to work within the established staff-training programme, whereas training in the home had to be adapted to suit the constraints of the family. The research worker was in no position to demand a particular form of cooperation if the parent was unwilling to provide this. It seems unlikely that the strategies used in some North American projects in which financial or other incentives are used will be acceptable in the service context in the United Kingdom.

It was found difficult to check on the effectiveness of advice and training if the parents were reluctant to keep records. Of the twelve sets of parents only two kept useful records of their programmes, and two made attempts at recording. A further two parents agreed to keeping records on several occasions and were provided with simple recording sheets, but the records were not kept outside supervised training sessions. In the light of this kind of problem it is difficult to make objective evaluations of parents as change agents in both the research and training context.

Teachers

On the teacher side the problems of liaison with parents are problems of

200

technology and attitude. In the Centre, communication between teachers and parents is patchy. It consists of weekly Home/School books, in which the information which can be passed is usually superficial, supplemented by occasional crisis information, and an irregular system of telephone calls and letters. Teacher attitudes are confounded by the poor communication. The teachers naturally feel inadequate as advisers on the home setting when they have little knowledge of the home situation. Teachers do not operate across the two environments and do not generalize school-based attitudes. Thus if a child is exhibiting problem behaviours at school this is readily seen as a situation that needs to be remedied by the application of effective training, but the same kinds of behaviour at home may produce a far less positive attitude to change. There is a strong feeling that home is different from school and the same rules need not apply.

The teacher may not be thoroughly convinced of the value of the model and so be unlikely to pass on her expertise to the parents. We have found that acceptance of the operant approach is closely related to the previous training of the teachers. Those with an alternative philosophy, deriving from what might be called a traditional nursery-school ethos, appear less willing to accept the approach. This is not necessarily reflected in effectiveness of these teachers within sessions but it is reflected in the priority given to training sessions over non-programme activities, such as general stimulation, e.g. trips to the park. It also affects the readiness and conviction with which the ideas are transmitted to other teachers.

Joint problems

Once parents of a handicapped child have managed to obtain treatment for their child they are usually the focus of many conflicting sources of advice, from both the health and education side. Teachers also are usually at the end of the advice chain within educational establishments (by the term 'teacher' we refer to the person who teaches the child, regardless of actual professional status) although they too may be offering advice to parents. If all the sources of advice are in the same place there should be potential for collaboration and a unified approach, but even then there are strong barriers to this degree of cooperation.

Most people agree that 'experts' should confine their advice to their own field of expertise. This often does little to solve the problem if definitions are blurred or there are overlapping areas or aspects of the child's behaviour. Agreements to collaborate and consult are important in planning the overall aims for each child and in making members of each profession aware of the implications of their advice on the other aspects of the child's programme. It is only through joint discussions that decisions can be made on priorities when there is conflict in the short term between the requirements of various professions. We have found that a 'holding' procedure is also needed to prevent hasty action in one part of the child's programme that would affect progress in another area. By this arrangement teachers accept advice from experts but do not act on it until the implications for the child's full programme can be discussed with others involved in that programme. If there is then a conflict, a meeting can be arranged with the expert who gave the original advice and others involved, to work out priorities. This kind of procedure could be adapted for use with parents but we have not done so yet; it has proved possible with teachers only when they have achieved sufficient confidence in their own role to resist immediate compliance with passing suggestions from experts.

Parents often relay back to the teacher the advice they have had from experts outside the school context not so much so that it can be discussed but so that it can be acted on. This is useful in that it gives an opportunity to check on the compatibility of the advice being given to parents with the programmes and a chance to get them to re-examine the advice. Sometimes there are straight misunderstandings which can be dealt with; a mother telephoned a teacher one day with instructions supposed to emanate from a speech therapist that the staff were only allowed to speak two words to her child all day. After the initial hilarity caused by suggestions as to which two words were appropriate the teacher found out from the speech therapist that the actual suggestion was to use simplified language in addressing the child and to use two-word sentences whenever possible.

When programmes are being conducted by more than one person, as happens when the same programme is run at home and at school, the need for good communications and a 'team' approach becomes crucial. This is difficult to achieve unless behaviour is continually monitoring in both settings. Verbal descriptions of the procedure being adopted are often not accurate indices of what is actually occurring. Even if it is possible to get both teacher and parent to record, the behaviour needs to be checked for validation of the records. One example of the misunderstandings that can arise comes from a child whose toileting programme was started (and recorded) at school and then taken up at home. To facilitate data collection, record sheets which had presented no problems at school were provided and explained for use at home. The toileting programme was unsuccessful at school. We were therefore surprised to find that when the first record sheets from home were returned the child had performed consistently each time he was placed on the pot and has only one or two 'accidents' in between. On a home visit the methods used were discussed and it emerged that the child was kept on the pot at home until he performed—often over an hour—which explained the discrepancy in the results. Obviously a more detailed record sheet might have picked up this information, but it is difficult to get records kept at all and so we tend to use the simplest forms possible.

Two possible solutions offer themselves. The parents or teachers could be shown video-tapes of the child's performance in other settings thereby allowing them to appreciate possible subtle differences in discriminative, setting or reinforcing stimuli. We have used this technique with some success discussing differences between the situations as sources of differences in behaviour.

The second possibility is to attempt transfer only when the behaviour in one setting is very well established. This procedure is sometimes necessary. It depends for its success on ensuring that discriminative and reinforcing stimuli are clearly identified. However, it is clearly the negation of the idea of collabora-

202

tion. This is nearer to work-sharing, which is desirable but theoretically and practically a different thing.

Other problems of home/school collaboration relate to differences between goals in the two situations. There may be verbal agreement over goals but the actual behaviour of parents and teachers may show that there are real differences. For example, a parent who cooperated in the training of a behaviour which is being taught at school may find that training interferes with the reinforcement the child is giving to him. The parent may then either refuse to cooperate or manipulate the entire situation to restore the overall level of reinforcement. We have an example of a parent who expressed concern for the independence of her child and seemed to share a common goal with the school in this. Acting on this and teaching the child skills to increase his independence in school resulted in the mother finding new 'reasons' to maintain the child's dependence. The child, who was being trained to walk quite successfully at school, was kept in his wheelchair at home even when a video-recording of the child's progress at school had been shown. The justification for this was that the mother felt that the child was virtually blind (although she would accept demonstrations of what seemed to be perfectly normal eyesight) and might injure himself if he moved around. The conclusion reached was that the covert as opposed to the verbally expressed goal of the mother was to retain a dependent relationship which she found rewarding.

General problems

The sometimes lengthy procedure necessary to get the child admitted to the Centre after what may have been months or years of difficulty at home leads quite naturally to enormous relief once a place has been gained. It is likely that parents consider that the child is now someone else's responsibility (in educational terms, anyway) and associate any resumption of educational responsibility with the probable return of his initial difficulties.

Similarly it may be argued that having a handicapped child increases the need for parents to develop joint interests outside the home. Certainly it seems unfair that they should be penalized for having a handicapped child by being denied the opportunity for outside interests. A lack of such interests may even militate against the child's welfare in the long run.

A final problem concerns attitudes to parents as educators. Attitudes tend to polarize: some see the parents as the prime educating agents, others feel that parents should not involve themselves at all, either because they lack professional competence or because they should be complementary to the teacher. But parents are perforce educators at some level and the question is one of how much this parental role should be structured. There is a case to be made for home being a discriminative stimulus for kinds of behaviour that are not necessarily acceptable in a wider social context; the opportunity to enjoy the freedom this represents that is surely one of the features of a home. One overall goal might be to teach which behaviours are appropriate to which settings.

We would suggest that parents are concerned with providing a looser environment in the sense that more alternatives are available than at school and in allowing the child more control of the environment. This control can generally be allowed because there are fewer individuals with whom it may interfere and the goals are less rigid. This is possibly the best situation in which to develop new behaviour. All of this, of course, depends on the particular home conditions; there may be social or physical conditions that make home *more* restrictive than school. The role of the interventionist here might be to see if a less restrictive environment could be produced by controlling some of the child's behaviour more. One child punished his mother for taking him out by screaming every time his push-chair stopped. This resulted in fewer and fewer trips. By being trained to ignore tantrums as attention-seeking stimuli and to respond readily to other bids for attention, the mother was able to exert more control over this aspect of his behaviour and was then able to re-introduce outings.

We would reject a model for parent–school collaboration that would depend centrally on the role of parents as educators. We would favour a model which would encompass and even encourage such a role but which would provide adequate education for the child in the school independent of the training at home. The role of parents could then range from active participation in goal-setting and training to providing an environment favourable to the practice of skills taught entirely at school.

We would consider it the right of the mentally handicapped child to receive a high-quality education regardless of the capacity of the parent to function as an educator. Similarly, the parent should have the right to opt in or opt out of the education of the child. Parents have complex problems of balancing their own needs, those of the siblings, and those of the mentally handicapped child. We would see their active involvement in programmes as an added bonus for the child. The main educational burden should be shouldered by the school.

Assuming that it is accepted that parents may take on some educational function if they wish, the question of who is to train them for this role arises. The psychologist might seem the most appropriately trained of the relevant professionals, but they are thin on the ground and not always open to this kind of role. Social workers could be used since they are already liaising between the home and school environments and have established advisory roles with the parents. Unfortunately, few social workers are open to the kind of approach to problem solving that operant work implies, and even fewer are trained to take on this role. Teachers have traditionally closer contact with parents and would seem to be the obvious group. However, the role of the teacher would need re-defining to encompass this further aspect, and they would need to be given adequate means to carry out this role. The training of parents is not a 'one-off' operation but needs a heavy commitment of time.

In rural areas peripatetic teachers could be employed to fill this role, and some counties and boroughs are already employing teachers in this way, although not within an operant framework as far as we know. The need in such situations would be to give the teacher experience of the child in the school as well as the home. Whether the teacher who trains the parent is attached to school or not, it is doubtful if an effective role could be played without a back-up from 'experts' in physiotherapy, behaviour modification and other relevant disciplines. As we have already noted, our experience with experts has been mixed. The model suggests that experts should function in an advisory rather than a controlling capacity if teacher motivation is to be maintained. Programme modifications required by day-to-day changes in behaviour should be in the hands of the teacher or the parent. In other words the immediate control of programmes needs to be in the hands of a group who may meet only once a week or less.

The wider implications of this suggestion are that we should be aiming at improvement in skills on the part of teachers and parents rather than simply increasing numbers of experts. The transfer of control to the teacher or parents needs to be monitored, and ways of putting in new information devised.

CONCLUSIONS

From an operant viewpoint the model of parent/school collaboration is highly desirable. However, several problems have been raised in teacher training, organization of school education, communication, and parent attitudes and training. It seems possible that the full model will not be possible for more than half of the parents. Consequently the school must still be seen as the prime educational agent for the child. Great value could however accrue for the child and his parents from increased contact, help and general advice.

The ideal service pattern might involve elements already developed in the normal school system, for instance the teacher/social worker role may be extended to special education. If this pattern were adopted, a small teaching group and home visits would be necessary.

These home visits would have to be seen as part of the normal working day of the teacher and not just added on by extra-conscientious teachers. It seems likely that additional resources of advisers on teaching and management within the school would also be necessary. The H.I.P. team have functioned as 'trouble-shooters' on programmes. In this capacity they have been successful only when they could devote time to problems and possibly take over a component of a programme from a teacher in order to identify difficulties. We would suggest that at least one such advisor/troubleshooter is necessary per 25 children.

We hope that this paper has raised some significant problems and suggested tentative conclusions which will give rise to more articulated thought. The paper represents a mass of speculation and untested hypotheses, but this seems to us to be substantially a reflection of the field of parent–school collaboration at its current state of development.

REFERENCES

CRAFT, M., RAYNOR, J. and COHEN, L. (1972) *Linking Home and School*, 2nd ed. Longmans, Harlow, Middx.
FUCHS, J. (1974) The impact of mentally handicapped children on family routine, with particular reference to siblings. Unpublished Masters thesis, University of London, Institute of Education

KIERNAN, C.C. and JONES, M.C. (1974) Development of an assessment battery for use with profoundly retarded. Final Report to Department of Health and Social Security

KIERNAN, C.C. and RIDDICK, B. (1973) *A Draft Programme for Training in Operant Techniques. Volume 1: Theoretical Units.* Thomas Coram Research Unit, London University Institute of Education, London

RIDDICK, B. and KIERNAN, C.C. (1973) *A Programme for Training in Operant Techniques. Volume 2: Practical Units.* Thomas Coram Research Unit, London University Institute of Education, London

SHARROCK, A. (1972) Research on home–school relations. In Craft, M., Raynor, J. and Cohen, L. (*op. cit.*)

TAYLOR, W. (1972) Family, school and society. In Craft, M., Raynor, J. and Cohen, L. (*op. cit.*)

Commentary

PETER MITTLER

POTENTIAL AND PERFORMANCE IN PARENT–SCHOOL COLLABORATION

The paper by Saunders, Jordan and Kiernan provides an illuminating account of their work in the Hornsey Intervention Project (HIP) and at the same time raises some fundamental problems about parent–school collaboration which deserve detailed study by everyone involved in special education, whether their approach is 'traditional' or 'behavioural'. Although there are points of detail that might be raised about the project itself, discussion will be largely confined to the model proposed by the authors, and to its assets and deficits as they see them.

Nevertheless, one immediate question concerns the extent to which a model which arises from one particular project can validly serve as the basis of generalizations to other projects, particularly since HIP is in many ways far from typical of what might be attempted in 'ordinary' local authority settings. It is atypical insofar as its authors appear to exercise an unusual degree of influence (if not control) on organization and curriculum; they could choose to work intensively with 24 children, select certain parents for direct participation in the project and reject others. And how often does such a large research team descend on a school?

Since the authors have also decided, for better or worse, to evaluate their work by means of a group design involving experimental and control groups, I would have welcomed more evidence in support of the statement that the parents represented 'a rough cross-section of the community at large'. What about years of education completed, age, number of siblings and perhaps details of housing? It would also be useful to know on what basis the 24 control (i.e. non-HIP) families receiving 'the normal varieties of local authority provision' were selected; these details will no doubt be available in later reports from the project. In the meantime, one remains intrigued and challenged by the spectacle of a committed behaviourist group returning to 'classical' research designs.

Despite these reservations, the project's use of an unselected parent sample is excellent, since other projects have either used volunteers, paid parents to participate or persuaded them to enter into formal contracts with project staff. In doing so, however, they invited the difficulties which they frankly and honestly describe and which are probably typical of the problems yielded by any unselected parent sample (in fact, the same problems have also been reported by people working with self-selected volunteer parents), especially problems of finding time and keeping records (O'Dell 1974).

It is clear that the team did everything they could once the project started to prepare and encourage the parents, in the light of their aim of finding out "whether it was possible to break down initial resistance and shape collaborative behaviour in the parents." Since the notion of active collaboration between home and special school is comparatively recent, some of the parents may have been a little surprised to find that they were being asked to play a more active part in collaborating with the school than they might have been expecting. It seems important to emphasize for the future that schools which place a strong emphasis on active parental participation should make it clear from the outset that parents will be asked to play a fuller part in working with the school than they were perhaps expecting or than is usually the case in normal schools. This should help them to come to terms with the fact that although the child is now in skilled professional hands, his full development can only come about as a result of a very close working partnership between home and school.

In this connection it is at first surprising that the authors should feel that parents as a group can only be expected to meet the requirements of the third element of their model—"to provide a generalized interaction with the child which will encourage the development of new operants and the use of existing skills in new ways." They add, however, that parents who are able to participate in more structured teaching should be encouraged to do so both for their own sake and for the sake of the child.

The conclusion seems a little pessimistic, because the second element of the model also appears to be critical to a working collaboration between parents and teachers, since it refers to transfer of learned behaviours from one environment to another; similarly, the first element specifies that certain behaviours cannot be modified under *normal* classroom or home conditions and therefore calls for "individual sessions in specially engineered environments to allow the initial establishment of new responses". Whatever the degree of optimism, the authors deserve to be congratulated for the unusual frankness with which they have listed and discussed the problems at a time when early learning, behavioural approaches to education and parental involvement have all the makings of the bandwagon syndrome.

Parent–school collaboration has so far only been developed on a very limited scale and has not been comprehensively evaluated. What is clear, however, is that all attempts reported so far have differed greatly and that while distinctive features may be found, no common pattern is discernible. In a review of 70 studies, O'Dell (1974) lists a variety of training approaches that have been used, including educational groups, individual consultation and controlled learning environments. A distinction is also made between training content that concentrates on a verbal approach to principles and one that tries to teach behavioural skills directly. Use has been made of lectures and didactic instruction, films, programmed texts, direct cueing, modelling and behavioural rehearsal. All these techniques have produced positive changes, but O'Dell reports that paradoxically little attention has been given to the establishment, maintenance and generalization of parental motivation. "It has taken several years for some parent trainers to realise parents need reinforcement too" (p. 425).

Jordan and her colleagues are well aware of motivational problems, and stress that not all of these are amenable to intervention—e.g. domestic difficulties, psychiatric disorder, or housing problems. Finding the time to work with the child is obviously related to motivation, but the kind of teaching model suggested is also relevant. It is often physically or motivationally difficult for parents to set aside a definite time each day; on the other hand, the teaching model might stress the need to be opportunistic and to exploit the incidental teaching opportunities that occur during ordinary everyday activities. This is in fact the third element of the HIP model which is felt to be most relevant.

However, even if we restrict the parental role to this third element, certain problems arise from its interpretation. In particular, how can parents be expected to 'recognize new operants' without having a fairly detailed knowledge of child development and observational techniques? Obviously, the appearance of clearly identifiable new skills will not be missed, e.g. the attainment of major milestones such as walking, but many other new behaviours are slight and subtle and require considerable sensitivity or training to spot. The first appearance of finger–thumb apposition, visually directed reaching, fear of strangers, hand-to-hand transfer, not to mention the acquisition of minimal additions to the ability to vocalize or imitate voice or gesture, may be missed unless the parent has some kind of observational framework or model available. These may take the form of detailed criterion-reference or developmental charts; ideally, parents should have assessed their own child on such charts, and had an opportunity to compare their assessments with those carried out by teachers or research workers. Discussions based on agreements and disagreements between parents and teachers might then form the basis of a useful working relationship.

The main point here is that experience of normal children is not necessarily enough to enable parents to become skilled and sensitive observers or to recognize the developmental and cognitive significance of new behaviours (see Mittler (1974) for an elaboration of this point). On the other hand, the establishment of a working partnership between parents and professionals can achieve this objective and also help parents to maintain their skills even after contact with a specialist team has been lost because of change of school or for any other reason. In other words, the parents can be helped to 'internalize the model' and use it in new situations (Cunningham and Jeffree 1971).

The use of a framework based on normal development carries a number of risks and disadvantages (see p. 22). However, given a full awareness of the limitations of developmental charts, they can be adapted for use with parents and constitute a viable basis for a working dialogue between teachers and parents.

The paper rightly highlights problems of structure, organization and communication which are inevitably central to the success of any enterprise of this kind. We came to similar conclusions in Manchester and set out in some detail the organizational framework which we developed for our own workshops (Cunningham and Jeffree 1975). Our experience of school-based parent workshops has been that these require even more careful preparation, organization and co-ordination for precisely the reasons given in the paper: parents, teachers, 'expert' advisers, visiting lecturers—not to mention the children at the receiving end—may have different aims and differing degrees of priority. It is essential to clarify aims and objectives both in writing and in practice in order to avoid failures of communication. Perhaps an essential member of the team is someone skilled in the social psychology of systems and organizations.

IMPLICATIONS FOR PRACTICE

The authors usefully conclude by looking beyond Hornsey to consider the problem of home–school collaboration from a wider perspective of developments in special education – a timely problem that must surely concern the current Warnock Inquiry. Assuming that there would be general agreement to the proposition that active collaboration between parents and special educators is desirable and feasible, how can it be brought about?

Several approaches are possible, but it may be unwise at this stage to become too involved in discussions of professional responsibility. For children attending school, however, the head teacher must clearly be seen as the key figure from an organizational point of view, even though much of the day-to-day work may be delegated. If, therefore, we as experts take the view that home–school collaboration can be recommended as an important contribution to the future of special education, we shall need to convince directors of education, special education advisers and head teachers that the attempt is worth while. The Department of Education and Science might even be persuaded to issue a circular on the subject and to organize study groups and seminars for LEA staff involved. It is essential that the problem be tackled realistically and with a full appreciation of the many practical and intangible problems that arise when attempts are made to secure an effective and working partnership between home and school.

My personal view would be that the establishment and maintenance of an active working link between home and school should be one of the aims of special education (Mittler 1974); that the head teacher should be encouraged to develop such a link and be given every assistance by the education authorities. Much greater emphasis should be given to this question in both initial and in-service training of teachers, and opportunities should be available for teachers to discuss their anxieties and reservations in respect of any proposed new role vis-à-vis parents. Encouragement might also be given to the setting up of various pilot schemes in selected special schools, with some degree of monitoring and evaluation, not with a view to making formal comparisons between the effectiveness of various approaches but with the aim of providing detailed descriptive accounts of what they actually do and how they work. At least one member of staff of each school should be given special responsibility for working with parents in addition to any work that individual teachers might do. Ideally, he or she should have special training and experience in working with families but should be able to call on other advice freely and have opportunities for meeting others engaged in similar work to share ideas and pool resources.

The Hornsey project has made an important contribution to the discussions to come.

REFERENCES

CUNNINGHAM, C.C. and JEFFREE, D.M. (1971) *Working with Parents: Report of a Workshop for Parents of Preschool Mentally Handicapped Children.* National Society for Mentally Handicapped Children, and Hester Adrian Research Centre, University of Manchester

CUNNINGHAM, C.C. and JEFFREE, D.M. (1975) The organisation and structure of workshops for parents of mentally handicapped children. *Bull. Br. Psychol. Soc.* (in press)

MITTLER, P. (1974) Parental involvement in the education of the handicapped. *Teaching and Training, 12,* 74–84

O'DELL, S. (1974) Training parents in behavior modification: a review. *Psychological Bulletin, 81,* 418–433

Discussion

Jordan: Some of Peter Mittler's points overlook the fact that this was not a research study aimed at an ideal situation but a study of what is likely to go wrong in the real world when you offer to unselected parents as much as they can take, and demand from them only as much as is reasonable. In most cases this boils down to getting them to practise newly-learnt skills with their children rather than looking for new operants.

Saunders: Much of the pressure to provide improved services comes from articulate, well-motivated parents. If you yield to this pressure and develop a service particularly suited to them, you run the risk of providing nothing of value to the others.

Cunningham: Social class seems to me a red herring. In our parents' workshops we found just as many well-motivated, conscientious parents in social class III as in social classes I or II.

Saunders: We have the same experience. Two of our parents are graduates in the social sciences; they, and similar parents, are happy to discuss their children's problems at length but are not nearly so ready to get on and work with the child in the ways we suggest as are some of the less well-educated parents.

Mittler: I withdraw 'middle-class'. What I meant was parents who are not totally overwhelmed by appalling economic and housing problems.

Jordan: About imposing conditions of admission to the programme: there was no way in which we could do this, and in any case I don't consider it right to make educational help for any child conditional on its parents' undertaking to do far more than is expected of parents of normal children.

Mittler: My suggestion was that it might be wise to warn parents at the outset that this was an unusual school and that you might be making more demands on them than they might have been expecting, rather than admit the child and then gradually build up the demands.

Kiernan: However, it has been reported that parents find it difficult to sustain the demands even when they have accepted initial conditions.

It should be emphasized that the Hornsey project, unlike the Manchester parents' workshops, is a child-orientated system. Every effort is made to collaborate with the parents, but if the parents choose to opt out or prove unable to maintain standards, the teachers concentrate thereafter on working with the child.

Yule: In the home-based project (Howlin *et al.* 1973) for training parents of autistic children we are experiencing the mirror-image of what Chris Saunders and Rita Jordan have been describing: parents who yearn to collaborate with the schools but find the teachers unreceptive to their expectations and demands. It's not the teachers' fault, it's ours: we are presenting them with unrealistic goals. We expect them to grasp instantly what we are aiming at, forgetting that it's taken us months to train ourselves and the parents. We must think much more in terms of shaping the people we want to work with, rather than giving up and saying they're not the prime targets of our programme. I found this paper was too pessimistic, both on this score and on one other: to reach 50% of the parents on the first trial is not a failure but in fact very good going.

Barton: Have you tried training a parent with a handicapped child other than his (her) own? We have one such experience—a mother employed in a classroom other than her child's—and with beneficial results.

Corbett: In the Juniper Gardens project in Kansas, parents are trained in this way with the idea of starting them working with a child on the basis of a more objective relationship.

Cunningham: That's all very well for training parents in particular behaviour modification skills, but Saunders and Jordan are trying to teach them to develop content and goals, and I would have thought their motivation would be too weak with other people's children.

I'm interested that you too have encountered the problem of the parent's over-expectation of your expertise. When we tried to teach school teachers to train parents on our workshop model, we found that they unconsciously assumed the role of experts, partly because of their customary classroom activity, partly because the parents forced it on them, and partly because of their insecurity with the model, so that they were afraid to say "I don't know". Now I am very much aware, as I'm sure everyone here is, how strong is the parents' desire to regard you as an expert. We think it essential to start out with a parent by establishing a relaxed, giving relationship in which the parent can take our advice, but with a pinch of salt.

Mittler: One is, however walking a tightrope, because if one starts out by saying "You are the experts, not us", parents may say (or feel) "My God, if you don't know what is going on, who on earth does?" The right degrees of mutual trust and scepticism can be arrived at only after many weeks of working together.

REFERENCES

HOWLIN, P., MARCHANT, R., RUTTER, M., BERGER, M., HERSOV, L. and YULE, W. (1973) A home-based approach to the treatment of autistic children. *J. Aut. Child. Schiz.* **3**, 308–336

Behaviour Modification in the Hospital School for the Severely Subnormal

ELIZABETH SPINDLER BARTON

Meanwood Park Hospital, Leeds

ABSTRACT

Published work on the use of behaviour modification in the classroom is considered with reference to hospital schools for the severely mentally handicapped. Typical programmes are given and representative cases discussed for problems in toileting, dressing, instruction following, play, verbal comprehension, locomotion and vocalizations. There is a strong case for the use of behaviour modification in classes for the severely retarded.

It has been remarked (Haskell 1974) that conferences of this nature do little to aid the teacher or the nurse who is trying to cope with the problems of the severely subnormal. This paper presents an account of published work on such problems followed by some applications of behaviour modification techniques in an ESN(S) classroom.

Many problems are encountered in the classroom with severely subnormal children. Operant techniques provide some answers to them, both in enabling the child to learn new behaviours and in providing the teachers with methods of control so as to produce an atmosphere more conducive to learning.

LITERATURE REVIEW

Of the many studies of behaviour modification in the classroom, this review will cover only those where the pupils are mentally handicapped or where the procedure or situation is relevant to the mentally handicapped. Bijou (1968) emphasizes that physical abnormalities and reinforcement histories should be borne in mind when one approaches the training of the mentally handicapped child. The child who can only lie on his back will be severely limited in stimuli; further, he may look ugly and so people may reject him; this could lead to social deprivation, which limits language development and experience with social contingencies, e.g. approval and praise, which may thus later prove to be inadequate reinforcers. A mentally handicapped child may well have an inadequate reinforcement and discrimination history. Environment with few oppor-

213

tunities for reinforcement and discrimination produce children with limited repertoires; such environments may use only infrequent reinforcers or, more likely, indiscriminate reinforcers (for example, where parents mistakenly pander to every whim). Restrictions to a child's development can also occur where the child is treated as abnormal or chronically ill—exemplified in literature by the boy who had convinced himself and his nurse that he was a hunchback in *The Secret Garden* (Burnett 1970) and so remained in bed all day. Abnormal parents, for example deaf mutes, may also restrict a child's possible learning experiences, as may deprived economic and social circumstances. If undesirable behaviour is inadvertently reinforced by unknowing or desperate parents it can reach a high rate and in itself prevent the child from learning more, for children who display obnoxious behaviours can be considered unteachable. Severe aversive stimulation from violent parents can also retard development by depressing a number of behaviours.

Hall, Pangan, Rabon and Broden (1968) pointed out that student teachers were often ill equipped to cope with behaviour problems resulting from factors such as these. These authors gave the teachers a short introduction to operant conditioning and then instructed them in specific procedures to employ in their classroom. The teachers were given feedback as a reinforcer for applying various types of reinforcement (attention, length of break, classroom games) themselves, and a fairly well-designed study (ABAB and reliability) showed that the teachers could accept and successfully apply behaviour modification principles. Bijou's points underline what difficulties a poor reinforcement history can lead to. Many other authors emphasize how much a teacher can alter a child by arranging for a good reinforcement history. The aim is to make teachers aware of the effect their behaviour has on their pupils, so that they can arrange to apply reinforcement appropriately.

CONTINGENCIES

The most commonly reported contingency is that of token reinforcement. Birnbrauer and Lawler (1964) described the use of sweets and tokens to shape and reinforce desirable classroom behaviour in young retardates, using time out as a consequence of undesirable behaviours. The behaviours involved were entering quietly, hanging up coats, sitting attentively, and working and were improved in 37 out of 41 children.

The procedures were tested more rigorously in BAB design by Birnbrauer, Wolf, Kidder and Tague (1965), who aimed to study the value of tokens given for correct responses, together with 10-minute time out for undesirable behaviour. The tokens were employed for 3 months, withdrawn for a month, and reintroduced for a further month. There were fifteen mildly retarded subjects, aged 8–14 years. The behaviours under study were: percentage errors in assignments, productivity, and amount of disruptive behaviour. After improvement on introduction of tokens, three reactions were observed upon their withdrawal. Five students showed no change in behaviour rate, six students increased in errors and four increased in both errors and severe disruptive behaviours. All students improved on reinstatement. This paper shows the value of the tokens but introduces the problem of fading out tokens, which difficulty is echoed through many of the papers which followed.

O'Leary and Becker (1967) decided to use a token reinforcement programme to try and reduce the deviant behaviour of the eight most disruptive children in an adjustment class. After baseline observation, the teacher was instructed to go from desk to desk giving ratings exchangeable for sweets and trinkets. There were dramatic results with all eight students, though the design is only an AB one. Reliability of observation was 75–100%. The authors comment on the lack of reversal or similar control and say a replication is planned in another class.

Zimmerman, Zimmerman and Russell (1969) compared the use of tokens and praise on instruction-following behaviour in seven moderately retarded students. They concluded that tokens improved the behaviour of four of the students considerably, whereas two others appeared to do equally well on tokens or praise. One student responded to neither reinforcer. The study used only a few sessions in each experimental condition and thus showed the immediateness of response in most, but not all, subjects.

Dalton, Rubino and Hislop (1973) reported the effects of token rewards on school achievement of mongol children. The thirteen subjects lived at home, were 6–14 years old and had IQs between 30 and 64 on the Leiter scale. They were divided into control and experimental groups and their behaviour was rated on a conduct scale as positive or negative, the reliability of raters being checked. Language and number skills were also tested before and after the experiment and a year later. The experimental group received tokens (poker chips) on an intermittent schedule (VR5) and praise continuously for correct answers in arithmetic and language programmes, the tokens being exchanged at the end of the session. Control children received identical treatment but no tokens. The procedures were in effect $3\frac{1}{2}$ days a week for 8 weeks for $2\frac{1}{2}$-hour instructional periods. All token students, except one, showed gains in both language and arithmetic; all control students also showed improvement on language, but only two in arithmetic. A year later the token group's improvements were more sustained, some over-learning presumably having taken place. Thus, tokens were somewhat stronger reinforcers than praise alone. One wonders whether a greater difference might have been seen had the tokens been distributed on a continuous reinforcement schedule. Although the advantages of intermittent reinforcement need to be assessed this would be better done if we knew the effects of continuous reinforcement, particulary on follow-up.

In 1971, Axelrod concluded in a review article on token reinforcements in special classes covering mental handicap, drop-outs, and emotionally disturbed children that most token economies in special classes were effective, but that one must programme against extinction when tokens are withdrawn and that it is best to use existing reinforcers (as did Phillips 1968 in the achievement home). However, as tokens are operative in adult life, it is difficult to see why children should be expected to operate without them—although the schedule could be made intermittent and the back-ups considerably delayed for practical reasons and to guard against extinction. Axelrod also criticizes the experimenters for failing to demonstrate that it is the contingent reinforcement that is effective because they have not used a reversal or similar design; however, this is more applicable to the early than the later studies, many of which employed some controls (as described). His criticism that large numbers of personnel and/or electronic equipment are required which are not normally available in the classroom for mentally handicapped children is not justified as regards the more severe degrees of handicap, as the teacher usually has at least one helper. The token system therefore appears to benefit several different groups and the criticisms raised so far seem to be largely surmountable.

An even more economic contingency is that of Premack, where a low-rate behaviour is reinforced by the opportunity to engage in a high-rate behaviour. Homme *et al.* (1963) used the Premack principle to control the behaviour of nursery school children. The children were 3 years old and spent much time in running and screaming. These activities were therefore made contingent upon desired behaviour such as sitting still. Later on, the subjects earned tokens for carrying out low-probability behaviours; the tokens could then be exchanged for the opportunity to engage in high-probability behaviour. With these procedures behavioural control was evident in a few days, though no data or reliability data are given; as the authors conclude, in this informal application, the principle was shown to be both practical and effective.

Experiments on particular behaviours

Three particular types of behaviours have been placed under behaviour control in the classroom: instruction following, undesirable behaviours and academic behaviours.

Two studies concentrated particularly on instruction following. Whitman, Zakaros and Chardos (1971) and Schutte and Hopkins (1970). Contingent attention from the teacher increased instruction following from 60% to 80% in kindergarten subjects (Schutte and Hopkins 1970). In the study by Whitman *et al.* the aim was to assess the efficacy of using physical guidance plus reinforcement in order to produce appropriate motor responses to instructions. The subjects used were both severely retarded, a boy of $4\frac{1}{2}$ years and a girl of 7 years. Ten instructions were given to each subject for training, and ten were used as a generalization test. The reinforcement was verbal praise and cereal; the manual guidance was gradually faded out. Short training sessions were given each day, with the full twenty instructions presented at the end in a probe session (without guidance or reinforcement). An ABAB design was used with data checks and reliability. The results show that instruction following increased considerably when reinforcement was in effect and there was quite good generalization to the unreinforced instructions. The authors recommend that the child should know the words before they are presented in instructions in order to get the best results. Instruction following is the most basic requirement in classroom behaviour and it is encouraging that the behaviour is amenable to reinforcement.

Many papers have, of course, been concerned with the elimination of disruptive behaviours, usually centring on talking out of turn and aggression towards other pupils. Patterson (1965) described an attempt to control hyperactivity in a 9-year-old boy of borderline normal intelligence. The hyperactive behaviour complained of consisted largely of talking, pushing and hitting. A small box with a bulb and an electric counter were placed on the boy's desk. If he avoided disruptive behaviours for a certain period of time (which increased as the trials progressed), the light flashed and the counter clicked. At the end of each session, the number of points on the counter was exchanged for money or sweets which were then divided up between the class. Eight fewer disruptive behaviours per minute occurred during conditioning (which was significant, $P < 0.01$).

Perline and Levinsky (1968) were interested in controlling the classroom behaviour of four severely retarded subjects (SQ 22–38), mean age 8 years. The maladaptive behaviours were aggression toward peers, out-of-seat behaviours, aggression toward the teacher, aggression toward objects, and stealing. Tokens were given contingent upon behaviours which were compatible with the maladaptive behaviour in response to instructions from the teacher. Tokens were removed when a maladaptive response occurred; a 5- to 15-minute time out was also used for half the subjects. Maladaptive rates decreased, though not to zero; those subjects who had had both tokens and time out showed no greater improvement. However, the study can be criticized on three counts: firstly, it was only an AB design; secondly, the time out was not complete (the child was merely restrained within the same environment); and thirdly, from the data given, the procedure was apparently much more effective with one than with the other three subjects and this point was not discussed.

With respect to the use of behaviour modification to improve academic skills, Warren (1963) pointed out that although it was long thought that SSN children could not learn basic academic skills, a survey of the academic attainments of 177 pupils (IQ 35–58) showed that reading and spelling and simple arithmetic, though limited, were attainable.

Mein (1967) reviewed the experiments by Hermelin and O'Connor (1960) on the reading ability of the severely subnormal and concluded that such children might be able to learn to read. Hermelin and O'Connor's work shows that high-frequency words tend to be learned more easily. Ten subjects with a mean age of $12\frac{1}{2}$ years and mean IQ of 43 could be taught to transfer the ability to read a word with a picture to reading the word presented alone. Furthermore, once they had learned to transfer, successive transfer became quicker and quicker (4.7 presentations for the first word, 1.9 for the second and 1.1 for the fourth). When the transition from picture to non-picture proved difficult, the size of the picture was gradually reduced to aid transfer. These studies all encourage the teaching of reading (particularly important signs) to the severely subnormal.

Rydberg (1971) experimented with reading discrimination in six children aged 6–16 years, IQs 22–46. In seventeen training sessions the children were reinforced for correctly reading words on cards (with the pictures on the back). The sessions were from 3 to 35 minutes. Follow-up tests were carried out 24 and 48 days later. The higher mental ages learned best, with little drop on follow-up.

217

The lower mental ages, however, did learn a few words, particularly their own names, but forgot quite a lot on follow-up. Rydberg concluded that it was quite possible to train visual discrimination by reinforcement.

Brown *et al.* (1970) believed that children with IQs under 50 could learn a lot more than basic self-help skills, if appropriately taught with the use of contingency management. In the first of their papers they describe the training of a 12-year-old girl, IQ 47. She was presented with 57 words printed on individual cards; on baseline she could read 6 of these words. Training used modelling and reinforcement techniques. Each word was presented and labelled, then the girl was asked to repeat the label and given reinforcement or brief time out as appropriate. The criterion of success was spontaneous naming on three consecutive occasions, and the successes were graphed on the classroom wall. As this method was successful Brown et al. carried out a further study with six subjects, aged 12–14 years, IQs 36–49. The aim of the study was to determine whether group or individual training was better. Ten words were printed on index cards, five for group training, five for individual training. The reinforcers were sweets and peanuts. After baseline, the subjects were taught one set in group sessions and one set in individual sessions. The results from the group were better; the authors suggest the reason may be imitation or social reinforcement. However, the methodology of the paper is inadequate (there is no reliability assessment, no test of generalization, no breakdown of scores subject by subject) and there may have been other variables operating. It would be interesting to repeat the study, however, as group training is more economical than individual training in teacher time. Barton (1972, unpublished) found no difference between individual and group training in a similar study.

There are few studies on the teaching of addition skills to severely retarded subjects; one of them is that of Brown and Bellamy (1972), who taught four subjects a sequence of arithmetic skills which led to the consistent solution of simple problems. Their procedure was based on learning theory, with behavioural analysis and systematic environmental manipulation and measurement. If the subject's initial response was incorrect, an established sequence was employed to give the least help necessary to elicit and reinforce the correct response.

Many papers describe the excellent results which can be obtained from the use of behaviour modification to teach self-help skills and speech. Few papers relate these to classroom programmes, and so an extensive review of this work will not be given; the techniques, however, are of considerable value in the hospital school for the severely subnormal, where the children have in many cases not developed self-help or communication skills.

In conclusion, the papers on the use of behaviour modification procedures in the classroom are very encouraging, particularly to those involved in the teaching of children for whom learning is not fun and is not therefore a reinforcement in itself. Socially inadequate or handicapped children do not necessarily fail to make progress because they *cannot* learn but because their behaviour is too disruptive for any teaching to take place, and the teacher has to spend his whole time achieving some semblance of classroom control. Even when such children are taken individually and their attention is gained, learning and academic tasks have a negative connotation as they have been aversive events in the past because of failure or frustration. These children should not be denied the benefit of learning because they cannot see the situation as reinforcing in itself; reinforcement and time out provide the contingencies to help the child learn.

METHOD

Meanwood Park Hospital, Leeds is a medium-sized subnormality hospital (550 beds). Amongst the hospital patients are 60 children, who together with 10 day pupils (who have generally been found impossible to place in the regular ESN(S) schools) attend the Meanwood Park School daily.

The children all received a full psychological assessment of (as appropriate) intellectual or developmental level, language skills, social skills and, occasionally, perceptual motor development. They were 3–17 years old; there were 50 boys and 20 girls. The results showed they could be grouped as follows:

TABLE 1

Number of school children in each intelligence quotient (IQ) and social quotient (SQ) category

Level of retardation	No. of standard deviations below the mean	IQ	SQ
Borderline	−1	0	0
Mild	−2	0	2
Moderate	−3	5	7
Severe	−4	12	11
Profound	−5	36	33

TABLE 2

Number of children in each class and the mean age and intelligence or development quotient

Class	No.	Mean IQ or DQ	Mean CA
1	16	5	8
2	10	19	8.5
3	12	21	11
4	6	10	13.5
5	9	31	14.5

Examination of the social skills revealed that 38% could not feed themselves, 61% could not dress themselves, 52% were not toilet trained, 57% had no speech, 36% were non-ambulant, 7% had severe behaviour disturbances.

It was, therefore, decided to plan individual programmes related to each child's most educationally disruptive problem or difficulty which it was at the same time a reasonable ambition to overcome or teach. The programmes were to be carried out on an individual or classroom basis as appropriate. Originally a control group design was planned but this was later dropped in favour of own-subject or multiple-baseline designs. For staffing reasons, it was impossible to start all the children on programmes at once and the number involved is being gradually increased. The behavioural problems initially chosen for behaviour modification programmes were as follows:

Poor instruction following	:	4 children
Inability to feed self	:	3 ,,
Inability to dress self	:	3 ,,
Inability to toilet self	:	5 ,,
Lack of communication skills	:	13 ,,
Inappropriate speech	:	1 child
Running away	:	2 children
Poor locomotion, reaching and vocalizations	:	7 ,,
Lack of response to environment	:	19 ,,
Stereotypy and self-injury	:	3 ,,
Poor number	:	1 child
Not using both hands	:	1 ,,

As programmes were instituted, the child was observed for a baseline period during which reliability checks were made using independent observers. Data were not accepted until reliability was at least 85%. Baselines of different length were recorded, as appropriate to multiple-baseline designs.

Instruction-following

Three children from class 3 were placed on instruction-following programmes of two different kinds: (a) a limited number of specific instructions to be followed each day and (b) reinforcement for compliance with any instruction given in the classroom.

The first procedure was used with a 15-year-old moderately retarded schizophrenic girl who was completely out of control when she was admitted to the school. She had been in an adult psychiatric hospital for a year and seemed to be deteriorating in that situation. She was therefore admitted to the school for a trial period. After several days of negativistic, aggressive, demanding tantrum behaviour a simple programme for instruction-following was instituted. She was given a weekly token card on which were written between 7 and 10 instructions with which she was asked to comply each day, e.g. obtaining and eating lunch. As these tasks were completed they were initialled by a supervisor and at the end of each day the initials were converted into money (1 p per instruction). The money was spent immediately in the school shop on reinforcing items (usually toiletries). That the programme was a success can be seen from the completed cards, which show all instructions completed on most days and few losses of tokens (i.e. initials) for bad behaviour. The card system is quite flexible as tokens can also be earned for not breaking rules, as well as following them;

220

further it was not found to be a disruptive or onerous procedure in the class-room.

Two younger (aged 10 and 12 years) and less able (IQs 28 and 30) Down's syndrome children were also placed on an instruction-following programme. A multiple-baseline design with different lengths of baseline was chosen to try and demonstrate the effect of the procedure a little more rigorously than is usually possible in the classroom. The children had been thought of as almost impossible to work with because of their negativistic, disobedient behaviour which made learning most difficult. It was decided to reinforce compliance to any instruction given in the classroom with a token. Tokens were chosen because of their advantages of speed, flexibility, lack of satiation, security and the possibility of fining which it was thought could be introduced at a later date. Observations were made by sampling as it was impossible to record all instructions and the response thereto. During the baseline period the children were observed for 15 minutes each day (time of day randomly chosen); during the reinforcement phase 15-minute samples were taken once or twice a week. The children were largely unaware that their behaviour was being recorded, as they were very used to observers in the classroom.

We taught the children the value of the tokens by trading them immediately for the first few days and gradually delaying the trade-in to the end of the session (2 hours in all).

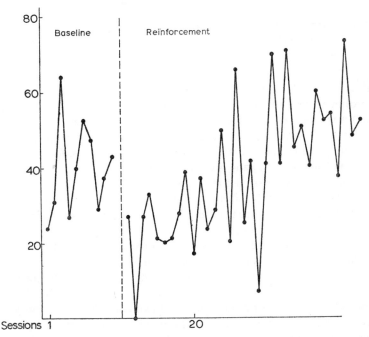

Fig. 1. Percentage obedience by a 10-year-old severely retarded girl to instructions given in the classroom.

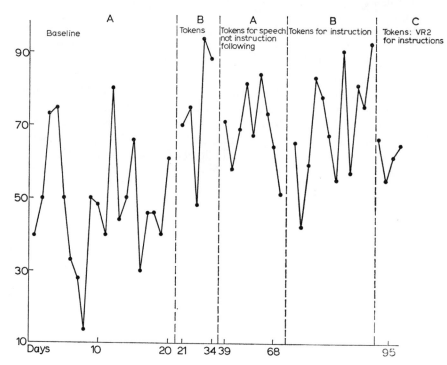

Fig. 2. Percentage obedience by a 12-year-old severely retarded boy to instructions given in the classroom under five different conditions. VR, variable reinforcement

Results. Shirley (Fig. 1) received 13 baseline sessions and has been on token reinforcement ever since (8 months); results are from about 30 sessions. John (Fig. 2) was observed for 21 baseline sessions; he then went onto token reinforcement for instruction following for 16 sessions. This was judged to be so successful by the teachers that the tokens were gradually reduced to minimize extinction (Axelrod, 1971) and given instead for speech and individual working for the next 50 or so sessions; instruction-following was assessed during 9 of these sessions. Tokens for instruction-following were reinstated for a brief period and then the reinforcement schedule was reduced to approximately 50%.

Discussion. Although the plan was to reinforce each obedient operant with a token, in practice this proved impossible and in fact the children were reinforced on a variable ratio of anything from 50% to 90%. This intermittent reinforcement was probably responsible for the very slow progress made by Shirley—the less intelligent and more negativistic of the two children. John's progress was quite clear and he was soon able to move onto his next programme (spontaneous speech). The results underline the importance of dispensing consistently and frequently.

Toileting procedure

Class 4 had 6 children whose mean IQ was 10, and mean age $13\frac{1}{2}$. These children were all incontinent and it was decided to turn the class into a toilet-training unit, as incontinence was the most significant and disruptive aspect of the children's behaviour.

Commodes were obtained and placed within the classroom; a time-out area was delineated and the subject's reinforcers were recorded and obtained. After a baseline period of 3 days, during which account was taken of accidents and successful visits to the toilet, a concentrated training package of the Azrin type

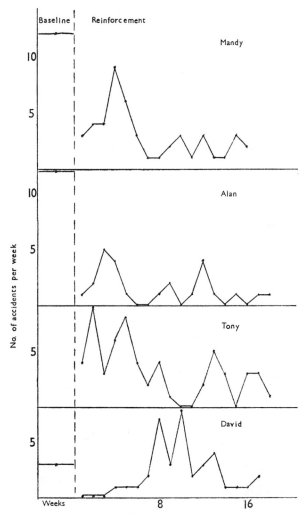

Fig. 3. *Number of toilet accidents per week in three profoundly retarded children and one severely retarded child (David).*

223

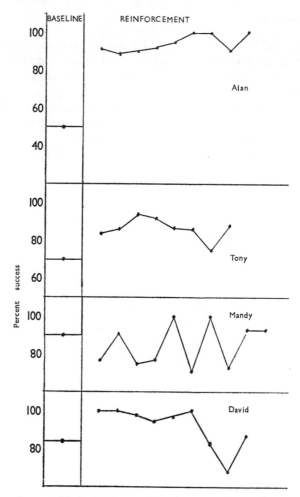

Fig. 4. Number of successful eliminations in the toilet per week by three profoundly retarded children and one severely retarded child (David).

(Azrin 1973, Azrin and Foxx 1971, Foxx and Azrin 1973) was put into effect. During school hours the children were taken and placed on the commodes every half hour. They remained until elimination or for 15 minutes, whichever was the earlier, and were reinforced for success with extra fluids, sweets, biscuits, praise and attention. In between visits to the commode they sat at a table with a teacher and played with various attractive toys and during this time received attention and fluids as long as they remained clean and dry. Accidents resulted in time-out from this reinforcing situation for half an hour. A time-out chair with a seat belt was placed away from the group in a corner of the room.

All successes and accidents were recorded.

Results. Two of the six children did not complete the training period through repeated illness. Results are given individually for the other four (Figs. 3 and 4), as each child responded differently. No child achieved complete dryness, though accidents were reduced to as few as one per week; one boy, David, after an initial good response showed a complete relapse. In all cases, progress was erratic. These children are all severe epileptics or have behaviour disorders as well as being profoundly retarded and, as is often the case with non-laboratory studies, this leads to uncontrolled variables. We concluded, however, that the procedure was manageable in the classroom and the results were worthwhile. The procedure was demanding of the teachers' skills but resulted in significant progress of the child.

Dressing

Though dressing is not a skill traditionally taught in school, it was thought appropriate for the severely subnormal classroom for three reasons: it would be of considerable use to the child, it provided an easy way to develop an instructional control and reinforcing relationship between the teacher and the child, and it reduced the time taken up during the school day in helping children on and off with coats, knickers, shoes, etc.

The children learned to put on easy items of clothing despite low IQ (down to 8) and extra handicaps of deafness and poor sight. A typical prompt-and-fade procedure was used, the child learning by backward chaining and expected to carry out more of the dressing action each time to gain the reinforcer. The younger, profoundly retarded children were reinforced with spoonfuls of a milky sweet chocolate pudding which had the advantages of being quickly

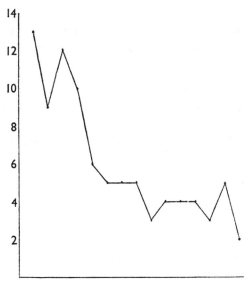

Fig. 5. Number of prompts per 20 trials required in teaching a severely retarded girl (IQ 22) to put on her pants.

swallowed and leading to satiation only slowly. Large, loose, elasticated clothes were chosen.

A typical result (Fig. 5) shows the progress made by a 10-year-old girl (IQ 15) in putting on her pants.

The dressing programmes were carried out individually, the children being withdrawn from the classroom by the teacher and trained in a small bare room while the rest of the class was engaged by the teaching assistant in a holding activity (records, painting, jigsaws etc.). Dressing programmes were usually completely successful and showed generalization to the ward, though if the child was not required to dress himself at all for several weeks he required retraining. This usually took less time than before.

Inappropriate speech

A phenomenon occasionally met with amongst severely and profoundly retarded children is that of clear but confused and inappropriately applied speech. Some earlier work (Barton 1970) suggested that one can alleviate this by reinforcing appropriate speech. The present subject was a 15-year-old profoundly retarded girl (IQ 11), Liz, who mechanically repeats a small number of stereotyped phrases ('mucky cat', 'mucky bugger' etc.) and tunes ('Edelweiss' ad nauseam); she also confuses the names of simple objects, calling a shoe a teddy bear and so on. A reinforcement programme for appropriateness was attempted with a limited number of pictures of items she regularly confused. Liz was seen for 15-minute individual sessions three or four times a week. She was presented with a picture and asked to name it; if she failed she was prompted and then the card was presented again. Successes were reinforced with sweets.

Results. Fig. 6 shows Liz's slow progress after the introduction of the reinforcer. Twelve cards were presented. A complete success scored 2, and 1 point was given when prompting led to success on the second presentation (maximum score, 24).

Discussion. Liz improved in appropriate labelling but showed persistent difficulties in the discrimination of one or two items: these were cat and dog, a boiled egg (which it was later discovered was never served her) and a toilet. These failures underline the need for a most judicious choice of items in teaching programmes for these children. We are now repeating the programme for Liz, using concrete objects so as to determine the most efficacious mode.

Running away

A common and exceedingly disruptive behaviour in the ESN(S) classroom is that of running out of the classroom and away, with teachers following in haste. The reinforcer is, of course, the thrill of the chase and as such is built in and impossible to remove. Severely subnormal children often take no heed of

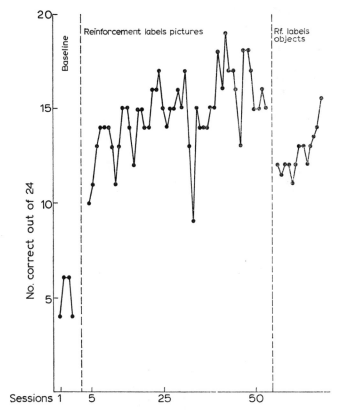

Fig. 6. Number of correct i.e. appropriate responses in labelling pictures and objects by a profoundly retarded brain-damaged girl.

traffic, so that the behaviour cannot simply be ignored where the child is also adventurous and enjoys the escape even if not chased.

Mark, 12 years old, IQ about 26, persistently ran out of the classroom or slipped through a window and was on two or three occasions returned by bewildered policemen from several miles away. The behaviour was rather variable as Mark is a severe epileptic, and before each seizure Mark becomes lethargic and disinclined to run away. A long baseline was therefore taken and it was decided to reinforce appropriate and meaningful trips from the classroom as a behaviour incompatible with the inappropriate and purposeless running away. Mark was sent on 1 to 15 errands each day, and successful completion of the errand (i.e. his return to the classroom) was rewarded by a token.

Results and discussion. Fig. 7 shows number of escapes per day during baseline and contingency phases; Fig. 8 shows the percentage of errands which were successfully completed. The procedure was largely effective, though Mark continues to be variable in his behaviour. The teachers are pleased because not

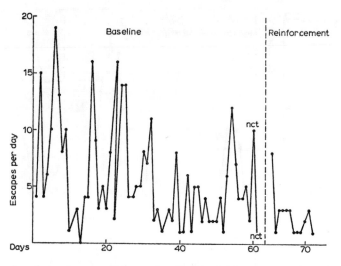

Fig. 7. *Number of occasions on which a profoundly retarded boy ran away from the classroom per day. nct, non-contingent tokens.*

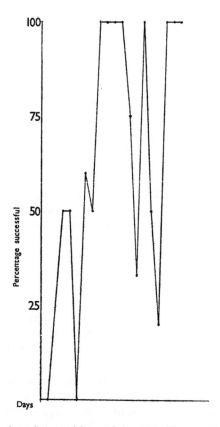

Fig. 8. *Number of successful errands completed by a persistent escaper.*

only do they not need to keep a constant guard on windows and doors but also because Mark is available more often for other learning experiences.

Special care children

In the school about 25 % of the children fall into what is known as the special care category. These children are both physically and mentally profoundly handicapped. The mental ages are rarely greater than 9 months and are generally much lower. It is difficult to decide what sort of training programme can be recommended for these children. Two basic aims are evident: first, that they should move about more and emit more behaviour; secondly, that they should be made more aware of their environment. Typically these children lie passively and make little movement or response.

A major difficulty in working with this type of child is that of finding a suitable reinforcement. Some work has been carried out at Meanwood (Myrvang 1974, unpublished) on the use of vibration as a reinforcer for special care children. One case will be briefly described. The subject was an 8-year-old girl with a developmental age of 3 months, who was given 35 fifteen-minute sessions over a two-month period. The behaviour involved was vocalizations, i.e. voiced sounds not including crying, sneezing etc. Reliability of observations was assessed using

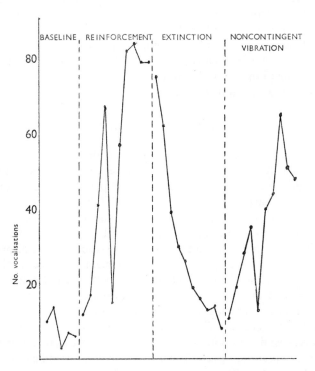

Fog. 9. Number of vocalizations per 15-minute session made by a profoundly handicapped 8-year-old girl when vibration was used as a reinforcer.

229

naive observers. The design composed five baseline sessions during which vocalizations were merely quantified, then ten sessions with a 10-second burst of vibration (using a large, vibratory pad (Niagara) placed under the child) contingent upon vocalization; this was followed by ten extinction sessions and then by ten sessions of non-contingent vibration.

Vocalizations remained steady during baseline (Fig. 9), increased under contingent reinforcement, and decreased during extinction. There was some increase during non-contingent reinforcement which may be due to the non-contingent reinforcement having the effect of intermittent reinforcement. The results are encouraging in suggesting a potentially useful exploration tool for development.

Verbal comprehension

A common problem amongst severely subnormal schoolchildren is that of poor language skills; the children have difficulties both with comprehension and expression. With the less able children work is often begun with simple comprehension tasks where the behaviour desired can be easily promtped. Such a programme has been carried out with a number of children in the school. Initially, a familiar object is chosen and placed on the table in front of the child and he is asked "Give me the X"; this is soon extended so that he has two objects to choose from, and so on. Then prepositions and combined phrases can be taught e.g.: put the ball on the plate. The children are usually withdrawn from their classroom and taught individually in this type of programme, which under ideal circumstances is carried out daily. A session usually lasts 15 minutes or less, according to the child's interest.

Some results are shown in Fig. 10.

BRIEF DISCUSSION

Examples of the value and application of behaviour modification to problems occurring in the hospital ESN(S) school have been described. Many other examples could have been given. The important point is that each of these programmes has been carried out in school by the child's regular teacher. Although a number of these programmes do require individual work, this is not impossible where a teaching assistant can keep the other children in a holding activity.

One of the major problems in the ESN(S) classroom is that of poor instruction following. The children find the environment more rewarding for undesirable behaviours, as these are the ones to which teachers often have to pay most attention and the class can deteriorate into a continuous and unrelieved prevention of unwanted behaviours. Such a situation is not conducive to learning even if the children found such learning easy. Some ESN(S) children can, therefore, spend their schooldays without ever settling to a learning activity other than the ubiquitous jigsaw. The use of behaviour modification to improve instructional control is, therefore, invaluable.

Teachers are often reluctant to use reinforcement, as they feel embarrassed

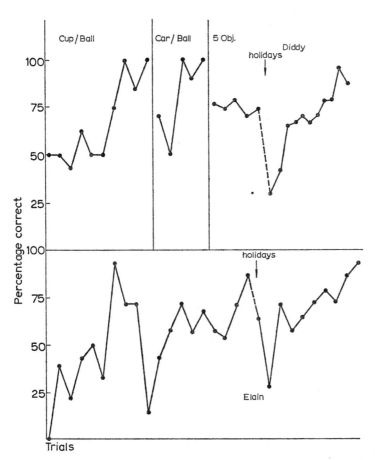

Fig. 10. Number of correct actions performed in response to simple commands in a verbal comprehension programme.

that they cannot by their teaching art alone interest the child in the task and have to resort to bribery. It is necessary to discuss this problem fully, pointing out the role of praise with the normal child; otherwise, in my experience, the teacher devotes more effort to thinning out the schedule of reinforcement than to developing new behaviours.

In conclusion, I think there is a strong case for the use of behaviour modification in the ENS(S) classroom, that the subjects described in this paper demonstrate this and also show its practicability, but that the problem of introducing it into a traditional classroom cannot be minimized.

APPENDIX

Organization of the school

Meanwood Park School has at present a staff of eighteen, which consists of

1 head teacher and 6 qualified teachers (3 of whom have the Diploma of Education of Backward Children), 3 unqualified teachers and 8 general helpers.

There are between 6 and 21 children in each class. Numbers vary slightly, as children admitted for short-term care to the hospital also attend the school. Each class has at least one qualified teacher. Other staff is distributed according to need. The school is run on a team-teaching system.

Organization of the sessions

An old store room in the school was converted in 2/3 cubicles each containing a table and two chairs. The teacher takes the child from the class and brings him into this quieter setting for his teaching programme. Ideally each child on a programme would receive a 15-minute session each day. In practice, they usually receive 3 per week. The sessions are planned out beforehand with printed forms to ease data taking. Codes for scoring etc. are devised previously. If the teaching material is to be presented randomly this is worked out beforehand according to coin tosses or tables of random numbers, and printed. If a fading or shaping technique is being used, the fades are previously worked out and numbered so that if several people are carrying out sessions with a child they can number the *next* form to be used with the fade level they reached in their particular session. Files for data are kept close to the individual teaching areas so that the forms stand more chance of survival.

REFERENCES

AXELROD, S. (1971) Token reinforcement programs in special classes. *Except. Child. 37,* 371–379

AZRIN, N.H. (1973) Toilet training and mealtime behaviour. Paper read at the International Behaviour Modification Conference, Bangor, Wales, Aug. 1973

AZRIN, N.H. and FOXX, R.M. (1971) A rapid method of toilet training of the institutionalized retarded. *J. App. Behav. Anal. 4,* 89–99

BARTON, E.S. (1970) Inappropriate speech in a severely retarded child: a case study in language conditioning and generalisation. *J. App. Behav. Anal. 3,* 299–307

BIJOU, S.W. (1968) The mentally retarded child. *Psychol. Today 2,* 46–51

BIRNBRAUER, J.S. and LAWLER, J. (1964) Token reinforcement for learning. *Ment. Retard. 2,* 275–279

BIRNBRAUER, J.S., WOLF, M.M., KIDDER, J.D. and TAGUE, C.E. (1965) Classroom behavior of retarded pupils with token reinforcement. *J. Exp. Child. Psychol. 2,* 219–235

BROWN, L. and BELLAMY, T. (1972) A sequential procedure for teaching addition skills to trainable retarded students. *Train. Sch. Bull. 69,* 31–44

BROWN, L., HERMANSON, J., KLEMME, H., HAUBRICH, P. and ORA, J.P. (1970) Using behavior modification principles to teach sight vocabulary. *Teach. Except. Child. 2,* 120–128

BURNETT, F.H. (1970) *The Secret Garden.* New ed. Heinemann, London

DALTON, A.J., RUBINO, C.A. and HISLOP, M.W. (1973) Some effects of token rewards on school achievement of children with Down's syndrome. *J. App. Behav. Anal. 6,* 251–259

FOXX, R.M. and AZRIN, N.H. (1973) Dry pants: a rapid method of toilet training children. *Behav. Res. Ther. 11,* 435–442

HALL, R.V., PANYAN, M., RABON, D. and BRODEN, M. (1968) Instructing beginning teachers in reinforcement procedures which improve classroom control. *J. Appl. Behav. Anal. 1,* 315–322

HASKELL, S. (1974) Review of 'Assessment for Learning in the Mentally Handicapped'. (Mittler, P., ed.). *Bull. Br. Psychol. Soc. 27*, 320

HERMELIN, B. and O'CONNOR, N. (1960) Reading ability of severely subnormal children. *J. Ment. Defic. Res. 4*, 144–147

HOMME, L.E., DEBACA, P.C., DEVINE, J.V., STEINHORST, R. and RICKERT, E.J. (1963) Use of the Premack principle in controlling the behavior of nursery school children. *J. Exp. Anal. Behav. 6*, 544. Reprinted in *Control of Human Behavior Vol. 2* (Ulrich R., Stachnik, T. and Mabry, J., eds. 1966). Scott Foreman, Glenview, Ill.

MEIN, R. (1967) Recent investigations into reading with the severely subnormal. In *The Assessment and Education of Slow-learning Children* (Brown, R.I., ed.). University of London Press, London

O'LEARY, K.D. and BECKER, W.C. (1967) Behavior modification of an adjustment class: a token reinforcement program. *Except. Child. 33*, 637–642

PATTERSON, G.R. (1965) An application of conditioning techniques to the control of a hyperactive child. In *Case Studies in Behaviour Modification* (Ullman, L.P. and Krasner, L., eds.), pp. 370–375. Holt, Rinehart and Winston, New York

PERLINE, I.H. and LEVINSKY, D. (1968) Controlling maladaptive classroom behavior in the severely retarded. *Amer. J. Ment. Defic. 73*, 74–78

PHILLIPS, E.L. (1968) Achievement Place: token reinforcement procedures in a home-style rehabilitation setting for pre-delinquent boys. *J. App. Behav. Anal. 1*, 213–223

RYDBERG, S. (1971) Beginning reading discrimination taught at IQ 35 by conditioning. *Percept. Mot. Skills 32*, 163–166

SCHUTTE, R.C. and HOPKINS, B.L. (1970) The effects of teacher attention of following instructions in a kindergarten class. *J. App. Behav. Anal. 3*, 117–122

WARREN, S.A. (1963) Academic achievement of trainable pupils with five or more years of schooling. *Training Sch. Bull. 2*, 75–86

WHITMAN, T.L., ZAKARAS, M. and CHARDOS, S. (1971) Effects of reinforcement and guidance procedures on instruction-following behavior of severely retarded children. *J. App. Behav. Anal. 4*, 283–290

ZIMMERMAN, E.H., ZIMMERMAN, J. and RUSSELL, C.D. (1969) Differential affects of token reinforcement on instruction-following behavior in retarded students instructed as a group. *J. App. Behav. Anal. 2*, 101–112

Commentary

CHRISTOPHER WILLIAMS

I must preface my discussion on Elizabeth's paper by stressing that in many respects Meanwood Park Special School is unique amongst special schools in its use of behavioural techniques in an educational setting. Whereas it would follow from a knowledge of the experimental analysis of behaviour that *all* interaction between individuals either modifies or maintains behaviour, it is rarely demonstrated or used as explicitly as in the studies described in this paper.

The prescriptive use of this approach is rightly emphasized, for a practical approach to education must surely have greater utility than any descriptive theoretical approach, however sophisticated. In her review Elizabeth highlights the extent of the literature on behaviour modification and it should be a source of concern that this information has had only a relatively minor impact so far on educational practice and teacher training. When Bijou (1968) emphasized faulty reinforcement history as an important factor in the development of handicapped children he unfortunately diminished the importance of other equally important factors. It must be made more clearly apparent that the reinforcement history of an individual is itself a function of a number of variables: the physical characteristics of the environment, the reinforcer preferences of the individual himself, and the skill and knowledge of the reinforcer dispensers. Each of these factors needs to be considered when designing an educational setting for handicapped children. One crucial factor will be the appreciation of a distinction between unwitting and planned reinforcement of behaviour. As Mrs Barton says, teachers should be aware of the effect of their behaviour on their pupils so that they can arrange to apply reinforcement appropriately.

In quoting the Birnbrauer et al. (1965) study it is important to pinpoint the fact that they reported maintenance of performance following token withdrawal in five of their 15 subjects, whilst the remaining ten showed some degree of deterioration. All of the subjects showed improvement on reinstatement. The questions that are left unasked concern the predictability of maintenance following token withdrawal—can this be predicted from behaviour during training? Should they have been 'weaned' off tokens with a period of intermittent reinforcement? Should behaviours have been developed that will eventually be brought under the control of the 'natural' environment (Tharp and Wetzel 1969)? Is it possible to shape extended chains of behaviour using social reinforcers? Generalization and maintenance of behaviour following token reinforcement have both been demonstrated by O'Leary et al. (1967) and O'Leary and Becker (1967).

It cannot be stressed strongly enough that the child who learns appropriate behaviour only in the presence of a specific person has not been taught any generalized independent living skills.

When reviewing studies on particular behaviours Elizabeth mentions the Whitman et al. (1971) study on developing cooperative behaviour with severely retarded children. It is axiomatic that unless cooperation can be established it will be difficult if not impossible to teach higher-level skills. This target for systematic teaching is often omitted in curriculum design for handicapped children, and children can sometimes be excluded from full-time special education because of their lack of cooperation, under the guise of their 'not yet being ready' for school.

It is of concern to note that, although Elizabeth refers to the existence of many studies demonstrating the efficacy of behaviour modification principles to teach self-help skills, she points out that few of these studies refer to actual classroom programmes. This is not surprising when it is noted that in a recent (1974) Department of Education/Department of Health and Social Security circular on the education of mentally handicapped children and young people in hospital no specific mention is made of the teaching of self-help skills, these being considered to be part of 'ward routine' and as such should not 'interrupt while school is in progress'. And yet in a previous (1972) DHSS circular, figures for children in hospitals for the mentally handicapped showed that of children 5 to 9 years old some 71% were severely incontinent and some 75% needed assistance in feeding, dressing and washing. Due priority should be given to the teaching of these early independence skills, and the necessity for such an expertise should be acknowledged in the training of special school teaching staff.

The descriptions of the teaching programmes at Meanwood Park School raise some interesting discussion points.

Classroom programmes

The first requirement of any group programme is that it be both feasible and practical in terms of staff availability and classroom numbers. Token systems seem to correspond to these requirements, given that the staff have aims consistent with a reinforcement approach to learning. This is clearly the case in the studies presented here. It might have been helpful to the discussion had Elizabeth considered the tokens not only as acquired reinforcers in their own right but also as the means whereby the staff are cued in to give social reinforcement for specified and appropriate target behaviours.

Toilet procedure

Incontinence is such a severe problem with special education that it is not uncommon to hear of schools where children cannot be accepted for full-time education until they are toilet trained. It is promising to see that this is now less the case than in previous years. Nevertheless, it still happens that an incontinent child is handed over to the *least* trained member of the school personnel for training, whereas as Foxx and Azrin (1973) have shown, toilet training can be effected using techniques that should be part of the expertise of all special teachers. That this is possible is shown by the data presented on the children of class four.

Dressing

It is significant to note that the design for this programme allowed the class teacher time to work individually with a child on dressing while the teaching assistant carried on the more traditional group teaching. This is a clear departure from the more usual approach in which the teaching assistant would have been responsible for dressing and undressing the children in preparation for their 'education'. The case studies presented also emphasize the necessity for a maintenance programme to be considered since it cannot be assumed that a skill will continue to be emitted unless it becomes part of the general requirements of independent living.

Special-care children

It can be predicted that over the years an increasing proportion of the children in mental handicap hospitals will fall into the category of 'special care' and that special techniques will need to be developed in working with such children. One particular group will be the multiply handicapped. Maiden (1974) has recently prepared an extensive series of assessment and management programmes for use with such children, and it is hoped that increased resources for research and innovation for such children will be forthcoming.

The work on the use of sensory reinforcers cited by Elizabeth appears to be a promising area of further study.

In conclusion I should like to add that it is encouraging to note that many innovative methods now being introduced into special education are based upon theoretical models of learning and are substantiated by empirical data. Since education is primarily concerned with the development of behaviour it is therefore a natural setting for behavioural programmes leading to the design of therapeutic environments in which the *science* as well as the *art* of teaching can take place.

REFERENCES

BIJOU, S.W. (1968) The mentally retarded child. *Psychol. Today 2*, 46–51

BIRNBAUER, J.S., WOLF, M.M., KIDDER, J.D. and TAGUE, C.E. (1965) Classroom behavior of retarded pupils with token reinforcement. *J. Exp. Child Psychol. 2*, 219–235

DEPARTMENT OF EDUCATION AND SCIENCE and DEPARTMENT OF HEALTH AND SOCIAL SECURITY (1974) *The Education of Mentally Handicapped Children and Young People in Hospital.* HMSO, London

DEPARTMENT OF HEALTH AND SOCIAL SECURITY (1974) *Census of Mentally Handicapped Patients in Hospital in England and Wales at the end of 1970.* HMSO, London

FOXX, R.M. and AZRIN, N.H. (1973) Dry pants: a rapid method of toilet training children. *Behav. Res. Ther. 11*, 435–442

MAIDEN, D. (1974) The next step on the ladder—assessment and management of the multi-handicapped child. Part I: Method of assessment (a guide for the professional worker); Part II: A programme for parents and professionals. Institute of Mental Subnormality, Kidderminster

O'LEARY, K.D. and BECKER, W.C. (1967) Behavior modification of an adjustment class: a token reinforcement program. *Except. Child. 33*, 637–642

O'LEARY, K.D., O'LEARY, S. and BECKER, W.C. (1967) Modification of a deviant sibling interaction pattern in the home. *Behav. Res. Ther. 5*, 113–120

THARP, R.G. and WETZEL, R.J. (1969) *Behavior Modification in the Natural Environment.* Academic Press, New York

WHITMAN, T.L., ZAKAROS, M. and CHARDOS, S. (1971) Effects of reinforcement and guidance procedures on instruction-following behavior of severely retarded children. *J. App. Behav. Anal. 4*, 283–290

Nurse Training in Behaviour Modification

C. WILLIAMS and M. W. JACKSON

Lea Hospital, Bromsgrove, Worcs. and Institute of Mental Subnormality,
Kidderminster, Worcs.

ABSTRACT

Before any scheme of training in professional skills can begin, both the individual to be trained and the job for which the individual is to be trained should be explored. The early material in this paper describes something of the current situation in hospitals for the mentally handicapped in the United Kingdom. The problems and priorities are highlighted with respect to training needs. Initial attempts to develop nurse training programmes are described. The development of a formal training course by the Joint Board of Clinical Nursing Studies is described and an outline curriculum presented. Nurses are currently trained according to a syllabus laid down by the General Nursing Council which is so worded as to allow the inclusion of training in behaviour modification. An in-service practical training module for student nurses is outlined for an introductory course in behaviour modification in preparation for post-registration training

INTRODUCTION

The context in which nurses' training in behaviour modification is to take place and the area in which the skills will be practised is an important variable in deciding the content of the training. The behavioural characteristics of the individuals currently resident in hospitals for the mentally handicapped in the United Kingdom should determine the priorities of the training syllabus.

The Department of Health and Social Security (1972) has recently surveyed the subnormality hospital population, about 60,000 individuals at that time, of whom some 20% were totally incontinent, 23% were unable to wash, dress or feed independently and 21% had never spoken more than a few words. The figures for children are more relevant, as they may reflect the future hospital population. For children 5–9 years old ($N = 2187$), some 85% were not toilet-trained, 95% were not able to wash, dress or feed independently and 91% had not spoken more than a few words. A survey of this type will, however, include individuals who will never attain independent self-help skills because of gross physical handicap or defect. An informal survey of a group ($N = 32$) of children without such handicap, all of whom were fully mobile and had intact sensory systems, showed that of these some 75% were not fully toilet-trained, 72% were not able to dress alone, 44% were not using at least a fork and spoon for eating, 84% were not able to wash themselves and brush their teeth independently and some 78% did not use sentences of three or more words. The level of attainment on these skills was based upon criteria taken from the Fairview Self-Help Scale (1970). From these data it is clear that one major goal of training must be to enable trainees to teach self-help skills and language to children of this kind.

Such a goal cannot be introduced without first considering the environment in which the skills are to be practised. One limiting factor will be staff numbers. There is no point in training staff who will be unable to utilize their skills because of staff shortages. All too often through sickness, leave and other commitments a theoretical staff-resident ratio of 1:2 becomes in reality 1:12 at any one time. With such ratios the number of staff-resident contacts must be low, even if the quality of those contacts is high. Harmatz (1973), in a study of ward staff behaviour in an institution for retarded children in the United States, observed that only 24% of available staff time was spent in child-related activities involving actual contact; 21% of time was spent watching the children or attending to physical care, whilst more than half the time was spent in activities that were not child-related: paperwork, housekeeping, linen storing and talking to other staff. The staff–child ratio was 1:8. Harmatz points out that the visibility of the task tends to determine whether it will be done. It is easier to observe when the linen has been stored away than when a child has achieved a small step towards independence, and staff members are more likely to perform those tasks that produce some observable change in the environment, either because they are rewarded for doing so or (more probably) because they are reprimanded for not doing so. One obvious solution is to make any changes in the child's behaviour resulting from the nurse's interaction more visible by specifying more clearly the behavioural goals for the children in their care. However, increasing the nurse-child interaction time by employing additional staff to undertake activities not related to the children will not lead to improved development of those children unless the quality of the interactions is high.

One must also consider the physical environment in which the residents live and the staff work. No longer should administrative criteria overrule the basic need for an environment in which new adaptive skills can both be taught and maintained. Sleeping, eating, toileting, recreational and educational areas must be planned so as to allow the training of handicapped children in a one-to-one situation in the wards, not another part of the hospital. At present, emphasis is often wrongly placed on preparing individuals for 'training' in some other hospital area. This can often lead to those block treatment practices designed to produce well-fed, clean and neatly dressed, but dependent children that King, Raynes and Tizard (1971) rightly criticized. Behaviour modification training for nurses cannot, therefore, be treated as an isolated goal in mental handicap. Little will be gained by training unless attention is also paid to the other limiting factors (Gunzburg and Gunzburg 1973).

Three major needs can be identified:

1. *Organization* – ward management practices need to be organized to emphasize the training needs of the residents more than the residential routine.

2. *Expansion of services* – both the manpower resources and the physical environment need to be expanded to provide realistic settings for the teaching of independent living skills.

3. *Utilization of skilled personnel* – individuals whose training is based upon behavioural principles will be needed.

The rest of this paper is concerned with the third of these. It describes methods used by a specialized teaching unit to explore various means of implementing staff training projects.

We felt that the efficacy of a behavioural approach had been well enough established (Gardner 1971; Thompson and Grabowski 1972) that we could afford to develop practical skills rather than demonstrate their usefulness yet again. We have, therefore, concentrated on providing practical experience in a clinical setting supported by theoretical teaching at regular intervals.

SHORT WORKSHOPS FOR TRAINING

One of our main methods has been, and is, the 3-day introductory residential worskhop where at most eight students, usually with different training and background experience, are taken for a full 3 days of theory and practical experience. No illusions are held that in 3 days we can train individuals to become competent behaviour therapists. We can, however, introduce them to various behavioural programmes that are being run by nursing staff in both specialized and general wards. The course is outlined below.

Programme outline for 3-day introductory residential workshop

Day 1

Basic operant theory – lecture	$1\frac{1}{2}$ hr
Self-help skills – observation	1 hr
Self-help skills – lecture	1 hr
Self-help skills – supervised sessions	$1\frac{1}{4}$ hr
Ward-based token systems – lecture	30 min
Self-help skills – film	40 min

Day 2

Ward-based token systems – observation	30 min
Language development – lecture	1 hr
Token systems – ward visit	30 min
Play and motor skills – lecture	1 hr
Token systems – ward visit	45 min
Self-help skills – ward visit	45 min
Early language skills – lecture	45 min
Language and play skills – practical	45 min
Home intervention programmes – lecture	1 hr
Teaching language – film	40 min

Day 3

Token systems – ward visit	30 min
Ethical aspects – lecture	1 hr
Solving problems of implementation – lecture	30 min
Language and play programmes – solo practicals	30 min
Self-help skills – solo practicals	30 min
Ward-based practicals – ward visits	45 min
Journal review – seminar	30 min
Course review – seminar	30 min

To date, 11 of these workshops have been held; a further six are planned in the coming year. Most students have reported that they gained most from the practical sessions and that implementation of programmes at their own hospitals has been difficult without sufficient staffing levels and support from senior staff.

One limitation of this form of workshop, which aims to provide a high proportion of practical experience, is that only a small percentage of the staff from any one hospital can attend the course. We have experimented with sending a group from the teaching unit to visit a hospital for two days. In these two days only the flavour of the behavioural approach can be imparted; a restricted programme has reduced practical experience for course members to a morning session of demonstrations in the ward (with patients chosen by the ward staff themselves).

Programme outline for 2-day visiting workshop

Day 1

Basic theory – lecture	$1\frac{1}{2}$ hr
Self-help skills – lecture	1 hr
A 'language' programme – lecture	45 min
Token systems – lecture	45 min
Play and motor skill training – lecture	45 min
Teaching language – film	40 min

Day 2

Ward-based practical demonstrations	3 hr
Self-help skills – film	40 min
Ethical considerations and problems of implementation – discussion	1 hr

We have found that this type of course has little impact unless a programme is already in progress in the host hospital.

The Joint Board of Clinical Nursing Studies (1974) has recently published a curriculum for behaviour modification in mental handicap for registered nurses. Our 6-month course based on this outline has been approved; it attempts to integrate theory and practical experience closely. Initially, 6 students will be selected and grouped into three pairs for practical sessions, each lasting 5 weeks in three training areas in succession. These will include practical experience with both children and adults in the ward, in day centres for adults, in ward-based token systems, in community care programmes and in individual intensive teaching programmes. A project week has been included during which time each course member will have a session in which to present both a literature review and a treatment description. A significant departure from standard practice for post-registration courses has been the inclusion of a 6-week supervised practical period for the students in their own seconding hospitals, the intention being to provide experience of the real problems to be encountered in developing functional behavioural programmes, but with the help and support of the tutorial team.

The successful completion of such a course will earn a certificate of competence from the Joint Board of Clinical Nursing Studies. The course graduates should be well equipped to work cooperatively with psychologists and psychiatrists in developing independent behavioural treatment programmes in their own hospitals.

Until sufficient numbers of trained staff are available, individual hospitals will have to utilize existing staff and training methods, one of which is the current syllabus for the General Nursing Council training for the Registered Nurse in Mental Subnormality. It is to this part of pre-registration training that one of us (M.J.) has applied himself in developing an in-service training course for student nurses at Lea Hospital.

TRAINING OF STUDENT NURSES

It has been argued that the General Nursing Council 3-year training course for student nurses in mental handicap still retains the traditional medical approach as opposed to the social model. Many now consider this training, with its emphasis on clinical experience, irrelevant to the needs of the mentally handicapped, which are mainly social and educational. In fact, however, the 1970 G.N.C. syllabus for the 'Registered Nurse for the Mentally Subnormal' examination already covers practically the whole of the material to be included in the Joint Board of Clinical Nursing Studies post-registration syllabus on behaviour modification. We believe that although the theory section of the G.N.C. syllabus contains all that is necessary for the learning of behaviour modification techniques, the actual teaching of it is usually neglected. In the practical section of the syllabus the subject is lost amongst a mass of clinical nursing exercises. We suggest that the nurse who reaches the ward will rarely be called upon to exercise the specialized clinical skills which she has already practised excessively in the nurse training school, but will be in a situation where *practical* skill in behaviour modification would be beneficial.

Many subjects are included in the 1970 G.N.C. syllabus which are directly relevant to the application of behaviour modification. Reference is made to:

Behaviour therapy
Operant conditioning and use of rewards

Objectives of care and training
Behaviour disorders
Assessment and continuity

Also mentioned is the role of the nurse in the training of the mentally handicapped in:

The family setting
Teaching the family techniques of habit and social training
Instructing children and severely subnormal adults in dressing, washing and
feeding.

Sections of the syllabus refer to the use of monetary and other rewards; the management of various behaviour disorders, overactivity, destructiveness, aggression and self-injury; making observations; and keeping records.

Thus, the 1970 G.N.C. syllabus includes sufficient material to form an excellent training in the care of the mentally handicapped. However, it is essential that a practical course in behaviour modification should be provided during the student nurse's time in the training school. We describe below a 6-week training period to embrace theory and practice in behaviour modification for student nurses.

Our behaviour assessment and treatment unit is run on a 5-day week, children referred by consultants within the area attending for daily sessions. Parents usually accompany the child for the first day to allow the completion of various behavioural and developmental assessments. The children are also taken through the toileting, washing, feeding and dressing programmes and are assessed on their performance. The parents are given a detailed, structured interview by a psychologist and a member of the unit's nursing staff to help identify and assess the difficulties of the child and family. This information provides us with a pre-treatment baseline from which to develop our treatment objectives and programmes. A short time after the first assessment, two members of the unit team make a home visit to boserve and record the child interacting with members of the family. The parents are asked to take the children through specified procedures required in self-help skills. These interactions are sometimes also recorded on video tape for later use in discussion with the parents.

The student nurse's training is divided into four sections:

Practical training
Formal assessment methods
Theory training
Miscellaneous skills

Practical training

The practical training includes programmes in self-help skills, language, play and motor skills. Staff training records of the following form are provided:

Self-help skills

Programme	Observation	Supervised	Solo
Toilet training			
Washing			
Dressing/undressing			
Feeding			

The student is shown how to take a child through each of the training programmes and assess the level of performance attained.

The aim of the self-help programme is to teach the children to become independent in these skills. The aim of the language programme is to develop receptive and expressive language. Exercises are provided in:

Attention and cooperation
Physical imitation
Auditory discrimination
Object discrimination
Concept development
Sound imitation
Echoic vocabulary
Non-echoic vocabulary
Verbal contingencies

and the student progresses through observation, supervised and solo sessions in each area. At the end of this section the student will be able to help to assess a child's performance of these skills, carry out a previously designed training programme and record the training sessions.

Students are shown the importance of play in the development of social skills. They are taught how to run individual and group play sessions and how to teach basic motor development and pre-academic skills (eye-hand coordination, shape and colour discrimination). The aim of the play and motor-skill programme is to develop gross and fine motor skills, social skills and basic concepts and to teach new behaviours that are incompatible with non-productive and non-adaptive behaviour.

Theory

The theory of behaviour modification is taught with the aid of lectures, reading lists, films and video tapes. Subjects covered are: the operant model, teaching of self-help skills, language development, play and motor skills, token systems and ethical considerations. The student is required to reach a 75% pass level in a questionnaire on these topics.

General

Within the 6-week training period the students visit various other wards and departments with behaviour modification programmes. They also accompany the psychologist on school and home visits for initial assessment and follow-up of children, presenting this information at weekly care review meetings. Video and tape recordings, role-playing and one-way mirrors are used to facilitate the training sessions. Whenever possible, the 6-week training programme is followed by placement on the wards with behaviour modification programmes.

CONCLUSION

The preceding paragraphs imply that there is satisfactory progress towards a substantial increase in training in behavioural techniques for nurses in mental handicap. However, several factors may well limit such expansion. It is illogical to establish extensive nurse training courses without first establishing sufficient numbers of qualified individuals to provide the training. At present the clinical psychologist in mental handicap, by virtue of his training in the theories of learning, should play a major part in developing behavioural training programmes. However, Hall points out the marked shortage of psychologists in the National Health Service and emphasizes that few psychologists are in fact sufficiently experienced to be able to teach behaviour modification. A cohort of teachers must be developed before any significant impact on the training of nurses can be expected. It is hoped that the products of the Joint Board of Clinical Nursing Studies course may well be able to function partly in this role of training other staff. From our experience we believe that a behaviour modification module can and should be included in the pre-registration training for the Registered Nurse for the Mentally Subnormal.

Finally, to reiterate a point made earlier, unless the physical environment of the resident is also modified to enhance and maintain independent living skills in our hospital population, the resources employed in training specialist behaviour modifiers will largely have been wasted.

REFERENCES

DEPARTMENT OF HEALTH AND SOCIAL SECURITY (1972) *Census of Mentally Handicapped Patients in Hospitals in England and Wales at the end of 1970* (Statistical and Research Report series No. 3). HMSO, London

GARDNER, W. I. (1971) *Behaviour Modification in Mental Retardation: the Education and Rehabilitation of the Mentally Retarded Adolescent and Adult.* University of London Press, London

GENERAL NURSING COUNCIL (1970) *Syllabus of Subjects for Examination for the Certificate of the Nursing of the Mentally Subnormal.* GNC, London

GUNZBURG, H. C. and GUNZBURG, A. L. (1973) *Mental Handicap and Physical Environment: the Application of an Operational Philosophy to Planning.* Baillière Tindall, London

HARMATZ, M. G. (1973) Observational study of ward staff behaviour. *Except. Child.* 39, 554–558

JOINT BOARD OF CLINICAL NURSING STUDIES (1974) *Outline Curriculum in Behaviour Modification in Mental Handicap for Registered Nurses. Course No. 700.* JBCNS, London

KING, R.D., RAYNES, N.V. and TIZARD, J. (1971) *Patterns of Residential Care: Sociological Studies in Institutions for Handicapped Children*. Routledge and Kegan Paul, London

THOMPSON, T. and GRABOWSKI, J. (eds.) (1972) *Behaviour Modification of the Mentally Retarded*. Oxford University Press, London

Commentary

ELIZABETH BARTON

I think we all accept the need to offer training in behaviour modification to nurses, parents and teachers. Not only are the techniques reasonably effective with these patients but also they can improve the nurse's or teacher's morale by showing that there *is* something they can do with even the most handicapped patient. The authors outline a number of ways in which nurse training might be done. Perhaps the following points would be worthy of discussion:

Priority in nurse education. In view of the quite extensive curriculum covered by the student nurse in mental handicap, how much emphasis can be placed on behaviour modification? Should behaviour modification skills play a large part, or be one of many nursing skills? If the latter, should not nursing training in general be improved? Can something be left out? Some nurses receive lectures on dreams and theories of personality, genetics and skin diseases. Are these important, or even relevant?

Length of training. If nurses are trained in behaviour modification, at what level of training should we aim? What would be the role of the psychologist in a hospital with such highly trained nurses? Is a high level of training possible, given the low status of the job and poor recruitment figures?

Nurse reinforcement. Is the reinforcement of having a patient achieve a new skill sufficient to the nurse? I know many who feel it is not worth the effort.

Short courses. What is the function of the 3-day workshop and 2-day road show. Are these useful techniques in furthering the cause, or solely 'entertainments'? I know there have been some follow-ups on people who have attended these, perhaps Chris Williams can give us some data.

Putting skills to use. Will such training of the junior nurses be effective when after training they are under the guidance of senior nurses who may not know anything about behaviour modification?

Senior staff. What about the problem of the Number 7, 8 and 9 nursing officers? These are the people who will have to encourage, reinforce and advise the ward staff. How can they do this when they may know nothing of the skills and techniques involved? Particularly as some traditional nursing procedures

245

are diametrically opposed to what behaviour modification would suggest, e.g. what to do when a patient has a tantrum. You can invite such staff to meetings (as M.J. says) but you can't force them to attend.

Who should modify?   Are nurses the right people to carry out behaviour modification training? What about a new profession of behaviour modification trainers? In many hospitals few patients remain in the wards during the day; they attend school, O.T., I.T. and playgroups—perhaps these staff would more usefully be trained in behaviour modification techniques.

Discussion

C. Williams: I would like to take up some of Elizabeth Barton's points.

On what basis should we set goals? Despite what has been said here, I still think we have to use normal developmental scales until someone produces something better.

As for the training of clinical psychologists, those who come to us all go through the same 6-week training as do the student nurses. I am a little unhappy about the suggestion that these skills should be taught in the training school, because there are so very few registered tutors at the moment.

I have no way of knowing yet whether 6 weeks or 6 months is enough for the training: we shall have to wait and see. I am not convinced that children's development will act as sufficient reinforcement for nurses: peer reinforcement is much more effective. As to whether nurses are the right target for the training at the moment, I would have thought they were, just in terms of their numbers.

Mittler: To what extent have you tried to involve industrial-therapy staff, occupational therapists, and other non-nursing staff along with the nurses? These are the people with whom residents spend a great proportion of their day.

C. Williams: We are working mostly with children, and we always involve a teacher from the hospital school along with each nurse or group of nurses. IT and OT staff in our own hospital who work with adults are trained specifically only in terms of the token programme which they operate.

Mittler: I would like to put forward the view that long-stay hospitals may have a role in the future *provided* they are regarded as educational communities. Now if you accept that, it follows that we need to develop a whole set of educational techniques, and I hope I won't be too unpopular if I say that I see behaviour modification as only one of those techniques.

Hogg: What others do you have in mind?

Mittler: Well, for example, planned stimulation and play experiences that do not involve the use of contingent reinforcement. The skill of the educational planner would reside in deciding when the more structured contingent-reinforcement methods are suitable and when they are not. I am completely convinced of the value of the behavioural approach, but I would not like to see the educational development of residents in hospitals for the mentally handicapped construed solely in behaviour modification terms.

Kushlick: In what other terms could it be construed?

Mittler: I can't answer that briefly. But I am concerned that we may be going along too narrow a path, and neglecting a wider educational framework.

Harzem: There are two kinds of contingent reinforcement: that provided by the behaviour modifier and that which results from the constraints of the real world.

Patients should be exposed to natural contingencies, and play situations provide opportunities for such exposure.

Mittler: This is why I mentioned play, and perhaps the need to train nurses to observe play and even structure it without necessarily using behaviour modification techniques.

Berger: To what extent are you, in training nurses, going to make them aware of the external factors, which King, Raynes and Tizard (1971) describe as institutional management factors, that control what a child is to wear, for example, in addition to training them in how to teach children dressing skills?

C. Williams: Consideration of the nurses' institutional environment is included in the syllabus, but there is no time in a 24-week course for them to learn to apply questionnaires and rating scales. We must concentrate on what the nurses will actually be doing, namely working with individuals.

Kiernan: Forgive me, but I think that is taking too limited a view. Many of us are worried by the prospect of many well-meant behaviour modification projects failing because there has been no attempt to modify the organizational framework into which they are inserted. The appalling staff turnover to which Geoff Thorpe alluded, and which was also experienced in the E6 project at Queen Mary's, Carshalton, may be avoided by suitable negotiation with the hospital authorities. You can do a lot if you understand the potential ill effects of a hospital environment, know exactly what you want, and can make people see why you want it.

C. Williams: To some extent we are securing the cooperation of the nurse's second-ing institution by requiring that that institution accepts them back for a 6-week period in which they put into practice what we have been teaching them. We also hope that people surrounding the nurses who have been trained will pick up and extend their work, so that the trained nurse will be at the centre of a snowball effect; and finally we hope that in due course these nurses will be climbing the ladder of their career structure and will themselves be in a position to influence decisions.

Yule: Perhaps we should not be too pessimistic about behaviour modification projects failing to thrive in a hostile environment, since as Alison Tierney told some of us at another meeting recently [Action Workshop No. 2, Institute for Research into Mental and Multiple Handicap, 24–25 October 1974 (unpublished)], she had found 15–20 such projects operating satisfactorily in Scotland a year after the nurses who initiated them had been to a three-day workshop on the subject. We mustn't think that everything has to be started by psychologists.

Hogg: Others have had the opposite experience, though, in observing hospitals where a short workshop has had neither a positive nor a neutral effect but the negative one of inducing feelings of guilt in the nurses who were unable to implement what they had heard and were convinced that it would be right for their patients.

Chris William's thought that those surrounding the nurse who has been on the course will somehow cash in on her experience and help her will, I fear, be no more than a pious hope unless it is programmed in some way.

REFERENCE

KING, R., RAYNES, N.V. and TIZARD, J. (1971) *Patterns of Residential Care.* Routledge and Kegan Paul, London

Token Economy Systems

J. G. THORPE

The Manor Hospital, Epsom, Surrey

ABSTRACT

In this paper the feasibility of establishing token economy units in the hospitals for the mentally handicapped is examined. The view is presented that such units are not viable therein for several reasons. Although some of these arise out of the unsuitability of the administrative structures built into the National Health Service as a whole, the main reason lies elsewhere. It is to be found in the need for a change in the philosophy underlying the treatment of the mentally handicapped. The traditional view that they are sick needs to be replaced by the view that they are primarily in need of social training, so that behaviours which are socially more acceptable will be developed and brought under their own control. Such a radical change in orientation is unlikely to occur as long as the mentally handicapped are cared for in hospitals.

"Forget about the literature review, forget about the general aspects of token economies, forget about selling them to the unconverted. Concentrate instead upon the issues and problems which occur when we attempt to institute token economy programmes with the handicapped." So, with some license, reads my brief. I also note that my presentation should serve as a provocative basis for informal discussion. I accept both these invitations willingly.

It should come as no surprise to learn that I shall be concentrating my efforts upon token economies within the National Health Service since I am employed in that Service. It would, however be unfair to interpret my criticisms as applying specifically to any one hospital; discussion with colleagues indicates that the problems to which I shall be drawing attention are exceedingly widespread.

It would be difficult to find a more concise summary of the implications underlying the institution of all token economies than that provided by Stewart Agras (1972) when he introduces Ayllon and Roberts' chapter in his book *Behavior Modification.* Agras writes: "Instituting such an economy implies total environmental control. If privileges are to be used as reinforcers, then they must only be obtainable via a token exchange. This means that the hospital or school administration must agree with the aims of the project and take the necessary administrative measures to allow for such control. Moreover, staff at all levels must be educated in the use of the token system and be convinced enough of its advantages to work willingly within it. Thus, the first steps in starting a token economy are to seek administrative support and to educate the staff. The newcomer to the field is advised to seek consultation ... or to visit an operating token economy to familiarize himself with the myriad of small operational details that can make or break such an endeavour. The mere giving of tokens is not a token economy. Properly done, the token economy is a complex motivating environment."

My concern here will be to develop some of these points, to draw out some of the wider and deeper implications, and to formulate provocative conclusions in accordance with my brief.

Agras in the above quotation pleads for the appropriate education of all those who are to be employed in such a system. Nor is he alone in this regard. We find this sentiment expressed by Leonard Krasner (1968) when he writes "The experience of the author as well as other investigators in this area indicates that staff training is the most important element in the success of the token economy programme," while Kuypers, Becker and O'Leary (1968) go as far as saying that if you want your token economy to fail, don't train your staff and you will succeed!

The problem of staff training, however, leads us to ask who are these people who are in need of training, how are they to be selected, who is going to train them, and what training procedures should be used?

At first sight these are simple questions, and the answers come easily. In a hospital setting it is nurses on the ward who need to be trained, and this they will receive by seconding them for 6 months to one of the approved courses outlined by the Joint Board of Clinical Nursing Studies (1974), and on their return be given further specific instruction in the hospital in which the token economy is to operate. At the moment of writing only one course has been approved by the Board. Moreover, not all psychologists are equipped to give training in behaviour modification locally. Training facilities are therefore in short supply. Nor, I believe, should we confine our training to the nurses on the ward. It is imperative that senior nurses to whom the ward nurses will be responsible should also have a considerable understanding of the procedures and approve of them. Which leads us to the problem of selection. How are the nurses who are to work on the ward to be selected, and by whom? It seems reasonable that the person to whom the nurses will be responsible should have the responsibility for their selection. Nurses can therefore be expected to be selected by senior members of their profession who may not have even heard of behaviour modification, or who have got no further than understanding a token economy as the mere giving and spending of tokens—a view which will be reinforced if they read in the ward reports 'tokens (iii) given'!

In Watson's opening talk at the Bangor Conference on Behaviour Modification in 1973 many questions were asked about staff selection and staff training. From Watson's replies it would seem that these difficulties are formidable in America also and that there more emphasis is placed upon selecting the right people for training than upon attempts to convert existing staff who have been both selected and trained within the framework of a differing philosophy of treatment—which is perhaps the most fundamental of all our difficulties.

I am not the first to point out that token programmes (and one may include all behavioural approaches) require a radical change in the entire philosophy underlying treatment of the people whom we regard as patients. This has two distinct aspects. Firstly, the traditional view of the individual as a sick person incapable of developing responsible behaviour must give way to a new percept —that of a responsible individual who needs to be brought into a position of full control over his behaviour (Krasner 1969). And this brings in its wake the need for change in our perception of the roles of the staff employed to bring about this change. Such staff are required to see themselves as 'behavioural engineers' (Ayllon and Michael 1959) rather than as traditional nurses. And both of these changes have to occur in a *hospital* in which *patients* are the legal responsibility of *doctors* who have been trained to make out *prescriptions* for their *nursing staff* to administer! One can, of course, no more blame doctors for applying their medical expertise than one can blame psychologists for applying their psychological expertise, or indeed blame nurses for being nurses. The question is not one of attaching blame but one of establishing relevance. I would submit that traditional medical and nursing training is by and large inappropriate for most of the behaviour problems displayed by the mentally handicapped residents of the National Health Service—who find themselves in a *hospital* only because society will not accept them and they have nowhere else to go.

In spite of Sir George Godber's recent remarks (1973) in which he asked his fellow doctors: "Do we not in this field of medicine, as indeed in some others, underestimate the value of the contributions these other professions can make?," tradition dies hard, and in the meantime mentally handicapped individuals show a progressive deterioration of behaviour which dedicated doctors and nurses are unable to prevent by virtue of the inappropriate philosophical foundations of their expertise.

The literature contains many references to the thorny problem of who should staff token economy units, and Johnson, Katz and Gelfand (1972) list those who have already been employed in these units. They mention housewives, high-school students, college students, and teachers. They continue by outlining their own procedure for selecting and training psychology undergraduates for this role. They write that the "advantages of such a scheme are many. Patients benefit by more intensive attention and more systematic treatment programming which in most cases resulted in dramatic improvement or even discharge." They also found that "the morale of the nursing staff improved as the students took over many of the more difficult problems..."

The same authors in another publication (Katz, Johnson and Gelfand 1972) investigated the most efficient ways of training the staff within a token economy programme. This research revealed that of three separate approaches to training (instructions, verbal prompts, and monetary reinforcement) the monetary one was by far the most effective approach, the other two having little or no effect.

The issues raised in these two reports pose problems. It is hard to see such a general use of psychology undergraduates or postgraduates in this country. Even clinical psychologists, some of whom have had considerable experience in token and general behavioural approaches, cannot always be assimilated in this way. As one nursing officer put it, he didn't quite see how psychologists could help because they had received no training in nursing procedure!—and in fairness to him there is no mention of psychologists in the new 'Salmon' structure. Further, as long as Responsible Medical Officers come under the scrutiny associated with public enquiries the most recent of which was published only a few months ago, we should not be surprised to find them taking their responsibilities seriously and sometimes finding it impossible not to intervene in a patient's programme for what is genuinely seen as a medical reason.

But what of the financial bonuses which Katz et al. require to facilitate the training of the token economy staff? Clearly, within the National Health Service no-one has the authority to apportion salaries in this way. Indeed, with the present Whitley regulations it may not be possible even to allow nursing staff to go home a little earlier, or to have a couple of days off duty, as alternative reinforcements for their work. Perhaps we should take note of McNamara (1971) who reinforced his staff with special tokens which could be exchanged for a beer at the end of a day! But who will pay for them?

Lest it be suspected that I would wish to exclude the nursing profession completely from all token economy ventures, let me quickly refer you to a paper by Johnson and Groves (1972) entitled 'The token economy: a challenge to nursing'. They write "Perhaps the most obvious feature of token economy programmes is the central role of nursing personnel. They more than other staff are in a position to oversee all aspects of a token programme, including the coordination of observations, administration of reinforcers, and programme planning. This is a remarkable change in the role of the psychiatric nurse in an acute unit and one which represents considerable challenge to the field. In this capacity nursing staff would be responsible for the operation of token programmes for individual patients or units and use social workers, psychiatrists, and psychologists as consultants." They conclude "Currently the education of nurses desiring work in a psychiatric setting represents a small portion of their total programme. In many cases there is no formal contact with behaviour modification in the curriculum. *If the field of nursing is to maintain its leadership in all aspects of the care of psychiatric patients, more attention must be given to the application of behavioural principles in patient care and management* [my italics]." I submit that these conclusions are equally relevant to the field of mental handicap, but for reasons already given the practical difficulties are enormous—though less, one would hope, than the strength of the challenge.

Those of us who have been required to show visitors round our token economy wards are bound to have been asked how long this particular form of treatment is supposed to last. Although we have come to expect this question it does of course indicate a complete misunderstanding of the rationale of human behaviour. It also gives us a lead into the problem of stimulus generalization. Do the behaviours acquired under token regimes continue when those regimes are discontinued? One can see no reason whatever why they should. Quite apart from the fact that to discontinue token issues is to put the project immediately into reverse, if the discontinuation of tokens also means transfer to another ward which may be staffed by the traditionally trained then a new learning situation is in operation in which any and every behaviour which is emitted is met with new consequences and strengthened or weakened accordingly. The token economy has for this reason been labelled prosthetic rather than therapeutic (Zimmerman, Zimmerman and Russell 1972)—a distinction first made by Lindsley (1964). Prosthetic environments show changes only during treatment conditions, and removal of these results in a loss of treatment effects. Therapeutic environments show changes which are maintained after the treatment conditions are discontinued. This distinction is an important one, and Zimmerman et al. are clearly of the opinion that token economies do not produce effects which generalize to new situations. With this I would agree. It seems unreasonable to expect that a behaviour pattern established as a result of a particular set of reinforcement contingencies and subsequently changed through a manipulation of those contingencies in a token economy will continue in their changed form if the original contingencies are reinstated. From this it follows that a token economy in a large hospital for the handicapped must be continued in isolation—at least until a second unit designed to maintain the behaviour established by tokens has already been set up. In this regard we can refer to an observation made by Leo Krasner (1971) that tokens serve several purposes —including that of providing a vehicle for training the key environmental figures how to observe the behaviour of others, and how to use their own behaviour to reinforce the behaviour of others.

An existing token economy is therefore a good training ground for the staff of subsequent units. There are a number of procedures designed to increase stimulus generalization, but without the adequate training of the new staff who will take over the responsibility for these patients little can be expected. Taking Ayllon and Azrin's Relevance of Behaviour Rule for instance (1958), which states that we should 'teach only those behaviours that will continue to be reinforced after training', this cannot be relied upon in a subnormality hospital if most of the nursing staff have a traditional orientation.

Similar pessimism can be expressed towards other techniques designed to *programme* the continuation of behaviours produced in a hospital token economy ward in the patients who have left it. One technique has been that of pairing verbal praise and token reinforcement (O'Leary and Becker 1967), which has proved promising. We need to be reminded, however, that verbal praise sometimes has to have its reinforcement value increased and also that such praise needs to be given contingently upon the target behaviours which are being maintained, and again we have the problem of training the reinforcement dispenser first. Even if we decide to programme our generalization by having our subjects spend increasingly longer periods of their day out of the programme, a procedure employed by Henderson and Scoles (1970), the problem remains.

By far the most promising approach to generalization is to prevent the need for it by training the relatives, first in the administration and then in the con-

253

tinuation of important contingencies as soon as the mental handicap has been detected. For this reason it has been developed by Watson and his colleagues and has been much emphasized in the Behaviour Modification Conferences over the past few years. To train parents in this way should ultimately considerably reduce the need for their children to be hospitalized and also reduce the incidence of so many of the self-destructive and socially unacceptable behaviours which are frequently produced in growing youngsters who model themselves upon their hospitalized elders. Such a development would, however, more properly be categorized as token reinforcement, and takes us away from the token economies with which we are concerned.

Most of the definitions of the token economy make explicit reference to its self-correcting nature. It cannot be set up a priori. To quote Ayllon and Roberts (1972) "It is a continuous self-corrective procedure that enables the therapist to abandon any misconceptions about the presumed effectiveness of the ongoing therapeutic procedures." It is hardly necessary to point out that the self correction to which these authors refer is brought about by the continuous assessment of the efficiency of the programme by a responsible staff member. Such a staff member should be present within the framework of the economy at all times. According to the Direct Supervision Rule, say Ayllon and Azrin in their epoch-making book, he should be the one who is charged with the final responsibility for the accuracy of the continuous assessment to which we refer. He would also be available to standardize the procedures and prevent the bending of the rules referred to in a previous publication (Thorpe 1974). A token economy which operates in the absence of such a staff member or such continuous assessment does not qualify for the title, and on this criterion the number of token economies, particularly in the U.K., would drop considerably.

The usual problems of circumnavigating the reinforcement contingencies are inevitable in any unit. Tokens are lost and found, or stolen and returned. Relatives visit and bring along gifts for non-contingent distribution, but how completely complex contingencies need to be controlled is an empirical question to which Burchard (1969) has drawn attention.

If we are correct in our understanding of the development and maintenance of the behaviours of the mentally handicapped, and if our suspicions that much of the maladaptive and undesirable behaviour seen in our hospitals has developed subsequent to admission, it ought to follow that all our efforts should be concentrated upon the younger members of the hospital population. But how easily can token economy units be established for mentally handicapped children in a hospital? Not very long ago this could perhaps have been achieved. I say 'perhaps' because the problem of selecting teachers would have had to be added to that of selecting nurses. Since 1972, however, children under sixteen have become the responsibility of the Educational Authorities for their traditional education, while continuing to be 'nursed' in their wards out of school hours. Such a bifurcated administration makes the establishment of token economy systems difficult in the extreme.

I have said, I think, enough to make it clear that I hold that token economy systems in the hospitals for the nation's mentally handicapped are not a viable proposition. They are not viable for three main reasons. Firstly hospitals, as the very name suggests, are staffed by doctors and nurses whose predominant framework is that of medical diagnosis and pharmacological treatment for those who are ill. As we have suggested, there are good reasons for believing that the majority of the mentally handicapped in our hospitals are there for a different reason—that neither their families nor society will accept them.

Secondly, the management structure of the National Health Service prevents the satisfactory inclusion of specialists. There is no way in this country of delegating any responsibility to the psychologist as long as the Responsible Medical Officer continues by law to be responsible for all aspects of his patients' welfare, including all aspects of the behaviour modification approach with which he may be completely unfamiliar.

Thirdly, it has been noted that the new management structure for nurses (Ministry of Health and Scottish Home and Health Department 1966) does not make possible any working relationship between themselves and psychologists. Nor are their conditions of service sufficiently flexible to make possible the administrative requirements of a behaviour modification approach.

It seems sad to have to draw conclusions such as these, particularly when there are so many doctors and nurses up and down the country who can be counted as one's friends. Being aware of their dedication to the welfare of their patients, however, I can hope that this paper will be accepted in the spirit in which it has been offered. For it is a like concern for the mentally handicapped that has prompted this paper.

REFERENCES

AGRAS, W.S. (1972) *Behavior Modification: Principles and Clinical Applications.* Little, Brown, Boston

AYLLON, T. and AZRIN, N.H. (1968) *The Token Economy: A Motivational System for Therapy and Rehabilitation.* Appleton-Century-Crofts, New York

AYLLON, T. and MICHAEL, J. (1959) The psychiatric nurse as a behavioral engineer. *J. Exp. Anal. Behav.* 2, 323–334

AYLLON, T. and ROBERTS, M.D. (1972) The token economy: now. In AGRAS (*op. cit.*), pp. 59–86

BURCHARD, J.D. (1969) Residential behavior modification programs and the problem of uncontrolled contingencies: a reply to Lachenmeyer. *Psychol. Rec. 19*, 259–261

GODBER, G. (1973) The responsibilities and role of the doctor concerned with the care of the mentally retarded. *Br. J. Psychiat. 123*, 617–620

HENDERSON, J.D. and SCOLES, P.E. (1970) A community-based behavioral operant environment for psychotic men. *Behav. Ther. 1*, 245–251

JOHNSON, C.A., KATZ, R.C. and GELFAND, S. (1972) Undergraduates as behavioural technicians on an adult token economy ward. *Behav. Ther. 3*, 589–592

JOHNSON, W.G. and GROVES, G. (1972) The token economy: a challenge to nursing. *J. Psychiat. Nurs. 10*, 10–13

JOINT BOARD OF CLINICAL NURSING STUDIES (1974) *Course No. 700.* JBCNS, London

KATZ, R.C., JOHNSON, C.A. and GELFAND, S. (1972) Modifying the dispensers of reinforcers: some implications for behaviour modification with hospitalised patients. *Behav. Ther. 3*, 589–598

KAZDIN, A.E. and BOOTZIN, R.R. (1972) The token economy: an evaluative review. *J. Appl. Behav. Anal. 5*, 1–30

KRASNER, L. (1968) In *Role of Learning and Psychotherapy* (Porter, R., ed.), pp. 155–174. Churchill, London

KRASNER, L. (1971) Behavior therapy. *Ann. Rev. Psychol. 22*, 483–532

KUYPERS, D.S., BECKER, W.C. and O'LEARY, K.D. (1968) How to make a token system fail. *Except. Child. 35*, 101–109

LINDSLEY, O.R. (1964) Direct measurement and prosthesis of retarded behavior. *J. Educ. 147*, 62–81

McNAMARA, J.R. (1971) Teacher and students as sources for behaviour modification in the classroom. *Behav. Ther. 2*, 205–213

MINISTRY OF HEALTH and SCOTTISH HOME AND HEALTH DEPARTMENT (1966) *Report of the Committee on Senior Nursing Staff Structure* (Chairman: B. Salmon). HMSO, London

O'LEARY, K.D. and BECKER, W.C. (1967) Behavior modification of an adjustment class: a token reinforcement program. *Except. Child. 33*, 637–642

REPORT OF THE COMMITTEE OF INQUIRY INTO SOUTH OCKENDON HOSPITAL (1974) (Chairman: J.H. Inskip). HMSO, London

THORPE, J.G. (1974) In *Proceedings of the one-day symposium on Behaviour Modification, Lea Hospital, Bromsgrove, March 1973*, pp. 17–22. Institute of Mental Subnormality, Kidderminster, Worcs.

WATSON, L.S. (1973) *International Behaviour Modification Workshop*. University College of North Wales, Bangor

ZIMMERMAN, E.H., ZIMMERMAN, J. and RUSSELL, C.D. (1972) in KAZDIN and BOOTZIN (*op. cit.*)

Commentary

M. W. JACKSON

"Token economy systems in hospitals for the nation's mentally handicapped are not a viable proposition." This would certainly appear, as Dr Thorpe suggests, a provocative basis for discussion. The main reason given is that the clients reside in hospitals and that they are cared for by nurses who are unable, because of their management structure, to have a working relationship with psychologists and because the clients' welfare is the responsibility of Medical Officers.

The problem areas are staff selection, staff training, the education of senior nursing personnel and the shortage of psychologists with relevant clinical experience. I think that we would agree that all these are problem areas. It is also true that the rationale behind 'treatment' needs changing from custodial care to developmental care and that staff education is largely inappropriate for mental handicap. The training framework is an evolutionary phenomenon and is under constant pressure to change.

We would not expect a token system to be fully operational from the word go. We see it as making a start, then gradually moving towards a goal in a shaping procedure, shaping not only the clients but also the staff, the support needed initially being faded out when possible, as the programmes become established as ward routine.

Staff training

It would not be practicable to wait for all the necessary staff to be trained before starting the programme because staff turnover is high, particularly of student nurses in training. Sisters and Charge Nurses, as the key staff, should be well trained. They will then train the new staff (Hall 1974).

Staff reinforcers

One of the main reinforcers for nursing staff is peer approval, particulary when related to patient progress (Watson 1972). Key staff (nursing and Senior Nursing Officers) must therefore be familiar with the programme and be active supporters of the ward staff. They should be drawn into periodic assessment and continuity meetings of programme efficacy with programme members.

School and other departments

The dichotomy between school and ward is not helpful for children unless specific steps are made to make it so, such as a gradual extension of the token system into the departments attended by the clients. Administrative structures can be changed either formally (by coercion) or informally (by consent). Working relationships can be a function of other variables apart from management structure, as with inter-professional meetings to plan goals of performance.

Generalization

It appears that generalization must be built into the programme by bringing new behaviours under the influence of 'natural' reinforcers. This presents us with the problem that most of the 'natural' reinforcers in institutions tend to be negative—"stop it," "put it back," "no," "sit down," "do as you're told." It may well be necessary specifically to build in positive reinforcers as part of the 'natural' environment.

Johnson and Groves (1972) stress the nurse's central role in token economy programmes. They are in a better position than many others to oversee all aspects of a token programme. These authors also stress the need for a radical change in the philosophy of treatment and the role of the nurse, with a changing emphasis in current nurse training.

We believe that the nurses in the mentally handicapped field will accept this challenge and are in many cases welcoming all that this entails, providing that they are given the opportunity and the necessary skills.

REFERENCES

HALL, J. (1974) *Training Nurses in Behaviour Modification: an Analysis of Current British Practice.* Unpublished report: University of Leeds

JOHNSON, W. G. and GROVES, G. (1972) The token economy: a challenge to nursing. *J. Psychiat. Nurs.* 10, (May–June), 10–13

WATSON, L. S. (1972) *How to use Behaviour Modification with Mentally Retarded and Autistic Children: Programs for Administrators, Teachers, Parents and Nurses.* Behavior Modificaton Technology, Columbus, Ohio

Discussion

Tizard: Well, I warned Geoff that I was going to be very critical of this paper. I would like to make five points:

1. I find the assumptions, and particularly the quotation, at the beginning of Geoff Thorpe's paper very chilling. As a statement of objectives it might sound all right for the Gulag Archipelago or Dachau, but as a way of thinking about patients and people it is unacceptable.

2. Like Geoff, I am critical of most token economies. The only one I've seen was a very well-known American programme, and I was appalled. Bored and cynical behaviour technicians were giving tokens to bored and cynical patients. Nobody had been discharged from the unit and the work in the unit as a whole was greatly inferior to what was being done elsewhere by the very nurses to whom the behaviour technicians were so condescending.

3. I am doubtful of the specificity of the effects of token economies, where they exist. One of John Hall's most interesting papers (Baker, Hall and Hutchinson 1974) showed that non-contingent reinforcement by tokens given to a small group of schizophrenics was as effective as contingent reinforcement by tokens, which suggests that the model itself is a grossly over-simplified one. Thus, we have naive assumptions on which it is proposed to base an unacceptable way of life for human beings.

4. I deprecate the denigration of colleagues and find Geoff's characterization of the medical model a caricature. I don't think one can make such sweeping generalizations about whole professions, without inviting similar generalizations about psychologists.

5. This paper makes no suggestion that we should look at the quality of patients' environment and of their life. Programmes are regarded as ends in themselves rather than means to enhance the quality of patients' lives. The basic weakness is to take behavioural engineering as the basis for the formulation of a way of life. We have seen what engineering does when it is allowed to dictate town planning: it destroys the quality of the environment. The same will be true of behavioural engineering, unless we are vigilant in relating it to the value of people as individuals.

Thorpe: I am surprised at Jack Tizard's reaction. I wouldn't have thought token economies were different from any other form of behaviour modification, in that all require a reformulation of our thinking. In any of our procedures you come face to face with the problem of the individual's freedom. To a behaviourist, freedom is an awareness of the behaviour–consequence contingencies and an ability to choose between different behaviours in the light of that knowledge. Now the trouble in our subnormality hospitals is that either the patients are not aware of the contingencies, or the contingencies are determined by traditional nursing—e.g., if you have a temper tantrum you will be comforted by a member of the staff. If patients can become aware of more logical contingencies, this seems to me a gain, not a loss of freedom.

That some token economies contain bored and cynical attendants does not damn token economies as a whole, it merely condemns that one token economy.

I am frankly amazed to be accused of denigrating colleagues, which was the last thing I had intended. My point was simply that a dedicated, good nurse can do immeasurable harm precisely because of his or her training, which is not conceived of in terms of learning theory.

On the quality of life, there is nothing to prevent anyone from selecting target behaviours relevant to his concept of enhanced quality of life and putting those target behaviours into a token economy system.

Tizard: The token economy ward I mentioned was on view because it was thought

258

to be something special and important. The fact that it was so much less effective than what was being done without the benefit of the knowledge and experience of the research psychologists seems to me to say something loud and clear.

Barton: Tokens are useful, flexible and convenient reinforcers, but I think that the complete control of life on a ward by tokens is both unnecessary and inappropriate for mentally handicapped patients. Massive effort is put into organization instead of into patients, and the whole concept assumes the population of a ward to be much more homogeneous than it ever is.

C. Williams: I do want to stress the usefulness of tokens for reinforcement in learning particular skills, especially work skills, before the condemnation of the total token economy engulfs this idea.

Yule: They can also be useful in a project such as Achievement Place (Phillips *et al.* 1971; 1973) which aims at rehabilitation into the community. But there again you have only a partial use of tokens; the children go off to ordinary school every day.

Kiernan: Chris Williams seems to be saying that it's all right to use tokens provided you only set goals in one particular area, but there is a danger, of course, that someone else can come along with a Gulag Archipelago philosophy for the others. It seems important to use tokens only for educational goals aimed at increased self-determination.

Yule: We often talk about differentiating the technology from the goals, but I think we must be very concerned to note that when a token economy goes wrong it goes badly wrong. The techniques at their simplest are readily learned and can be put to bad use.

Jordan: A factor which makes for an intolerable environment is the assumption that reinforcement has to be contingent. I think this is yet to be proven, and that it is much more likely that reliable contiguity is sufficient—which can be provided in a humane environment.

Thorpe: However, it is difficult to ensure in hospital that the reinforcer—be it a token or other reinforcer—is given for a particular behaviour, and the fact is that you do see the behaviour of those admitted to mental subnormality hospitals deteriorating because the wrong behaviours are reinforced. So I am convinced the only way to solve the problem is never to admit them to these large hospitals in the first place. One characteristic of these places is the appalling staff turnover—in 3 years on our token economy ward for 24 patients, with 4 nurses on duty at any one time, there were 289 different nurses! And another is the totally inappropriate orientation, which makes a scandal out of a patient who is not acutely ill being still in bed at 11 a.m.

Harzem: I think Rita Jordan is right: the early token economy systems were unnecessarily totally controlled because they were pioneer efforts, just as we now know Pavlov took unnecessary precautions in his early conditioning experiments. We can probably demonstrate that a token economy need not be rigid in order to be effective.

REFERENCES

BAKER, R., HALL, J.N. and HUTCHINSON, K. (1974) A token economy project with schizophrenic patients. *Brit. J. Psychiat.* 124, 367–384

PHILLIPS, E.L., PHILLIPS, E.A., FIXSEN, D.L. and WOLF, M.M. (1971) Achievement Place: modification of the behaviors of pre-delinquent boys within a token economy. *J. Appl. Behav. Anal.* 4, 45–49

PHILLIPS, E.L., PHILLIPS, E.A., FIXSEN, D.L. and WOLF, M.M. (1973) Achievement Place: behavior shaping works for delinquents. *Psychol. Today* (June), 75–79

III The context of programmes

This section deals with the broader issues arising out of the application of a behaviour modification approach.

If the practitioner using behaviour modification is to be able to rise above the level of a technician and an exponent of the educational and social system in which he functions, he needs to define new, independent goals for his programme and consider carefully the ethical issues raised by these goals. Kushlick and Paul Williams both address themselves to these points.

The practitioner also needs to consider whether and how to change the organization in which he operates, since it is unlikely that improvement through behaviour modification can be brought about in a totally hostile environment. Georgiades and Phillimore's paper discusses the types of move necessary if change is to be facilitated.

Improving the Services for the Mentally Handicapped

ALBERT KUSHLICK

Health Care Evaluation Research Team, Winchester

During the course of this study group and at a meeting convened earlier this year by the Institute for Research into Mental and Multiple Handicap, contributors have presented papers on experiences in, or plans for, providing training courses in behaviour modification to enable staff and parents caring for mentally retarded people to do so more humanely and effectively. The size of the training task has been shown to be enormous and the obstacles to improving the environment which handicap the trainers, the staff and the retarded have been shown to be formidable. This paper aims to reexamine some of these problems, and to present ways of breaking them down into what may be manageable tasks. In doing so, I will present and illustrate some recently published work by people working in the field of experimental analysis of behaviour which have enabled my research colleagues and me to formulate our own future programme.* This work may also clarify some of the options open to people developing behaviour modification training courses with the general aim of improving services for the retarded and their families.

THE PERFORMERS

The paper assumes that the contributors to the symposium share an interest in improving these services and that they have a wide range of skills in teaching individuals who are themselves retarded, as well as skills of teaching others —nurses, teachers, parents, and other professionals—to teach individuals who are retarded. It also assumes that they define teaching as accelerating the rate at which their students acquire skills or knowledge by arranging their environments (Bijou 1973), and that they share the aim of doing this with a minimum of negative reinforcing or punitive contingencies. Finally, it assumes that the consequence of such teaching is seen as increasing the extent to which the student can control his or her own environment and reinforce a wide range of creative behaviours in others with whom he or she interacts.

---

* Roger Blunden, Senior Research Officer in charge of our work on Care of the Elderly, has played a major part in the development of our programme.

THE CONDITIONS UNDER WHICH THEY WORK

These teaching activities are at present being carried out under conditions which constitute obstacles to the carrying out of any planned programmes. Some of these obstacles will now be identified, both in order to clarify them and to suggest ways in which we may attempt to change them.

1. The number of people skilled in behaviour modification is very small, much smaller than the number of nurses, teachers and parents of the retarded.*

2. Teachers of the experimental analysis of behaviour now have the benefit of well-designed teaching material. However, the range of skills and knowledge, concepts and procedures which can be taught has widened considerably, as well as the number of methods for teaching them. Therefore, the problem of choice arises: of selecting what to teach people, and the methods to be used.

During this study group contributors have spoken of the difficulties of evaluating the effectiveness of teaching programmes. Some of the difficulties may be related to the magnitude of the desired changes in the students' behavioural repertoire and the desired degree of generalization to situations in which the students will find themselves after their training.

3. Everyone agrees that skills and knowledge developed in the teaching situation may be extinguished or even punished by the prevailing conditions under which the student works or the retarded person lives.

ANALYSIS OF THE OBSTACLES

Can we specify some contingencies which mitigate against the introduction of behaviour modification procedures? If so we may be able to change our own performance and that of others in ways which help the retarded to acquire the social skills essential for the exertion of control over their own environment.

It may also be possible to meet some of the criticism currently being levelled at behaviour modifiers by people outside the field (Cohen 1974) and within it (Holland 1974). These suggest that behaviour modifiers are using their procedures to develop, in people who lack power, conforming behaviour that maintains those conditions which contribute to their lack of power. Such conditions may also force behaviour modifiers to make use of 'unnatural', culturally unacceptable procedures. These practices are not limited to procedures where the use of punishment is designed to weaken behaviour. Where environments provide so few social reinforcers (or choices of reinforcing activities or materials) for strengthening behaviour, edible reinforcers, made more powerful by deprivation procedures, have been used instead. Token economies operating under such conditions have been criticized because certain reinforcers (visits, recreational activities, access to therapists) have been provided for residents

---

* The numbers of retarded and the staff caring for them appear impossibly large if presented as total numbers in the country as a whole (Hall 1974). When converted into rates per 100,000 of the population the numbers appear much more manageable but they are still formidable (Kushlick 1973).

contingently on their acceptable conduct. Civil rights codes are being drawn up which specify that such reinforcers must be made available non-contingently (Wexler 1974).

It should also be possible to avoid 'explaining' the existence of inadequate environments for the retarded by reference to such constructs as 'organization structure', 'attitudes of staff', 'the prevailing value system', or by the pejorative use of the terms 'bureaucracy' and 'hierarchical'.

The first step is to attempt to specify those people whose performance (or deficits) in specific situations affect or indeed constitute the conditions under which others have to act (Skinner 1953, 1968, 1969). Let us examine in this way some of the conditions which affect the preparation of plans for training people working with the retarded.

The DHSS policy document 'Better Services for the Mentally Handicapped' (Cmnd. 4683) was published in 1971. The writers identified and described publicly some features of the existing service which were preventing retarded people, their parents and direct-care staff from developing and maintaining a wide range of activities or which were actually causing the retarded to suffer. They outlined plans by means of which officers at the DHSS, Hospital Authorities, Local Authority Social Service and Education Departments, could begin to provide new services and improve existing conditions. They predicted that more money and resources would be made available to implement the policies outlined. As an early step towards this they requested officers of Health, Education and Social Service Authorities to prepare joint 10-year plans for implementing specified features of the policy and to submit these statements of intent to the DHSS for approval and funding.

Despite many of its weaknesses (see later) Cmnd. 4683 is a unique document in the way it specifies a wide range of things to be done by people at many levels of different agencies. The sequel to its publication highlights specific deficits which are interesting because they suggest who might do what to try and change them.

There is no document easily available to professionals or public which would enable them to monitor the extent to which the proposals have been implemented and to give praise, positive feedback or reinforcers where they are due. There is some evidence of failures which contribute to the conditions under which the staff, the retarded and their parents live or work, and to the conditions which influence those who are planning training courses.

Only 5 out of 15 Regional Hospital Boards returned 10-year plans jointly with the Local Authorities in the Region to the DHSS. Contrary to the policy document's statements of intent:

large *new* hospitals serving catchment areas having a total population of more than 250,000 are being funded;

hospitals with more than 500 beds are being enlarged by the provision of 'temporary' accommodation which is *not* domestic in character, *not* locally based, *not* staffed as recommended, and *not* part of a comprehensive service for people living at home as well as those in hospital;

attempts are being made to remodel old wards that have many of the unsatisfactory characteristics spelled out in the document. This produces disruption to staff and residents without altering many of the unsatisfactory features. Funds, as well as the time and resources of builders and designers, are consumed to provide environments which fail to maintain or develop a wide range of skills in clients or staff;

policies on alignment of hospitals and sectorization of wards (i.e., relocation of residents on the basis of areas in which their families live to enable them, their parents, other professionals from the local area to jointly set, monitor and attain individualized goals for clients at home and in institutions) are not being implemented.

there is no clear guidance to officers of Regional Health Authorities and Local Authority Social Service Departments on how to ensure that people implementing Cmnd. 4683 policies, or the monitors and supervisors or direct-care personnel in any of the professions, are supported, or that people implementing contrary policies are restrained from doing so and aided in carrying out the policies as defined; and

even before the latest 'financial crisis', the capital expenditure on mental handicap in the hospital service as a proportion of the total was decreasing despite statements of intent to spend more. It is possible that this trend in expenditure was not noted by the people responsible for providing funds because of the lack of monitoring instruments to detect changes in levels of allocation towards these services.

Since the financial 'crisis', services for the retarded have suffered further in the general cuts on health, education and social services. Because of existing deficiencies in methods of monitoring expenditure, the effects of these cuts are not clear. There is some evidence that services for the retarded will be particularly damaged by the stopping of small projects, which can always be terminated more easily than large projects. Such small projects include the building of small locally-based units by both Hospital Authorities and Local Authority Social Service Departments as specified in Cmnd. 4683.

THE DEVELOPMENT OF BEHAVIOUR MODIFICATION
TRAINING PROGRAMMES

I will return later to the problems of implementing Cmnd. 4683 and the way in which these influence the development of behaviour modification training programmes. I want now to look at the task of designing and evaluating such training programmes.

The work of Robert F. Mager (Mager and Pipe 1970) has been particularly helpful within our research team in clarifying our task of developing and evaluating services. Mager identifies the tendency of people working in large organizations who want other people to do something other than what they are doing to formulate the problems as 'The other people are *poorly motivated*, have *bad attitudes*, and *lack skills*. Therefore what is needed is a training programme.' He further identifies the tendency of such people to state what the *other* person should or should not be doing very imprecisely—i.e. in the form of what he calls a 'fuzzy' (Mager 1972). The test he describes for distinguishing 'fuzzies' from valid 'performance statements' is called the 'Hey Dad' test which fuzzies fail but performances pass. Examples of fuzzies which fail this test are:

'Hey Dad, let me show you how I can ...
    develop my full potential
    develop a mature approach
    develop self-awareness
    increase my sensitivity to the environment
    change the organizational structure
    develop new attitudes
    manage with enthusiasm
    give people autonomy.'
Examples of non-fuzzies or performances which pass the test are:
'Hey Dad, let me show you how I can ...
    smile a lot
    say favourable things about others
    recognize symptoms
    assemble components skilfully
    write reports
    codify rules
    design records
    produce training packages
    list materials.'

The consequences of distinguishing fuzzies from performance statements are many.

An imprecise statement of an intended performance (a fuzzy) may set the occasion for a wide range of responses from different people at the same time, or from the same person at different times. For example, a person may be unable to make any response to a fuzzy; others may respond in different ways to the same fuzzy with consequences which cancel each other out; in a group situation, failure to clarify a fuzzy may lead to responses with conflicting consequences and to further misinterpretations. Thus in most group situations (like the present study group), long and often heated discussions take place apparently on a single topic. No initial attempt is made to clarify the different performances to which each is referring. The participants interpret the same fuzzy as different performances. They punish or argue with others who are interpreting it differently. The debate is often extended as each participant adds more fuzzies which in turn set the occasion for further misinterpretations.

For example, our discussions have concerned training courses for the mentally handicapped, for direct-care staff and for parents. It has been stated that it is very difficult to evaluate the effectiveness of any training course that has been set up or that may be set up. Mager's analysis would suggest that one possible reason for both concentrating on the development of training programmes and for debating at length whether or not we can evaluate them is that we have been discussing fuzzies and have not identified the intended performances of teachers, students and the mentally handicapped.

Mager demonstrates that it is possible to transform fuzzies into fairly clear performances which pass the test. The list of such performances may itself be tested: 'If all of these performances are carried out, will the fuzzy have been achieved?' The resulting list may be very long and the performances themselves may be fairly complex. Moreover, some of the performances identified in this way may indeed conflict with one another.

The next step, therefore, involves arranging the performances in order of their importance. It is then possible for a group of individuals who appear to have major disagreements when discussing how to implement fuzzies to reach agreement not only on the performances required but also on their priority.

In the next step, the question is posed 'If the life of the person who should carry out the performance but is not doing so were at stake, could he or she succeed in doing it?' If the answer to this question is YES, the problem is *not* one of lack of skills and the solution does *not* lie in a training programme. Other solutions may be more relevant; Mager discusses these in detail. One solution is the design of a job aid—a manual, a guide, a map, etc. which simplifies and clarifies the performance. Another is to remove punishing obstacles which face the person required to perform. Yet others include ensuring that there is a pay-off to the person carrying out the performance, and removing punishers which follow the goal activity. Finally, one may attempt to ensure that there is no pay-off for *not* performing or for doing something else which is incompatible with the desired performance. (All of these procedures are recognizable as identifying the problem performances and the contingencies maintaining them, and as changing these contingencies of reinforcement to attain the intended changes in performance. See also Lindsley 1964a,b).

If the answer to the question is NO, the problem is one of lack of skill. It may yet be possible to solve the problem by means other than a training programme —i.e. by simplifying the task, or making it unnecessary by changing other conditions in the situation. If, however, a training programme *is* chosen as the solution, it is important that its objectives are clearly determined in order to enable the specified performer(s) to carry out defined performances in the specified situations. This immediately clarifies questions of 'what should be taught'. In addition, it becomes possible to evaluate the effectiveness of a training programme by the extent to which it enables people in a defined situation to attain criterion performance. If there are several ways of teaching available, they can be evaluated comparatively.

Our team in Winchester is faced with the task of developing and evaluating health and social services for the retarded and for old people. We have found it helpful to simplify the task by breaking it down into small manageable components. One useful step has been to identify people in the services as (1) providers and planners; (2) monitors or supervisors; (3) direct-care personnel (these include parents and relatives of clients who live at home); and (4) clients themselves.

THE USE OF JOB AIDS IN CHANGING PERFORMANCE

This study group is concerned with the training of direct care personnel and clients. One of our present activities involves enabling these people to attain their intended purposes by building on their existing skills and knowledge. This involves the design of what constitute job-aids in Mager's analysis.

We have come across two outstandingly good aids. The first set (Thomas and Walter 1973; Carter 1973; Gambrill, Thomas and Carter 1971) has been developed by a group at the School of Social Work, Ann Arbor, Michigan, for interventions with individuals in a wide range of settings. The user is given a number of clearly specified sequenced steps to follow. These start with recording the clients' problems in the form of fuzzies stated in the client's own words or those of his relatives, friends or teachers. They proceed with the clarification of the fuzzies into performance deficits or excesses in specified situations, the rank ordering of these into priorities, and behavioural specification of those chosen for intervention so that baselines can be determined and antecedent and consequent events identified. Only when all of these steps have been completed and contracts have been agreed with the client and his relatives is the intervention plan formulated and implemented. The effectiveness of the intervention is monitored by referral to the baseline data. A maintenance and follow-up plan complete the intervention package. A similarly designed set of guidelines has been developed for use with groups of adults (Lawrence and Sundel 1972).

These packages for intervention at individual client level have features which resemble very closely those outlined by Mager for interventions designed to introduce changes in large-scale organizations. They also incorporate features which safeguard the clients' rights and which counter the criticism that the technology of behaviour modification procedures must necessarily involve selecting and imposing arbitrary changes on clients without their participation in goal setting.

As in the Mager guidelines, these authors point out the tendency of therapists to commence intervention procedures at too early a step and without involving the clients and those who implement the programmes. The dangers or ineffectiveness of so doing are stressed.

The other job-aid has been designed by two psychologists working in Wisconsin (Shearer and Shearer 1974). This package is designed to enable parents of pre-school children with developmental delays to strengthen selected specific appropriate responses in the child through simple interventions lasting about 10 minutes two or three times per day.

The package consists of a developmental checklist from which the parent ticks off the skills which the child already has. The skills covered are cognitive, psychomotor, self-help, social and play. One or two responses which are just within or above the child's skill levels are then chosen to work on at any time. The package also contains a pack of cards on which each response on the checklist is specified in performance terms. The card also contains 3–5 simple instructions for the parents on how to help the child attain the target criterion with respect to the response. A consultant helps to fix the criterion, models the parental response with the child and parent present, instructs the parent on how to chart the outcome of the training exercises and leaves the parent to get on with the programme. The consultant visits the homes weekly to check that the records have been completed, to test whether the parent is able to conduct the trials and to clarify procedures if there are difficulties in implementing them. If the performance steps are too big, the consultant breaks them down and prepares another card.

By this method one consultant can supervise a number of parents. This number can be increased if the consultant supervises other professionals who visit the families (e.g. health visitors or social workers) and who have learned how to supervise the parental performances with the job-aid. The parent, over a period, should develop skills of pinpointing responses which can be increased or decreased in frequency, of giving clear instructions, of presenting social or tangible reinforcers immediately following the response, and of recording and graphing the response. They also learn how to find time to conduct training sessions within the schedule of a busy day. They will also have practice at task analysis. Watson and Tharp (1972) have provided a most useful monograph which teaches the reader the concepts and operations of experimental analysis in the context of self-modification programmes.

The job-aids so far described allow a wide range of people with different levels of skill to directly implement behavioural programmes with individual clients.

Further 'organizational' problems arise in attempts to coordinate activities when the intervention programmes require organic or medical investigation and treatments as well as behavioural interventions, and when more than one professional is concerned with implementing the programme. The problem-oriented medical record of Weed (Weed 1969; Cross 1974) is being used increasingly as a job-aid to overcome these problems.

In our research plans we intend to develop and test packages of such job-aids for direct-care personnel. These will include intervention guidelines and records for the joint setting, monitoring and attaining of goals with individuals. The importance of the problem-oriented medical record is that it increases the probability that medical interventions are limited to identifying and manipulating only those organic variables which can be manipulated, because for each 'problem' identified there must be a 'plan' specified. Both the procedures for implementing the *plan* and for recording the *consequences* of these procedures in solving the problem (e.g. reducing the blood pressure, reducing the blood sugar level) must be carefully charted on separate flow sheets. The problem list and current plans must be continuously brought up to date.

The availability of adequate records for the implementation of intervention programmes on individual clients also enables monitoring and supervisory staff to assess the extent to which their support and allocation of resources allows direct-care staff to carry out their activities.

The design of the client's record and the method by which it is completed might contribute further to joint goal setting and to higher quality of care if clients and their relatives were to have legal right or access to the record. This legal right is already recognized in the USA.

270

'Recent litigation has established that the record developed by any professional or agency is the property of the client. Under the concept of the right to know, records must be available to parents and clients upon demand. Records, therefore, should record objective data and observable behaviors, rather than inferences, assumptions, and interpretations that may not be defensible. Under the concept of privileged communication, an agency staff member may withhold specific material that is in the client's record. However, the client must be told what material is being withheld, and due process must always be observed. The agency should have a staff person present to interpret the record to the client and his family.'
(Accreditation Council for Facilities for the Retarded 1973.)

ENVIRONMENTAL OBSTACLES TO TRAINING PROGRAMMES

Earlier in this paper I mentioned that conditions under which direct-care staff work may often impede the implementation of individual intervention programmes. It is becoming increasingly clear that insofar as it is possible to implement programmes for individuals, the time available for their actual implementation cannot take up more than a small fraction of the clients' total day. Yet it is the clients' interaction with the environment during the whole of the waking day that will determine whether or not acceptable skills and knowledge will be developed and maintained, or whether these will be extinguished or punished and disruptive and emotional repertoires develop.

The quality of care section within our team is developing packages with which it should be possible for monitors and supervisors to measure aspects of the quality of the day-long environment from the extent to which the environment generates activities of the clients. Measures of the extent to which clients engage in 'appropriate' or other forms of behaviour during different activity periods throughout the day constitute one *dependent variable*. Measures of the extent to which direct-care staff contact clients during these activities constitute a second dependent variable. It should be possible to identify the extent to which interventions of the monitoring and supervisory staff, such as allocation of staff, changes in staff-client ratio, methods of staff rotation, methods of staff supervision, sequencing of client and staff activities, staff training, job-aids, etc. (i.e. changes in *independent variables*) also change the above *dependent variables*.

My colleagues Ron Whatmore and Lyn Durward have piloted one such measure in residential units for retarded children (Durward and Whatmore 1975; Whatmore, Durward and Kushlick 1975). The behaviours of the children are categorized as Disruptive, Inappropriate, Neutral or Appropriate (D.I.N.A.) with respect to different activity periods throughout the day. Reliable scores can be obtained by time-sampling observations throughout the day. The higher the 'quality of care' on this score, the greater the proportion of appropriate (as opposed to D.I.N.) behaviour the residents exhibit. In addition, the higher the proportion of contact with children by staff during periods of appropriate behaviour, the higher the quality of care. Conversely, the higher the proportion of contact by staff during D.I.N. behaviour, the lower the quality of care.

It has been necessary to specify for severely mentally retarded children which activities at specific activity periods (from getting up to going to bed, including mealtime and recreation time) are D.I.N. or A. It has also been necessary to specify differently, in some instances, according to whether children are ambulant or not. Methods of sampling have been assessed and clear differences shown between two units which appear different on commonsense intuition. The problems of time sampling and training observers have been described (Durward and Whatmore 1975).

The Living Environments Group of Kansas University Department of Human Development has developed very useful concepts and procedures for monitoring levels of quality of care and for evaluating the effectiveness of interventions (Cataldo and Risley 1974, 1974b; Doke and Risley 1972; LeLaurin and Risley 1972; Risley and Cataldo 1973). In their work, the main dependent variable is the level of 'wholesome' client activity generated or sustained at different periods throughout the day: the higher this level, the higher the quality. Risley and his colleagues have demonstrated that it is possible using clear, simple and reliable methods (which require very short periods of observer training before reliable scores are obtained) to rate environments ranging from those in which there are *no* specified activities for clients to those where the activities are carefully programmed. In environments without specified programmes (Cataldo and Risley 1974b) ratings are made of what the clients are touching with their hands throughout the day (e.g. nothing, themselves, non-manipulable objects, manipulable objects, other people), as well as what they are looking at, their position, and whether or not they are vocalizing. In environments with programmes, certain forms of response are specified by the staff as the 'appropriate' or 'engaged' behaviour for that activity period (Risley and Cataldo 1973). Counts are made at 3-minute intervals throughout the observation period of the number of clients present in the activity area and the numbers who are 'engaged' at the end of each 3-minute period. It is likely that 'engagement' also reflects the extent to which care is being tailored for individuals. The assumption here is that activities in which the client engages are reinforcing to the client (Premack 1959).

Details are described in a number of papers. The most exciting aspect of these techniques is their simplicity, clarity and applicability to a wide range of residential and day-care facilities of groups of clients ranging from infants (Cataldo and Risley 1974a and b; Doke and Risley 1972; LeLaurin and Risley 1972) to very old people in geriatric facilities (McLannahan 1973). We have begun to use these concepts in examining the quality of care in psychogeriatric facilities (Felce, Samuel and Whatmore 1974).

'ORGANIZATIONAL' OBSTACLES—ROUTINES

These developments are relevant to some of the problems discussed in this study group as 'organizational'. These are features of the environment which influence the extent to which staff who have had different forms of training are able to set and attain individual goals for clients in the real situation. The

272

studies have highlighted the relevance of various routines—domestic (cleaning and tidying), health care (feeding, bathing, toileting, preparation and distribution of medication), and security (prevention of accidents, locking of doors, fire prevention)—in determining whether any staff time remains available for the setting, monitoring and attaining of individual goals for clients in these settings. It is now clear that unless the environment allows these staff routines to be carefully and efficiently carried out, the priority which staff must give to them will ensure that staff spend most, if not all, of the available time carrying them out. These are also the activities which are monitored most closely by the outside community. It is also clear that if we label them as 'institution-' or 'administrative-oriented' activities, as opposed to the 'client-oriented' activities of conducting individual training programmes, we merely punish direct-care personnel who have to carry out these activities. Moreover, we may make it less likely that direct-care staff will seek skills in individual training methods or attempt to implement individual programmes if trainers set performance goals for direct-care staff but fail to take into account the key conditions under which such programmes must be carried out.

In one of their papers, Cataldo and Risley (1974b) describe for an infant day centre the way in which the efficient design of health care routines (feeding and nappy changing), receiving and departure routines, and sleeping routines can contribute to high quality care in these areas, encourage parental participation in this and still leave time for play and recreation activities.

MATERIALS FOR THE ENGAGEMENT OF CLIENTS

In generating a wide range of planned activities (engagement) of clients throughout the day, it is important that suitable material which attracts the clients is prepared, displayed and available to clients at all times of the day and particularly when staff are *not* available for implementing individual programmes. These activities do not necessarily teach clients new responses or increase the strength and frequency of those already in their repertoires. However, they are likely to maintain those already present.

Moreover, engaged activities are incompatible both with the loss of existing repertoires and with activities which are so disruptive to the physical and social environment that they occasion the exclusion of clients from the environment. Disruptive conduct of clients may also lead to the removal from the environment of potentially dangerous materials (cutlery, crockery, curtains, etc.). These materials may be important to the clients' habilitation or rehabilitation. They set the occasion for a wide range of skills required by the community, i.e. for normalization. In addition their presence is likely to be attractive and their absence makes the environment unattractive, to the direct-care personnel working in the environment and to clients' relatives and volunteers.

When the environment can sustain high levels of engaged activities throughout the day, and once staff can complete their domestic, health-care and other routines without feeling harrassed, and if time is available, it becomes possible to implement the individual training programmes.

The development of materials and programmes for making these routines efficient is a priority and its effectiveness can be monitored by the extent to which engagement levels of clients improve (Quilitch and Risley 1973). Similarly, the identification, preparation and display of materials which engage the clients must become another priority. Their effectiveness can be similarly monitored.

CONTACT BETWEEN CLIENTS AND DIRECT-CARE PERSONNEL

Alongside these activities is the priority of simply and effectively ensuring that, between their other activities, direct-care staff contact the clients differentially and frequently during 'engaged' or 'appropriate' activities and ignore clients differentially during 'inappropriate' or 'disruptive' conduct. The State of Florida has recently published an excellent document (to which Risley is a contributor) outlining how this can be proceduralized and monitored (May, MacAllister, Risley et al. 1974). A most important section of this document deals with guidelines for weakening disruptive behaviours of clients. Procedures for doing this in ways that are likely to be widely considered acceptable and likely to lead to improvements in the daily living environment are described in this document in the way that they would appear in a training manual for staff. This makes it possible to design training courses for staff, if necessary, with the sole objective of teaching them those priority skills.

'ZONING'

Another key independent variable has been identified as determining levels of client engagement throughout the day. This is the planning of activities in physically demarcated 'zones' at any time of the day, and the 'manning' of these zones by one or more staff members who are responsible for the preparation of the activity and for engaging whichever clients are present in the zone. The evidence suggests that if three zones are 'open' at any time of the waking day (e.g. getting up, toileting and eating; toileting, eating and recreation; recreation I, toileting and recreation II; etc.) clients can move from one engaging activity to another at their own pace.* Clients move from one zone to another at *their* initiative and staff 'man' a particular zone for which they have prepared the relevant materials, displayed them and devised rules for their availability.

This not only enables the monitors and supervisors to allocate staff on a planned basis and to check whether the tasks are being carried out; it also enables personnel concerned with staff training to teach specific skills relevant to the preparation, display and rendering available of materials for different zones and for the engagement of clients within these zones. As not all clients need be in the same zone at the same time (e.g. eating, recreation or toileting)

---

* If only one zone is open and manned by staff at any time, those clients not engaged in activities are forced to 'wait around' in the area until the staff have completed all of their activities with *all* of the clients. It is during these waiting periods that direct-care staff must lock doors to prevent client movement and that non-engaged clients tend to behave disruptively

the rooms can be smaller and special equipment available in each room. Felce et al (1974) have developed a simple technique for describing the zoning of activities in an existing facility.

Since clients of different skill levels and interests are engaged by different materials (Felce et al. 1974), there are important tasks required in the development of suitable materials for clients with particularly limited or unusual behaviour repertoires.

SOME PRIORITIES FOR TRAINING PROGRAMMES

On the basis of these analyses, training programmes for staff might take the form of:
(a) courses for supervisors and monitors in assessing levels of engagement and allocating staff and other resources so that health care and other routines can be effectively carried out while high levels of client engagement are maintained;
(b) courses for direct-care personnel on:
    (i)   differential reinforcement of appropriate behaviours;
    (ii) procedures for weakening disruptive behaviour;
    (iii) opening and closing activity zones;
    (iv) preparing, displaying and making rules for the availability of materials for clients in different activity zones;
    (v) the use of job aids for individual intervention programmes planned jointly with clients (when possible), relatives and other professionals.

This paper has dealt so far with the performances of direct-care staff and supervisors and monitors in residential and day facilities. In our team, John Smith and David Felce are now developing these concepts and procedures for application in ordinary family settings.

PERFORMANCES OF PROVIDERS AND PLANNERS

Finally I would like to illustrate an application of goal analysis to performances of providers and planners of courses. This will be done by reference to the policy document 'Better Services for the Mentally Handicapped'.

My colleagues and I were recently invited to produce a Unit for the Open University course on 'Handicap in the Community' on preparing or setting goals in health and social service settings as a first step in attaining them (Kushlick, Blunden, Horner and Smith 1974). We have suggested that a well-prepared goal (or statement of intent) will contain the following elements:
(i)   A general *statement of aim*. This may be stated in the form of a 'fuzzy'.
(ii) A *Performer*.
(iii) *Target Performances*. Specific performances to be carried out by the performer if the goal is to be attained.
(iv) *Conditions*. Identified limitations in the situation in which the performer will be required to perform, e.g. rules defined in policy documents, resources available—people, money, job aids, other commitments of the performer, etc.

275

(v) *Criteria.* Characteristics of each performance which are measurable and allow the performer or others to check whether the performance has been achieved, e.g. 500 words written by a given date; 10 steps walked unaided in 30 seconds.

(vi) *Consequences* of the performance to specified people, e.g. the performer, the performer's colleagues, relatives, friends, etc., or to others (specified).

We suggest that by the time a goal statement has been prepared in this manner, it will not only constitute a job aid to the performer, it will also enable other people—the performer's colleagues, the performer's clients, the monitors and supervisors of the performer—to scrutinize the goal statement, to agree to it and to take steps to assist in its attainment, or to modify or even change it altogether.

A second advantage of this form of goal preparation is that, once written, it is possible to set subgoals which include altering the *conditions* which limit the attainment of the *performance*. For example, if the resources available in the *conditions* section suggest that the criteria will not be met, it may be necessary either to abandon the performance, change the criteria, or to prepare a subgoal to change the conditions, e.g. to 'increase the resources'.

Finally, once the consequences are spelled out, it may be possible to examine whether there are simpler ways of attaining the intended consequences without going through the named performance, or whether, given the judged importance of the consequence, any of the suggested performances are worth pursuing at all.

The spelling out of the immediate, medium- and long-term *consequences* for the performer is a crucial element of goal setting. During this study group it has been suggested that goal setting is 'only a technology', i.e. it is alleged that it does not assist in considerations of 'content' or take into account the ethical problems raised by interventions. However, we can, if we wish, make a rule that consequences to performer must always be spelled out and that:

the medium- and long-term consequences of any intervention must enable the performer to *expand* or maintain the range of his or her engaged activities, i.e. they must *not* decrease this range, and

any such desired changes in performance must be capable of being maintained in the performer's daily living environment without the use of punitive contingencies.

Goals set according to these rules should be such that both the performances chosen and the means of attaining them are ethically desirable. Moreover, as long as those involved in attaining the goals have also been party to the setting of goals prepared according to these criteria, the performances should also be attainable. Where clients cannot participate in the setting of goals, their relatives or advocates should do so.

We have found it useful to analyse texts using this format. It is particularly useful to do this with policy texts, as these are, in the framework of experimental analysis of behaviour, rules or discriminative stimuli (S^D's or $S^\triangle$'s) which set the occasion for the responses of others (Skinner 1969). David Felce and I have undertaken an analysis of Cmnd. 4683 into the categories: Performer, Performance, Conditions, Criteria, and Consequences.

Earlier in this paper I listed the failures to implement aspects of the Cmnd. paper policies as important unfavourable *conditions* under which direct-care staff had to care for their clients. I also listed aspects of the policy on which it was not possible to say whether or not policies have been implemented. You will recall Mager's guidelines: identify a performance which ought to be taking place but is not. If this is not due to lack of skill, remove the obstacles to the performance, or remove the pay-offs for not performing or for performing incompatibly. Provide positive feedback for performances which are on target or approaching target.

Cmnd. 4683 is an important document in this respect. The performances involve personnel at all levels of health, social service and education agencies. Members of most professional groups take part at all levels of the agencies concerned. Cmnd. 4683 is a unique document in the extent to which it spells out a long list of target performances which are to be carried out. It also lists performances which are *not* to be implemented.

Our analysis reveals an important weakness—few performances pass the 'Hey Dad' test—i.e. they are 'fuzzies'. One of the advantages of the analysis into Performer, Performance, etc., is that it highlights the extent of their imprecision, whereas this is often obscured in the ordinary text (Table 1). It can be seen that in the key areas of assessment (paras 128–139) and family counselling (paras 140–145) the performer is not always clear, the performances are very unclear, and the consequences, if mentioned at all, do not stand out as being positively reinforcing to the performer, the client, or to the others concerned.

The examples with respect to educational policy (Table 2) (paras 151–153) illustrate the very wide range of performances covered. Some of these are more imprecise than others. Moreover, the negative performance 'will not exclude' in paragraph 152 is possibly countered by the positive performance 'will transfer ... more flexibly' in paragraph 157.

The examples in Table 3 (paras 238–246) illustrate some much more precise performances and negatives. The degree of precision is illustrated by the extent to which quantitative criteria are spelled out. Paragraph 239 also illustrates how quantitative features of the services to be provided are defined by reference to other sections of the document. However, paragraph 244 also illustrates more 'flexible' criteria which could substantially affect the performances of the RHB officers viz. 'districts not exceeding 250,000 (possibly more in densely populated urban areas).' The note at the end of paragraph 246 highlights a major deficit in the document, namely that no clear policy has been enunciated for the profoundly handicapped and severely disruptive clients who will be the main responsibility of the future hospital service.

The tables have *not* been presented to ridicule the document either for the performances specified or for their degree of imprecision. As policy documents go, Cmnd. 4683 is outstanding for the range of performers and performances it attempts to cover and for the specificity with which at least some of the performances are defined. The examples have been provided to illustrate that:

The categories of provider and planners, supervisors and monitors, direct-care staff and clients and relevant others are identifiable even in so complex a document;

The performances vary in their degree of imprecision;

Each 'fuzzy' is capable and is indeed in need of further clarification into specific performances for which consequences can be spelled out; and

Once they have been so specified, it should become possible to:

(a) identify those performances which constitute priorities because of the positive consequences resulting if they are achieved, and the positive consequences which will be held up or the adverse consequences which will follow if they are *not* attained.

(b) identify the priority performances for which performers require job aids, training courses, or both (and collaborate with the performers in doing so).

(c) design methods for measuring existing performance levels (i.e. baselines) and identify variables (antecedents and consequences) likely to be controlling these performances.

(d) intervene and measure the effectiveness of the intervention strategies used, i.e. evaluate the interventions used.

CONCLUSION

Insofar as the policy document identifies performances of personnel at any level, the job of devising training courses for staff arises when, and only when, there is reasonable evidence that the performance is relevant or important ('What will be the consequence of it not occurring?') and when the performers lack the skill.

If there is no other way of avoiding consequences of the performance deficit identified, a training course can be devised to teach the relevant skill specifically and the effectiveness of the training performance evaluated.

The new techniques for monitoring quality of care during the client's waking day have highlighted the priorities of designing job aids for monitor and supervisory staff as well as for direct-care staff. Training courses will be needed to enable staff to use these job aids effectively.

An important research task is the development and field testing of such job aids for staff at different levels within the hierarchy, for the parents and relatives and for the clients themselves.

The concepts and procedures of experimental analysis of behaviour were developed in the past to modify the behaviour of retarded people in laboratory type settings. Problems, both ethical and procedural, have been encountered in implementing these procedures in the existing unsatisfactory daily living environments in residential settings. Developments in concepts and procedures can now be focused on changing these unsatisfactory conditions. Using these techniques it should also be possible to arrange facilities in ways which optimize the effectiveness of the activities of client advocates intent on improving these environments and maintaining these improvements. Moreover, it should be possible to test empirically and sensitively the effectiveness of these arrangements.

TABLE 1

Analysis of assessment and counselling paragraphs in Cmnd. 4683

Condition	Performer	Performance	Criteria	Consequence
Paragraph 128 *Given* young children at special risk	?	Will provide developmental screening	Regularly	Will detect deviant mental development as early as possible.
Paragraph 130 *Given* young children at special risk + list of 11 preventive measures + any new measures developed	(From Appendix) Doctors in child health clinics + Obstetricians + Paediatricians + Other specialists + G.P's	Will : - 1) Know the preventive measures 2) Use the preventive measures	?	?
Given young children at special risk + list of 11 preventive measures + any new measures developed	G.P's + nurses in domiciliary services and in hospital + social workers and others in touch with parents or prospective parents	Will be concerned with this	?	?

TABLE 1, *continued*

Condition	Performer	Performance	Criteria	Consequence
Given ditto + coordinated organization e.g. reliable recording system on children at risk of developing mental or physical handicaps	ditto	Will achieve this e.g. will keep children under review		
Paragraph 131 *Given* that a defect is detected or suspected	? Assessors	Will do comprehensive assessment of: – a) the nature of handicap(s) b) the needs of the handicapped person c) the problems of the handicapped person d) the needs of the family e) the problems of the family	?	?
Given age of child	? Assessors	Will consider age-appropriate medical, educational, psychological and social aspects	?	?
Given (that) no one person can be expected to possess range of skills required	? Assessors more than one person (? more than one discipline)	Will use multidisciplinary approach	?	
Given (that) child or adult grows or develops +	? Assessors	Will repeat multidisciplinary assessment	At intervals	?
Given handicapped person's age and current problems	?? Coordinator	Will vary the members of the assessment team		

TABLE 1, *continued*

Condition	Performer	Performance	Criteria	Consequence
Given young child with detected or suspected mental handicap	? Coordinator	(Will select) important members of the assessment team	i) Paediatrician concerned in the assessment and care of handicapped children ii) Consultant in psychiatry iii) Other experts in medicine, education, psychology, nursing and social work iv) G.P. v) Others concerned with support for family, e.g. health visitor and social worker	
Given young child with detected or suspected mental handicap	Assessment team members	Reassess progress	Frequently	?
Paragraph 139 *Given* handicap first detected	? Counsellor	Must tell parents	Sympathetically, skilfully	Parents to understand:- i) nature of child's handicap ii) what to expect from child iii) likely problems as he grows older iv) how family can best help the child to develop his ability to the full
Given services available including voluntary services	?	Must give i) an appraisal of services available ii) information on how to obtain them		
Given coordinated multidisciplinary approach				Parents will not receive conflicting advice.

TABLE 1, *continued*

Condition	Performer	Performance	Criteria	Consequence
Paragraph 140 *Given* parents' problems i) own feelings towards a handicapped child (disappointment, sense of failure, anxiety about the future, concern for any other children in the family) ii) rejection of the child or iii) over-protection of the child which may have lasting effect on the child's future.	? Counsellor	i) Will take into account the total family situation ii) will give advice to parents		i) Parents avoid preoccupation with the child and therefore ii) normal children avoid: – a) deprivation b) undue strain
Paragraph 141 *Given* that many people from many disciplines (GP, SW, psychiatrist, paediatrician) have a contribution to make + their work must be coordinated + social worker is in the best position to coordinate	Social worker	i) will act as coordinator ii) will take part in the multidisciplinary team iii) will maintain a continuing relationship with the handicapped child and his family	as soon as handicap is suspected	?
Paragraph 143 *Given* that family needs practical assistance of many kinds e.g. home help, domiciliary nursing, laundry service for the unit, sitters-in, play centre, day nursery, nursery school, youth club, temporary residential care for the person in emergencies and holiday	Voluntary workers Social workers	Will help i) will invoke help of volunteers ii) will coordinate their help		

282

TABLE 1, *continued*

Condition	Performer	Performance	Criteria	Consequence
Paragraph 144 *Given* that some families will also qualify for attendance allowance	?	?	?	?
Paragraph 145 *Given* family need for skilled evaluation of real needs of family and particularly mother	?	i) will tell family about the services ii) will advise them on their use		
Given times when mother needs reassurance and guidance on how to care for her child herself +	Health visitor + Social worker	Will give reassurance Will give advice		Others from outside will not give advice
other times when : — family needs a period of total relief from the daily routine of caring for the handicapped child +	?	?	?	?
essence of good community care is availability of someone				Family members can confidently expect understanding and help to meet every situation

TABLE 2

Analysis of educational policy in Cmnd. 4683

Condition	Performer	Performance	Criteria	Consequence
Paragraph 151				
Given the educational foundations laid by the health and hospital service	?	1) Will make available educational advice	more than before	
+				
the change to responsibility of the Education Service	?	2) Will train teaching and other staff	i) more fully ii) more professionally	
+				
children who up to now have been on the borderline behaviour/education/health	?	3) Will transfer children from one setting to another	more flexibly (easily)	
Paragraph 152				
Given children with mental handicap	Educator in educational system	Will *not* exclude		
Given that there are mentally handicapped children in hospitals who should attend schools in the community together with children living at home	These children in hospital	Will attend schools in the community	Together with children living at home	
Given proposals to build new schools	School planners	Will plan schools	Numbers specified for children at home and in hospital	It should become easier for children in hospitals to attend schools in community.
+				
the information on this dual intake (children in hospitals/children in homes)				

284

TABLE 2, *continued*

Condition	Performer	Performance	Criteria	Consequence
Given that fewer children will be admitted to large isolated hospitals + that more will be in smaller units in population centres recommended later	Children from home and institutions	Will intermingle	increasingly	
Given children in hospital who in the past have often been denied education for a) lack of a 'school' in the hospital b) lack of teaching staff to visit them on the ward	?	Will arrange to provide education Will provide education	i) in the wards ii) for children who were denied education in the past	
Paragraph 153 *Given* the description of special care and the functions of special care units for children and adults in paras 62–63	LEA officers + LHA officers + LA SSD officers + Hospital officers	Will jointly arrange ?provision ?operational policies ?running of special care units	1) for children but 2) especially for adults	

285

TABLE 3

Future pattern of hospital services, according to Cmnd. 4683

Condition	Performer	Performance	Criteria	Consequence
Paragraph 238 Given differences of opinion (see 189–192) about best size and location of hospitals or hospital units for m.h.	Government ?	Encourage someone to develop alternative lines		Experience with different solutions provided.
Paragraph 239	RHB's	Must provide assessment services and treatment services	i) type out-patients day-patients in-patients ii) on lines of Chap 5 iii) on principles of Chap 3 points (xi)–(xiv) para 40 iv) size and location paras 24 etc.	
Given request by DHSS	RHB	Must provide these		
Paragraph 241 Given that best of the present hospitals and those improved by i) relief of overcrowding ii) more staff iii) better living conditions will provide necessary experience of large specialized hospitals	RHB	Will *not*, for the time being, provide any new hospitals	i) large ii) specialized	a) prevent increase in numbers of in-patients b) allow comparison of experience of new alternatives with existing provision.
		Will *not*, for the time being, enlarge hospitals of	500+ beds	
Paragraph 242 Given that hospitals of 500+ patients on one site are overcrowded	RHB	Will provide new building to relieve overcrowding	located in areas of population elsewhere in the hospital's catchment area	

TABLE 3, *continued*

Condition	Performer	Performance	Criteria	Consequence
Paragraph 243 *Given* that in hospitals of 500+ patients on one site it is necessary to vacate existing wards to upgrade them	RHB	Will provide additional residential space on site	i) occasionally ii) very limited iii) one system-built unit per site iv) provided unit can be staffed	
Paragraph 244	RHB	will provide new units	site: i) in units for m.h. with a hospital containing other departments as well, or ii) in separate hospitals or units size: i) small or medium-sized hospitals ii) small or medium- size units	
	RHB	a) will ensure that staff of each unit contribute to a range of defined facilities for m.h.	i) from a defined district ii) district not exceeding 250,000 (possibly more in densely populated areas) iii) district coincides with district served by one (possibly 2) general hospital	
	Staff of each unit alone or with others (defined by RHB)	b) will provide a range of services: in-patient, out-patient, day-patient	relation to other services: i) from a defined district ii) district not exceeding 250,000 population (possibly more in densely populated areas)	
Given staff in these new hospitals and these new units for the m.h.	RHB Officers	c) will arrange close operational links	i) general hospital (staff) serving the same district ii) existing m.h. hospital staff	

TABLE 3, *continued*

Condition	Performer	Performance	Criteria	Consequence
Paragraph 245 *Given* planning figures in Table 5 + 200 places will eventually be necessary for populations well in excess of 250,000 + hospital serving population of more than 250,000 would be too remote from many of the population	RHB Officers	i) will provide new units ii) will provide additional day places	i) none more than 100–200 beds ii) many considerably smaller	
Paragraph 246 *Given* patients who i) require specialist medical supervision ii) are capable of going out daily to a special school or ATC iii) are capable of going out daily to employment or iv) have friends or relations nearby	RHB Staff in the units	will provide some of the smaller units will design and build these smaller units will site these smaller units will provide social activities for the m.h. residents	i) for such patients similar to LA homes, homely in character (as in para 163) preferably in a residential area i) similar to LA homes (as in para 163)	
Note: the Command Paper makes no mention of: – *Given* patients who i) *do* require specialist medical supervision ii) are *not* capable of going out daily to a special school or ATC iii) are *not* capable of going out daily to employment iv) do *not* have friends or relations nearby	RHB Staff in these units	will provide some of the smaller units will design and build these smaller units will site these smaller units will provide social activities for the m.h. residents		

TABLE 3, *continued*

Condition	Performer	Performance	Criteria	Consequence

No mention of
1) Criteria—'require specialist medical supervision', 'capable of'
2) who will classify?
3) who will monitor } classification?
     arrange
     supervise }				

ACKNOWLEDGEMENT

I should like to acknowledge the help of colleagues Roger Blunden, David Felce, John Palmer and Geraldine Cansick, for their advice during the preparation of the text; thanks are also due to my secretary, Janice Broadbridge, for the typing of various drafts. I am grateful to Professor Sidney Bijou for drawing my attention to the job-aid package mentioned on p. 269.

REFERENCES

ACCREDITATION COUNCIL FOR FACILITIES FOR THE RETARDED (1973) *Standards for Community Agencies serving Persons with Mental Retardation and other Developmental Disabilities.* Joint Commission on Accreditation of Hospitals, Chicago

BIJOU, S.W. (1973) Helping children develop their full potential. *Paed. Clin. N. Am. 20,* 579–585

CARTER, R.C. (1973) Outline for procedural guide to behavioral case management. Unpublished

CATALDO, M.F. and RISLEY, T.R. (1974a) *Evaluation of Living Environments: the Manifest Description of Ward Activities.* (in press)

CATALDO, M.F. and RISLEY, T.R. (1974b) Infant day care. In *Control of Human Behavior Vol. 3* (Ulrich, R., Stachnik, T. and Mabry, J., eds.), pp. 44–50. Scott Foresman, Glenview, Illinois

COHEN, S. (1974) Human warehouses: the future of our prisons? *New Society 30,* 407–411

CROSS, H.D. (1974) The case for problem oriented medical records. *Br. J. Hosp. Med. 11,* 65–79

DEPARTMENT OF HEALTH AND SOCIAL SECURITY (1971) *Better Services for the Mentally Handicapped. Cmnd. 4683.* HMSO, London

DURWARD, L. and WHATMORE, R. (1975) Testing measures of the quality of residential care: a pilot study. *Behav. Res. Therap.* (in press)

DOKE, L.A. and RISLEY, T.R. (1972) The organisation of day-care environments: required vs. optional activities. *J. Appl. Behav. Anal. 5,* 405–420

FELCE, D., SAMUEL, A. and WHATMORE, R. (1974) An example of an evaluative method from data collected on two psychogeriatric wards. Appendix C. In *Proposals for the Setting up and Evaluation of an Experimental Service for the Elderly: a Document for Discussion* (Kushlick, A. and Blunden, R.). Wessex Regional Health Authority, Winchester

GAMBRILL, E.D., THOMAS, E.J. and CARTER, R.D. (1971) Procedure for socio-behavioral practice in open settings. *Social Work 16,* 51–62

HALL, J. (1974) Training nurses in behaviour modification. An analysis of current British practice. *Behav. Mod.* (6), 17–24

HOLLAND, J.G. (1974) Political implications of applying behavioral psychology. In *Control of Human Behavior Vol. 3* (Ulrich, R., Stachnik, T. and Mabry, J., eds.), pp. 413–419. Scott Foresman, Glenview, Illinois

KUSHLICK, A. (1973) The need for residential care. In *Action for the Retarded,* pp. 13–26. National Society for Mentally Handicapped Children, London

KUSHLICK, A., BLUNDEN, R., HORNER, D. and SMITH, J. (1974) *Goal Setting. Unit 9.* Prepared for the Open University Course *The Handicapped Person in the Community.* Open University Press, Bletchley, Bucks

LAWRENCE, H. and SUNDEL, M. (1972) Behavior modification in adult groups. *Social Work 17,* 34–43

LeLAURIN, K. and RISLEY, T.R. (1972) The organisation of day-care environments: 'zone' versus 'man-to-man' staff assignments. *J. Appl. Behav. Anal. 5,* 225–232

LINDSLEY, O.R. (1964a) Direct measurement and prosthesis of retarded behavior. *J. Educ. 147,* 62–81

LINDSLEY, O.R. (1964b) Geriatric behavioral prosthetics. In *New Thoughts on Old Age* (Kastenbaum, R., ed.). Springer, New York

McLANNAHAN, L.E. (1973) Recreation programs for nursing home residents: the importance of patient characteristics and environmental arrangements. *Therap. Recreat. J. 7,* 26–31

MAGER, R.F. and PIPE, P. (1970) *Analysing Performance Problems*. Fearon, Belmont, Calif.

MAGER, R.F. (1972) *Goal Analysis*. Fearon, Belmont, Calif.

MAY, J.G., McALLISTER, J. and RISLEY, T.R. et al. (1974) Florida guidelines for the use of behavioral procedures in state programs for the retarded. Unpublished

PREMACK, D. (1959). Toward empirical behavior laws: 1. Positive reinforcements. *Psychol. Rev. 66*, 219–233

QUILITCH, H.R. and RISLEY, T.R. (1973) The effects of play materials on social play. *J. Appl. Behav. Anal. 6*, 573–578

RISLEY, T.R. and CATALDO, M.F. (1973) *Planned Activity Check Materials for Training Observers*. Center for Applied Behavior Analysis

SHEARER, D.E. and SHEARER, M.S. (1974) *The Portage Project*. Paper presented at the Conference on Early Intervention for High Risk Infants and Young Children, Chapel Hill, North Carolina, 5–8 May 1974. Cooperative Educational Service Agency, Portage, Wisconsin

SKINNER, B.F. (1953) *Science and Human Behavior*. Free Press, New York

SKINNER, B.F. (1968) *The Technology of Teaching*. Appleton-Century-Crofts, New York

SKINNER, B.F. (1969) *Contingencies of Reinforcement: a Theoretical Analysis*. Appleton-Century-Crofts, New York

THOMAS, E.J. and WALTER, C.L. (1973) Guidelines for behavioral practice in the open community agency: procedures and evaluation. *Behav. Res. Therap. 11*, 193–205

WATSON, D.L. and THARP, R.G. (1972) *Self-directed Behavior: Self-modification for Personal Adjustment*. Brooks/Cole, Monterey, Calif.

WEED, L.L. (1969) *Medieal Records, Medical Education and Patient Care*. The Press of Western Reserve University, Cleveland, Ohio

WEXLER, D.B. (1973) Token and taboo: behavior modification, token economies and the law. *California Law Review 61*, 81–109

WHATMORE, R., DURWARD, L. and KUSHLICK, A. (1975) Measuring the quality of residential care. *Behav. Res. Therap.* (in press)

Commentary

JACK TIZARD

Albert Kushlick's comments on the response to the publication of the White Paper are very telling. The misfortune—to the mental handicap services—is that Cmnd. 4683 was treated as though it was a Royal Commission report or a discussion document rather than a Command Paper. The reasons for this would repay analysis: and for this purpose I think we might still find it informative to use the old-fashioned 'fuzzy' terminology and concepts of social administration and political science as well as the more specific, and certainly more long-winded, descriptions which a 'performance' analysis would entail. A performance analysis, strictly interpreted, eschews all but the most primitive concepts or general notions; it replaces them by descriptions of 'behaviours'. But unless the list of behaviours exhausts all possible performers, target performances, conditions, criteria and consequences—which would be impossibly tedious even if it were feasible—we are also bound to use more general terms. We must, I think, see behaviour modification and performance analysis as part of the great empirical tradition of science and not as something which replaces it.

The paper brings out two important sets of problems which have to be tackled if we are to improve the services for the mentally handicapped. One is to move from the general notions of the White Paper to the more specific plans and policies which would put them into effect. The examples given illustrate the sort of steps that are required: in one way or another most of them would entail a much crisper definition of the problems. They would also require us to take much more seriously than we do today the implications of the now much talked about concepts of accountability in the National Health Service and Local Authority Social Services Departments. Our medical and social services are slowly, but only slowly, coming to accept that it is their responsibility to provide services which meet the needs of the *whole* population. The guiding principle is that of equity, that is of fairness and justice. And a consequence of good epidemiological research is that it draws attention to the extent to which existing services fail to do this. Without epidemiological studies we inevitably delude ourselves as to the adequacy both of the coverage of our services and their quality.

Now in Britain we are very good at epidemiological research. Where we fall down is in using the data it provides as a basis for planning. Dr Kushlick is pointing out that research can help us here in two ways. One is through planned experimental variation in the *form* in which services are provided; the second is through the use of corrective feedback to improve the *quality* of what is provided. The Wessex studies themselves make a notable contribution to both types of research, and the American work cited provides other examples.

Discussion

Kushlick: I would just like to question the usefulness of vague terms like 'sensitive awareness to the reality of a situation' and 'autonomy'. If they can be defined operationally, as you did in *Patterns of Residential Care*, well and good; but unless they are carefully redefined for each situation, they can lead the listener astray. For instance, in the study by King, Raynes and Tizard (1971), autonomy of the caring staff was regarded as a 'good' thing; it was measured (amongst other criteria) by the *infrequency* with which the next immediate supervisor visited the living units. Yet if important changes were being introduced in a residential unit, and if the supervisor had important skills to provide, infrequent visits would have a negative effect upon the quality of care.

Tizard: Agreed, but without these high-level concepts which you call vague, one remains constantly at the level of the particular and unable to draw general conclusions. The definition of autonomy which my wife Barbara used in her work on nursery schools was rather different, but the concept she was talking about was essentially the same, and it was valid and useful to use and extend it in this way.

Cunningham: I like the concept of specifying the consequences of interventions, as it may help us to get around the frequent problems of relating aims—the general intent and direction of a programme—and objectives, which are measurable behaviours adding up to the whole child or a whole situation. We may need systems analysis to put it all together, but specifying consequences at least helps to define objectives and to assess whether we have achieved them.

Kushlick: Specifying can be dangerous to the specifier because it exposes him to criticism, both on his definitions and on his performance—since unlike the people who keep out of trouble he has specified what he is trying to do. On this account specification is a highly aversive behaviour for many people.

Walker: That's right. A person may be content in his position because he feels he has autonomy. But if the person above him in the hierarchy defines the areas in which he is autonomous, that behaviour can be highly aversive because the supervisor's knowledge seems to rob the junior person of his autonomy.

Kiernan: It has become very clear to me that the person applying behaviour modification to a child over any length of time must have considerable autonomy to respond to the changing situation as he or she sees it. With parents, too, a most important source of motivation comes from feeling in control of the situation.

Tizard: Whether autonomy is good or bad depends on the operation you are trying to run. In acute nursing in a general hospital, there is little room for autonomy —and rightly so, because if some test is done idiosyncratically and gives the wrong result, someone will die. But in long-stay institutions, that sort of lack of autonomy can have a very bad effect. Perhaps my distaste for the token economy is that everything is so closely specified that the staff are not free to make decisions, and this is bound to lead to low morale.

Thorpe: I sympathize with that, although the purpose of token economies is surely to release nurses from the chores of toileting and dressing and making beds in order that they can become autonomous in higher-level activities.

Berger: My experience with certain teachers is that they don't want this autonomy and the responsibility it entails. They want very clear, structured guidance on what to do in any given situation.

Hogg: Accepting guidance isn't accepting control, and the teachers who seem to you so dependent during courses are aware that they can withdraw from that situation, whereas if they were under your direct supervision and control they could not do so.

Yule: You can have control and yet retain the feeling of having responsibility for everyday decisions, which was I think the important factor in King, Raynes and Tizard's concept of autonomy.

Kushlick: Let me illustrate another difficulty with respect to the concept of autonomy in residential living units. We observed that when a residential unit was put in the community, where parents could pop in and out, the amount of direction and control exercised by the more distant hospital was less – from which one might be tempted to infer that the staff 'had greater autonomy' – but the frequency of contact and control by parents was very considerable. When it became punitive in one instance, it was quite intolerable to the staff. In this setting 'autonomy' would have had to be redefined to fit the situation if it were to be useful analytically or procedurally.

REFERENCE

KING, R.D., RAYNES, N.V. and TIZARD, J. (1971) *Patterns of Residential Care.* Routledge and Kegan Paul, London

293

The Development of Social Competence

PAUL WILLIAMS

Castle Priory College, Wallingford, Oxfordshire

ABSTRACT

This paper considers the proposition that social competence is something that most of us lack in social situations that include handicapped people. Social education in this respect is as necessary for non-handicapped people as for the handicapped. What kind of education is needed and how it might be provided is discussed in relation to two subgroups of mentally handicapped people—the profoundly handicapped and those who are relatively mildly handicapped. The relevance of a behavioural approach is outlined. Behaviour modification is viewed as a technique for strengthening mutual social relationships rather than as a method of moulding the behaviour of individuals to conform to a desired model.

In addition, the apparent 'credibility gap' between our present knowledge of successful educational techniques and the lack of resources to implement them is discussed, taking a wide view of the applicability of behavioural analysis to predict possible ways of improving services.

The paper is intended to stimulate discussion on ways of making individual social interaction with the handicapped, and societal provision of high standards of service for the handicapped, more rewarding for non-handicapped people.

I have prepared this paper with some trepidation. I fear that I have departed seriously from my brief; I have decided to present at a scientific gathering a paper that contains more philosophy than science, more opinion than fact, more questions than answers. Moreover, I have made no attempt to meet the criticism that is often levelled at the publications that emerge from such occasions as this—that little is said which is of immediate relevance and use to the hard-pressed teacher, nurse, parent or therapist who is trying to cope with enormous day-to-day problems. In presenting may paper I am conscious of a feeling of embarking on a journey in a leaky boat, but I hope that others may, perhaps now and perhaps over a longer period of time, strengthen the boat so that it ultimately may reach some useful destination.

As I imply in my final paragraph, the enormous problems that we have got ourselves into in trying to solve the 'problems' of mental handicap require us at least to consider solutions that may seem larger than life. I hope at least that a number of issues will be brought out which will fire the discussion and will not be considered too irrelevant to the main theme of this study group.

I am going to consider throughout the question of relationships. I will present a very simplistic account of relationships and link this to discussion of ways of developing social competence, not just for handicapped people but for all of us. In doing this, I have taken my cue from the title of this study group: Behaviour Modification *with*, not of or for, but *with* the Retarded.

Relationships between people vary on two dimensions. In a strong relationship the behaviours of the individuals involved are mutually reinforcing; in a weak relationship they are not. In an appropriate relationship the behaviours which are reinforced are appropriate, in the sense that they are behaviours which are also likely to be reinforced in other social situations and are themselves likely to be useful as reinforcers of other people's behaviour. An inappropriate relationship is one in which behaviour is reinforced which is not likely to be reinforced in other situations or which is not likely to be useful for reinforcing the behaviour of others.

Another important variable is the extent to which the individual's involvement in a relationship is maintained by reinforcement from sources outside the relationship. The degree of this support required to maintain a relationship will vary according to the nature of the relationship. Strong relationships will require little external support, though if support is lacking the relationship may well weaken over time. Weak relationships will require a great deal of external support or they cannot be maintained. They will only be entered into because of the existence of external reinforcement.

All of us, if we live in any group or society, have to be involved in relationships with other people to survive. Most of us are also involved in a myriad of informal and less vitally necessary relationships which enable us to live productively, creatively and happily in society. Without these relationships we might survive physically as individuals but we would not survive as members of society. Our society has as a very high priority the reinforcement of relationships necessary to maintain physical life; the reinforcement of relationships that maintain social life is not regarded as such a high priority. Some relationships are therefore always considered to be necessary and will always be supported; other relationships, while considered to be desirable, will not necessarily be reinforced.

When two people meet, their social competence will be reflected in their ability to form a strong, appropriate relationship. If a person does not have the ability to ensure that the relationships he is involved in are strong, he will be identified as socially incompetent. Relationships necessary for his physical survival will be externally supported, but other relationships may not be. The possibility of his entering into relationships other than those necessary for physical survival may be drastically curtailed. If a person is involved in inappropriate relationships, this is likely to reduce his ability to make new relationships strong. Again, necessary relationships will be externally supported, but the possibility of other relationships will be severely reduced.

296

External support for relationships can be positive: people can be given rewards for maintaining relationships with other people. It can also be negative, and quite often is: relationships are maintained through the avoidance of unpleasant consequences by so doing. Society itself, through the processes of law, will sometimes administer punishment for failure to maintain certain relationships. In the case of relationships necessary to maintain physical survival, a failure in the relationship will be identified through a reduction in the health or physical well-being of the person for whom the relationship is necessary. Failures of other social relationships are not generally identified and dealt with in the same way.

Relationships that are externally supported will not necessarily become strong, nor will they necessarily be appropriate.

Let us look at some examples to illustrate this analysis:

Suppose I cannot feed myself. In order to survive I must have a relationship with another person who will feed me. This responsibility, through operation of agreed procedures within society, will be vested in someone: parent, relative or friend or an employee of some service agency that exists to ensure that people who cannot feed themselves do not die. The relationship between me and that person may be strong. The person may find that my response to his behaviour is a pleasant one and that the reward of seeing me behave in the way that I do is sufficient to cause him to want to do the same on the next occasion. No doubt I will find that his behaviour in feeding me is a pleasant consequence of my behaving in the way that I do. On the other hand, the relationship may be weak. The person feeding me may find that my response to his behaviour is not pleasant. In this case he will only come back to feed me on the next occasion if the consequences of his not doing so are even less pleasant, or if he is receiving material or social rewards for his behaviour from someone else: his wife, his friends, his employer. The relationship, whether strong or weak, may be appropriate; he may get his rewards from me or from others only if he feeds me in a certain way which is a useful way in that it also brings forth rewards when it is practised in other situations; similarly I may get my food only if I smile or sit still or turn my head towards him, which is a useful way to behave when other people are feeding me. Alternatively the relationship may be inappropriate, whoever is providing the rewards for the other person: he may get his rewards even if he hurts or neglects me, which will not get him similar rewards in other situations; I may get fed even if I scream or throw the food on the floor, which will not be helpful behaviour for me to exhibit elsewhere.

Now let us suppose I take a bus ride. A pretty girl enters, smiles at me and sits next to me. I have a habit of making peculiar noises and banging on the window, which I proceed to do in response to her smile. She does not find this a rewarding response and frowns. I like that response and I grunt and tap again. A weak, inappropriate relationship has been quickly set up. The girl is not being reinforced for her behaviour by anyone else and there is no threat of sanctions if she terminates the relationship, which she proceeds to do by getting up and going to sit at the opposite end of the bus.

Later my neighbour enters the bus. She smiles at me and sits next to me.

I grunt and tap. My neighbour believes that I exhibit that behaviour when I am happy and she feels good that she has produced this response. She smiles again and begins to talk. I like that and I continue to grunt and tap. She continues talking. Here is a strong, inappropriate relationship. We both feel good, but I and being rewarded for behaviour that is not likely to be rewarding to many other people and which is not likely to be rewarded in other situations.

I arrive at the psychologist's office for a therapy session. The psychologist who meets me first proceeds to smile and talk to me only when I look at him and handle the materials in a certain way. If I grunt and tap the window he turns away. I want him to smile and talk and so I look at him and handle the materials increasingly often. He however does not find the experience particularly pleasant. He is behaving in the way he does because the approval of his senior colleagues depends on his altering my behaviour. If this were not so he would much prefer to smile and talk to me non-contingently or to terminate the relationship and work with someone else. This is a weak though appropriate relationship, externally supported.

He is called away and my friend the lady psychologist comes in. She likes me and finds it very rewarding when I respond to her behaviour by looking at her and working with the materials. She enjoys our relationship irrespective of gaining external approval. Ours is a strong appropriate relationship. I learn from her, and she learns from me, behaviours that are appropriate in other settings too; and we are both motivated to resume the relationship on another occasion.

Mentally handicapped people are often involved in strong, appropriate relationships, with members of their families, with staff of services, or with other handicapped or non-handicapped people. The quantity and range of such relationships is usually much more restricted than for the rest of us. Sometimes important relationships between the handicapped person and his parents, or between him and staff providing services, are weak or inappropriate. Often, informal relationships with unfamiliar people will be weak and will not be maintained. We tend to explain this situation in terms of a lack of ability or adaptability on the part of the handicapped person, and since examples of the breakdown of relationships are prevalent and easily noticeable when a handicapped person is involved, we talk of such a person lacking social competence, or being socially incompetent.

Society has a number of ways of dealing with people who are identified as socially incompetent, i.e. have difficulty in forming and maintaining a wide range of strong, appropriate relationships. In a previous paper (Williams 1973) I have described these, after Scott (1966), as follows.

– Accommodation: the modification of the behaviour of the incompetent individual in a direction that increases his competence. This is done by ensuring that relationships involving the individual are appropriate, though they may still be weak.

– Locomotion: removal or restriction of the individual to an environment in which relationships can be maintained, by restricting the possibility of relationships to those with persons who are able to make them strong or by structuring and formalizing the environment so as to reinforce essential relationships externally.

– Construction: the modification of the behaviour of others that the person is likely to meet, so that relationships formed can be made strong, or the provision of external support for potential relationships in the individual's present environment.

The problem with accommodation as a strategy is that it is likely to be of only limited success. This is not of course to deny the importance of increasing the competence of the individual who is incompetent, but it recognizes that the more severely handicapped a person the less likely it is that the attainable goal of such training will be his rehabilitation into society, in the sense of being able to initiate and maintain more than a small number of strong, appropriate relationships.

The problem with locomotion is that it represents an abandonment (sometimes temporary but often permanent) of the goal of social rehabilitation. Persons who are admitted to long-term residential care have been described by Miller and Gwynne (1972) as 'socially dead'. With the strategy of locomotion, the maintenance of relationships will be to a greater or lesser extent restricted to those relationships that are necessary for physical survival.

I wish to consider primarily how we might make greater use of the strategy of construction. Our goal is to ensure the initiation and maintenance of as many relationships as possible between the handicapped person and other people. Let us look again at the reasons why relationships between handicapped people and others may be weak.

In relationships involving a handicapped person most of us lack the ability to make them strong. Since such relationships form a very small, and usually, as far as we are concerned, dispensable proportion of the total number of relationships in which we are involved, we do not regard this as a reflection of our social incompetence. For the handicapped person a high proportion of potential relationships run the risk of being weak. However if we consider the small subgroup of our own relationships that include a handicapped person, then a high proportion of those also run the risk of being weak. It seems to me to be helpful and enlightening to regard ourselves as lacking social competence in these relationships. Our lack of competence in this respect does not affect our lives to a very great extent, but it does affect the lives of handicapped people.

Let us for a moment have a go at reversing the usual conception of where the lack of competence lies in relationships between ourselves and mentally handicapped people. Such relationships are often weak because the behaviour of one of the participants does not reinforce the behaviour of the other. Put the other way, one participant does not find the behaviour of the other rewarding. This reflects a lack of ability to find such behaviour rewarding. Mentally handicapped people appear to find a great deal of our behaviour rewarding. Some research workers (e.g. Whatmore et al. 1973, who also quote Allen and Harris 1966, for experimental evidence) have found it fruitful in carrying out behavioural analyses of interaction between very severely mentally handicapped children and non-handicapped adults to regard any contact between adult and child as potentially reinforcing, regardless of the nature of the contact. When mentally handicapped people are described as 'less inhibited and more open' than most of the rest of us (e.g. Campaign for the Mentally Handicapped, 1974), this can be interpreted as meaning that they do not respond so readily with avoidance behaviour to approaches from us as we do to approaches from them. Many mentally handicapped people seem to have an ability to find the behaviour of other people rewarding in many situations where the rest of us lack that ability.

This way of putting things may seem like cheating, since the lack of inhibition of mentally handicapped people can be interpreted as a lack of ability to discriminate between stimuli that most appropriately and functionally cue avoidance behaviour and those that most usefully cue approach behaviour. This may be so, but remember we are considering relationships that involve handicapped people and in these situations if we respond in the usually appropriate way to such cues we may well remove any possibility of involvement in strong relationships for the handicapped.

This is exactly what we wish to avoid. It seems to me more fruitful to suggest that our responses to such cues are often so rigid and inflexible that we become unable to form relationships with handicapped people. Again, it is we that lack the social competence.

I am suggesting that the education of most of us is such that we indiscriminately interpret certain behaviours on the part of other people as cues for avoidance behaviour—such behaviours are indiscriminately non-reinforcing of our previous approach behaviours—whereas a fully educated man should be capable of much greater flexibility in finding the behaviour of other people rewarding or not, depending on the circumstances. Can we learn anything from mentally handicapped people in this respect? Can close contact with handicapped people teach us to be more tolerant and less inhibited in our relationships generally?

Let us look at some of the possible characteristics of behaviour that many of us are likely to find non-reinforcing. I will consider two characteristics of such behaviour: its predictability and its tolerability. The two are closely linked. One way to guarantee that the consequence of a piece of behaviour is non-reinforcing is to make it not only unpleasant but unpredictable. We can tolerate —i.e. not show avoidance behaviour towards—situations which we can predict. We come to be able to predict outcomes not only as a result of past experience, but as a result of information given on the spot. We tolerate the absence of a payout from a one-arm bandit because we can predict that a payment will eventually come, either from past experience or from watching someone else play or from reading the instructions on the machine.

We may be unable to predict the outcome of our initiating a relationship with a mentally handicapped person in two senses: we may find that his response to our initial behaviour is unexpected, and we may be unable to predict that a favourable response will eventually be forthcoming as a result of a certain chain or pattern of behaviours on our part. Moreover, because of the latter inability to predict an eventual pleasant outcome, the immediate short-term outcome may be intolerable.

I believe that the subjective experience of many people who find themselves in a position where a relationship with a handicapped person is initiated, is one of incompetence—inability to predict outcomes and inability to tolerate immediate responses.

What can be done about this? How can we increase people's ability to predict and tolerate the behaviour of the mentally handicapped? The ideal is for handicapped people to be fully accepted in society, for them to be able to go into situations without any risk that all the relationships that will be initiated will be weak. This will require at least a minor revolution in the general education of everyone, in so far as our education for relationships with handicapped people is so poor at present. It would seem to me to require an abandonment of social policies of segregation in schooling and in residential care. In my view the biggest argument in favour of integration of handicapped children in ordinary schools or provision of small, locally based, dispersed, mixed residential, work and educational services for handicapped people is not so much in terms of the immediate benefit to the handicapped themselves. Evidence is accumulating that very good education can be provided for mentally handicapped children in special schools and that very good residential care can be provided in village communities or in some hospital units. Segregated provision, however, denies non-handicapped people the experience of meeting handicapped people and learning with them, working with them and living with them. Hence the social incompetence of many non-handicapped people in forming relationships with the handicapped.

Even in the present situation, however, I believe we could do more. Most opportunities for non-handicapped people to form a relationship with a handicapped person arise in situations where another person is present who is familiar with that person—a parent or friend or a member of staff of a service agency. Often, it seems to me, the opportunity is lost because of the inability of such people to provide information that will enable the non-handicapped 'layman' to predict the outcome of his behaviour and to tolerate short-term outcomes. How typical, for example, is the following exchange?

Visitor to staff member: "How do you do?"
Staff member to visitor: "How do you do?"
Visitor to handicapped person: "Hello, what's your name?"
Staff member to visitor: "I'm afraid he can't talk." Embarrassed silence.
Visitor to staff member: "Well, I'll let you get on with your work, goodbye."
Staff member to visitor: "Goodbye."

Should we not be aiming for a position where each handicapped person has a behaviourally-orientated assessment to discover effective ways of initiating appropriate behaviour (i.e. behaviour that is rewarding to others) and effective ways of responding to that behaviour so as to reinforce it? This information should be known to all those in regular contact with the person and they should in turn inform newcomers. Something perhaps along these lines:

Visitor to staff member: "How do you do?"
Staff member to visitor: "How do you do? This is John and we are trying to teach him to look at other people when they approach him. Please sit down so

301

that you are on the same level and are facing him. Call his name until he looks up into your eyes. You may have to call him several times before he does this. When he does look at you, rub the back of his neck and make it clear to him that you are pleased, by smiling and telling him that you approve."

Visitor to handicapped person: "Hello, John, John, John, John. That's great. Well done. I'm glad to meet you."

Staff member to visitor: "That's very good. You've got him to respond to you."

Here is the making of a strong, appropriate triadic relationship between visitor, staff member and handicapped person. The chances of the dyadic relationship between handicapped person and visitor being maintained if they meet again is much greater than before. In the above encounter, the staff member is not only providing some initial external support for a relationship which, because of its general unpredictability for the visitor, is likely to be quite weak, but he is in the process teaching the visitor to be more socially competent in that situation.

I believe that it is helpful if we can teach parents and staff to teach us—ordinary members of society—in this way. This is difficult to do unless the parent or the staff member himself has a strong relationship with the handicapped person. Most teaching programmes, including behaviour modification programmes, concentrate on increasing the competence of the handicapped person through provision of structured appropriate relationships. This process, however, should be accompanied by attempts to enable other people with whom the handicapped person comes into contact to form and maintain a strong relationship with him.

Let me turn now to the question of tolerance. This seems to me to have a number of components. An event acts as a cue for avoidance behaviour (i.e. is intolerable) if avoidance is the one behaviour from a number of possible choices that will gain for the person the most reward. A long-term task is to adjust the reinforcement contingencies that exist in society so that avoidance behaviour towards the handicapped is not rewarded but is frowned on. It should be part of our general education that we learn not to reinforce each other for this. However, events are intolerable if they arouse in us feelings of anxiety or unpleasantness; these feelings arise because in our past experience we have found approach responses to have non-reinforcing consequences. These consequences seem to me to fall into two main categories: 'aesthetic' and time or energy consuming. The behaviour of mentally handicapped people often looks odd: this is sometimes compounded by the fact that the person may be dressed in a non-reinforcing way, may have an unpleasant smell, may be exhibiting the behaviour in aesthetically poor surroundings. Hence the importance of handicapped people smelling nice, looking nice and being encountered in pleasant ordinary surroundings. I believe for example that ordinary people are often quite tolerant of the behaviour of individual handicapped people: what turns people off is seeing large numbers of such people in one place at one time. Not only is such a sight aesthetically displeasing, but the chances of any sort of relationship with an individual in such peculiar circumstances are really minimized. Any environment in which there are more than one or two handicapped people is an environment that is not conducive to tolerance of individual oddities of behaviour by the ordinary person.

The consequences of approach responses to certain behaviours of handicapped people may be a commitment of time and energy which a person may have earned more rewards for if they were employed elsewhere. Relationships with people who are hungry and cannot feed themselves, or who have full bladders and are not toilet-trained, or who are unoccupied and cannot occupy themselves, will tend to involve a person in activities that are time-consuming and energy-consuming. Again, it seems to me that a major additional factor in making such situations intolerable for many people is their feeling of lack of competence. Any aids or assistance that can be provided for people at these times, and any increase in their own practical competence, will enhance the possibility of the relationship being maintained and being strong. To give an extreme and perhaps unlikely example in illustration, I am not quite so likely to get up and run when the person next to me on a bus is sick if I am well experienced in clearing up the mess and proper effective cleaning aids are available and I know where they are, have easy access to them and know how to use them. Actually, this situation is not so bizarre. I have visited units where mentally handicapped people are being cared for and have begun to form some small relationship with someone, when it has suddenly become clear that he has been incontinent. Such behaviour on his part puts an immediate end to the relationship, or at least severely interrupts it. Is it impossible that such an event could have been predicted and for me to have been given an idea of what to do without breaking the relationship? In that situation I am incompetent, not only through lack of skill but through lack of knowledge of where the bathroom is, where the cleaning materials are, where his clean clothes are, what to do with the dirty clothes, etc. Invariably I am not given the opportunity, even with help, to continue the relationship in this way. Yet perhaps I should be. Perhaps it is a vitally necessary part of my education which should accompany any attempts to toilet train my friend. My competence, as well as his, is the key to his social habilitation.

Of course not everyone is incompetent in relationships with handicapped people. Often the experts are other handicapped people. Furthermore, some not inconsiderable number of people find it fun, and inherently very rewarding, to work with or to teach or to live with mentally handicapped people. Can we apply functional analysis of the factors that produce this reward for some people, in order to extend it to many of the rest of us? Unfortunately, again, our social institutions, because of their history based on segregationalist philosophies (Wolfensberger 1969), militate against most of us coming into sufficient contact with mentally handicapped people. We cannot as individuals naturally explore the rewards of relationships with handicapped people because social policy prevents us doing so.

I would see perhaps in the future the setting up of units where handicapped people themselves, their families, staff who work or wish to work with the handicapped, and the general public (through further education programmes for adults or school-based educational programmes for children) attend the same unit for general social training in competence for situations where handicapped people are present.

Behavioural or functional analysis of what occurs in such gatherings should point to effective ways of teaching the required skills or eliminating undesired behaviour for all those who participate.

The components of a behavioural approach that I believe would be particularly useful are: the identification of effective reinforcers, the experimental study of the ways in which people control or modify each other's behaviour—in this case, the way in which handicapped people control the behaviour of non-handicapped people, and vice versa—, the setting of goals and the careful monitoring of progress towards them, and the careful breaking down of the teaching process into adequately small steps. In the sort of setting I envisage, behaviour modification would not be seen as a method of moulding the behaviour of individuals to conform to a desired model so much as a technique for strengthening mutual social relationships.

Mentally handicapped people of course form a very heterogeneous group. Is it meaningful to talk of social relationships with the most profoundly handicapped people who may show very little evidence of responsiveness? I believe that it is – indeed very much so. Firstly it seems to me that many parents with profoundly handicapped children, many teachers in Special Care Units and many nurses and other staff in hospitals, do form relationships with even the most severely handicapped people. For many of them the relationship is clearly strong, in that their behaviour towards the profoundly handicapped person is rewarded by that person's response, however small or insignificant, or even invisible, that response may seem to an observer. Similarly, there is often evidence on close observation that profoundly handicapped people do respond differently to different people; in many cases they quite clearly exhibit small but noticeable responses to particular pieces of behaviour by particular familiar people. To those involved in these relationships and to those who observe them it is meaningful to say that the relationship is a strong, mutually reinforcing one.

The strength of a person's contribution to a relationship can be measured in terms of the extent to which the other person's behaviour is maintained by his responses to that behaviour. Viewed in this way, however small the responses of very profoundly handicapped people may seem, the strength of those responses is often great. The potential for learning by the rest of us would seem to be at least as great here as in any situation.

Some people appear to achieve fulfilment and happiness in their lives through close relationships with profoundly handicapped people. While we should not expect anyone to restrict his relationships to those with a profoundly handicapped person, any more than we expect anyone to restrict his relationships to those with any one person, we can learn not only to share the caring tasks with those who do find such relationships easy, but to enjoy and benefit from the experience too. In this way, 'community caring' (in the sense described by Michael Bayley (1973)) may become a greater and more universal reality.

However, my own conviction that we could all do with social training for competence in social situations which include handicapped people arises from a number of conferences for mentally handicapped people, organized by Campaign for the Mentally Handicapped, in which I have been privileged to be involved. Reports of three of these conferences have been published (Campaign for the Mentally Handicapped 1972, 1973, 1974). The aim of the conferences has been to provide the opportunity for mentally handicapped people and non-handicapped people to participate in activities and discussions on a completely equal basis. The handicapped people have been relatively mildly handicapped and the non-handicapped people have mostly been staff of services who have had extensive experience of work with the mentally handicapped. Nevertheless the conferences have demonstrated both the difficulties and the rewards of encouraging greater and more equal participation between the two. Instances of socially inappropriate behaviour in such a setting (i.e. behaviour that was unlikely to be reinforcing of desired behaviour of others) were exhibited just as much by the non-handicapped people as by the handicapped. The mentally handicapped people were generally less 'inhibited'—i.e. they exhibited greater competence in raising important issues and going to the heart of the matter, rather than evading issues, and they tended to behave as if they found everything that was going on interesting and rewarding, rather than expressing boredom or displeasure. The reports, of course, represent unsystematic and subjective accounts of the proceedings; it can also be argued whether the differences in the behaviour of the handicapped and non-handicapped people reflected well or badly on either group. Nevertheless I am convinced that if the complexity of such social situations could be overcome and a behavioural or functional analysis made of what was happening, there would be an evident need for increasing the competence of the non-handicapped people to enable them to form better relationships with the handicapped. I include myself in that.

I see the concept of social education for all, to enable us to form stronger and more appropriate relationships with handicapped people, as applicable in relation to all degrees of handicap. I also advocate a behaviourist approach because I see behaviour modification as concerned with the analysis, not of the behaviour of individuals, but of relationships between people—i.e. how we control or modify each other's behaviour. If we set out to encourage and strengthen relationships that involve handicapped people we cannot for long, or with any chance of major lasting success, concern ourselves solely with the behaviour of the handicapped; we must turn our attention also to the behaviour of us all in situations where we meet with handicapped people.

The nature of the relationship that is the goal of behaviour modification programmes is that of a 'gift system' (Hamblin et al. 1971). The behaviour of each person can be regarded as a gift to the other, being pleasurable and reinforcing. In an appropriate relationship the gifts are common currency that can be used in other situations.

The widespread encouragement of gift relationships has been suggested by Ann Shearer (1974) as part of the answer to the problem of resources in services for mentally handicapped people, to which I now wish to turn.

Because of the widespread use of locomotion, as earlier defined, as a solution

305

to the perceived problem of the existence in society of people deemed to be incompetent, we have set up social institutions whose primary function is to guarantee the maintenance of relationships that are essential to the physical well-being of individuals. This is done by the employment of people who are put under contractual obligations to maintain these relationships. The relationships themselves may often be weak, but they are externally and powerfully supported. Increasingly however we have come to accept the importance of a whole host of other relationships not essential to life but essential to the social and psychological well-being of the individual. We have tried to ensure the maintenance of these relationships by extension of the locomotion system—i.e. by widening the job descriptions of employees of services and by externally supporting a much wider range of relationships than merely those essential to life.

The pressure to extend the scope of these relationships still further is always increasing. The demand is always increasing for more staff with better skills.

There do unfortunately appear to be limits to the number of people who find it an acceptable job to form relationships with handicapped people which they cannot make strong but which are externally supported through their terms of employment. There are also not the resources available, without a revolution in the determination of social priorities, to support the required system even if sufficient people were forthcoming.

At present much of the excitement about the potential of behaviour modification programmes seems to me to be due to two factors. The techniques offer a more effective method of carrying through as far as possible the social policy of accommodation, as defined earlier; we are more sure about how to increase the competence of handicapped people. Also, the introduction of behaviour modification programmes—and this is of course related to their effectiveness—is a way of gaining greater resources for a particular group of people in a particular unit. Part of the detailed planning required for the introduction of behaviour modification programmes involves the detailed working out of what resources are required; the consequences of a failure to provide these resources can be more clearly seen. Resources have been increased in recent years for two main reasons. One is as a result of negative reinforcement for so doing—scandals have been avoided. The other is positive reinforcement for so doing in terms of the observable and recordable improvement in behaviour and competence of individuals within special treatment programmes. The great potential breakthrough of behaviour modification, even in the limited sense of modifying the behaviour of handicapped people to conform more to a model, is that it enables society, through the agencies involved, to regard the services being provided as educational and treatment-orientated in nature, rather than being an enormous baby-minding service.

However, despite the increasingly acknowledged value of programmes of training and a marked move in the orientation of services away from locomotion towards accommodation as a solution to the 'problem' of mental handicap, one can still visit units where twenty, thirty or forty people are living in an environment where the possibilities of relationships with non-handicapped people are virtually non-existent, with the presence at any one time of only one or two staff and a spasmodic trickle of visitors and volunteers.

There is an enormous 'credibility gap' here which, unless we can find a solution to the problem of resources, may in the long run discredit behaviour modification programmes. The history of services for the mentally handicapped shows a pattern of periods of optimism followed by pessimism as a result of lack of forthcoming resources.

In order to be motivated to provide extra resources, those in a position to do so need to be able to predict the effect that extra resources will have. The monitoring and evaluative approach that is so much a part of behaviour modification offers the possibility of this. Yet there is still doubt as to whether the results will be sufficiently impressive to reinforce the provision of sufficient extra resources on a continuing basis. Moreover, unless society as a whole cares about what happens to mentally handicapped people, the power of negative reinforcement for greater resource provision will be limited. Several major scandals in recent years have still not resulted in resource provision even to meet the limited goals of the White Paper *Better Services for the Mentally Handicapped* (Department of Health and Social Security 1971).

Ann Shearer's solution is for us to begin to see mentally handicapped people as givers rather than always as receivers; i.e. to offer them the opportunity to enter into gift relationships. The importance of this idea can also be seen in Michael Bayley's analysis of services for families with handicapped members (Bayley 1973). He points out that effective community help given to families by their relatives, neighbours and friends is often reciprocal help, i.e. it enables the families to give in return, which is something that official services fail to do. Effective help offers families the opportunity to enter a gift relationship.

"Everyone has a contribution to make to the daily fabric of life in any residential establishment. Our first task should be to encourage and support that contribution at whatever level it may be offered. To find ways of accepting what the receivers of care have to offer is one of our most urgent tasks. The person receiving care must be helped and encouraged to make his contribution to the pattern of life which he and his staff are sharing" (Shearer 1974).

Ann Shearer describes how this philosophy works at L'Arche, a community for mentally handicapped people in France.

This community is staffed almost entirely by untrained people and professional help is sought as necessary from outside. "Staff are seen not in terms of job functions but first of all as people with something to contribute. Their right to give in other than contractual terms is not only recognized but is essential to the whole place. Each week people who want to work at L'Arche are being turned away for fear of swamping the handicapped people with helpers."

I am not particularly enamoured of village communities, because I am optimistic that the ordinary community can, and often already does, care. Yet because our social institutions have resulted from pessimistic philosophies of segregation, segregated services are still in great demand. Social education of all of us seems to me the only effective long-term answer. Can we as behaviourists take the first faltering steps in this direction? Can our work with individual mentally handicapped people lead us on to attempts to transform cultural patterns and educational priorities? Can we have the faith in the wider applicability of the methods we have discovered to work towards the genuine acceptance by society of all its members, no matter how severely handicapped?

Let us not be too romantic or impractical, but neither let us be too parochial or limited in our vision. The continuing presence of 60,000 people in segregated residential units, the continuation of a system of special education that enables a non-handicapped child to complete 12 years of schooling without meeting a handicapped child, the enormous difficulties of families with handicapped members—all these seem to me to require solutions at societal level: solutions that are a challenge to all of us and must involve us all.

REFERENCES

ALLEN, K.E. and HARRIS, F.R. (1966) Elimination of a child's excessive scratching by training the mother in reinforcement procedures. *Behav. Res. Therap.* 4, 79–84

BAYLEY, M. (1973) *Mental Handicap and Community Care: a Study of Mentally Handicapped People in Sheffield.* Routledge and Kegal Paul, London

CAMPAIGN FOR THE MENTALLY HANDICAPPED (1972) *Our Life.* CMH, London

CAMPAIGN FOR THE MENTALLY HANDICAPPED (1973) *Listen.* CMH, London

CAMPAIGN FOR THE MENTALLY HANDICAPPED (1974) *A Workshop on Participation.* CMH, London

DEPARTMENT OF HEALTH AND SOCIAL SECURITY (1971) *Better Services for the Mentally Handicapped. Cmnd. 4683.* HMSO, London

HAMBLIN, R.L., BUCKHOLDT, D., FERRITOR, D., KOZLOFF, M. and BLACKWELL, L. (1971) *The Humanization Processes: a Social, Behavioral Analysis of Children's Problems.* Wiley, New York

MILLER, E.J. and GWYNNE, G.V. (1972) *A Life Apart: a Study of Residential Institutions for the Physically Handicapped and Young Chronically Sick.* Tavistock, London

SCOTT, A.W. (1966) Flexibility, rigidity and adaptation: toward clarification of concepts. In *Experience, Structure and Adaptability* (Harvey, O.J., ed.). Springer, New York

SHEARER, A. (1974) Making the most of scarce resources: sharing-consumer participation. *Residential Social Work 14*, 354–357

WHATMORE, R., DURWARD, L. and KUSHLICK, A. (1973) The use of a behaviour modification model in attempting to derive a measure of the quality of residential care. Some methodological problems. Health Care Evaluation Research Team, Winchester. Unpublished

WILLIAMS, P. (1973) Social skills. In *Assessment for Learning in the Mentally Handicapped* (Mittler, P., ed.), pp. 163–191. Churchill Livingstone, Edinburgh

WOLFENSBERGER, W. (1969) The origin and nature of our institutional models. In *Changing Patterns in Residential Services for the Mentally Retarded* (Kugel, R.B. and Wolfensberger, W., eds.), pp. 59–171b. President's Committee on Mental Retardation, Washington, DC

Discussion

Thorpe: Paul seems to be suggesting changing the behaviour of the whole of Society. Isn't that rather a tall order? Isn't it more practical to think in terms of changing the behaviour of the mentally handicapped in the direction of the norm in Society? Does your suggestion imply a recommendation for complete integration of the handicapped into Society? I sometimes wonder if that isn't a very cruel policy in view of what we know about how much children who deviate even slightly from the average suffer at the hands of their peers.

P. Williams: I agree that the concept of integration has to be looked at critically and attempts at integration must be carefully evaluated, but I think that pilot experiments such as the school project in Bromley and the residential centre project with non-handicapped children at several Dr Barnardo's homes in Lancashire, even though they are as yet far from fully evaluated, are already showing that the problems are not as great as were expected, especially in terms of the handicapped child being bullied or left out of things.

Thorpe: I'm afraid I suspect that these projects tend to show us what we want to see, and that they bear little relation to what integration would actually mean in the real world.

Mittler: Perhaps we ought not to debate the merits of integration and segregation at this point. Paul's paper assumes that there will be a greater degree of integration in the future. On that assumption, he's asking "Can we make a start by training members of the staff (who are after all paid to work with the mentally handicapped) to be more socially skilful?" One aspect that I'd like to hear your comments on concerns underexpectation. I have seen a teacher behaving in what I interpreted as a highly segregating way even though on paper the two SSN children in her class were totally integrated with it. The teacher asked a question of the group and then shut everybody else up, saying "I know *you* all know the answer, but you see Johnny and Billy don't." Would you like to comment?

P. Williams: I'd like to look at it slightly differently. I would like to see that class regarded as an opportunity for the non-handicapped children to learn what is appropriate behaviour in the presence of mentally handicapped children. They should be encouraged to think that they may learn something by shutting up occasionally and listening to the handicapped child who may have something unusually valuable to say. That the opportunity for this kind of learning is virtually non-existent is a matter of grave concern to me.

Jordan: Peter Mittler is saying that non-handicapped children are not going to be encouraged in those attitudes unless you educate the adults in the situation first.

Hogg: Teachers are always having to restrain the responses of children who find a particular task easy until the slower ones catch on. I don't find her behaviour particularly discriminating or traumatic.

Kiernan: Although I subscribe to the thesis that the mentally handicapped should be treated as human beings with rights and wishes to be respected, the main problem with Paul's argument is that normal adults are conditioned by a lifetime of reacting to the range of people they normally encounter. It is therefore not going to be effective to appeal to people to love and be natural with the mentally handicapped: being natural would involve rejecting their unusual behaviour. We are all aware of the dichotomy often encountered between stated positive attitudes on the part of caring staff and their actual behaviour. It seems to me that you have to train the non-handicapped to behave in new ways rather than to be 'natural'.

P. Williams: I have argued in my paper that our aim should be to encourage relationships that are not only appropriate but are also strong. It seems to me that if we can offer maximum opportunity to form relationships with mentally handicapped people to those who know or believe that they have something to offer the handicapped and that the handicapped have something to offer them, we have a powerful basis for the establishment of strong, mutually reinforcing relationships. We can then help people to be more perceptive within these relationships. We can point out, after analysis of what is happening, that some behaviours are not appropriate or of general social value. We can help people to teach the mentally handicapped while retaining relationships which are mutually reinforcing. It would be interesting to see whether it is easier or harder to introduce a more behavioural approach in a place like L'Arche than, for example, in a hospital ward. I have suggested that, unfortunately, the social policy which has led to the present structure of services for the mentally handicapped tends to deny ordinary people the opportunity to form relationships with the handicapped, and cuts out large numbers of people who may well find such relationships easy and mutually beneficial. The impression is sometimes given that only a small group of highly trained professional people are capable of handling and forming relationships with the handicapped. This is untrue. One can look at families and siblings of mentally handicapped people or at volunteers within the services or at new or untrained staff of services and find ordinary people who have, without training, formed relationships with mentally handicapped people. Such relationships are very often not only strong but perfectly appropriate. Of course, where relationships are inappropriate, intervention may be necessary. I believe we should take care to do this in such a way that the strength of the relationship is not reduced, i.e. that the relationship remains a mutually reinforcing one. Thus, while it is true that it is not enough *simply* to require people to be natural, be themselves, love others, etc., we should certainly not imply that they are required to be unnatural or to be other than themselves or to suppress their love for others. This impression will lead to the behavioural approach being seen as cold and inhumane—a quite unnecessary and, one hopes, invalid perception of the nature of the approach. We should try to get people to change their behaviour without trying to change their positive motivations for involvement. This, it seems to me, is what good training is all about.

By all means let us define what is 'natural' and 'loving' in behavioural terms, but let us also have as our aim in doing so that people should remain 'natural' and 'loving' while adopting a behavioural approach.

Cunningham: We have to distinguish between having a positive attitude towards mentally handicapped people and having the technique to form appropriate and mutually satisfying relationships with them. Since we are not as sure of our ability to change attitudes as some people would like to make out, we should surely start with the people who have positive attitudes and work out behaviour modification techniques to reinforce their skills in making relationships.

Jordan: However, you may find that the positive attitude is contingent on the handicapped person's dependent status. If you train out the normal person's overprotectiveness his positive attitude may go out of the window with it.

Cunningham: It is true that we have seen this with parents of handicapped children as they acquire a measure of independence.

Yule: I disagree with Cliff Cunningham when he says that the attitude has to be right before you can affect behaviour. This has surely been the main therapeutic mythology for the past 50 years, with not a shred of evidence to support it as far as I can see. Are we not constantly showing that behaviour can be changed without attacking the attitudes first, and that attitudes change thereafter? I believe behaviour modification is now coming of age in becoming able to take into account the *reciprocity* of relationships, and handle much more complicated interpersonal reactions in which one person's response is the other's stimulus. What we need as a start is a behavioural analysis of the approach behaviour of the non-handicapped person to the handicapped one.

Harzem: Sheila Damon and I have recently completed a study (Harzem and Damon

1975) which bears on the point. We observed the interactions of retarded individuals and staff in the day room of a small hospital for the retarded at various times of the day over several weeks. We were able to classify patients quite easily into high, intermediate and low interactors. The high interactors emitted aversive behaviour which ceased when they got attention from staff members, whereas low interactors emitted aversive behaviour patterns when staff members approached. One feature of behaviour modification is that it often requires people to refrain from doing what comes naturally, and this is a case in point. If staff keep avoiding the low interactors because they emit aversive behaviour when they approach them, which is the natural thing to do, those patients will remain low interactors for the rest of their lives. Behaviour modification is in some ways a prescription for doing the unnatural thing, especially on the part of trained staff.

Hogg: Paul's paper does something which Zigler (1973) has criticized quite heavily, which is to attribute a common personality to 'the mentally handicapped' as if they were a homogeneous group. The paper almost suggests that mentally handicapped people all react alike in approach–avoidance terms. Peter Harzem's study, just referred to, clearly shows that they don't. Our own observations of classroom behaviour and analysis of teacher questionnaires also provide evidence of considerable diversity.

For this reason, to take Bill Yule's point, we are not going to be able to produce a general prescription to improve approach behaviour, only individual programmes to train certain non-handicapped and handicapped people to relate to one another.

Kiernan: What is critical, to my mind, is the implicit or explicit goal set by the non-handicapped person for the mentally handicapped one, in other words the content of the curriculum being taught. I think that to neglect discussion of curriculum content —what do you want for the mentally handicapped—and to stay at the level of generalities like 'We must have a positive approach' or 'We must have normalization' is dangerous. Only when you go into details of programme content do you find out that one person's positive approach is another's institutional straitjacket.

Mittler: Paul has done us a great service by indicating the difficulties of reconciling his humanitarian position with what we know about the behavioural approach. He is of course unique amongst us in being in a position to affect staff training and attitudes. We have nowadays far superior techniques to the T-groups, sensitivity training and holding of each others' hands which were until recently the main means of developing a greater awareness of one another as human beings. There are, for example, video recordings and simulated situations between staff and residents, discussion of either of which can be powerful developers of social skills. So Paul is not producing this paper in a vacuum; he's thinking of it in relation to the task in which he is engaged. And in doing so he forces us to face our own inadequacies not as behaviour modifiers, psychologists or teachers but as human beings.

REFERENCES

HARZEM, P. and DAMON, S.G. (1975) Social interactions of a group of severely retarded people with staff and peers in a hospital setting. *Psychol. Rep.* (in press)

ZIGLER, E. (1973) The retarded child as a whole person. In *The Experimental Psychology of Mental Retardation* (D.K. Routh, ed.), pp. 231–322. Aldine, Chicago/Crosby Lockwood Staples, St. Albans, Herts. (1974)

The Myth of the Hero-Innovator and Alternative Strategies for Organizational Change

NICHOLAS J. GEORGIADES and LYNDA PHILLIMORE

Department of Occupational Psychology, Birkbeck College, University of London

ABSTRACT

The paper cites evidence from educational and industrial training situations which demonstrate the unreliability of traditional forms of training as a means of generating innovation and change in work-organizations. Some strategy guidelines are suggested to assist managers of change in the preparation of organizational climates which would facilitate and perpetuate innovation and the effects of change.

This paper deals not with the form and content of training syllabi for personnel about to embark upon behaviour modification programmes in hospitals and community settings, but with different strategies for the implementation of innovation and change in these institutions. The first part of the paper addresses the question of whether training is the complete answer to inducing innovation and change into various settings; the second suggests some alternative strategies to accomplish the same objectives.

It would have been convenient if we could have presented a theoretical package on this topic which would have answered most if not all practical questions. However, it has been suggested that most of the theories in the field of organizational change are attempts to explain the unknowable in terms of the not worth knowing. As in most of the applied behavioural sciences, research and theory on planned organizational change *follow* practice. This may reflect either the difficulties of doing the necessary research, or the impotence of research in creating practical theory and contributing to improved practice (cf. Friedlander and Brown 1974). Whatever the reason, we find ourselves devoid of a presentable theory, and thus will turn to the question of whether the traditional forms of training are adequate to achieving the objective of change.

Particular reference will be made to evidence on educational innovation drawn from educational research. Although it is true that the rate of change inside educational institutions has increased (for instance, in 1930 it was estimated that 15 years need to elapse before something like 3% of schools adopted a particular change, while in 1960 it was estimated that 7 years need elapse before 11% of schools adopted an innovation), it remains a fact that innovation and change in schools is slow (cf. Miles 1964). Schools are still everywhere in need of change and improvement. We believe this is due primarily to continued emphasis upon training as the predominant change strategy: training not only for newcomers to the profession but also for those who are already in schools with some experience. The assumptions behind training as a strategy for inducing organizational change are based upon the psychological fallacy that since work-organizations are made up of individuals, we can change the organization by changing its individual members. There is a plethora of evidence to refute this proposition; not only the generalized psychological research relating to the nature of resistance to change at the workplace (cf. Watson 1969), but also specific research into the evaluation of training programmes.

Morrison and McIntyre (1969), summing up the effectiveness of teacher training, said: "Almost every relevant investigation, whatever the instrument used, has found that the changes in expressed attitudes during training are followed by changes in the opposite direction during the first year of teaching." Morrison and McIntyre (1967) had previously found that for 3-year-trained students, this reversal of attitudes far from cancelled out all the changes that occurred during the training period, but for 1-year-trained graduates the overall effect was of a return to original attitudes by the end of two years on the job. They conclude: "Changes in the direction of increased naturalism, radicalism and tender-mindedness among teachers in training are to some extent reversed as a result of full-time teaching and this reversal is taking place within a relatively brief period after leaving the training college."

Turning to industry we find that Fleishman (1953) reported a similar study in the International Harvester Organisation. He showed that despite first-class training of supervisory personnel the greatest influence upon how the supervisor actually behaved back home in the plant was the leadership of his immediate supervisor. Fleishman says "an implication of these results seems to be that if the old way of doing things in the plant situation is still the shortest path to approval by the boss, then this is what the foreman really learns. Existing behaviour patterns are part of and are moulded by the culture of the work situation. In order to effectively produce changes in the foreman's behaviour some changes in his back home-in-the-plant environment would also seem to be necessary. The training course alone cannot do it."

The same point was summarized even more effectively by Katz and Kahn (1966). They say: "The essential weakness of the individual approach to organizational change is the psychological fallacy of concentrating upon individuals without regard to the role relationships that constitute the social system of which they are part. The assumption is being made that since the organization is made up of individuals we can change the organization by changing those individuals. This is not so much an illogical proposition as it is an oversimplification which neglects the interrelationships of people in an organizational structure and fails to point to aspects of individual behaviour which need to be changed."

This then is the myth of the hero-innovator: the idea that you can produce, by training, a knight in shining armour who, loins girded with new technology and beliefs, will assault his organizational fortress and institute changes both in himself and others at a stroke. Such a view is ingenuous. The fact of the matter is that organizations such as schools and hospitals will, like dragons, eat hero-innovators for breakfast.

What guidance can occupational psychology offer to ensure that such organizations receive newly trained hero-innovators without gobbling them up? We offer two general points and six specific guidelines which may be of some assistance.

THE GENERAL POINTS

1. To initiate a planned programme of change inside hospitals or community settings, the initiator must consider very carefully the question "Who is my client?" It will become increasingly necessary for managers of planned change to cease regarding the individual patient as the client and move to a more systems-orientated view of the entire organization in which the patient is to be treated as the client. The objective increasingly will be to move away from the one-to-one treatment relationship into the role of *organizational change agent* or manager of change. This may well mean leaving the treatment role to the newly trained experts, whether they be psychologists, nurses or teachers. The manager of change must concentrate her or his attention upon preparing the culture in which these experts are to work.

2. Secondly, and this follows from the first general point, it may be necessary to radically reappraise the time scale upon which you work. Organizational change that is to be permanent is a lengthy business, and results cannot be achieved hastily. Currently it is estimated that 3–5 years are needed for a fundamental organizational change in commercial or industrial organizations. There is no reason to believe that hospitals or schools would be any more amenable to change.

The implications of these two general points are clear. Although it is possible to initiate a special (usually called experimental) ward or teaching environment very rapidly by cutting through the bureaucratic red tape, by concentrating one's attention upon the technical competence of the personnel and the all too often glaring needs of patients, the prognosis for such units is poor. Lack of attention by the manager of the change to the needs of others in the total system, and an understandable desire for haste in order to alleviate patient conditions, may produce a situation in which the support for the experimental situation (both financial and emotional) is at best half-hearted and at worst grudging. It also follows that the manager should not necessarily regard step one of the process as the training of key personnel: what might be called the cultivation of the host culture is the primary step. Training can of course proceed concurrently. Preparing the way for trained personnel may take as long as 12 months, but to plant them in an unprepared and hostile environment may do their cause more harm than good.

THE SIX GUIDELINES

These six guidelines are intended more as a checklist or reminder rather than a comprehensive treatise. Our concern is only with the strategy of change and not the goals which the strategies might achieve. We have been strongly influenced in the preparation of these points by an unpublished paper by R. Harrison (1971) and Margulies and Wallace (1973). There are at least two major strategic goals with which these guidelines might help.

The first is to gain influence based upon the expertise and ability which you undoubtedly have rather than try to exert influence through channels of authority and power which you may or may not have, and by doing so deploy your limited economic and human resources in order to maximize your impact. The second strategic goal is to maintain your team as a team, particularly when members come up against strong effects of pressure or stress. It will be necessary for them to retain high morale as an intact group even when troubles set in.

Guideline 1

The manager of the change effort should work with the forces within the organization which are supportive of change and improvement rather than working against those which are defensive and resistant to change. It is far better to find someone who wants to help and wants you to work with her or him than it is to try and convince sceptics that they need your assistance. Wherever possible, follow the parth of least organizational resistance to achieve your goals rather than confronting the resistance.

This guideline requires you to be sensitive to the psychological needs of those in the organization with whom you interact, particularly to individual and group needs which promote resistance to change. The key skill in this process is the ability to listen. The guideline also implies no large-scale, across-the-board, activity: no mass training, no mass public-relations exercises. As manager of change you will probably have limited resources available to you and these are weakened and absorbed by the organization if you attempt such full frontal attacks. The results are invariably disappointing.

Guideline 2

Try to develop what has been called a 'critical mass' in each change project. The manager of change should aim to produce a self-sustaining team of workers which is self-motivated and powered from within. The action implications of this guideline are again two-fold. First, always work on the principle of building teams (or Groups in the social psychology sense): never allow individuals to be isolated. Try and build a team of workers in a particular ward or school situation who are all committed to the same ideology and have the same level of technical skill. Never place an individual in a confronting or possibly hostile and threatening situation without the support of colleagues. Secondly, try and locate key people in the organization through whom the team will be able to

316

work. It may be necessary to spend some time on locating these key people and developing their interests systematically. This internal support system will help you to maintain the progress of your entire project, particularly in times of crisis.

Guideline 3

Wherever possible, the manager of change should work with the organization-ally 'healthy' parts of the system which have the will and the resources to improve (for a more complete definition of organizational health see Georgiades 1972). The team should avoid being seduced or pressured into working with or for parts of the system which might be regarded as lost causes—individuals or groups in the organization which have lost the ability to cope with the situation as it is. For instance, try not to accept people to be trained as key personnel simply because the system cannot find anything else to do with 'her' or 'him' or because the individual sees your programme as a way of escaping from previous conflicts or stress. Further, try not to accept wards or classes where previous innovations have failed or where absenteeism or staff turnover is the highest. Usually, change requires *additional* energy and talent during the period of transition. Performance in change situations (however measured) worsens, even after the most beneficial changes, until everybody learns how to make the change work up to its potential. Persons or groups whose performance is sub-standard or barely adequate usually cannot afford and are not allowed the additional resources and the period of further decreased performance which is usually required to change successfully. These people are unusually defensive in their reactions to outsiders who offer help.

Guideline 4

The manager of the change team should try to work with individuals and groups who have as much freedom and discretion in managing their own operations and resources as possible. It profits little to work out an agreed change with someone who turns out not to have the authority to carry it out.

Guideline 5

This guideline is clearly linked to Guideline 4, and it concerns the level of commitment and involvement of the top management team in the change pro-gramme. The manager should try to obtain appropriate and realistic levels of involvement by key personnel in the hospital or school system. This does not mean that the highest levels of management need necessarily be totally involved in the programme. Individuals at the top level in bureaucratic organizations are often too personally identified with the status quo for this to be possible. Often the best supporters of innovation and change are among the ranks of people just below the top, where the personal commitment to the present is less and where the drive for achievement may be higher than at the very top. At the very minimum, however, the manager should have received *permission* for the change to occur by those in a top management position. Frequently the unspoken qualifier in this situation is "It's OK as long as we don't have to do anything differently." Of course, if it is possible to enlist top management's support and encouragement so much the better, but this is frequently a much more difficult proposition.

Guideline 6

The last guideline concerns the role of the manager of the change in protecting the members of the team from undue pressure and stress. Arrangements should be made for most of the team to work in small groups or pairs for mutual learning and support. People should not be expected to work alone in highly stressful situations until they are quite experienced. Attempts should be made to prevent premature evaluation of the team's activities. The senior manager should attempt to absorb a large proportion of the pressure from above and outside himself. He should make a special effort to build strong personal support relationships amongst the unit members. Frequent group meetings should be held in order to allow the team to discuss their own anxieties and doubts about the kind of work that they are doing. Presentations and demonstrations of new techniques and processes by outsiders as well as attendance at professional meetings and courses should be built into the timetable of the team. Finally, the manager of the team will also have to assume the responsibility of not only being supportive to individual members but also of developing the kinds of relationships which will facilitate the graceful egress of those who feel that they are not making the right kind of progress or that are finding the going just too rough.

In this paper we have attempted to show that traditional forms of training, directed at producing innovation and change in hospital or community settings, tend to be inadequate. Evidence was cited from studies of education and industrial training which indicates the need to place greater emphasis upon 'back-home' situation of the newly trained innovator. To assist managers of change to create a more appropriate organizational climate, which will facilitate and perpetuate innovation, we have suggested six guidelines. These are based broadly upon the need to obtain influence and credibility within the organization and the needs of the innovating group to maintain high cohesion in the face of contrary organization pressure.

The predominant emphasis has been upon the re-examination of the role of the psychologist as team leader in change projects together with a more realistic appraisal of the time scales of organizational change.

We hope that the paper represents an attempt to bridge the artificial gap which appears to exist between the work of the clinical, educational and occupational psychologists.

REFERENCES

FLEISHMAN, E.A. (1953) Leadership climate, human relations training and supervisory behaviour. *Personnel Psychol.* 6, 205–222

FRIEDLANDER, F. and BROWN, L.D. (1974) Organization development. *Ann. Rev. Psychol.* 25, 313–341

GEORGIADES, N.J. (1972) The new organisation men. In *Social Problems of Modern Britain* (Butterworth, E. and Weir, D., eds.). Fontana Collins, London

HARRISON, R. (1971) Strategy guidelines for an internal organisation development unit. Unpublished.

KATZ, D. and KAHN, R.L. (1966) *The Social Psychology of Organizations.* Wiley, New York

MARGULIES, N. and WALLACE, J. (1973) *Organizational Change – Techniques and Applications.* Scott-Foresman, Illinois

MILES, M.B. (ed.) (1964) *Innovation in Education.* Teachers College, New York

MORRISON, A. and McINTYRE, D. (1967) Changes in opinion about education during the first year of teaching. *Br. J. Soc. Clin. Psychol.* 6, 161–163

MORRISON, A. and McINTYRE, D. (1969) *Teachers and Teaching.* Penguin Books, Harmondsworth, Middx.

WATSON, G. (1969) Resistance to change. In *The Planning of Change* (Bennis, W.G., Benne, K.D. and Chin, R., eds.), 2nd ed. Holt, Rinehart and Winston, New York

Final Discussion

DEVELOPMENT OF REINFORCERS

Barton: How does one set about devising a reinforcer for someone who seems not to care about food, drink, cigarettes, warmth, cold or pain?

Kushlick: Couldn't you work from a list of things that other patients have found reinforcing?

Barton: That seems extremely time-consuming: the list could be almost infinitely long.

Kiernan: We tend to go along with the nursery school teachers who maintain that presenting a stimulus is not enough: one has to get the child to experience it. This you do by introducing the experience—cuddling, say, which most people find reinforcing—by slow degrees when, and only when, the child is in a pleasant frame of mind. Thus you may sit with the child quite passively for a long time and then hold your hand at a little distance from his until eventually he moves his hand to make contact. After that moving moment you can increase the intensity of contact by further slow degrees.

Hogg: It is often not a question of finding a reinforcer but identifying a whole range of setting conditions, and I think we often extinguish available behaviours by removing the child from a natural setting to a comparatively barren experimental cubicle. We should try to analyse the setting more thoroughly first.

Barton: I agree that the setting can be important, but the patients I am thinking of seem to be responding to internal reinforcement and rejecting all external reinforcement.

Corbett: Can't you observe some self-stimulating behaviour which you can then use as a reinforcer, using the Premack principle?

Kushlick: What about a complete description of the child's behaviour from the time he gets up?

Barton: Well, one little girl I am thinking of, once she is unstrapped from the bed, bites and kicks the staff as they wash her, spits out the food they try to feed her, and only seems happy when she is left alone in her playpen where she fastens her own legs and arms under the bars and goes off into her own little world.

Corbett: Chris Kiernan made reference to a child who seeks restraint and finds it reinforcing. We have come across this problem many times, but there is surprisingly little published about it.

Barton: The child described certainly likes restraint, but not so much that it can be used as a reinforcer.

Kiernan: Some of the profoundly retarded children at Queen Mary's, Carshalton were so unaware of any kind of structure in their environment that we had to magazine-train them as you would a rat—with flashing lights *immediately* contingent on an event—before they could begin to perceive any kind of structure in their environment. Until you have this awareness of structure, reinforcement has no meaning.

Kushlick: I am still convinced that if somebody watches the child for a whole day and makes an extremely detailed record of what she is looking at and touching, and what positions she assumes, you will end up with a list of her favourite activities.

Jordan: If it's going to be that idiosyncratic, how is the work going to be useful to anyone else, or for the next handicapped child?

Yule: Yes, can we afford the man-hours to do it, particularly once the simpler cases get solved and we tackle the more difficult and less generalizable ones?

Kushlick: You don't need skilled personnel to carry out the detailed observation.

Kiernan: Perhaps we are talking about two kinds of problem: (*a*) with the profoundly handicapped child and (*b*) with the child who has been locked away and rejected and has learned maladaptive responses to human contact. Social reinforcers are not going to be much use in the latter case, so you switch to material reinforcers, and if you can't find one that they are interested in, you're in trouble.

Kushlick: We are beginning to look at people who apparently respond to nothing, and we are finding some sort of pattern in their lives. One patient with a history of violent behaviour and likely to be transferred to a State Security Hospital spends much of his time walking about alone, no trouble to anyone, but without a single verbal reinforcer, praise or a smile ever coming his way. His only behaviour which brings about any interaction with another human being seems to be self-induced vomiting. This occurs about 3% of his waking day. When it happens, staff members ask him to clean it up: he doesn't, and they do it for him. I think his problem behaviours are maintained by this interaction.

Yule: Yes, and don't the problems of Elizabeth Barton's child arise from another sort of interaction? It is astounding that in 1974 a child should have to be strapped into bed: would that be necessary if she were not still housed in a hospital with 60 beds to a ward?

Corbett: The answer is yes. We at Hilda Lewis House have had to restrain children on occasion, and we don't have crowded wards.

Barton: The ones we have to tie down are usually those who have been admitted to hospital from home.

Corbett: Quite so: they are in hospital because their behaviour is intolerable.

322

It's not that their behaviour is intolerable because they are (and have been for a long time) in hospital.

Yule: Isn't this search for reinforcers something that behaviour modification was engrossed with 10 years ago, and haven't we got beyond that?

Corbett: I would urge very strongly that this is not an out-of-date problem. The patients in care who do not respond reduce the level of care which their fellow-patients receive. Even though the number of such difficult cases is dwindling, it is worth spending the time on them, just as it is worth spending time studying heart transplantation even though this can never benefit more than a few people.

Kiernan: And if solutions to this research problem could be found in a specialized unit such as Hilda Lewis House it would be widely helpful to those who apply behaviour modification in less unusual environments, for whom the problem of choice of reinforcer comes up time and again. We know that from our training courses.

Berger: Are we over-emphasizing external reinforcers and neglecting the use of internal ones?

Walker: I have a suggestion based on laboratory experience. Though you won't find this in the textbooks, some rats refuse to eat a rat food pellet unless it is presented regularly, in a comfortable situation, until they are used to it. Only after that can you use it as a reinforcer. Perhaps you should present potential reinforcers regularly and non-contingently for a long time before you give them up as useless. Secondly, why isn't more done with automated reinforcers to save man-hours? With a child who is at least aware of his surroundings, one could rig up a machine to vibrate every 10 minutes (or at other frequencies) until the child got used to it, missed it if it were turned off, and would then find it rewarding and reinforcing. This would be especially useful for the patient who finds all human contact aversive.

C. Williams: We have used a vibrator with deaf–blind children, thereby providing the sensory input that much of their waking life is devoted to seeking through self-stimulation. The children quickly learned to press a panel to produce vibration, and it competed out self-stimulatory activity. On Mike Berger's point, we have tried to involve ourselves with whatever a non-responsive child was doing—even if it was stereotyped behaviour—on the theory that the behaviour was intrinsically reinforced and that by becoming associated with the primary reinforcer we might become reinforcing too. In one case it seemed to work.

BEHAVIOUR MODIFICATION IN THE HOSPITAL SERVICE

Corbett: I would like to put in a plea for more university-affiliated facilities in this country. We at Hilda Lewis House are very conscious of the university resources we can call on and the great difficulties people working in hospitals divorced from university departments undergo without such resources. Yet we and the Hester Adrian Research Centre seem to be the only university-affiliated units in the country with facilities for clinical research on this topic.

323

Hogg: I'm not sure to what extent we draw on the resources of the university. We provide a link, if you like, in that we all work in school or hospital service settings and combine academic work with providing a service.

Mittler: One great advantage of this approach is that researchers can be seen rolling up their sleeves and doing a useful job, perhaps with the aid of a high-powered piece of technology unavailable to the regular staff, but on the spot where regular staff members can discuss with them simpler ways of achieving the same ends. Thus the demonstration project takes shape right within the service setting.

Kiernan: The success of a demonstration project depends on the researcher having control of—or if you want to wrap it up more pleasantly, taking responsibility for—the situation and any decisions that need to be made.

Mittler: Another way to ensure success is to arrange conditions not so as to approximate to the ideal but to reflect in as many ways as possible the imperfections of the service as it exists at present. Hundreds of people went to look at the Slough project, but few local authorities copied it—not because they thought it was a bad model, but because the level was too high. People said "Well, given those resources and those staffing ratios, we could produce as good results or better!" Perhaps the answer is to start with the ideal and then fade out the unattainable elements before asking people to come and look at it.

Hogg: I shall worry about that when people in research come along and say I have done something which is worth passing on! One difficulty we labour under is that as research workers we are supposed to assess alternatives with an open mind, but at the same time we are supposed to deliver the goods in a short time, and this tends to influence you to present your favourite solution in the best possible light.

Kushlick: The work surely has to go in two stages: development, in which you may well need extra resources, and field testing, in which a scheme known to be within the present system's capabilities is devised and offered for trial.

Yule: Let me commend the Achievement Place model here (see p. 259). Those people took 6 years in the development stage; only then did they feel competent enough to start replicating. There are now about 30 Achievement Place homes, all under tight contractual control to be evaluated at first every 3 months and later every year.

Kiernan: Systematic replication is crucial.

Kushlick: And so is a clear statement of predicted outcome in your 'Consequences' column, so that everyone knows what they are working towards.

Cunningham: Well, it all sounds very nice, but the technology for evaluating programme packages has been around for some years now, and I don't see many first-class well-evaluated programmes on the market.

Kushlick: That may mean that good evaluation has shown the thing evaluated to be no good, so it never sees the light of day. For example, it may be too complicated or too aversive for staff to use.

Cunningham: But there are degrees of unsatisfactoriness, and one is still left with value judgments over whether to put out a programme which reaches 70% of criterion or spend twice the time bringing it up to 90%.

Yule: To come back to the question of university-affiliated facilities: I'm not sure that being part of a university is an unmixed blessing. In a university, and especially in a teaching hospital where there are too many faculty members chasing too few patients, it can be much more difficult to get a new line of work going than out in the hospital service where resources are scarce.

Corbett: I am not saying that service research should necessarily be university-*based*. It's only that subnormality hospitals with departments of psychology often lack effective links with neighbouring universities in this country. A lot of useful things have come from such links in the United States, and I think we should take due note of that.

Index